I HAD A HAMMER

HENRY AARON

with
LONNIE WHEELER

I HAD A HAMMER

The Hank Aaron Story

HarperCollins*Publishers*

FIRST EDITION

Designed by Helene Berinsky

Library of Congress Cataloging-in-Publication Data

Aaron, Hank, 1934–
    I had a hammer/by Henry Aaron with Lonnie Wheeler.
        p.   cm.
    ISBN 0-06-016321-6
    1. Aaron, Hank, 1934–   . 2. Baseball players—United States—Biography. I. Wheeler, Lonnie. II. Title.
GV865.A25A3   1991
796.357′092—dc20
[B]   90-55521

91 92 93 94 95 DT/RRD 10 9 8 7 6 5 4 3 2 1

*For the people who have always stood by me
when the going was rough—my wife, Billye; my
parents, Herbert and Estella Aaron; and my
children, Gaile, Hankie, Lary, Dorinda, and Ceci.
I love you all.—H.A.*

*For all those Negro League and sandlot players
who might have been Hank Aarons if they'd only
been given the chance.—L.W.*

ACKNOWLEDGMENTS

We would like to humbly thank all of the people who contributed so much to the book by sharing their memories and points of view:

From Hank's childhood—Herbert Aaron Jr., Sarah Aaron, Gloria Aaron Robinson, Alfredia Aaron Scott, Cornelius Giles, Ed Scott, Robert Driscoll, Lefty Morris, Punkin Smith, Alphonse Gordon, Ralph Powe, Edgar Powe, Theodore Gordon, and the fellow Mobilians who became his major-league contemporaries: Billy Williams, Willie McCovey, Frank Bolling, Amos Otis, and Cleon Jones.

From the Negro League—Jim (Fireball) Cohen, Buster Haywood, Buck O'Neil, Reuben Williams, Buck Leonard, Sam Jethroe, Dick Powell, Jim Zapp, Henry Kimbro, Sam Hairston, Cy Williams, Andy Porter, Chico Renfroe, Excell Moore, Charles Franklin, and Mrs. Ed Hamman.

From the Northern League—John Goryl, Marion Adair, Dick Bezanson, and Reuben Stohs.

From the South Atlantic League—Joe Andrews, Jim Frey, Dick Butler, Chief Bender, Tom Giordano, Ray Crone, Maury Fisher, Jim Bolger, and Spec Richardson.

From the Puerto Rican League—Mickey Owen, Charlie Neal, and Brooks Lawrence.

From the Milwaukee Braves years—Warren Spahn, Mal Goode, Ernie Banks, Bill Bruton, Lew Burdette, Lee Maye, Bobby Thomson, Jim Pendleton, Vada Pinson, Ernie Johnson, Joe Nuxhall, Sam Lacy, Red Barber, Bobby Bragan, Bob Allen, and Father Michael Sablica.

From the Atlanta Braves years—Dick Cecil, Dusty Baker, Ralph Garr, Darrell Evans, Paul Casanova, Pat Jarvis, Bill Acree, Calvin Wardlaw, Tony Gonzalez, Dave Bristol, and Frank Hyland.

From the Milwaukee Brewers—Bud Selig and George Scott.

From the front-office years—Ted Turner, Rubye Lucas, Sharon Richardson Jones, Jondelle Johnson, and Bob Hope.

And those whose invaluable, wide-ranging testimonies enriched numerous phases of the book—Gaile Aaron, Eddie Mathews, Felix Mantilla, Donald Davidson, Joe Kennedy, Wes Covington, Del Crandall, Bill Bartholomay, John Mullen, and Bill White.

And especially those who sacrificed their time most generously and whose contributions were particularly vital: Herbert and Estella Aaron, Horace Garner, Don Newcombe, Carla Cohn, and Barbara Aaron.

In addition to all of the people who played a part in the book through interviews, we would also like to acknowledge others whose assistance helped us put it all together:

Alan Pollock, son of former Indianapolis Clowns owner Syd Pollock; Charles Luhn, an unofficial but ardent Aaron archivist; Kevin Grace of the University of Cincinnati archives; Jon Blomquist, Bill Deane, and Pat Kelly of the Baseball Hall of Fame; Robert E. Johnson of *Jet* magazine; David Bur and Ron Buckli of the *Eau Claire Leader-Telegram;* Joe Overfield of Buffalo; author Bill Heward, formerly of the Indianapolis Clowns; historian Jules Tygiel; historian Phil Smith; collector Tom Steinhardt; Dick Miller of Kentucky, for opening up his personal library; Jim Riley of the Society for American Baseball Research; JoEllyn Reitman of the *Milwaukee Journal* and *Sentinel;* Valerie Lyons of the *Atlanta Journal-Constitution;* Jay Higginbotham of the Mobile Municipal Archives; Susan Bailey, Hank Aaron's secretary; editor Daniel Bial; attorneys Ken Norwick and Sam Frankel; and, most notably, two people without whose tireless and dedicated efforts the book would not have gotten off the ground—literary agent David Black and Alicia Berns of Pro Star Management.

And, of course, our support system and first line of proofreaders, Martie Wheeler and Billye Aaron.

INTRODUCTION

Hank Aaron is almost twenty years older than I am, which is just about right. I have no baseball memories that predate him, and he is an eminent presence in the earliest ones. Actually, they are glimpses more than palpable memories, single-frame impressions of a figure who was at the same time remote and salient. I recall listening to the radio beyond my bedtime as the Cardinals tried to protect a lead against the Braves in the late innings and thinking what a fearfully difficult thing that was with Aaron, Mathews and Adcock in the middle of Milwaukee's lineup. I recall Aaron's unlined, innocent face on my baseball cards. And I recall sitting on a picnic table at the Art Gaines Baseball Camp in rural Missouri as the coaches talked about hitting a baseball hard—not high and far but *hard*—and raising my hand to tell them that I had been to Busch Stadium in St. Louis and seen Hank Aaron hit a ball that banged off the left-field wall quicker than, well, I don't know what, but quicker than anybody else alive could make a baseball bang against an outfield wall. I knew that would impress them, because they were baseball people and they would know that Hank Aaron was the right name to drop in that situation.

In most company, though, the popular argument back then was Willie Mays or Mickey Mantle, and the popular choice was either of them. Hank Aaron had nothing to do with pop culture; he was just the best guy at swinging a baseball bat, whether or not they appreciated it on the coasts. He was a hitter for the heartland. We knew him as consummately that and nothing more than that, and never would, until he broke Babe Ruth's record for home runs. Even then, Aaron showed us only what he cared to. He seemed a featureless hero, an impenetrable icon whose effortless grace on the playing field was often taken for indolence and whose wary reticence off the field was sometimes mistaken for indifference. When he broke Ruth's record, he was little more than the quiet man who broke Ruth's record.

But how could it be left at that? How could that be all there was to Hank Aaron? There was too much background behind him to leave it at that—too much baseball, too much history, too much America. How could a man hit 755 home runs and have nothing more to offer? How could a person come out of Alabama as a black teenager in 1952 and not have a perspective for the rest of us to consider? How could he play in the Negro League and not have an experience that speaks to our culture? How could he integrate a Southern minor league and not have stories to pass along? How could a fellow go through all that Hank Aaron had gone through in Milwaukee and Atlanta, in the outfield and the front office, in obscurity and in fame, and not have memories and points of view to submit? It wasn't possible.

Other writers told me that Hank Aaron would have little to say. I didn't believe it, and I didn't care. His life was eloquent enough. He personified so many things that have been so symbolic to the social history of modern America: the South—he grew up in the deepest part of it, as the damndest color; the Negro League—he started his professional career in it when only a handful of moribund teams remained, and two decades later, when the Negro Leagues were a bygone of Americana, he was the last remnant of their legacy; the fifties—he gloried in them, playing on pennant winners and coming of age in the fiftiest town in America; the sixties—he was the most conspicuous athlete in the city that centered the South and headquartered the civil rights movement; the home run record—he was the object of a polarizing racial controversy that brought out the vicious side of white society and told America more than it wanted to hear about itself.

Hank Aaron was a living metaphor for all of these things, and he was willing to talk about them, as well. More than willing, he was determined to talk about them. To him, it was vital that his experience be brought to light, where it could at least illuminate the past and at best beacon the future. The multifarious forces within him all wanted out. He had a fundamental desire to make a statement with his life, an abiding urge to make a difference, and a consequent need to expose the ignorance, cruelty, and fear that had blackened his fifty-seven years. He had things to say. He had a book in him.

And so we met time and again over the course of nearly two years—in Atlanta, Milwaukee, Florida, Philadelphia, New York, and Cleveland. I smelled the collard greens simmering on his mother's stove in Mobile and drove the black neighborhoods with his tireless father, turning home on Henry Aaron Loop. In Jacksonville, Florida, I looked into the smart green eyes of his first wife for six straight hours. I spoke with five Hall of Famers, six managers, three owners, ten Aarons, nineteen Mobilians, eighteen Negro Leaguers, and twenty-eight teammates, among others—more than a hundred people, in all.

But the book came from Aaron—from his life, times, and reflections. Aaron's deep Alabama voice accented the details and anecdotes with urgency, worth, and a gentleman's candor. We had the same book in mind, and his recollections were persuasively reinforced by the most reliable of the other sources. This was not a point to be taken for granted, because the popular versions of Aaron's past were not always consistent with the facts. The media, for instance, commonly advanced the notion that Aaron never spoke out about civil rights until his second marriage and pursuit of Ruth. But Aaron maintained that he had stepped forward on racial issues throughout his career, and the old articles bear him out; he was on record in behalf of black managers and desegregated training camps as far back as the late 1950s. Similarly, critics had little sympathy for his wariness of the press, yet the old articles supply abundant cause for this, referring to him repeatedly in plantation-hand terms.

Of course, Aaron's memory, like most people's, was not unfailing. There were elusive details that neither he nor the written record could pin down. As an amateur and semipro in Mobile, for instance, he played on numerous, almost interchangeable teams that received little or no coverage in the newspapers. It would have been triumphant to find a journalistic verification of the game in which the Indianapolis Clowns discovered him playing for the Mobile Black Bears as a seventeen-year-old shortstop, but it doesn't exist, and the imprecise oral legend will have to suffice in its stead. It would have been a winning moment, also, to locate a published account of the doubleheader in Buffalo, New York, which moved the Boston Braves to sign Aaron despite the fact that he batted cross-handed. But none was available, and I collected five far-ranging oral versions of this afternoon before a former Braves official sent me a copy of the letter that the Boston scout filed after the games. Aaron's entire Negro League season is obscured by the scarcity of reporting, and some of that which exists only obfuscates the truth more deeply. To wit, it has been passed down through the years that Aaron led the Negro American League in batting, and, in fact, he was atop the published list at the time he joined the Braves' organization in mid-season. The list, however, was more than three weeks old at the time of its printing, and Aaron had slipped far out of the lead in the intervening period. Moreover, the flow of misinformation didn't stop when Aaron reached the big leagues. For a player with such sweeping historical connotations, Aaron's legend is surprisingly rife with canards.

Given the long-past and loosely chronicled status of some of his richest years, the testimony of Aaron's old friends and team-mates was indispensable in the recording of his complete story. Beyond that, it was inspiring. One by one, the old ballplayers poured out precious memories and profound affection for a man whose friendship is a highlight of their lives—from Hall of Fa-mers like Ernie Banks and Billy Williams to big-league journey-men like Dusty Baker and Ralph Garr and George Scott to lesser-leaguers like Fireball Cohen of the Indianapolis Clowns and Hor-ace Garner and Joe Andrews of the Jacksonville Braves. There was a consistent reverence in their voices—awe, in some cases—that I hadn't expected. To them, Aaron filled an unlikely double role—friend and model.

There was another unmistakable message in the conversa-tions of the black players who were Aaron's contemporaries. To a man, they felt powerfully, as he does, that baseball's heritage of racial discrimination must be addressed in unqualified terms. Their eagerness to contribute to Aaron's autobiography was mo-tivated in part by the knowledge that Aaron will not compromise the facts of baseball's bigotry. This sentiment was expressed most vividly by Don Newcombe, a former Dodger who was Aaron's opponent and Jackie Robinson's closest teammate. "Young kids have got to be made to know what Henry and Jackie and I endured," Newcombe said. "Henry's got guts. He'll say what he feels. And it's important that he does, because there aren't many of us around anymore who went through it. It's up to guys like him and me. We've got to tell it the way it was. If I call somebody a goddamn bigot, you can take out the goddamn if you want, but don't take out the bigot, because that's what they were."

As the steadfast unity of former black ballplayers is a testament to the merit of their cause, the loyalty of Aaron's countless friends is a testament to the merit of Aaron. By nature, he is not a man who makes friends casually. He has always been wary of people and uncomfortable in crowds. As a ballplayer, he seldom partied with his teammates, finding that, when they drank, they tended to say things they wouldn't say sober. Recently, a white friend of more than twenty-five years imposed a racial slur on a black friend of Aaron's while drinking. Aaron takes personally all offenses toward his race and his friends, and as is his custom when such an incident occurs, he has remained out of the old pal's presence since then. Even his best friends know that Aaron is not to be crossed, and they are ever alert to the chilling communications he can convey using nothing more than his eyes. And yet, his eyes can be warm as a grandmother's. They can also blaze with delight when he pulls back his face in a gold-medal smile. He loves to laugh and smile and to be around people who make him do it. Aaron is a private man, but not solitary. He is repelled by crowds, but attracted to quiet companionship. His friends give him release and shelter, and they range from celebrities and politicians to local merchants and maintenance men. Most of us have a handful of close acquaintances whom we can call on the telephone and begin talking to without introducing ourselves—Aaron has dozens. He is, in fact, a softly sociable person, spending large portions of his days on the phone or lingering contentedly at errands. But he also requires his own time every day. The part of his afternoon that he is loathe to miss is his long daily run, when he can be alone with his legs and ruminations.

He runs also because he cannot sit still for an entire day.

Aaron has always been a man who expresses himself in action, and he continues to be. For that reason, our book sessions took place not in concentrated multi-hour interviews but in itinerant conversations that spanned the morning and night. We got together often when he had spare time during his travels. We would meet for breakfast, read the paper, talk a little, ride in the car, talk a little more, stop at the drugstore; he would make some calls; I would work a little; we would ride in the car again, stop at the record store, each lunch, talk a little, stop for ice cream, make some calls, talk again, go back to the hotel, take a break; he would run; I would work; we would meet for dinner, walk a little, talk, watch television, knock off, and do it again the next day. I seldom got all the material I wanted that day, but invariably stumbled over some that I hadn't expected. Often, it would be in the form of transitory glimpses that were nonetheless revealing. Like the time in Florida when the waitress came to our table, looked straight at me as if I were alone, and asked if everything was all right or did I want more coffee. I saw Aaron's eyes flare up when she did that. It might have been innocent discourtesy on her part, but Aaron said it happens often when he eats with a white person.

There was also the time we were walking back to our motel in Mentor, Ohio, after a day at the Cleveland Browns' training camp, and he commented that he envied musicians because musicians never die—their music is preserved and played for eternity. Aaron is immortal in the baseball sense, but none of his 755 home runs will ever happen again, and the question of his legacy is one that he has not subdued. He has no self-doubts about his enduring qualifications as a ballplayer, but wonders where ball-playing fits in the greater scheme—in effect, where *he* fits in the greater scheme. I was startled to realize the depth of this doubt one night as we were pulling into the parking lot of the Palm Hotel in West Palm Beach and he suddenly asked, "Do you think I've gone from here to here?" He moved his hand from knee level to shoulder level as he spoke. It was a question I hadn't anticipated from the most decorated player in baseball history, and it discomfited me in its naked vulnerability. "Since when?" I asked. "Since I left Mobile." Realizing, of course, that he wasn't talking about baseball, I proceeded clumsily to rattle off all the marks Aaron has made in other areas. I mentioned the night before, when his wife had called him in his hotel room to ask him to help the son of a friend from Atlanta. The friend's son was living in another city and had locked himself in the bathroom while under a chemical influence. Aaron quickly got on the telephone with the young man's roommate and talked him through the situation. It should have been, and was, important to Aaron that he was the one the friend turned to—not because he is famous, but because he is a man to whom people turn.

In measuring his contribution to the world, Aaron looks first at two concerns that are really one—children and civil rights. Although the matter of racial discrimination has underpinned his entire life, by now he addresses it largely in terms of abolishing it for the emerging generation. His disposition toward civil rights is a considered one, but his affection for children is a natural one that colors his days, whether by taking his grandson to baseball practice or asking old teammates about their kids and knowing all their names. Officially, he has been a major player in the Big Brother/Big Sister movement. Unofficially, he simply cares about kids. I caught a fleeting manifestation of this one day at the Browns' training camp, when we were walking to the car just as a young girl came running toward the parking lot and clotheslined herself on a wire strand. Aaron was kneeling at her side before I even comprehended what had happened. She got up, brushed herself off, and proceeded on her way, seeming fine, but before we could drive off, Aaron insisted on watching her from the car until she had walked out of our sight.

The reason we were there in the first place, incidentally, is that Aaron is a hopeless Browns fan. He seems to be more interested in the Browns than he is in himself, which I discovered one summer afternoon at his home in Atlanta. We had spent several hours in his attic, rummaging through old photographs, clippings, contracts, keepsakes, and boxes of letters he hadn't seen in decades. To me, it was a treasure trove of materials. To Aaron, it was a mess in the attic. When we were finished, he came downstairs carrying one item that had caught his attention—a year-old copy of *Browns News*. He wanted to review the previous year's draft to see how it had panned out.

He was in his glory at the Browns' training camp—as long as he could stay away from the crowds. Aaron will never say no to an autograph request—if he can't stop to sign, he might say that he'll be right back—but he will do his best to steer clear of autograph conditions. This is a necessary measure of self-defense. Having witnessed what it's like when Aaron steps out in public, I am convinced that if he stopped in a crowded place to sign autographs and kept signing as long as people came up to him, he wouldn't leave his spot until the area was vacated. As it is, autograph hounds presume him to be at their service. One woman, noting Aaron signing in a crowd, approached him with her materials ready and said, "I don't know who you are, but you must be famous." Occasionally, in that situation, he will sign "Willie Mays." Although the two look nothing alike, he is mistaken for Mays surprisingly often.

When he is not cornered by a crowd, Aaron enjoys being out in public. He is friendly with clerks and waitresses—if his waitress has gone off duty, he will seek her out to make sure she receives the tip—and revels in the moments that celebrity eschews him. He likes to tell the story of a fund-raising banquet he recently attended in Atlanta, when he shared the stage with well-known actors and statesmen. At one point in the evening, a woman approached with a flash camera and called his name. "I thought, 'Hey, this is great. I'm back in the spotlight.' Then she said, 'Mr. Aaron, will you move over just a little bit so I can take a picture of Denzel Washington?' " When we were in a sporting goods store in Canton, Ohio, I heard Aaron chuckling by the front window. Walking over, I found him looking out at the street with a huge smile on his face, holding a softball bat and assuming the stance from which he hit 755 home runs. As he explained it, "The man and woman in that car out there were laughing and pointing at me and saying, 'Look at that old man. He has no idea what to do with that bat.' "

In fact, Aaron doesn't swing a bat anymore. Although he remains in baseball as a vice-president of the Atlanta Braves and is ever concerned with the game's posture in racial matters, there are few signs about him that he ever played. His office is free of baseball artifacts, and in the main rooms of his home the most visible items from his old days are balls and pictures signed by Presidents. He is concerned with the past only insofar as it matters for the future. As a ballplayer, Aaron's career was characterized by perseverance, and the quality itself has perservered within him. Befitting a man of history, he harbors the hope that some of his greatest deeds are yet to come. He thinks perhaps this book might somehow play a part.

There have been other books on Aaron, well over a dozen. Only one other, published in 1968, was autobiographical. Most of them—including a later release of his first autobiography, with an addendum that he did not author—were timed around the home run record, which he broke in the first week of the 1974 season. Years later, James Baldwin expressed an interest in writing an Aaron biography, but it never materialized, and there remained no book that presented Aaron's story with the specificity and perspective he believes are pertinent to his mission. That's why he wanted so much to do this one, and to do it his way.

It's a delicate book, because it attempts to deal with a man's complaint without complaining. Aaron is compelled to file his grievances against baseball but has no urge to lash out at the game he loves and owes. He wishes to get his message across without the graceless effect of a soapbox or sandwich board. What he wishes, really, is to speak his piece and think out loud about where he's been that other's haven't, what he's seen that others couldn't, and how it all adds up. He wishes to write a book that will be his statement and story. And he says he'll never do another one, because this is it.

L. W.

I

The day I left Mobile, Alabama, to play ball with the Indianapolis Clowns, Mama was so upset she couldn't come to the train station to see me off. She just made me a couple of sandwiches, stuffed two dollars in my pocket, and stood in the yard crying as I rode off with my daddy, my older brother and sister, and Ed Scott, a former Negro League player who managed me with the Mobile Black Bears and scouted me for the Clowns. When we got to the station, Mr. Scott handed me an envelope with the name Bunny Downs on it. Downs was the business manager of the Clowns, and when I arrived at their camp in Winston-Salem, North Carolina, I was to hand him the envelope unopened.

My knees were banging together when I got on that train. I'd never ridden in anything bigger than a bus or faster than my daddy's old pickup truck. As we pulled out of the station and Daddy and Sarah and Herbert Junior and Mr. Scott kept getting smaller and smaller, I never felt so alone in my life. I just sat there clutching my sandwiches, speaking to nobody, staring out the window at towns I'd never heard of. It was the first time in my life that I had been around white people. After a while, I got up the courage to walk up and down the aisle a few times. I wanted to see what a dining car looked like, and I needed somebody to tell me where I wasn't allowed to go. Then I sat back down, listened to those wheels carrying me farther away from home, and tried to talk myself out of getting off at the next stop and going back.

I've never stopped wondering if I did the right thing that day. I was barely eighteen at the time, a raggedy kid who wore my sister's hand-me-down pants and had never been out of the black parts of Mobile. I didn't know anything about making a living or taking care of myself or about the white world I'd have to face sooner or later. I didn't know what I wanted to be doing when I was forty or any of the other things I needed to know to make a decision that would affect the rest of my life—except for one. I knew that I loved to play baseball. And I had a feeling that I might be pretty good at it.

I suppose that's reason enough for an eighteen-year-old boy to board a train and set off on his life's journey, and I suppose it's time I stopped second-guessing myself. But I'm not eighteen anymore, and two generations later I'm still living with a decision I made back when JFK was starting out as a senator. I live with the fact that I spent twenty-five of the best years of my life playing baseball. Don't get me wrong; I don't regret a day of it. I still love baseball—Lord knows, it's the greatest game in the world—and I treasure the experience. God, what an experience. But sometimes I have to wonder just how far I've really come since I took that envelope from Mr. Scott and walked onto the L&N. How far can a guy really go playing baseball? I guess that's what I wonder about. I can only thank God that I played the game well enough that maybe it meant something. Maybe in the end, I can do as much good, in my way, as, say, a teacher. That's what Mama wanted me to be.

With all of my wondering, I don't doubt for a minute what baseball has done for me. Let me put that another way: I don't doubt what my ability to *play* baseball has done for me. I realize that if I hadn't been able to hit the hell out of a baseball, I would have never been able to lay a finger on the good life that I've been fortunate to have. Playing baseball has given me all that a man could ask for—certainly a lot more than a timid little black kid like me ever dared to dream about. I've traveled the world, met Presidents, had my share of fortune and more fame than I ever wanted. I even have a place in history, if only for hitting home runs. The fact is, I have every reason to be content. My kids have all been to college. I don't know how I managed to stumble onto the great woman who is my wife. Everything is just about perfect. I don't even hear much about Babe Ruth anymore, thank goodness, and I haven't received a really nasty piece of hate mail in about fifteen years.

Believe me, I take none of this for granted, because there was a time when my life was very painful. One of my sons passed away as an infant. My first marriage was rough, and I was struggling to get over the divorce at the same time I was starting to close in on the home run record. The Ruth chase should have been the greatest period of my life, and it was the worst. I couldn't believe there was so much hatred in people. It's something I'm still trying to get over, and maybe I never will. I know I'll never forget it, and the fact is, I don't want to. I feel like if I forget about that and everything else I've been through in the last four decades, I'll be content. It would be so easy to be content. It would also be so unforgivably selfish that I can't let it happen. I used to have talks with Jackie Robinson not long before he died, and he impressed upon me that I should never allow myself to be satisfied with the way things are. I can't let Jackie down—or my people, or myself. The day I become content is the day I cease to be anything more than a man who hit home runs.

I might not feel this way if I weren't black. I'm sure this is a had thing to understand for somebody who isn't black; but what kind of a man would I be if I cashed in my fame and retired to a comfortable life with my wife and my trophies and my tennis court? See, I'm one of the lucky ones. I could do something that white people would pay to see. Singers, dancers, boxers, ballplayers—sure, we can make it in the white world. White people love to have us entertain them. But what about all the black teachers and mechanics and carpenters and janitors and waitresses? Am I supposed to say to them: Hey, folks, I know it's rough, but look at me, I made it? What am I supposed to do with my good fortune? Am I just supposed to say, thank you, Lord, and then get fat and sign autographs for fifteen bucks a shot? I don't believe that's the reason God gave me the gifts that he did. I think that if I were the kind of man to be satisfied with the way things are, he would have given my eyes and my hands and my mind to somebody who would put them to better use.

And so I make it my business not to be content. Of course, that rubs some people the wrong way. They say that I'm bitter. They say that I have a chip on my shoulder, that I read racism into every phrase and discrimination into every decision. But I don't think white people can understand that I have a moral responsibility to do whatever I can. With all of my worldly advantages, how can I look the other way? If I did that, how could I face the people I come from? How could I justify who I am?

Look, I don't have the vision or the voice of Martin Luther King or James Baldwin or Jesse Jackson or even of Jackie Robinson. I'm just an old ballplayer. But I learned a lot as a ballplayer. Among other things, I learned that if you manage to make a name for yourself—and if you're black, believe me, it has to be a big name—then people will start listening to what you have to say. That was why it was so important for me to break the home run record. Believe me, there were times during the chase when I was so angry and tired and sick of it all that I wished I could get on a plane and not get off until I was some place where they never heard of Babe Ruth. But damn it all, I had to break that record. I had to do it for Jackie and my people and myself and for everybody who ever called me a nigger.

And when it was over, my real job was only starting. Once the record was mine, I had to use it like a Louisville Slugger. I believed, and still do, that there was a reason why I was chosen to break the record. I feel it's my task to carry on where Jackie Robinson left off, and I only know of one way to go about it. It's the only way I've ever had of dealing with things like fastballs and bigotry—keep swinging at them. As a ballplayer, I always figured that I had a bat and all the pitcher had was a little ball, and as long as I kept swinging that bat I'd be all right. It worked pretty well. People said I pounded the ball as if my bat was a hammer, and they called me Hammerin' Hank. Well, I can't pound a baseball anymore. I'm fifty-seven years old. My back aches, my knees are weak, and I need glasses to read. These days, I couldn't hit a good slider with a snow shovel. But I can do what I can do.

The way I see it, it's a great thing to be the man who hit the most home runs, but it's a greater thing to be the man who did the most with the home runs he hit. So as long as there's a chance that maybe I can hammer out a little justice now and then, or a little opportunity here and there, I intend to do as I always have —keep swinging. I'm taking my cuts as you read this. I'm telling my story, and when everything's said and done, maybe it'll mean more than a bunch of home runs. I can only hope and keep hammering.

2

Herbert Aaron and his teenage bride moved to Mobile, Alabama, long before it was the fashion. That is to say, before the war. Fewer than 80,000 people lived in Mobile before World War II, and three years after Pearl Harbor there were more than half again as many. The work force nearly tripled over the same period, suggesting that the newcomers were not moving down for the gardens and golf courses—unless, of course, to maintain them. They were poor farm people looking for city work. For the most part, they were black people.

Herbert and Estella Aaron came from Wilcox County, south of Selma, and they brought nothing but ready shoulders and unspoken hopes. Both of them were raised close to the earth in large, deep-rooted church families to whom the outside world was the white side of Camden. A line of preachers preceded Herbert, but he was not of the same cloth. The urge was in him to cut loose and go somewhere. When he was working in the cotton fields one sweltering afternoon, an airplane had buzzed overhead. The cotton pickers held their bags and stared up in astonishment as the little plane roared over and then disappeared in the distance, and the vision of that flying machine never left Herbert Aaron. It would be several decades before he ever rode in an airplane, but the city down by the bay had all the things that Camden didn't—trolleys and boats and possibilities. He was going, and Estella would join him as soon as she was old enough to leave home.

In the 1920s, the black community of Mobile was just beginning to emerge on its own. There was a black postal worker named John LeFlore who in 1925 had the temerity to scuffle with a white man who tried to keep him off a city bus. There was a black musician from New Orleans named Jelly Roll Morton who was lured by the juke joints on Davis Avenue and stayed long enough to write the "King Porter Stomp." And there was a gangly black pitcher named Satchel Paige who was doing the most unusual things on the local ballfields, such as sending his infielders to the bench and telling his outfielders to sit down while he struck out the side with the bases loaded.

The young Aarons, though, were just looking for labor, and they took an apartment in the low-lying grid known as Down The Bay, which was home to Paige and much of Mobile's black population. Down The Bay was not a street-life sort of neighborhood, but its working people had more idle time than they would have prescribed. They were laid off in waves as shipbuilders, docks, and other bay businesses struggled through the Depression. In those years, maids and cooks made up the biggest group in Mobile's work force, but Estella Aaron couldn't spend all her time cleaning other people's floors. She was busy enough having children.

Her third, Henry, was born in 1934, on the day before Babe Ruth's thirty-ninth birthday. It was to be the Babe's last year with the New York Yankees, but his merry heroics were of little relevance where the Aarons lived. In Down The Bay, the big news that early February was that five Alabama Negroes, imprisoned in Montgomery for unrelated crimes, were being sent to the electric chair together in a mass execution.

Incidents such as those served as sharp reminders to Mobile's black people that they were indeed a part of Alabama. Such was its isolation and cultural autonomy that in many ways Mobile was removed from the customs of the state, making it seem but a suburb of the Deep South. Some think it is perhaps due to the seaport, which for centuries has brought a diversity of people and cultures to the city's door, that in matters of race Mobile has been a more accommodating place than its latitude might suggest. Some of the South's most liberal politicians found a forum in Mobile, and, although their positions were not generally electable, they spoke of equal opportunity long before civil rights was a popular cause. A local, private college, Spring Hill, was integrated prior to the Civil War. John LeFlore, the postal worker, organized a local chapter of the NAACP in the 1930s, and a few white folks even listened to him. The Mobile public library opened its doors to blacks before other Southern cities encouraged them to read. To be sure, segregation was dutifully observed in midcentury Mobile, but it was not wielded as a bone- and spirit-crushing weapon. As opposed to the hard-line South at large, Mobile's was a subtler discrimination, a provincial un- derstanding, a way of life that went with the azaleas.

This is not to say that Henry Aaron's hometown was a swell place to be black. In fact, the venting of liberal thought called forth some of the most zealous racism in all the South. Some local historians believed that if Martin Luther King Jr. had cho- sen to make his mark in Mobile instead of Montgomery, he might not have survived until 1968. Indeed, for all of its comparative tolerance, Mobile was not a safe place for a black man to pursue equality. Herbert Aaron feared for his life in 1942, when white workers rioted for two days at Alabama Dry Dock and Shipbuild- ing, where he worked, because black welders had been promoted in their stead. The situation was so threatening that guards were hired to escort the black workers to and from the plant.

But despite the tension there, the dry docks were living waters to men willing to work. They employed more than 40,000 people at the peak of the war, and rural blacks streamed down from hamlets all across the South to build and repair navy ships. There wasn't enough housing to accommodate such numbers, and soon there were tents and trailers and lean-to shelters made out of packing boxes behind almost every house in Down The Bay. Without decent roofs over their heads, the men took shelter in the bars and clubs of Davis Avenue, which, ironically, had been named for Jefferson Davis but became known as Little Har- lem.

Mobile's city limits ended near Davis Avenue, and on the other side was a village known as Toulminville, so rural that its garbage pickup was provided by the pigs on hand. It was known for its oak groves and for a country fair put on by its founder, General Theophilus Toulmin. By the early 1940s, a few blacks had begun to move out there to escape the crowding of the city, and Herbert Aaron reasoned that it was a good way to get around the nine dollars he had to pay for rent every month at 666 Wilk- inson. Estella, who had become accustomed to the city life, said *at first that she wasn't moving out to the woods, but by this time there were six Aaron children, and in the little house on Wilkinson they were beginning to crowd the bedroom.*

◆　　◆　　◆

I was eight when we moved to Toulminville in 1942. They were tearing down an old house close to where we lived in Down The Bay, so we grabbed up the lumber and Mama spent her days pulling out nails. Daddy bought two overgrown lots at $55 apiece and paid a couple of carpenters $100 to build us six rooms, which was twice as many as we were accustomed to. When the walls and roof were up, we moved in, and that was it—no rent or mortgage, it was ours. We were a proud family, because the way we saw it, the only people who owned their own homes were rich folks and Aarons. After the house was built, we just kept patching it up and putting on new layers—shingles, felt, brick, whatever we could get. When I made some money in baseball, we added a back room, and my parents still live there. I've told Mama I would buy her a big house in a new neighborhood, but she says she's not looking for any big house, she's just looking for Jesus.

There were only two or three houses on Edwards Street when we moved there. It was wide open, with a dairy on the corner and country things on every side of us—cows, chickens, hogs, cornfields, sugarcane, watermelon patches, pecan groves, and blackberry thickets. The streets were just mudholes that cars were always getting stuck in. We took out water from a well, and for heating and cooking we brought in whatever wood we could find. Sometimes we'd strip it off an old abandoned farmhouse. There were no lights in our house—not even windows. A kerosene lamp was all we needed. The bathroom was an outhouse in the backyard. It was a good outhouse—we built it ourselves—but Mama was always scared to death that one of us would fall down that hole.

Mama stayed at home and looked after the kids during the

day. Now and then she would clean somebody's house for two dollars, but she likes to brag that she never hired a baby sitter in her life—which is something to brag about, considering that there were eight of us. I often wonder how Mama and Daddy managed with all those kids. Nobody knew anything back then about family planning; they just kept having kids whether there was room and food for them or not. None of us ever had a bed to himself. And we almost never ate anything that was store-bought. I've gone many, many weeks with just corn bread, butter beans, and collard greens. Maybe we'd have a piece of pork to season the greens, but we were practically vegetarians before we ever heard of the word. We tried to keep a hog in the backyard to kill every year, and everything else came from the garden. You can believe the Aaron kids didn't have any fat on them. My sister Gloria was so skinny that I called her Neck Bone. My brother Tommie's nickname was Pork Chop, because he always wanted one. We all described ourselves as six o'clock—straight up and down. But we didn't know to feel sorry for ourselves, because everybody else was in the same boat. Nobody made fun of me for wearing my sister's hand-me-down clothes, because they were probably wearing their sister's clothes, too.

My father was a boilermaker's assistant at the dry docks, which meant that he had to hold up sixty-pound steel plates while somebody else riveted them to the ships. But it seemed like he was laid off almost as much as he was working. To make some extra money, he ran a little tavern next to the house, called the Black Cat Inn. It was the only tavern for black people in Toulminville, and it was a pretty lively place—music and dancing and people coming in and out all night. After a while, Daddy had to shut it down because the neighbors complained about the ruckus. But he always had something going on the side. He sold a little moonshine—white shinny, they called it. Once, some lawmen came busting into the house looking for that stuff, and they turned over Mama's bed with her in it. But they couldn't ever find it. Daddy would bury it in the potato vines, and he always kept a few bottles in a little space over the door. He could get to it by pulling on a nail that had the head cut off. When the law was in the house, he would always manage to excuse himself for a second and go around and yank that nail back from the other side so nobody could see it.

My sister Sarah, the oldest child, ran the tavern for my father. Herbert Junior was next in line, and he always had some job or another. For a long time, he worked for a lady named Miss Higgins in a grocery store on St. Stephens Road, which is the main road running past Toulminville. Miss Higgins would give Herbert Junior clothes and groceries. She helped raise him. I had a few jobs, too, but I wasn't a worker like Herbert Junior. I mowed some yards and picked some potatoes. The potato truck would come by at about seven in the morning; we'd hop on, and they'd take us out to the country, then bring us back around suppertime with eight or nine dollars in our pocket. I would have liked to work as a carpenter—before blacks started getting into the big leagues, that's what I really wanted to be—but the closest I got was mixing cement for a couple of bricklayers. The best job I had, though, was delivering ice. It would come in twenty-five-pound blocks, and we had tongs to carry it into the houses. Later on, I used to tell sportswriters that I built up my wrists by hauling ice up flights of stairs, but I doubt if that had anything to do with it. The truth is, I didn't have the job for very long. My mistake was that I told them I'd drive the truck, although I was only fourteen and didn't quite know how to drive yet. I was doing all right until I pulled away from a stop when I was on a hill and all the ice went sliding off the back of the truck.

After that, I pretty much just helped my mother around the house, tending the garden and cutting wood. Herbert Junior and I both had to cut wood for the stove, and I usually tried to sneak a few of my sticks onto Herbert Junior's pile so I could get out of there and play ball. It wasn't easy to get away, because Mama always had work for us to do. If we didn't feel like doing it, she'd let us cut a little switch off a tree. Then she'd braid it together like girls' hair and whale on us for a while. It got to where doing the chores didn't seem so bad, except that it wasn't baseball.

There wasn't much else that could keep me from playing ball. If nobody was around to get up a game or have a catch with, I'd find ways to play by myself. I could spend hours hitting a ball with a stick or throwing it on the roof and hitting it or catching it when it came down. I was so good at rolling that ball up on the roof that I could toss it over the house and run around and catch it before it hit the ground on the other side. We'd make our own baseballs by wrapping nylon hose around an old golf ball, or just use old rags tied together, or handlebar grips, or tin cans crumpled up. I still have a mark over my eye where Herbert Junior batted a tin can into the side of my face. I wailed when that happened, but Daddy told me to be quiet and take it like a man. I learned early not to show pain.

When I look back on my life, I can see that all through my childhood I was being prepared to play baseball. Whether you call it luck or fate or chance, it took one coincidence after another to get me to the big leagues, as if somebody or something was up there mapping it all out for me. Being born in Mobile was my first break, and moving to Toulminville was the second. I might have made it as a ballplayer if I had grown up in Down The Bay—Satchel Paige and Willie McCovey sure did—but there was no better place to play ball than Toulminville. When we lived on Wilkinson, all I had room to do was hit bottle caps with a broom handle under the big water oak in the front yard. Even then, I was so crazy about baseball that my father had a lady down the street—Miss Vivian—make me a little baseball suit. But it was in Toulminville that I became a ballplayer. There were open spaces in Toulminville, and before long, enough kids had moved in that we could generally get up a game. After we had been there a few years, they cleared the pecan grove that was on the other side of a vacant lot across the street from my house, and we carved out our own ball diamond. Then the city (Toulminville had been annexed to Mobile in 1945) built its own diamonds on that very spot—Carver Park, the first recreational area for blacks in all of Mobile. It was like having Ebbets Field in my backyard. I'd be over there every day after school and in the summer, usually with my neighbor, Cornelius Giles, and anybody else who could get out of his chores.

There are all kinds of theories on why Mobile turned out so

many good ballplayers in my generation, but I believe that Carver Park had as much to do with it as anything. As soon as the park was built, the city started a black recreational league that pulled teams from every black neighborhood in town. The league was formal enough to count for something and informal enough to leave us to our own devices. The result was that neighborhood teams were always challenging each other, and the rivalries were pretty hot—especially between Toulminville and Down The Bay. For a while, our teams kept getting pounded by the guys from Down The Bay, who always tried to push us around anyway. It didn't end with baseball—there would be gang fights now and then—but our group preferred to settle things on the field whenever possible. So we started spending every day at Carver Park, and pretty soon we were giving the boys from Down The Bay all they wanted.

> *The way I can still see Henry is like this. We'd be having a game on Saturday, and he was late most of the time, because his mother would have him doing chores. After a couple innings, you'd look out and see him running across that cornfield. He had a path beaten through that field, with vines growing up on either side. You'd see his head bobbing up and down over that corn, and in a few seconds everybody knew that Henry was coming. And whoever was batting for our team, he would just lay that bat down on the ground, because Henry was going to pinch-hit. I know, because it happened to me many times.*
> —Aaron's boyhood friend, Robert Driscoll

There was always some kind of ballgame going on in Toulminville. Before I was really old enough to play, my father ran a little team out of his tavern. I never saw Daddy play much; he's small, but he has always been wiry and quick, and probably would have been a hell of an infielder if he'd had the time to take the game seriously. Unfortunately, he never had that luxury. Even when he had his own team, he was more concerned with trying to make some money off the refreshments. That was where I came in. Occasionally, he would let me go out on the field and play, but my main job was to stand in the back of the truck and sell enough cold drinks that maybe we could buy ourselves a pound of bologna or something.

Until I was a teenager—and even then, up to a point—most of the organized ball I played was softball. All of the black kids played on softball teams, because that was what the recreation department offered. But when we were on our own, we played baseball, and although it never occurred to us that we were anything special, the record shows that we must have played it about as well as any kids in any city in the country. The only other place that turned out ballplayers who compared with ours was Oakland, which sent Frank Robinson and Vada Pinson and Curt Flood and a bunch of others to the major leagues. But I think even Oakland took a back seat to Mobile—at least, for one generation. I was the first of the line, not counting Satchel Paige, and after me came McCovey and Billy Williams—all three of us within five years of each other, and all three in the Hall of Fame. After Willie and Billy, there followed my brother Tommie and Cleon Jones and Tommie Agee and Amos Otis. There were even a few white players—Frank Bolling, who became a teammate of mine with the Braves, his brother, Milt, and later Jim Mason. Of course, back home we almost never played on the same field as the white boys, and if we did, it was off the beaten path where the police couldn't see us. Later on, Eddie Stanky, the former big-league player and manager who made his home in Mobile, would arrange a pickup game between black and white teams now and then. We played once against a team that had the Bolling boys on it—they whipped us pretty good, as I recall—but I never knew either of them until Frank and I had lockers next to each other in Milwaukee. As a rule, black people in Mobile didn't know white people unless they worked for them.

The black players eventually put Mobile on the baseball map, but we weren't the only ones in town who took the game to heart. In fact, Mobile was one of the few places in the Deep South— maybe the only place—where baseball wasn't completely overshadowed by football. Of course, black Southerners didn't worship football like white Southerners did anyway, because none of us could go to Alabama or Auburn or LSU, but in Mobile, football wasn't quite as important to the culture as it was in cities like Birmingham and Atlanta and hundreds of small towns. There wasn't a Southeastern Conference school closer than 200 miles away. On the other hand, there wasn't a major-league team within 700 miles, but we had our own little relationship with big-time baseball. Teams like the Dodgers and Yankees and Cardinals and Reds and Braves would stop to play in Mobile as they barnstormed their way north after spring training. My father climbed a tree to see Babe Ruth play at Hartwell Field in 1928, and he swears he saw Ruth hit a ball into the coal car of a train and they didn't retrieve the ball until the train pulled into New Orleans. Twenty years later, he took me to see the Dodgers, with the great Jackie Robinson.

Jackie Robinson was the hero of Davis Avenue—he and Joe Louis. When Louis would fight, everybody would get together and crowd around a radio, and when the Dodgers were on—a Mobile station carried pirated broadcasts from an announcer named Gordon McLendon—it was practically the same thing. The day Jackie Robinson came to town in 1948, I skipped shop class to hear him speak in the auditorium on Davis Avenue. That same day, I told my father that I would be in the big leagues before Jackie retired. Jackie had that effect on all of us—he gave us our dreams. He breathed baseball into the black community, kids and grown-ups alike. Before then, whenever I said I wanted to be a ballplayer, Daddy would set me straight. I remember sitting out on the back porch once when an airplane flew over, and I told Daddy I'd like to be a pilot when I grew up. He said, "Ain't no colored pilots." I said, okay, then, I'll be a ballplayer. He said, "Ain't no colored ballplayers." But he never said that anymore after we sat in the colored section of Hartwell Field and watched Jackie Robinson.

Hartwell Field was the home of the Mobile Bears of the Southern League. Back in the late 1920s, Satchel Paige worked out with the Bears occasionally, and they used to tell him that they would breeze to the pennant if only he could pitch for them. That was out of the question, of course, because no black man would ever throw a ball in the Southern League. As long as he was in Mobile, Satch pitched only for black teams against black teams. He had his own way, for the most part, but it wasn't as if there was no competition. Old-timers say that Satch used to hook up with a local pitcher named Ralph Donahue, and as often as not the games would be nothing-nothing until suppertime. Another fellow from Mobile was such a good pitcher and catcher that they called him Double Duty Radcliffe. Double Duty and his brother, Alex, hit the road when they were teenagers and became two of the best players in the Negro Leagues in the 1930s and '40s. But a lot of the great black players stayed in Mobile to work in the shipyards. Outside of south Alabama, nobody ever heard of most of them, but the local stories about them make you wonder how good they were. For instance, there was a shortstop named Peter Smith who, to hear the old-timers tell about him, could have been Ozzie Smith's grandfather.

There's no telling how many major leaguers Mobile might have produced if blacks hadn't been kept out of baseball until Jackie Robinson. I always thought that my Uncle Bubba—Bubba Underwood, from my mother's side of the family—could have been a star in the big leagues. When I was a kid, he was the best player in Mobile. I played against him a few times, and it was nothing for Uncle Bubba to hit a couple of home runs and a couple of doubles in the same game. He actually had a chance to go into organized baseball after Jackie signed, but he was a little old by then and he didn't much like the idea of being away from home. It was lucky for me that he stuck around, because if anybody helped me get started in baseball, it was Uncle Bubba. He would come over to the house, sit back, and say, "Man"—everybody in my family calls me Man, because I was such a big baby that some neighbor kid said I looked like a man—"Man, you just comb my hair a hundred times, and after that maybe we can go outside and have ourselves a catch." He was the first one to teach me anything about the game.

I have a feeling that my mother might have been a pretty fair athlete herself, but I never saw her play anything because she always had a baby in her arms and one or two others pulling on her apron. After me came Gloria, who was one of the best athletes in the family—a track and softball star in high school—and then

Tommie. Tommie was five years younger than I was, so we never played together much. But he was bigger, could hit the ball as far as I could, and was a better football player. When my life story started appearing in books and magazines and newspapers, it was often written that I was a football star in high school and could have gone to Florida A&M on a scholarship, but I was no football player. Tommie was the football star in the family.

The next brother, Alfred, died from pneumonia when he was two. He was already gone when Mama had another girl. She named her Alfredia. None of us cared for that, because we were afraid that it might mean something bad would happen to her, but Mama was insistent. To this day, she feels a special closeness to Alfredia, who lives near me in Atlanta. One of the things I'm most proud of is that I was able to help my parents send Alfredia and my youngest brother, James, to college.

Education was always very important in our house. Mama ranked it right behind family and church. Nothing else mattered to her. She hasn't even driven a car since she ran into a truck once—around 1932, as I understand. She doesn't dance or go to banquets, and she hasn't been to a party since she went to one about fifty years ago with a neighbor lady and the lady shot her own boyfriend. Mama had to climb the fence to get out of there and decided right then that she'd been to her last party. After the kids were out of school and on their own, she began devoting more time to her neighborhood church, Morning Star Baptist. We were all baptized there by Reverend Peterson, and it seems like the whole family was raised at that church. We'd spend the day there on Sunday, and Mama still does. Daddy doesn't like all the singing and carrying on, so he goes to an Episcopal church where he can get in and out in an hour.

It seems ironic that my father's family is the one with all the preachers. Even his mother became a preacher later in life. Mama Sis, we called her—tall and straight as a ramrod, with deep-set eyes and sharp Indian features. Her mother was half Indian, and I remember how peculiar we all thought it was when great-grandmother was buried Cherokee style—standing straight up in the grave. Great-grandmother was very old when she died, and

Mama Sis lived to be 101. She was quite a woman, strong and peaceful and the best cook there ever was. Mama Sis would set out that pork with rice and gravy, and I can still hear her calling me to the table: "Boy, sit down and eat." She didn't have to tell me twice.

My brothers and sisters and I used to go up to Wilcox County in the summers and stay with Mama Sis and Papa Henry, for whom I was named. I went there more than any of the others, probably because Mama and Daddy thought I needed to learn to work. Mama Sis and Papa Henry owned their own farm, with cotton fields and a smokehouse. We'd work all day every day until Sunday, when we rode the horse-and-wagon to church. Then I'd listen to Papa Henry stand up there and preach from his heart. People in my family say that I'm like Papa Henry in a lot of ways—deliberate and good at making decisions. I hope I picked up a few things from him, because he was a wise man. Papa Henry could see things that nobody else could see. He believed that his religion helped him look into the future, and he always predicted that Daddy's family would somehow be known forever. I don't know if he was talking about me, but I'd like to think that I made his prediction come true.

My father may not be the church man that his ancestors were, but he had his own values and he preached them to his kids. At the top of his list was respect. Daddy is the kind of man who takes off his hat when a funeral procession passes and who believes that people should not speak out of turn—especially his children. He always hammered that home to me, and when I left to play ball he reminded me that nobody would want to hear what I had to say until I proved myself.

Daddy used the same sort of approach with white people. He would say all the right things and go along with the system despite what he might have thought deep down. He didn't really have a choice. There were things that a black person in Mobile just had to put up with—things more subtle than riding in the back of the bus and drinking at the colored fountain. If you were in line at the grocery store, a white person could just step right in front of you and you couldn't say a thing. When you got paid at the end of the week, your salary was whatever they wanted to put in that envelope. Once when Daddy went into the courthouse to get a license, a deputy jumped all over him for not taking his hat off. Daddy told him that he was so scared he didn't know if his hat was on or off—which was exactly what the deputy wanted to hear. So the deputy got a big smile on his face and Daddy went on about his business.

Daddy had to worry about feeding a house full of kids, so he did all he could to avoid confrontations with white people. But wherever blacks and whites were together, there was the threat of trouble. Once he had a disagreement with a white man at work, and another white man defended Daddy. When that happened, his white friend was warned. They said, "You gonna take up for that Negro? You know, you got to come to work tomorrow yourself." Another time my father was on the bus—he didn't ride the bus often, because he had an old Model-T that he drove to work—when the driver moved the sign for the colored section farther back. After that, a black man got on, and when he saw there weren't any seats left for him—even though there were plenty of empty seats in the white section—the man took the sign and stuffed it in the driver's mouth, then walked off the bus.

When things like that happened, my father just kept quiet. But now it's different for him—the same way that it's different for me. He's well known around Mobile now, and he finally feels as though people will pay attention to what he has to say. So now he speaks up, even if it's just over small things. For example, after he retired from Alabama Dry Dock and Shipbuilding, he worked for the city recreation department, and one of his superiors there was a white woman who treated him nicely but still always made it clear that she was white and he was black. Once, she had some coffee left over and she said, "Aaron, you can have some of this." He said, "No, thank you, I don't drink leftovers." So a few days later she was having coffee with somebody else, and this time she said, "Aaron, we're having some coffee, why don't you come on in?" It was a little thing that meant a lot to my father.

He'll also hold his ground on public matters, which I found

out when Mobile decided to name a street after me. At first it was going to be Davis Avenue, but Daddy didn't think it was right to have my name on a street in a black neighborhood. He figured that we'd come far enough to get away from that—that if I was going to be honored in Mobile, it should be in a way that represented all of Mobile, not just the black part. So he made a fuss, and they ended up renaming a very prominent street that connects downtown to the rest of the city. He also made sure that the signs with my name on them were big enough to suit him. Davis Avenue, meanwhile, was renamed for Martin Luther King.

My father and I have a lot of the same instincts, which I suppose is why he always seemed to understand what I was up to when I was a kid. He understood that I had to play baseball. Mama was the one who had a hard time accepting it. It wasn't that she had anything against the game or against me playing it, but it bothered her that I was more interested in baseball than anything else, including schoolwork. She had her heart set on me going to college, and baseball was something that could get in the way. She would have preferred for me to play football, because football might have sent me to college. And that was one of the reasons why I stayed away from football—because I knew that if I got a football scholarship, it would keep me out of baseball. I did go out for football once in high school—to impress a cute majorette named Queenetta Jones, as much as anything—but there were some personal things that went on with the football team that I didn't care for, and I quit after a few days. The principal at Central High, Dr. Benjamin Baker, took exception to my decision, and we got into a little argument over it. He ended up chasing me down the hall, waving his cane at me.

Central didn't have a baseball team—none of the black schools did—but it had a fast-pitch softball team. I was a catcher, pitcher, and infielder, and managed to hit quite a few home runs. There wasn't a fence at our park, which meant that you had to run out your home runs. I thought I got around the bases in pretty good fashion, but I ran on my heels in a manner that must have looked peculiar to my friends. They called me Snowshoes. Looking back, it's strange that nobody said anything about the way I batted, which was cross-handed, with my left hand on top even though I was right-handed. But the fact is, I don't think anybody gave it a second thought. We were never told the right way to bat, and we didn't lose any sleep over technique. Coaching was something for white kids. I realized that I batted differently than other guys, but it felt right and it worked, so I saw no reason to change.

Softball was a big sport in the black communities, but to me, it was just something to do until I could play baseball. When the city started its rec-league baseball program, I was on a team called the Braves, ironically enough. Most of the guys on the Braves were older, but they made an exception for me because I had picked up a little reputation as a hitter. I suppose other people could see the talent I had, but I never thought I was any better than several other guys who played with and against us—guys like Lefty Morris and Marcine Chatman and Tin Cup Taylor and my friend Cornelius Giles. Lefty was the one everybody thought would make it big. He was a powerful first baseman from Down The Bay, and he later played some pro ball. He was the first black man to play in Johnson City, Tennessee, in the Appalachian League, and he was the best player they had. But he wasn't the kind of guy who could go along with everything that he had to put up with from coaches and fans and teammates, which was what it took if you wanted to make it. So he just hung on a few years in the Negro Leagues and then became a schoolteacher. It would have pleased Mama if I'd done the same thing.

Cornelius was a pitcher, and he played some Negro League ball with the Indianapolis Clowns. He also had a tryout with the Milwaukee Braves when I was with them, but his arm was shot by that time. He must have thrown it out pitching to me all those years. I learned to hit by hitting against Cornelius. When we weren't playing baseball at the park, we'd be playing with broomsticks and bottle caps in the yard or the street. I believe that my style of hitting was developed as a result of batting against bottle caps. Even in the big leagues, I never swung the bat like other power hitters. Most great home run hitters—guys like Mickey Mantle and Harmon Killebrew and Reggie Jackson—hit with their weight way back on their back foot. But I was the opposite. I had my weight on my front foot—especially early in my career

—and I got my power from lashing out at the last second with my hands. If you've ever tried to hit a bottle cap, you know that you can't sit back on your haunches. The way one of those things will dip and float, you've got to jump out and get it, and that's the way I always hit a baseball.

Cornelius and I were together all the time when one of us wasn't away at a relative's house. When it got dark and we couldn't pitch and hit anymore, we'd cook out in the yard. We'd build a fire and get some crayfish out of the ditch that ran in front of our house, pop their legs off, and boil them with anything else we could find in the garden—potatoes, turnips, okra, tomatoes, whatever. Of course, the pot didn't have a lid, so we boiled and ate all sorts of bugs along with everything else. For dessert, we'd sneak over to the neighbor's garden and get a couple of watermelons to bust open. If we ever had a nickel, though, our big treat was to go the grocery and get a cookie with icing inside. For a dime, you could get icing on the outside, too.

Other than playing ball and eating, we didn't do a whole lot. I'd lay on the floor at home and read Dick Tracy comic books for hours at a time. If Cornelius was over, we'd shoot marbles—I was as good as anybody in Toulminville. Other times, we'd just sit under the streetlights and brag. If we got bored, we'd fight. Cornelius would bite, and I would kick. At Christmas time, everybody roller-skated. And in February, the big event was the Colored Mardi Gras. I was a Boy Scout, and the Boy Scouts directed traffic during Mardi Gras. One year I had the honor of directing traffic at the busy corner of Davis Avenue and Lafayette. It was cold that day, and all I had was short pants because we couldn't afford to buy the long ones, but I wasn't about to give up my post at Davis and Lafayette.

Mama would have been a happy woman if I'd been as good at school as I was at Boy Scouts. I could always find my way back from the deep woods, and I was hard to beat at catching snakes. Almost every kind of snake could be found around Mobile, including rattlers, which we'd catch by tying a silk rag onto the end of a stick and dangling it in front of their eyes. When they bit down on the rag, we'd yank the stick and pull their teeth out. None of my friends were afraid of snakes—but a lot of us were afraid of water. I think it came from our mothers. They always told us to stay away from the bays and bayous. In my case, Mama had good reason to worry. Once, I slipped on a log and fell into a bayou, and I might have drowned if my friend hadn't pulled me out. I was lucky, at that, because he couldn't swim either.

Poor Mama—it seemed like if it wasn't the bayous, it was baseball. I guess she was afraid I could fall into baseball and drown, too, if she didn't watch out for me. And, in a way, she was right. Baseball might have ruined my life if I hadn't been good at it. I can understand now why Mama was so concerned about me, because I certainly made a mess out of high school.

I lost my enthusiasm for Central High after the principal chased me down the hall with his cane. On top of that, I knew I was going to be a ballplayer. There was no doubt in my mind. And so school didn't matter to me. School couldn't teach me how to play second base like Jackie Robinson. I could learn that better by listening to the Dodgers on the radio. So that's what I did. I would go to school in the morning, walk in the front door, walk out the back, and then go to Davis Avenue and shoot pool until the Dodger game came on or the movie house opened up. I skipped school something like forty days in a row, and finally Dr. Baker kicked me out. I was afraid to tell my mother and father about it, but somehow Daddy found out, and one afternoon he marched into the pool hall and signaled for me to follow him home. We had an old car parked in front of the house, and we must have sat in that old car and talked for an hour or two. He told me that he and Mama weren't going to let me quit school, and I told him I was going to be a ballplayer. Then he said that every morning he put two quarters in my pocket so I could go to school and have a good lunch, and he only took one quarter with him to work, because my education was more important than his stomach. He also said that he was going to enroll me in a private school, the Josephine Allen Institute.

But that would be the next fall. In the meantime, all I had to do was earn a little money and play ball. After a few games that spring in the rec league—mostly softball games—I caught the eye of a man named Ed Scott, who managed and played for a semipro team called the Mobile Black Bears. I knew that Mr. Scott wanted me to play for him, and I knew I'd get in trouble with Mama if I did. The Black Bears were mostly grown men, and, what was worse, they played on Sundays. So every time I saw Mr. Scott coming, I hid.

His mother kept telling me she'd let him play sometime, but not right now. I'd go by the house every weekend, and she would always put me off. My wife asked me why I just didn't leave those people alone. But I kept going by there. One time I saw him hiding around the side of the house, and when I looked over, he stepped back real fast. I didn't let him know I saw him. Well, I don't know how he worked it out at home, but the next day I saw him coming through the gate at Mitchell Field, where we played our games. He came up to me and the first thing he said was, "If I play for you, do I get a uniform?" I got him a uniform, and he played that day. He was only seventeen and the rest of us had wives and children. He was green as he could be. He stood up there at the plate upright, no crouch at all, and the other team figured he wasn't ready. The pitcher tried to get a fastball by him, and he hit a line drive that banged against the old tin fence they had around the outfield out there—nearly put the ball through the fence. They walked him the rest of the time.
—Ed Scott

That was 1951. Mama wouldn't let me travel with the Black Bears when they went out of town, but when they were at home in Prichard—just up the road from Toulminville—I was their shortstop every Sunday. The owner of the team, a man named Ed Tucker, paid the players ten dollars after every game. But he never paid me on Sunday. He would tell me to come by the house on Monday to get my money, and he or Mrs. Tucker would always stick a couple extra dollars in my hand.

To me, getting paid to play for the Black Bears seemed about as good as it could get for the time being. What I didn't realize was that Ed Scott did a little scouting for the Indianapolis Clowns of the Negro American League. Scott had played some Negro League ball himself with the Norfolk Stars, where the manager was a flashy little guy named Bunny Downs. By this time, Downs was the business manager of the Indianapolis Clowns, and Scott had been giving him reports on me. Then he arranged for the Clowns to come to Mitchell Field to play us, so Downs could get a look at me. I don't think I knew what was going on, but I hit the ball hard that day—a home run and maybe a double or two, as I recall—and after the game, Bunny Downs came up and asked me how I'd like to play shortstop for the Clowns. Well, I knew Mama wouldn't go for that one. I had to go back to school in the fall and try to stay there. But anyway, Mr. Downs came home and talked to Mama and said that when school was out next year he'd send for me. I figured I'd never hear from him again.

In the meantime, the Brooklyn Dodgers held a tryout camp in Mobile for black players late that summer. To me and my friends, the Dodgers meant Jackie Robinson and Roy Campanella and Don Newcombe. If there was any team that would give a black kid a fair opportunity, it was the Dodgers. I felt in my bones that someday I would join Jackie Robinson, and here was my chance. The problem was, I wasn't the kind of kid who stuck out in a crowd. Those boys from Down The Bay were good, and they were cocky enough to call attention to themselves. I was just a quiet, skinny boy who swung the bat cross-handed. Well, I got up there and took a cut or two, and the next thing I knew some big kid from Down The Bay was rushing me out of the box. One of the Dodger scouts told me I was too small, and that was it. Since that day, I've often wondered how many good black players were overlooked because a scout thought they were too small or too skinny. It was hard to scout black players then, because they didn't have the benefit of good coaching and there were no high school teams to watch. Those scouts should have looked me over and said to themselves, "What is this boy going to look like in a couple of years, when he starts eating and sleeping right and playing the game right?"

I had always been a Dodger fan, but I guess I changed my mind a little bit after that tryout camp. I wasn't disappointed when Bobby Thomson beat them out of the pennant with that famous home run about a month later. In fact, it was one of the greatest things I ever heard—not because the Dodgers lost, but because of the way it happened. Back then, you could walk down

Davis Avenue and hear the ball game playing on the radio in about every store you passed. When I heard that home run, I was so excited that I ran all the way home, imagining that I was Bobby Thomson on my way to home plate, where my teammates would pick me up on their shoulders and carry me off in front of thousands of cheering fans.

The reality, though, was that I was just a teenager having a hard time with high school. Part of the problem was that my mind was always on baseball. I kept wondering if the Clowns were really going to send for me, and after the first of the year I started checking the mailbox every day. By the end of the winter, I was sure they'd forgotten all about me. And then one day, there was the contract. It said the Clowns would pay me $200 a month, and I was supposed to meet the team for spring training in Winston-Salem, North Carolina. Of course, this school term wasn't over yet, but I couldn't miss this chance. I knew that if I waited around for a white scout to sign me, I might never get out of Mobile. Besides, I didn't think I'd make the team, anyway, and I'd probably be back in a week or two to finish school. I told Mama that if I made it, I'd still finish school in the offseason, and if I didn't make it, I'd go on to college. It wasn't easy for her, but $200 a month was a lot of money to a family like ours. It also helped that they threw in a couple of shirts for me and a suit for Daddy. I'm sure Ed Scott got some clothes out of the deal, too. The expression everybody used was, "Throw a little something on me."

In a few days, I was on my way to Winston-Salem, getting more and more frightened as the train took me farther away from Mobile and Mama. I kept wondering if I was doing the right thing, and what the Clowns would be like and whether I was any good. And I kept looking at that envelope Ed Scott gave me for Bunny Downs. I never did open it, but years later I found out what Mr. Scott had written. The note said, "Forget everything else about this player. Just watch his bat."

I guess I had a good reason to be scared. All I had going for me was my bat, and I didn't even know how to hold it.

3

When Jackie Robinson joined the Dodgers in 1947, it opened up a whole new world for black ballplayers and closed another. For the few carefully picked pioneers who followed Robinson over the next couple of years—Larry Doby, Roy Campanella, Don Newcombe, Satchel Paige, Monte Irvin, Hank Thompson, Willard Brown, Luke Easter—and for the hundreds who came along later, Jackie Robinson was the best thing that ever happened to their careers. But like so many historic passages, Robinson's didn't occur without casualties. For the hundreds who were already making a decent living in the Negro Leagues, Jackie Robinson was the beginning of nothing more than the end.

By 1952, when eighteen-year-old Henry Aaron joined the Indianapolis Clowns, only six of the major league's sixteen teams had broken the color line. And yet, the Negro National League was already a memory—it had broken up in 1948, when only Robinson, Campanella, Doby, and Paige had integrated the majors—and the Negro American League was a wheezing relic. From its first stirring moments, Robinson's quest consumed the headlines and hopes of the black communities, and the fallout crushed such teams as the Homestead Grays, New York Black Yankees, Baltimore Elite Giants, and Newark Eagles. The Eagles' attendance was reduced to less than half in the first year after Robinson joined the Dodgers. In the understandable excitement over baseball's long-awaited desegregation, the cultural and competitive heritage of the Negro Leagues was left behind in a darkened attic. While the black newspapers trumpeted the progress of the modern cause, Josh Gibson died in quiet agony and Cool Papa Bell returned unnoticed to the ghetto.

For more than three decades, though, the Negro Leagues had been a treasure of sport and Americana. Their heroes were legends, and their legends were epic. If the names and deeds of the Negro League stars were obscure to the white societies, they were folklore on the other side of town. And while, even now, formal history recognizes only a handful of the greatest Negro League players—the ones specially elected to the Hall of Fame—those who were there know that the company was fast, deep, and fancy. On one team alone—the Pittsburgh Crawfords of the mid-1930s—there were five Hall of Famers (Paige, Gibson, Bell, Oscar Charleston, and Judy Johnson) and at least four others (Sam Bankhead, Jimmy Crutchfield, Vic Harris, and Leroy Matlock) who would have certainly been major-league stars. The tales of Paige and Gibson are part of baseball's hand-me-down history, but common knowledge doesn't accommodate the fact that Turkey Stearnes hit as many home runs as Gibson, if not more, and that Mule Suttles hit them as far as Gibson, if not farther, and that Smokey Joe Williams was as good a pitcher as Paige, if not better, and that Bullet Joe Rogan threw as hard as Paige, if not harder. In the big-city ballparks of the North and the backroad sandlots of the South, the Negro Leagues filled the fields with since-forgotten players who, like Stearnes and Rogan, were earlier versions of the black Hall of Famers who would come later to the major leagues. But by 1952, the great Negro Leaguers had gone on or gone away—to big-time ball or back-lot oblivion. There was but one player of reckoning left in the Negro League, a schoolboy shortstop for the Indianapolis Clowns who batted cross-handed.

After Aaron, a few more Negro Leaguers would make it to the majors, but only one who made it big. Ernie Banks, who was in the army in 1952, returned the next year to play for the Kansas City Monarchs until he was signed and brought up by the Chicago Cubs late in the summer. The others were faintly remembered, transitory players such as Pat Scantlebury, Jehosie Heard, Lino Donoso, John Kennedy, and Pancho Herrera.

With teams coming and mostly going—Mobile was actually in the league for part of the 1957 season—the NAL played it out until the fifties were over. Then, only the Clowns were left. They barnstormed, and they clowned; they tried a woman second baseman, a woman pitcher, midgets, giants, white guys . . . and finally they, too, gave it up in the seventies. When they did, there

was only one last link to the old Negro Leagues—an aging out-
fielder for the Atlanta Braves who was closing in on Babe Ruth's
all-time record for home runs.

◆ ◆ ◆

They called it spring training, but there wasn't much training
involved and the weather in Winston-Salem didn't feel like any
spring I'd ever known. The wind ripped across the field without
mercy, cutting right through the threadbare shirt I practiced in.
The veterans had jackets, but they weren't about to hand one over
to an eighteen-year-old rookie.

The Clowns didn't think too much of rookies. They had a lot
of veterans on the team, and they had won the Negro League
championship the last couple of years without any 150-pound
teenagers. I was just a nuisance to most of them, a raggedy kid
who was in the way. They made fun of my worn-out shoes, and
they asked me if I got my glove from the Salvation Army. They
didn't bother to find out if I could hit. It was just like that Dodger
tryout all over again—every time I'd step into the cage, some big
veteran would come charging in and tell me to get out of there. I
couldn't do much of anything but stand on the sidelines shiver-
ing. At night, we stayed in rooms over a pool hall, and the older
players would hang around that pool hall talking about how fine
it would be when they could leave the little country kids behind
and start seeing some towns. Buster Haywood, the manager,
would wink at me when he said that, but I didn't take it as a vote
of confidence. I was sure that I would be back at Josephine Allen
in a couple of weeks.

Looking back on it, I can understand how the Clowns must
have felt about somebody like me. To start with, being as quiet as
I was and knowing as little as I did about the world, I was an easy
target. Back then, ballplayers were traditionally rough on rookies,
anyway, because every rookie who made the team cost a veteran
his job. For the guys on the Clowns, though, it was more than
that. They didn't have the luxury of concerning themselves with

something like tradition. The only tradition they knew about was getting kicked in the teeth. The best players on the team were twenty-five- and twenty-nine- and thirty-four-year-old men who had been in baseball since they were teenagers themselves and were better than half the guys who were making ten times as much money in the big leagues. They knew that they were going nowhere, and they also knew that if they were just ten years younger—if they were me—they would someday be up there with Stan Musial and Ted Williams and Jackie Robinson, whom they knew as the kid who used to play a little infield for the Kansas City Monarchs. They could see that a guy like me would get the chance they never had. In the meantime, all they could do was try to hang on with the Clowns for their $250 or $300 a month, and damn if they were going to make it easy for some kid who had never eaten a cheese sandwich on the bus to Greenwood, Mississippi.

There were no big-time stars on the Clowns anymore, but there were guys who could play the game. Buster Haywood himself was a good catcher, although not as good as our regular catcher, a guy named Piggy Sands, whom the Clowns had signed out of Sing-Sing. Piggy had played on Jackie Robinson's barnstorming team at the end of the previous season and had been named the most valuable player of the tour. One of our outfielders, Speed Merchant, had led the Negro American League in stolen bases a time or two. Our second baseman, Ray Neil, was the team leader and a polished ballplayer who had a tryout with the Dallas team of the Texas League just before he reported to us. The word was that Dallas let him go because he wasn't flashy enough. There had never been a black player in that part of the country, and I guess they figured that if they were going to have one, he ought to play like a black man was supposed to play.

I was the only player on our team who eventually went to the big leagues, but one of our pitchers, a big fellow named Jim Tugerson, signed the next season with Hot Springs of the Cotton States League. The problem was that most of the Cotton States teams were in Mississippi, and Tugerson wasn't allowed to play there. The other teams went so far as to kick Hot Springs out of the league until the president of the minor leagues got involved and reversed their decision. Maybe those Mississippi teams knew something, because Tugerson ended up winning about twenty-nine games for Hot Springs that year. But he wasn't any better than several other pitchers on the Clowns. One was his brother, Leander. There was also an older guy named Fireball Cohen who earned extra money by driving the bus. And our ace was a little lefthander named Ted Richardson, who was my traveling buddy.

I might never have gone on the road, though, if one of the regular infielders hadn't gotten hurt about the time we started playing exhibition games. When that happened, Haywood had to put me in the lineup—everybody else was either hurt or a pitcher —and as soon as I got to the plate the hits started to fall. As frightened as I was about everything else, it never occurred to me that I might not hit. I got one-hop singles through the infield, low-riding doubles through the outfield, and a home run to right-center now and then. I tried to act like it was nothing, but I could tell that people were noticing me. It was a small league, and it didn't take long to make a reputation.

The first time I saw Aaron, we were playing the Clowns down in Alabama or Louisiana during the spring. I noticed this young boy hitting in the fourth spot, and I said, "Buster, what's this kid hitting fourth?" He said, "Buck, you just wait and see him swing the bat." Well, I had some pretty good pitchers who had been around the block a few times, and the first time he came up I told the pitcher to throw this kid a good fastball. He threw a fastball, and the kid hit it up against the right-field fence. The next time he came up I had my best lefthander in there, and I said to him, now throw this kid a good fastball. He threw his fastball on the first pitch, and the kid hit it against the center-field fence. I looked over at Buster, and Buster was just laughing at me. The last time, I had the star of my staff in there, an old pro named Hilton Smith, and I told Smith to throw this kid some curve balls. The kid hit a curve ball over the left-field fence. I told Buster then, I said, "Tell you what. You and I both know that by the time you get to Kansas City to play us, this kid won't be with you anymore." No way a hitter like that was going to stay around the Negro League.—Buck O'Neil, manager of the Kansas City Monarchs

It was somewhere around that time that the owner of the Clowns, a man from Tarrytown, New York, named Syd Pollock, wrote a letter to John Mullen, who was the farm director of the Boston Braves. About the only way a Negro League team could make any money in those days was by selling players to organized baseball, and Pollock's best customer was Boston. He wasn't writing Mullen about me specifically, but at the bottom of the letter he added a note that said: "P.S. We got an 18-year-old shortstop batting cleanup for us."

Somehow, the New York Giants found out about me, too—probably through their great scout, Alex Pompez—and then a couple more teams. Pretty soon, there were scouts on every side of us. I knew I was going to have to make a decision before long, but I didn't know what to do, because I wasn't eager to leave the Clowns. I was having a good time. My teammates were even talking to me. Besides, none of the scouts were saying anything about giving me money for signing with them. But one night in Oklahoma, Ed Scott called me from Mama and Daddy's house and convinced me that if the opportunity came to sign with a big-league team, I couldn't pass it up. I guess that was when I told Mr. Pollock I would go to the Braves if he thought that was the best thing. So he and John Mullen made a deal over the telephone. It was just a verbal agreement for a thirty-day option. Either the Braves would sign me after thirty days or give up the option. That way, Mr. Pollock could keep me with the Clowns for a while. He said I was his drawing card.

I guess I was, at that, because they had posters made up with my picture on them. I even had top billing over King Tut and Spec Bebop, the guys who made the Clowns clowns. We were a serious baseball team, but the fans expected us to do some clowning to live up to our name. That was what had made the Clowns the top attraction in the Negro Leagues. They were the Globetrotters of baseball, and in fact, before I was with them, their big drawing card had been the famous Globetrotter, Goose Tatum. They say that Tatum was one of the fanciest first basemen you ever saw. The old Clowns also had a catcher named Pepper Bassett who would catch a couple innings sitting in a rocking chair, and a contortionist who coached first base standing on one hand. When I was there, we still did the shadowball routine, taking infield practice without a baseball. But after warm-ups, the players played and left the clowning to Tut and Bebop. Tut—Richard Tut was his name—was a former player himself, and Bebop was a dwarf who acted as Tut's sidekick. They would do routines where Tut would have a toothache and Bebop would yank it out with pliers, or they would pretend like they were fishing and the boat turned over, that sort of thing. They threw buckets of confetti into the crowd—all the same stunts the Globetrotters did. The fans ate it up.

The Clowns were also the best team in the league, and we drew well wherever we went—which was just about everywhere east of the Rockies except Indianapolis. I don't know why we were called the Indianapolis Clowns, because we never made it to Indiana as long as I was with the team. We took off from North Carolina and stayed on the bus all the way to Texas and Oklahoma, then circled back through the South and up the East Coast, only getting off long enough to play the ballgames every night. We never stayed overnight anywhere except Saturday nights. By that time, a bed looked awfully good. Later on in organized ball, they used to tease me that I could sleep anywhere. I learned how to do that by sleeping six nights a week on a bus full of loud, sweaty ballplayers. And I have to say, I was good at it. King Tut and Bebop and Piggy and some of the guys would be back there playing cards and listening to music and drinking and hollering, and I'd just close my eyes and wake up for breakfast. My roommate—whoever sat next to you was your roommate—was an outfielder named James Jenkins, who was quiet, like me. Everybody called him Preacher, because he was always reading the Bible and quoting it. Preacher taught me how to conserve my money. We all got two dollars a day for meal money, and he and I would put ours together to buy bread and sandwich meat or peanut butter. After we bought our food, Preacher would stick his extra dollar in an envelope and send it home to his wife. Somehow, I wasn't able to send home any of my meal money. In fact, I was always asking Bunny Downs for a few dollars' advance on my salary.

We almost never stopped in a restaurant, because it was hard to find one that would serve us. We just picked up some groceries when we saw a store and ate on the highway. Sometimes we'd be on the road for a week before we got a chance to wash our clothes. When we finally stayed over somewhere on Saturday night, most of the guys would take off on the town. You never knew what was going to happen on Saturday night, and Buster always made sure we left behind our Clowns jackets before we went out, just to be safe. The veterans had been in most of the towns before, many times, and they knew where to find good times and women. I tagged along with Richardson, but I couldn't keep up with the rest of the guys. They laughed at me because I drank Scotch and milk with a spoonful of sugar. I wasn't in their league when it came to partying—and not when it came to the ladies, either. Especially Bebop. Women were all over that little guy.

We'd been playing games for about two weeks when we got to Texas, which was where the scouts really picked me up. They started phoning my daddy's house in Mobile, and that was why Ed Scott called me in Oklahoma. Everybody seemed to know that I wouldn't be in the Negro League for long—everybody but me, anyway. I was no major-league infielder, but I must have been playing a good enough shortstop, because in one game against the Monarchs we set a league record with seven double plays. The first time my name was ever mentioned in the *Pittsburgh Courier,* the leading black newspaper for sports, it said, "Henry Aaron has been the shining light for the Funmakers in the early games. His batting and fielding have been a revelation." That was news to me. The only revelation I knew about was at the end of the New Testament.

After our southwest swing, we came back East—Sikeston, Mo., Kansas City, Chattanooga, Knoxville, Nashville, Cullman, Ala., Chattanooga again, Asheville, Spartanburg, Suffolk, and finally Baltimore. I was learning more about America than I ever would at Josephine Allen. I was also learning more about Josh Gibson. When I hit two home runs at Memorial Stadium in Baltimore—one of them after my top hand had slipped off the bat— it started everybody talking, and when people around the Negro League talked about home runs, they talked about Josh Gibson. It seemed like we heard Josh Gibson stories wherever we went. I still wonder sometimes how far that man must have really hit the ball. One thing I can tell you—he hit it a lot farther than I ever did.

The day after Baltimore, we were rained out of a big Sunday doubleheader at Griffith Stadium in Washington. We had breakfast while we were waiting for the rain to stop, and I can still envision sitting with the Clowns in a restaurant behind Griffith Stadium and hearing them break all the plates in the kitchen after we were finished eating. What a horrible sound. Even as a kid, the irony of it hit me: Here we were in the capital in the land of freedom and equality, and they had to destroy the plates that had touched the forks that had been in the mouths of black men. If dogs had eaten off those plates, they'd have washed them.

From Washington, we went up to Pennsylvania and then Buffalo, which was really more of a home base for us than Indianapolis, because it was closer to Mr. Pollock. I hadn't heard back from the Braves yet, but I wasn't suffering from lack of attention. The Chicago *Defender* said that "major-league scouts are swarming to parks where the Clowns are playing to get a good look at the young Aaron . . . All seem to agree that he stands at the plate like a Ted Williams."

> *Aaron was marked. Everywhere we went, he was the man. Birmingham had a pitcher named Dick Powell who had been in a big-league camp, and he didn't know anything about Aaron. When Aaron came up, his third baseman said, "Look, man, don't throw him nothing inside." I don't know what Powell threw him, but whatever it was, Aaron hit it right dead at the third baseman. He tried to turn away, and the ball hit him smack in the butt. That third baseman was all over Powell when*

that happened. After the inning, we told Aaron that the pitcher had been up with the big leaguers, and he said, "You mean to tell me he was getting by with that stuff up there?"

Aaron could hit anybody. And for a skinny kid, he was incredibly strong. Especially in the forearms and wrists. I remember one boy made him mad once about something, and Aaron just grabbed that boy by the wrists and held him up against the wall. And when he put those wrists into the ball, it would take off. It wasn't long before the scouts knew all about him. The Braves' guy, Dewey Griggs, followed us all around the East. I had a little deal myself with the Pittsburgh scout in Buffalo, Dick Fisher. He ran a sporting goods store there, and he told me if I put him on to a player that he signed, he'd give me a thousand dollars. If the player made the majors, I'd get five thousand. Well, as soon as we got to Buffalo, I went straight to the store and I said, "I think I got you a man." Fisher was supposed to go up to Canada with his wife, but I talked him into staying around to watch Aaron. We had a doubleheader the next day, and Aaron hit the ball all over the lot. I talked to Fisher afterwards and he said Aaron looked all right, but he didn't pull the ball. I told him he didn't get any pitches to pull, so he hit 'em over the right-field fence. He said, okay, he'd talk to Branch Rickey, who was running the Pirates then. I told him he'd better hurry up, because somebody was going to grab Aaron quick. I don't know if Rickey ever gave him the go-ahead, but it didn't matter. It was too late by then—Fireball Cohen of the Indianapolis Clowns

It rained in Buffalo, but I had a good day against the Memphis Red Sox. I hit a home run and had a few other hits in the first game, and between games I noticed a man with a hat standing by the rail. You could always pick out a scout. He called me over to talk to him, introduced himself as Dewey Griggs of the Braves, and told me he was a little concerned about my style of playing. I had a habit of fielding the ball on one knee, and I would sort of flip it underhanded to first base. He didn't know if I could really throw. Also, I used to ease around the field at about three-quarters speed most of the time, and he wondered if I could run. I said that my daddy had told me never to hurry unless I had to, and it was advice that I believed in. But if he wanted to see me run and throw, I'd do what I could. Mr. Griggs also suggested that I hold the bat with my right hand on top instead of cross-handed.

The first time I came to bat after that, I held the bat the right way and hit a home run. I never batted cross-handed again, except for now and then when a tough pitcher had two strikes on me. The next time up, I bunted to show Mr. Griggs that I could run. And whenever they hit a ball to me, I made sure I threw it overhanded to first base, as hard as I could. I guess Mr. Griggs was satisfied because he wrote a letter to John Mullen that night.

May 25, 1952

Mr. John Mullen
32 Gaffney St.
Boston, Mass.

Dear John:

Scouted the double header between Indianapolis and Memphis at Buffalo Sunday afternoon. Heavy showers in the morning left the playing field in a muddy condition and prevented good fielding.

Henry Aaron the seventeen year old shortstop of the Indianapolis club looked very good. In the first game he had seven chances, two fly balls back of third and five hard hit ground balls. Started one double play from short to second to first, hit three for five, two line drive singles over third and short and a perfect bunt down third base line. His only error was a low throw from deep short. These hits were made off a good looking left hander. Altho the official scorer gave the boy four for five, I gave the third baseman an error on the play.

In the second game he accepted five chances without an error, started one double play from short to second to first and hit three for four. Off the starting left hand pitcher he hit an outside curve ball over the right field fence, three hundred and thirty feet away and dropped down another perfect bunt. In the sixth inning he hit a low inside curve for a single over second base off a right hander with the bases loaded.

At the present time he is hitting around 400 and batting fourth for the club. He made no effort to go either to his right or left as the slippery infield made it impossible to make these plays. During the intermission I talked with Syd Pollock and the boy asking why he made all his throws to first either under handed or side armed when he had plenty of time to gun the ball from deep short over handed. Also why he aimed before throwing the ball on the double play. In the second game he rifled two good overhanded throws to first and made the double play without the slightest hesitation.

On June 15th Indianapolis plays two games with Kansas City at Buffalo and at that time I will give you a complete story on the boy. I am satisfied with the boys hitting. However I want to see him make plays both to his right and left and slow hit balls that he has to come in after. Also another look at his throwing. This boy could be the answer.

Sincerely yours,

Dewey S. Griggs

When the letter arrived in Boston, John Mullen realized that thirty days had passed since his telephone agreement with Syd Pollock, and he called Mr. Pollock right away to see about getting me under contract. Mr. Pollock was at a league meeting in Chicago, sharing a room with Tom Baird, the owner of the Kansas City Monarchs. When Mullen called the hotel, Baird answered the phone and said that Mr. Pollock was down in the lobby receiving a telegram from the New York Giants. Mullen called back in a few minutes, and Mr. Pollock told him that he was about to close a deal with the Giants. That was the last thing Mullen wanted to hear, because by this time his general manager, John Quinn, knew about me, and the Braves didn't want me to get away. They especially didn't want to lose another black player to the Giants. A few years before, the Braves were all ready to close a deal with the Birmingham Black Barons for Willie Mays when the Giants went in and signed Mays directly. Baseball's policy with the Negro Leagues was that you had to deal with the player's team, but the Giants had found a way around that—they learned that Mays wasn't really under contract with Birmingham. The Braves were still angry over that deal, and so Mullen wasn't about to back down on this one. Mr. Pollock informed him that the thirty-day option had expired, but Mullen didn't want to hear about technicalities. They went back and forth for a while, and finally Mr. Pollock agreed to honor the Braves' option if that was my choice.

On May 29, Mr. Pollock received telegrams from Mullen and John Schwarz of the Giants containing the details of their offers. The Braves would pay me $350 a month and send me to their Eau Claire, Wisconsin, club in the Northern League. The Clowns would receive $2,500 immediately and another $7,500 if the Braves kept me in the organization for thirty days. The Giants would pay me $250 a month to play for Sunbury, Pennsylvania, in the Interstate League. They would also pay the Clowns $2,500 immediately, $2,500 if I was promoted to Triple-A, $2,500 if I was promoted to the major-league roster, and $7,500 if I stayed on the major-league roster for thirty days. Mr. Pollock would have made more money in the long run if I had signed with the Giants, but there was no bonus money for me either way. I was aware that with the Giants I would have a chance to team up with Mays, who had been the last player to make it big from the Negro League—the Chicago *Defender* called me "the best prospect seen in the Negro League since Willie Mays"—but I never considered that I might have played next to him in the outfield. I was an infielder. On the other hand, I thought my chances to make the Braves were better and that they were being fairer to me, paying me more money to play in a lower classification. Besides, the Giants spelled my name "Arron" on their telegram.

When it came time to sign my Braves contract, I didn't realize that I was supposed to write my name in cursive. I printed a few letters until somebody told me to scratch it out and start over. My signature was not enough to make the contract legal, anyway. I was still a minor, which meant that my father had to sign it, too. The Braves sent a copy to Mobile, and Daddy carried it to a lawyer before he would sign it. I'm sure he paid the lawyer more than I got paid in that contract. But we got it done, and after we did, the Buffalo *Criterion* reported that "the Clowns have sold their star shortstop to the Boston Braves for one of the highest prices paid for an American League star in many years." I have to laugh when I read that now. It makes you wonder how much the other guys brought.

My reporting date was June 11, so I was with the Clowns for another two weeks after I signed. Somewhere during that time, I lost my lead in the NAL batting race. But it took about two or three weeks to get the new statistics reported, and when I left for Eau Claire, the newspapers were still writing about me as the leading hitter in the league. The final statistics from that season have disappeared—none of the black newspapers ran them, and the news service that compiled them doesn't even have a record—but I'm pretty sure I wasn't the 1952 NAL batting champion, despite what's been written all these years. And I didn't hit any .467, which was the number generally reported. That might have been the latest figure published at the time I left, but I had actually fallen well under .400 by then.

When the time came to report to the Braves, Mr. Pollock gave me a cardboard suitcase to mark the occasion. That was my signing bonus. We played a doubleheader at Comiskey Park in Chicago on June 8, and then I put that cardboard suitcase on the train for Milwaukee, where I caught a little North Central Air Lines two-engine commuter bound for fame, fortune, and Eau Claire, Wisconsin. I'll never forget that plane. It was the first flight of my life, and the worst flight. I was a nervous wreck, bouncing around in the sky over a part of the country I'd hardly ever heard about, much less been to, headed for a white town to play ball with white boys.

The team was on the road when I arrived in Eau Claire, and I checked into the YMCA. There were two other black players on the club, and they shared a room there—Julie Bowers, a catcher from New Jersey, and John Covington, a big, good-looking guy and lefthanded outfielder from North Carolina. Covington would later be my teammate in Milwaukee, where we knew him as Wes. It was obvious that he was a big-league talent and pretty obvious that Julie wasn't. Julie was a solid player, but he had no dreams about making the majors. He was the type of black player you always found on minor-league teams back then—an older guy who was there to provide company for the younger black players and keep them out of trouble.

We were not the first black players in Eau Claire. Two years before, Bill Bruton had been there along with a pitcher named Roy White. Bruton was named Rookie of the Year in the Northern League, and the next year the best rookie was another black player for Eau Claire, an outfielder named Horace Garner. Bruton and Garner—and to some extent, myself, although I didn't realize it yet—were the players who were being counted on to clear the way for all the blacks in the Braves' organization. Bruton certainly made things a lot easier for the rest of us in Eau Claire. He was a great outfielder, an exciting base runner, and a gentleman. By the end of his season there, he was the most popular player on the team—and that was no small thing in a town where the women and girls were warned not to walk down the street with him.

Eau Claire was not a hateful place for a black person—nothing like the South—but we didn't exactly blend in. The only other black man in town was a fellow who used to stand on the street corner flipping a silver dollar. Wherever I went in Eau Claire, I had the feeling that people were watching me, looking at me as though I were some kind of strange creature. I remember eating breakfast at a table next to a young family, and a girl about seven years old was staring at me so hard that she didn't touch her food. Another time, I was walking through the parking lot after a game, and I noticed a man just standing against his car gawking at me. It made you feel like you should start tap-dancing or something.

> I got hit in the head one game in Eau Claire and had to spend about three weeks in the hospital. I was the first black person who ever went into the hospital there. I felt like a sideshow freak. They assigned different nurses to me every day so they could all get the experience of being in my presence. Actually, I was treated very nicely. I received so many letters and flowers that they had to move me from a single room to a double. The nurses would open my mail and water the flowers for me. All but this one. One nurse, a lady who must have been sixty or

seventy years old, had the job of putting water in my pitcher every day. The pitcher was on a tray by the door, and I'd look up and see this arm coming around the door and picking up the pitcher. Then the arm would come around and put the pitcher back. I never saw anything more than the arm. Then one day I was out of bed when she came, and I looked at her. She just froze. I said something, and she just stared at me. She poured the water very nervously, then left. I asked somebody about it later, and they said she had just never seen a black person before and didn't know what to expect. Well, one day I was close enough to the door and I handed her the pitcher. Then she started to acknowledge me, like bowing her head real fast. Finally, she said something. After that, we had a little conversation, and by the time I left the hospital, she was sitting at the side of the bed talking to me like an old friend.—Wes Covington of the Eau Claire Bears

If it was strange for those white folks in Eau Claire to be around black people, it was just as strange for me to be around them. There was nothing in my experience that prepared me for white people. I wasn't much of a talker anyway, but in Eau Claire you couldn't pry my mouth open. It didn't take much to tell that my way of talking was different than the way people talked in Wisconsin, and I felt freakish enough as it was. I might not have said fifty words all summer if it hadn't been for Wes and Julie and a white family that sort of adopted me. They were big supporters of the team—Eau Claire was that kind of town—and for some reason, this family just took a liking to me. Especially the daughter. She was a teenager, like me, and we'd sit out on the porch holding hands. Nobody made a big deal about it, but we made sure we didn't go out in public together. Once she and I and Wes and Julie and a bunch of girls went up to a big hangout called Elks Mound, out in the country, and somehow a bunch of local guys found out and came looking for us. I don't know what they would have done if they had found us, but I wasn't eager to find out. The girls hid us in the bushes until they were gone.

But that sort of thing didn't worry me as much as the idea of playing ball against white boys. I never doubted my ability, but when you hear all your life that you're inferior, it makes you wonder if the other guys have something you've never seen before. If they do, I'm still looking for it. It didn't take long to find out that the ball was still round after it left a white pitcher's hand, and it responded the same way when you hit it with a bat. I batted seventh in the order, and when I came up in the second inning for my first time at bat in organized baseball, I was more nervous that it was my first time at bat against a white pitcher. That was the unknown, as far as I was concerned. When I hit a hard single over third base against a lefthander for St. Cloud named Art Rosser, I knew that everything would be fine. The next day, the Eau Claire *Leader* gave me my first press clipping in organized ball: "Hank Aaron, 18-year-old Negro League shortshop, made an auspicious beginning by banging out singles in his first two trips, driving home Collins Morgan, who had hit doubles to deep center field each time. Aaron handled seven chances but muffed a potential double play ball as St. Cloud scored the deciding runs in the sixth inning." As I read that now, I'm surprised they called me Hank, because I didn't think anybody called me that until I made it up with Milwaukee.

The next night, I ended the game by starting a double play, but Covington was the hero with two home runs, one of them a 400-foot grand slam. He was the power hitter on the team and the guy who drove in the big runs. I batted second in the order after the first night and didn't hit a home run until my second week. It was in the tenth inning against a lefthander for Fargo-Moorhead named Reuben Stohs, who later became a doctor of psychology and developed personality tests for major-league ballclubs.

> I remember our manager saying what a fantastic prospect Aaron was. I'd look twice at him and think, "What do they see in this guy?" He wasn't impressive physically, and his strike zone was from his shoes to the tip of his cap. But the quickness of his bat was amazing. When I pitched to him that night, I got him out on a curve the first time. In the tenth inning the count went to three-and-two and I threw a high fastball. I could see his eyes get wide. He went up on his toes to get that ball, and just whipped it out of the park.—Reuben Stohs of Fargo-Moorhead

That home run came at the right time for me, because I had been so depressed that I thought hard about quitting. It was something that a lot of black players went through in the minor leagues back then. You can't imagine how alone we felt. It was almost like being in a foreign country, because we couldn't do anything the way we were accustomed to doing it. When John Roseboro played in Sheboygan, he wrote to his parents and said, "Send me the clippers. These peckers don't know how to cut a nigger's hair." It was that sort of thing at every turn.

What made it worse for me in Eau Claire was an incident that affected me on the field. About a week after I got there, we were playing Superior when somebody hit a ground ball to our second baseman. He tossed the ball to me, because there was a man on first—a catcher named Chuck Wiles—and when I threw on to get the double play, the ball smacked Wiles square in the forehead. They carried him off the field in a stretcher, unconscious. I don't think he ever played ball after that. I felt horrible, and on top of everything else, they booed me in Superior every time I came to bat for the rest of the season.

Around the same time, I was taking batting practice left-handed, toying with the idea of becoming a switch-hitter, when the bat slipped out of my hand and broke the nose of one of my teammates. After that, I never again tried to bat left-handed. I regret that now, because after batting cross-handed for so long, I would have been a natural switch-hitter.

Anyway, I was feeling awful about all these things and was ready to pack everything into that cardboard suitcase and go back to Mobile. I called home and told them I was on my way. But my brother, Herbert Junior, took the phone and told me I'd be crazy to leave. He said there was nothing to come home to, and if I left, I'd be walking out on the best break I could ever hope to get. Years later, when I talked with other black players, I found out that a lot of them almost quit in the minor leagues. Billy Williams actually left his team in Amarillo, Texas, and went back home to Mobile. But when he got there, all his friends and kids from the neighborhood kept swarming around him and asking about pro ball, and he realized he was about to blow a chance that the rest of them dreamed about—which was exactly what Herbert Junior said to me.

I felt better after that, and after a few weeks I was leading the league in hitting. Around the end of June, one of the Braves' top scouts, Billy Southworth, came to watch us play. I thought I made a pretty good account of myself when he was there, but I was surprised to read in the local paper that, when he was asked about the best prospects on the team, the only player he mentioned was a first baseman named Dick Engquist. Covington and I were practically tearing up the league at the time. I'm not sure what the strategy was—things happened to black ballplayers that I still can't explain—but for some reason, he didn't want to single us out in the newspaper even though he knew we were the best players. I'm sure of this, because I've seen the report that he filed about me. He wrote, "For a baby-face kid of 18 years his playing ability is outstanding. I will see the remaining games but will send in the report now, 'cause regardless of what happens tonight, it won't change my mind in the least about this boy's ability."

Southworth's report was a little different from the one sent in by my manager, Bill Adair. The first thing I found out about Adair was that he was from Mobile, which I didn't receive as thrilling news. I knew how white people from Mobile thought about black people from Mobile, and I wondered if I could ever be the equal of a white player in his eyes. As it turned out, Adair was a fair and good manager—he was virtually a legend in Eau Claire— and he gave me every chance to prove myself. Apparently, though, I failed to impress him away from the batter's box. "Nobody can guess his IQ," he wrote, "because he gives you nothing to go on . . . The kid looks lazy, but he isn't. He may not be a major-league shortstop, but as a hitter he has everything." I suppose the comments about my intelligence and my laziness could be taken the wrong way, but Adair was just reporting on what he saw: I didn't have anything to say, and I didn't sprint around the field like Pete Rose. That wasn't my way; and it wasn't, or isn't, the way that a lot of black players do things. A lot of white people don't seem to understand—maybe Adair was an exception—that

it's just human nature for some black people to do things deliberately. Maybe that comes from pulling a mule twelve hours a
day and not getting paid: Why hurry?

In mid-July—a month after I reported to Eau Claire—I was
selected to play in the Northern League All-Star Game. The only
catch was that the game was in Superior, where they still hated
me for hitting Chuck Wiles with that throw. I singled my first
time up, but sprained my ankle trying to break up a double
play—something that the Superior fans didn't find to be too un-
fortunate. The whole night turned out to be like an omen for all
the All-Star Games I would be in during the next twenty-two
years.

Meanwhile, our team was turning things around. An infielder
named John Goryl, who later played with the Cubs and Twins
and also managed the Twins, arrived in Eau Claire at about the
same time I did, and we went on a ten-game winning streak. We'd
had a losing record before Goryl and I got there, but with the
whole team in place we started to put some pressure on Superior,
which led the league. We slowed down when Covington got hurt,
though, and it turned out that we were too thin in pitching to go
all the way. At one point, a guy named Bobby Brown—not the
future president of the American League, but a little lefthander
from Brooklyn—had to pitch both games of a doubleheader
against St. Cloud . . . and, amazingly, won them both. The same
day, Covington hit his fourth grand slam of the season. At that
point, if people had known that one of our players would someday be the all-time, major-league home run leader, everybody
would have assumed that Covington would be the guy. Wes was
loaded with natural power, but even so, he didn't lead the Northern League in home runs. That distinction went to a guy from
Fargo-Moorhead named Frank Gravino, who had a beautiful
swing but never made it in the big leagues because his eyes went
bad. I didn't end up leading the league in hitting, either. I batted
.336, but it wasn't good enough to hold off a black outfielder
for Duluth, a former Negro League player named Joe Caffie
who made it up with the Cleveland Indians a couple of years
later.

Our team finished third, and the only thing I won that season was Rookie of the Year. The Eau Claire *Leader* reported it this way: "Henry (Hank) Aaron, 18-year-old Mobile, Ala., colored shortstop for the Eau Claire Bears, has been named as the outstanding rookie in the Northern League for the 1952 season. In a poll of sports writers, managers and umpires, Aaron rolled up 75 points, an amazing total that more than surpassed the combined totals of his three rivals . . . Other players who got votes for first place included John Covington, Eau Claire colored outfielder, and John Goryl, Eau Claire third baseman . . . Aaron is the third of his race to win the George Treadwell–Duluth Dukes Memorial Award." The news was not that I was the third straight Eau Claire player to win the award—after Bruton and Garner—but that I was the third straight member of my race to win it.

I can't explain why I got so many more votes than Covington. I only outhit him by six points, and he had twenty-four home runs to my nine and drove in a lot more. Julie Bowers also hit over .300, but somehow we all knew that Wes and I were the ones being watched—we were on our way up the organizational ladder while Julie would be sticking around the low minors. Maybe the Braves took advantage of some of their black players that way—holding them in the minor leagues to look after the younger blacks. Maybe all the teams did. But at the same time, I know that John Mullen went out of his way to see that guys like Wes and me had clean shots at getting to the big leagues. He also looked after us in personal ways. For instance, I would have probably gotten in a lot of trouble with the draft board if it hadn't been for John Mullen. The Korean War was going on, and one of the first things Mullen told me after I signed was that I had to register for the draft. I told him, "Mr. John, I don't fool with them and they don't fool with me." In the South, sometimes blacks could take advantage of the stereotypes that way—turning things around to work for them instead of against them. I wasn't above doing that if I could get away with it. But Mullen said, "Henry, this is the law. You have to do it." I wasn't drafted right away when I registered, but Covington was.

When I was called into the army, Hank and I had to change our plans a little bit. All summer long, we were just two punks talking about the big leagues. The team would ride around Wisconsin and Minnesota and North and South Dakota in our Nash station wagons, and there was nothing but open road. We had lots of time to talk and dream, and before long, we had it all figured out how we would get to the big leagues. We'd do it together all the way up, winning batting titles and home run championships. Then I got drafted the next spring, and I told Hank I was going to have to go fight the war for him, but when I got out I would just do things right behind him—whatever he did, I'd come along and do the same thing. He said he'd do it better. Well, the next year he won the batting title at Jacksonville, and the first year I was back, I won the batting title at Jacksonville.

As it turned out, we weren't teammates again until I made it up with the Braves in 1956, and we were never really as close again as we were that summer in the Northern League. We went through a lot that summer and it brought us together, but Hank and I were really very different. I was talkative and adventurous, and Hank enjoyed quiet times. He'd bring a pocket radio on the road with him, and just lay back and listen. If we had a day off on the road, we'd find out what movie was playing in town. Movies were always a big thing with Hank. He'd just sit there with his popcorn and be content. In Eau Claire, there was a park with a nice lake right outside the stadium, and on game days Hank and some of the guys would bring fishing poles and just sit out there fishing until it was time to get in uniform. It didn't take much to keep him happy. Hank could get total relaxation out of things that other people would find boring.

He wasn't the kind of person who would jump into things. Hank was hesitant. He was a great observer of people, always observing them and sizing them up before he would speak. If somebody did something he didn't like, Hank would have nothing to do with them. One time we were eating out and somebody at the table chuckled or snickered at something Hank said or did. Hank didn't do anything about it at the time, but he never ate with that fellow again. That's just the way he was. You could tease him, but don't offend him. The important thing to Hank

was that he knew where people were coming from. If you were straight with him and he knew where you were coming from, everything was all right. He and I were about as different as two people could be, but we understood each other, and so I could get away with teasing him—which I did quite a bit. He was just a little skinny country kid and sometimes you had to laugh. I'll never forget one day when we were on the road. Hank had that cardboard luggage he'd gotten as a bonus, and I guess he was proud of that luggage. Well, one day, it's raining pretty hard and I look over at Hank and he's just standing there with a handle in his hand. I laughed about that the rest of the summer. That luggage didn't even get him through the Northern League.
—Wes Covington

If I was going to need new luggage every time it rained, I figured I'd better find some work in the offseason. So instead of going back to Mobile right away, I hooked on again with the Indianapolis Clowns. Back then, players often barnstormed in the fall—especially black players.

The Clowns had won the first half of the Negro American League season and the Birmingham Black Barons had won the second half, so the two of them were playing a best-of-thirteen World Series throughout the South. Negro League rosters were always changing from month to month, and by the end of the season, Ray Neil and Piggy Sands were gone. To compensate, the Clowns added Horace Garner and me. It seemed like Horace had played everywhere at one time or another. He had been with the Clowns a couple of years before, and he was the guy who had been Rookie of the Year in the Northern League before I was. Prior to joining up with the Clowns at the end of 1952, he had led the Three-I League in home runs while playing for Evansville. There were a few other fellows on the Clowns that I didn't know from the first time around, but the biggest change was in the coaching box. Spec Bebop was gone. In his place we had a one-man band named Boogie-Woogie Frisco.

The Series started in Birmingham, and from there we moved on to Memphis, Little Rock, Hot Springs, Nashville, Knoxville, and Welch, West Virginia. After all those big towns, I don't know why we played in Welch—a little place in the middle of the Blue Ridge Mountains—but it must have been a traditional Negro League stop. I realized that after I hit a home run that landed at the foot of a mountain and everybody started talking about Josh Gibson again. The old-timers swore that Josh hit one halfway up that mountain.

After Welch, we turned back to the Deep South, and in a few days we were in Mobile. It was the first time I had been back home since I had left in the spring, and they gave me a big welcome. I was honored by one of the black organizations, the Dragon Social Club, and they called it Henry Aaron Day at Hartwell Field. It seemed strange—I had never gotten to play at Hartwell Field before, and here they were naming the day for me. When the Mobile Bears or big-league teams played there, they would cordon off part of the ballpark as the colored section, but when we were at Hartwell Field for Henry Aaron Day, they reserved part of the grandstand for white fans instead. I guess they figured there wouldn't be many of them.

I don't remember what I did that day—the Mobile newspapers didn't bother to report the game, even though it was the Negro League World Series—but we won, and it got us back in the Series. The Black Barons had been ahead five games to three, but we ran off four straight victories and finally clinched the championship in New Orleans, the Clowns' third in a row. I finished the Series batting over .400, with five home runs.

It didn't take me but a couple of hours after the last game to be back in Mobile. I was eager to hear what Daddy and Mama had to say about my season. Daddy bragged on me to all his friends, and Mama felt a lot better about me playing baseball than she had when I left. But she still insisted that I go back to Josephine Allen and get my degree. I knew there was no getting around it. No matter what I did on the ball field, Mama wasn't going to cut me loose until I graduated from high school.

4

In 1953, the major leagues were no farther South than St. Louis and Cincinnati. Baltimore was still a year away from the American League, and there wouldn't be a team below the Mason-Dixon line until the Colt 45's set up in Houston in 1962. Big-league baseball didn't actually get to Dixieland—the real South—until the Braves moved to Atlanta in 1966. The fact is, Jackie Robinson did not desegregate professional baseball in all of the United States—just the northern ones.

It wasn't that Robinson didn't try to break down the South. Before he went north with the Dodgers in 1947—the year the color line was busted—Robinson and black pitcher John Wright were to accompany the team for an exhibition game in Jacksonville, Florida, a city where nearly half the population was black. Jacksonville, however, abided by a city ordinance which prohibited blacks and whites from competing together on city-owned property. Consequently, Jacksonville's Parks Commission voted unanimously to cancel the game. The Dodgers objected, of course, and after a few days of squabbling and circumvention, they showed up at Myrtle Avenue Park to go on with the game—only to find that the park had been padlocked, with policemen standing guard outside for good measure. After that incident, Robinson and the Dodgers persevered in other Florida towns. In De Land, the scheduled game was called off because the lights were not working—the curiosity being that it was a day game. In Sanford, Robinson actually made it onto the field and began to play until the police chief appeared and escorted him from the premises.

The South was stronghold of minor-league baseball, and its Jim Crow practices were a retardant to the major leagues' desegregation process. Visionary executives like Branch Rickey and Bill Veeck were impaired by the refusal of their Southern farm clubs to receive black prospects. Placing a black player in the South was dangerous, at worst, and, at best, scandalous. In 1952,

Rock Hill, South Carolina, of the Tri-State League employed a black outfielder named David Mobley, but after appearing in the lineup once, he was banned by the league. The Cotton States League went one step further when it tried to banish the entire Hot Springs franchise from its ranks during the Tugerson incident in 1953. The same year, Jacksonville Beach attempted to put black players on its Florida State League roster, but the local chamber of commerce wouldn't permit it. "No race prejudice is involved," explained a spokesman. "It's just that the patrons of the team felt they would rather have an all-white team."

There were a handful of players on the fringe of the Deep South as early as 1952. After Aaron's teammate with the Clowns, Ray Neil, was rejected in Dallas, the same team signed a black pitcher-outfielder named Dave Hoskins, who dominated the Texas League that year. The Florida International League fielded three black players in 1952—Dave Barnhill of Miami Beach, Claro Duany of Tampa, and Willie Felden of Fort Lauderdale. But even so, the prospect of playing in even a suburb of the South was terrifying to most black players—especially those from the North, to whom the South was a land of horror stories. An item from the New York Giants' training camp in 1953 subtly demonstrates this, as reported by the Pittsburgh Courier: "Doesn't Want To Go South! Perhaps the hardest-working player in uniform is Bill White, rookie first baseman. Reason? White wants to go to a Class C league in the North rather than face discrimination if he goes into the Carolina League." As it turned out, the future president of the National League was dispatched to Danville, Virginia, of the Carolina League, where he had to be removed from the field on several occasions for engaging in animated disputes with objecting white customers.

While the breakthroughs in the Carolinas and Florida were significant, the two minor leagues that carried the banner of the Deep South were the Southern and South Atlantic. Their members were located in the Jim Crow playing fields of Louisiana, Alabama, Georgia, South Carolina, and Northern Florida, where the notion of interracial athletic competition was unthinkable to many. In towns like Birmingham and Montgomery, it was against the law for blacks and whites to even play checkers or dominoes together.

To its very end, the Southern League held out staunchly against integration. The only black player who ever appeared in a Southern League game was Nat Peeples, who went to bat one time for the Atlanta Crackers in 1954. He failed to get a hit, and when the league closed down in 1961—in large part, because of its racial intransigence—it could say that a black man never made it to first base in the Southern League.

The South Atlantic League—the Sally League, as they called it, Mother of the Minors and Cradle of the Great—was made up of smaller towns than was the Southern. Its members were Montgomery, Alabama; Columbus, Augusta, and Savannah, Georgia; Columbia and Charleston, South Carolina; and the infamous Jacksonville. In 1953, the Sally League was observing its fiftieth birthday, ceremonially formalizing its place in Southern tradition. In many cultural respects, Aunt Sally represented the South at its deepest.

It was into this uncharted and forbidding territory that the Milwaukee Braves sent Henry Aaron, Horace Garner, and Felix Mantilla. The three unwitting pioneers were assigned to the Braves' Class A farm club in Jacksonville, the very city where Jackie Robinson had been welcomed with policemen and padlocks. At the same time, Savannah signed on a pair of black players named Fleming Reedy and Al Israel. And so, despite the efforts of Robinson and the others, it was up to Henry Aaron, Horace Garner, Felix Mantilla, Fleming Reedy, and Al Israel to break the color line in the most vividly racial corner of the country. Baseball wouldn't be truly integrated in America until these five young men had made it through a season in the Sally League.

◆　　◆　　◆

The Boston Braves moved to Milwaukee one day during spring training in 1953. John Quinn, the general manager, walked onto the field in Bradenton, Florida, and handed everybody a cap with an "M" on the front, and that was it. Or so I heard. I wasn't there. I was in Kissimmee, Florida, with the Milwaukee Brewers, which had been the Braves' top farm team before the move. When Milwaukee became a major-league city, the AAA club was moved to Toledo, and I would have played there in 1953 if I had made the team. But there wasn't much danger of that. I was only in Kissimmee as a courtesy for the season I'd had in Eau Claire.

It was the only time in my life that I failed to make a baseball team—although I can't honestly believe that the failure was mine. I hit the ball whenever I got up to bat. That was about three times, as I recall. My best opportunity was supposed to come one day when another black player and I went with the team to play the Red Sox in Winter Haven, but when we got there, the local authorities wouldn't let us off the bus. On the rare occasions when I did bat in Kissimmee, I had a double or two and a home run. The home run was my big mistake. It went over the right-field fence, which was the wrong way to impress the manager, Tommy Holmes. Holmes knew a lot about hitting, and one of the things he knew was that I would never be any good at it unless I learned to pull the ball. I'm sure he thought that the American Association was not the place for me to learn this. Before he actually had a chance to cut me, though, I went to John Mullen and asked that he reassign me to a lower team that would give me half a chance. Nice man that he was, he sent me to the Okefenokee Swamp, where the Braves had a minor-league camp outside Waycross, Georgia.

I rode to Waycross with Hugh Wise, who was the assistant minor-league director, and another player. We may have passed a living person or two along the way, but all I can remember is slash pines and saw grass. You couldn't see the mosquitoes, but you knew they were out there waiting for you. The only reason they didn't get me was that I had to stay in the car. The other guys brought sandwiches out to me, and I ate in the back seat. Finally, we came to a clearing in the woods—an old World War II air base that was our camp.

In those days, organizations had more farm teams than they

do now, and the Braves sent all their players from the Class A level or below to Waycross. We slept in barracks, blacks and whites in the same long room. The camp was far enough from town that none of the local people paid much attention to us, but living together like that was a pretty bold thing for that day and age. The Reds had a similar place nearby in Douglas, Georgia, and they kept the black players' quarters separate from the whites'.

The camp had almost everything we needed, which wasn't much. Food and Ping-Pong were about it. On weekends, a bus would take us into town so we could do laundry or get a haircut or shoot pool. The first weekend I was there, I went in for a haircut, but somehow I managed to miss the bus back to camp. It was a long walk, and it was getting dark by the time I got to the camp. You had to climb a fence to get onto the grounds and there was a long road to the barracks, but it was much shorter to go through the woods. I found my way through, and when I came out, the guard spotted me. All he saw was a black kid sneaking up on the barracks, so, without further ado, he opened fire. Bullets were flying past my ears. I could see my career ending right there in the red clay of Waycross, Georgia—to say nothing of my life. Somehow, I managed to crawl into the barracks without being hit. The next day, John Mullen gave me a Bulova watch and told me not to miss the bus anymore.

Other than being eaten alive and shot at, Waycross was great. We had four fields, with batting practice and intrasquad games going on all the time. I got to bat almost as much as I wanted, and nobody seemed to care if I hit the ball 400 feet to right field.

There weren't any fences on most of the fields in Waycross, but they had dirt piles out there that served as fences. They were way out there, deep. I was getting ready to hit one day, and I noticed this little black kid hitting the ball over those dirt piles. The first time, I didn't pay too much attention, because he wasn't a very big kid. But then he hit one over the center-field dirt pile, and I thought, hey, nobody else here has been doing that: who is this guy? Somebody told me it was a kid who played shortstop for Eau Claire the year before.—Jim Frey

As it turned out, it was a good thing I left Kissimmee when I did, because it gave me time to learn a new position in Waycross. Felix Mantilla, a Puerto Rican who had played at Evansville the year before, was easily the best shortstop in the organization, so right off they moved me across the bag to second base. That way, Felix and I could play on the same team, which is exactly what happened—except that we didn't know it would be that way until they announced it. In those days, with so many minor-league teams, they made assignments the way they gave out tour-of-duty orders in the army. You had hundreds of guys in camp—guys with numbers on their backs like 195F—and nobody knew where they were headed. Finally, they'd put up a list with every-body's assignment and call it out. It would be like: Henry Aaron, Bus 5, you're going to Jacksonville. Felix Mantilla, Bus 5. Horace Garner, Bus 5. They told us to pack our things and be on the bus the next morning, because we had to get to Jacksonville to play the Red Sox. They also mentioned that Horace, Felix, and I would be breaking the color line in the Sally League.

The game against the Red Sox was called a "historic event" in the Jacksonville newspaper, the Florida *Times-Union*. Since Jackie Robinson had been locked out six years before, black play-ers had participated in games there on four occasions, but never on Jacksonville's side. As we expected, there were some boos, and we heard "nigger" and "burrhead" and "eight-ball" and other friendly greetings, but the biggest problem that day was the Red Sox. They beat us, 14-1. I could take some satisfaction in the fact that our one was a home run I hit in the eighth inning—to right field, naturally—against Ike Delock.

Two days later, we played Tommy Holmes's Toledo team, and it pleased me to hit a 400-foot home run to center field. The fact was, we probably had more talent than Toledo, even though we were two classifications lower. With Horace in right field, Felix at shortstop, Joe Andrews at first base, Rance Pless at third base, Jim Frey in center, and Ray Crone and Larry Lassalle pitch-ing, we had the best roster that Jacksonville had ever seen. Jack-sonville hadn't been blessed with many good teams, and neither had our manager, Ben Geraghty. Ben was a baseball man through and through, and it meant a lot to him to get to manage a team like ours. He knew it was his big chance.

Before we started playing games, Ben sat down with Horace and Felix and me and said that he would love to have us on his team, but we ought to be aware of what we would be up against if we stayed there. It was nothing we didn't already know, but it was reassuring to hear that the manager was on our side. Ben wasn't much to look at—he was a small guy, with a long chin and hound-dog eyes—and he didn't speak the King's English. He was also nervous, he drank too much beer, and he didn't change his clothes as often as he should have. But in all the years I played baseball, I never had a manager who cared more for his players or knew more about the game.

There were a few open days before the season started, and we used the time to get acclimated to Jacksonville. Meanwhile, Jacksonville used the time to get acclimated to us. We went to stores and just milled around for a little while, maybe stood in the doorway for a few minutes so that people could see us and get used to us. We also found a place to live, a house near the ball-park owned by a black man named Manuel Rivera, who ran a tavern called Manuel's that was the local hangout.

A day or two after we moved in, I was lingering around the ballpark when I noticed a girl about my age going into the post office. Our clubhouse man, T. C. Marlin, knew everybody in that part of town—a black section known as Durkeeville—so I fetched him real fast and asked him who the girl was. He told me her name was Barbara Lucas, and she had just returned home from Florida A&M to attend classes at a local business college. I had him introduce me as one of the next great stars of baseball. I don't think she was impressed, but I asked her for a date anyway. She said I'd have to come home and meet her parents before she could think about going out with me. She lived in the projects across from the park, and whenever we were in town the rest of the summer you could usually find me on Barbara's front porch eating her mother's coconut cake. And if I was there, more than likely Felix was sitting right across from me, having a piece of Mrs. Lucas's lemon pie.

I don't know whether it was coincidence or not, but our first game was in Savannah, against the team that had the other two black players in the Sally League. It seemed to Felix and Horace and me that the whole South had its sights trained on us, and as we were getting on the bus to leave for Savannah, the mayor of Jacksonville came by to tell us that whatever we heard on that field, or whatever the fans tried to do to us, we had to suffer it quietly. It sounded a lot like the speech Branch Rickey gave Jackie Robinson the first time they met.

There were more than 5,500 people at the ballpark in Savannah—the biggest Opening Day crowd they'd ever had and the biggest in the Sally League that year. It would be that way all summer. Wherever we went, the fans poured out to the park. We set all kinds of attendance records that year, and opened up the Sally League to a whole new group of customers. There were so many black fans that they had to add room to the colored section in a lot of the ballparks. Columbia had a rickety old park, and one night the colored section got so full, and the people got to rocking it so hard, that it collapsed. It was like a party every night in the colored section. All we had to do was catch a fly ball, and everybody on the black side of the ballpark would whoop and holler like we'd won the World Series. Then the people in the white section would start yelling at the people in the colored section, and it would go back and forth—sometimes in a friendly way, but more often not. There was probably nowhere else in the South where so many white and black people could be found in the same place. Horace and Felix and I knew that we had to shut out everything else and play ball, but when we looked up at all those black and white faces screaming at us, we couldn't help but feel the weight of what we were doing.

Every park I went in, I was on pins and needles. I just felt it was my duty as league president to see what happened to those guys. Even though Savannah had black players, too, I traveled with Jacksonville because most of the focus was on Aaron. Aaron probably didn't know it, but all year long I followed Jacksonville and sat in the stands to sort of keep a lookout. You were never

sure what was going to happen. Those people had awfully strong feelings about what was going on. I knew, because they would call me all hours of the night to tell me. Before I took over as president of the league, I'd worked in Happy Chandler's commissioner's office in Cincinnati, and to the folks in the South that made me a Yankee. And since Chandler was the one who opened the door for Rickey and Jackie Robinson, I guess I was a damn Yankee. They'd call and tell me to get back up north and take my niggers with me. I was living in Columbia, and after word got out that we had blacks in the league, one of my friends quit speaking to me. A lot of the whites stopped coming to the ballpark. But Henry played so well that by the end of the year, they were coming back. My friend in Columbia even started talking to me again. Henry made Christians out of those people.
—Dick Butler, former president of the Sally League

We won the opener when Felix drove in a run in the ninth inning, and we kept winning—seven in a row before we lost one. We beat Augusta one night, 28-6. The Jacksonville paper wrote that we might be one of the greatest Class A teams ever assembled. And nobody could doubt that Horace and Felix and I had a lot to do with it. I hit well right from the start, although one of my teammates, Joe Andrews, led the league for the first month or so. Horace had a lot of power and one of the best throwing arms from right field that I ever saw. Felix was a flashy shortstop— much better than I was at second base—and a .300 hitter. The Braves had counted on the fact that all three of us would fare well in the Sally League, or they wouldn't have put us in Jacksonville. We had to clear the way for other black players to play down there, just as Billy Bruton and Garner made it easier for me and Covington at Eau Claire. The Braves knew, and we knew, that we not only had to play well, but if we ever lost our cool or caused an incident, it might set the whole program back five or ten years. When the pitchers threw at us, we had to get up and swing at the next pitch. When somebody called us a nigger, we had to pretend as if we didn't hear it.

All of that was harder for Felix than it was for Horace and me. We were both accustomed to it, being from the South, but

Felix never heard that sort of thing growing up in Puerto Rico. It wasn't as easy for him to turn the other cheek. What made it worse was that it seemed like he got beaned almost every night. When it happened, Felix would shout back at the pitcher, mostly in Spanish, and Horace and I would tell him to shut up. The papers wrote that he was a crazy Puerto Rican, carrying on like that. Finally, when he was hit one night in Macon, Felix put down his bat and went after the pitcher. Horace was in the on-deck circle, and he sprinted out there and grabbed Felix before he could get to the mound, put a bear hug on him, got right up to his ear, and said: "You dumb son of a bitch! I know you don't speak much English, but hear what I'm telling you. You're gonna get us all killed!" Meanwhile, the people from the white section along first base were coming over the railing and people from the colored section were headed over to the white section. It was real close to being a race riot. They called the police, and after order was restored, the policemen ringed the field and stood there with their hands on their guns.

The next night we were in Augusta, and after a couple of innings the fans in the right-field stands started throwing rocks at Horace. Horace always said he didn't mind the rednecks throwing rocks at him, but when they started hitting him, that was different. He called time and told the umpire, and the umpire made the mistake of grabbing the public address microphone and asking people to stop throwing things at the right fielder. That was all the fans wanted to hear. When he came up to bat, they were all over him, shouting things like, "Nigger, we're gonna kill you next time. Ain't no nigger gonna squawk on no white folks down here." Ben had to move Horace from right field to left, where the fans couldn't get to him. But we got our revenge that night. I was five-for-five, and between us, Horace, Felix, and I were on base thirteen times in fourteen times at bat.

That was the only kind of recourse we had. And laughing. After the games, we'd get back to our rooms and say, "Horace, what did you hear tonight?" We'd exchange our stories and just laugh all night at how stupid people could be. We'd laugh ourselves to sleep thinking about those people. They'd sit in the stands with mops on their heads. They'd throw black cats onto the field. You'd hear things like, "The big nigger [that was Horace], he's got to mow the owner's lawn on Saturday. Aaron's got to feed his hogs. And that other one, I don't know who he is, but he's a nigger to me." Of course, whenever somebody said something like that, it bounced off the walls and echoed through the whole ballpark. It was strange how it worked. Everything would be normal, then it would get real quiet for a second, and out of the hush you'd hear something like, "Hey, nigger, why you running? There's no watermelon out there." Horace hurt himself running into a fence one night in Macon, and as they were carrying him off the field, somebody shouted, "Put that nigger down. He can walk!" Joe Andrews, a white first baseman, was our buddy, and they even yelled at him. They'd say, "Hey, Andrews, every time you come to town you get blacker. You sleeping with Aaron's sister?"

My favorite incident was the time Horace caught a foul pop fly running into the crowd. We drew so well that they often filled the stands and put the overflow around the edge of the playing field. Well, one time there was a fly ball right down the line in right field and Horace and I went after it. Horace caught it on the run, and when he did, it carried him right into the crowd. He was about to run over this little kid, so to keep from knocking him down, he just picked the kid up and kept going for a few steps. And before he could put the kid down, this lady started shrieking: "My God! That nigger's running away with my baby!"

Not all of the incidents were quite so funny, though. We had death threats in Montgomery. People would send us letters saying things like they were going to sit in the right-field stands with a rifle and shoot us during the game on a certain night. Felix got one in Jacksonville that said, "Nigger, if you play tonight, they're going to carry you away in a casket." He showed it to the lady who owned our house, and she got hysterical. She called the police, and the police called the FBI, and within about ten minutes there were two FBI guys at the door trying to talk to Felix, who could barely speak English. They told Felix he should go ahead and play, and they would be sitting in the stands. Nothing happened.

I don't recall ever feeling that our lives were in imminent danger, but we took nothing for granted. When we were leaving the ballpark after a game, Joe Andrews would carry a bat with him and tell us to stick close. Ben Geraghty fathered us and kept us calm, but Joe was our protector. We couldn't talk back to the fans calling us names, but Joe could, and he damn sure did.

I believe I was arrested three times that year for arguing with people on Henry's behalf. We'd walk on the field and they would start up the chants: "Nigger! Nigger!" Places like Macon, they'd come into the ballpark with coolers of beer and they'd be half drunk by batting practice. I'd say, "These sick rebel suckers," and every now and then I'd just wander over to the screen to see what I could do for 'em. It was amazing the way Henry and Horace and Felix could take it. I'd be standing next to Henry in the infield and some yahoo would call him a nigger or something and I'd turn to Henry and say, "Did you hear that?" He'd look back at me and say, "What do you think, I'm deaf?"

It wasn't just the fans, either. We had a few Southern boys on our ball club, and they'd say things. Henry came up with a couple of men on base once when we were down by a run, and he popped up to end the game. Afterwards, somebody on our team said, "Well, when pull comes to tug, a nigger's gonna croak every time." I just started screaming. We didn't need to be worrying about our guys, because we had enough problems with the rednecks on the other side.

And believe me, there were some mean pitchers in that league. In Macon they had an old ballpark so big you could land a 727, and there was a tin fence that circled the park, but it was too deep for a home run fence, so they had a snow fence inside it. The first time up, Henry hits one over that snow fence for a home run. The next time around, I doubled and then Henry came up. Their pitcher was some old-timer from the Pacific Coast League or somewhere like that, and when Henry was up there the second time, the pitcher said, "I got four for your head, nigger." He threw the first one behind him. Henry just moved his head a little. Then the pitcher said, "I got three more here." I was standing on second base, so I just yelled out, "Hey, why don't you throw one at me?" I would have loved to take that guy on. But Henry didn't need me. The next pitch was right at his *head, and Henry just stepped back a little and tomahawked that thing right over my head. About two seconds later you could hear the ball banging against that old tin fence way out there. When we got to the dugout, Henry said, "Why was that boy mad at me?" I pointed out to the pitcher, who was stomping around the mound, and I said, "If you think he was mad before, take a look at him now."*

Henry was just so innocent, and such a nice kid. One time the pitcher was throwing at him and the other team was getting on him pretty bad and the fans were giving it to him, too, and I could tell it was bothering him. I said, "What's wrong, Henry?" He just shook his head and said, "I don't want to hurt nobody. I just want to play baseball."

The poor kid was only nineteen years old. He was so naive he didn't even know how to put on his uniform. Hell, he'd never had anything like sanitary hose before. And he didn't care anything about signs, or that kind of stuff. One time in Columbia he came up late in the game with us losing 1-0 and no outs and a couple of men on base. Ben gives him the bunt sign, and I see Aaron back out of the box and shake his head. Ben flashes bunt again, and Aaron backs out and walks halfway down to third base to meet him. They talk about something, and then Aaron gets back in the box and hits a rocket to right center to score both runs and we win the game. Well, the next day I get to the park and Ben calls me over and says, "You know what that son of a bitch told me? He said, 'I know this pitcher and I know what he's gonna throw me. Anybody else, I'd bunt, but I know this pitcher and I know I can hit him.' Well, okay. But then last night I'm sitting in the lobby of the hotel and he's down there standing on the street corner waiting for some girl to show up. But the girl he's waiting for is from Columbus! We're in Columbia, and he's waiting for some girl from Columbus to show up! Hell, how could he have known that pitcher? He didn't even know what town we were in!"—Joe Andrews

Horace and Felix and I never stayed with the rest of our teammates when we were on the road—never even ate with them. The team would stop at a restaurant, and the three of us would sit on the bus while Ben or Joe or some guy who rode the bench brought hamburgers out to us. We used to joke that the cows turned and ran when they saw us coming, we ate so many hamburgers. Once, we stopped at a little store and the white players got out to buy cold drinks. We stayed in the bus, but Felix wanted to get a drink out of the water fountain. There were two fountains, white and colored, and Felix took a drink out of the colored fountain. But it was hot water, and he spit it out. Then he moved over and took a drink from the white fountain. The problem was that the store owner saw him do it, and, being a good law-abiding Southerner, he called the sheriff. The sheriff was there before the team was back on the bus, and he said he was going to put Felix in jail. Ben talked to the sheriff for a long time before he finally convinced him to let Felix come with us.

Whenever we got to the town where we were going, the bus driver would take the white players to their hotel and Horace and Felix and I would just sit in the bus as the rest of our teammates filed out. It got real quiet when the white players had to leave us sitting there. I'm sure that if it had been up to them, we'd have stayed in the same hotel that they did. But Jim Crow made the rules, and we had to abide by them. Bear in mind, this was a year before the civil rights movement got rolling with the Brown vs. Board of Education decision. So after the white players got off the bus, we'd ride on to some private home on the other side of the tracks. Black people were happy to put us up, because we were big news down there. We were the closest they would ever get to Jackie Robinson.

The only place where we stayed in a hotel was Montgomery. Otherwise, Montgomery was the worst town in the league for black players. I could tolerate it only because my parents drove up from Mobile to see me play. When we weren't playing there, my father would go up about once a week anyway to read about the Sally League in the Montgomery newspaper. But even with Mama and Daddy nearby, I couldn't enjoy Montgomery. They had segregation down to an art in that town—the art of keeping the niggers down. It would be 100 degrees and black people would be standing on the sidewalks watching half-filled buses go by because there wasn't any more room in the colored section.

When I heard two years later that Rosa Parks refused to give up her seat to a white man, I understood perfectly.

The black hotel was called the Ben Moore, and as you might imagine, it was not in the high-rent district. It was located over a juke joint, and the noise kept us up most of the night. There was no air conditioning, the place smelled from the fish they were always frying downstairs, and if you opened a window the bugs would invite themselves in for a little picnic. The interior decorating consisted of a potted plant in the lobby. But after sleeping on the bus in the Negro League, the Ben Moore was like the Waldorf-Astoria to me. It was also a clubhouse to the black players, because the Jim Crow laws prevented us from putting on our uniform at the ballpark with the white players. Finally, near the end of the season, we said to heck with it and dressed at the park. As far as I know, the white players all went on to have normal, healthy lives after that.

Wherever we stayed, Ben Geraghty would always make it a point to come over and see us. He had nothing special to say—he'd just drink a few beers and talk baseball—but it meant a lot to us that the manager would go out of his way to make us feel like part of the team. One day in Columbus, the team was invited out to Fort Benning. When it came time to eat, suddenly Horace, Felix, and I were shuttled off to the kitchen. As soon as we sat down, here came Ben to join us. I've known white players and managers who will try to put on a good face around black players despite their real feelings, but there wasn't a phony bone in Ben's body. He was just a baseball man, and to him, we were just baseball players. Besides that, he liked us. He liked me and Felix because he knew we were headed for the big leagues, and he liked Horace because, in addition to being the best right fielder in the league, Horace was a good man who knew where to buy beer on Sunday. Horace always managed to find Ben a case of Schlitz for the long Sunday bus rides.

I guess it's not surprising that Ben drank a lot of beer, considering what he had been through. A few years before, he had been manager at Spokane when the team bus rolled down a hill and some players were killed. Ben climbed up the hill to get help.

The crash wasn't his fault, but he took it very hard. People who knew him then said that he wasn't the same after the crash—he was nervous and drank more—but as far as I'm concerned, he still would have made a great big-league manager. Ben was in the Braves' system for a long time, and he was interviewed at least once for the manager's job, but with his wrinkled clothes and plain way of talking, he didn't make much of an impression. I always thought that, in his way, Ben was discriminated against every bit as much as Felix and I ever were. He died in 1963. It's one of my biggest regrets that he never got a chance to manage in the big leagues.

As kind as he was with his players, Ben never forgot that he was the manager, and he knew how to chew a guy out if he made a mental mistake. He jumped all over Felix and me one night when we let a pop fly fall between us. And he was always on me for missing signs. Once, he wanted to try a squeeze play, but to disguise it he clapped his hands and told me to hit the ball out of the park. So I believed him and hit the ball out of the park. But the worst was the time I got picked off second base three times in one game. The first time up, I singled and stole second, and the second baseman tagged me out with the hidden-ball trick. The next time, I stole second again, and he used some other hidden-ball trick and tagged me out again. Ben let it go the first time, but the second time he was pretty hot. When it happened the third time, he let me have it. Of course, I deserved it. But Ben did something I appreciated—something I've always admired in a manager. Instead of screaming at me in front of the whole team —Lord knows, I was embarrassed enough already—he waited until he could get me alone after the game. Then he told me how stupid I had been, and I couldn't disagree with him. I was a better baserunner from that day on.

The only person Ben couldn't handle was Joe Andrews. Joe was a big guy who might do anything, and Ben was probably scared of him. One night, when Joe had been drinking, we stopped the bus at a gas station and Joe put a coin into the vending machine to try to get a drink. The bottle wouldn't come out, and Joe started hitting and rocking that machine like he was going to knock it over. Ben didn't want to go out there, so he sent Horace out. Horace was the one guy who could hold his own with Joe—they were great friends. Horace just put his own money into the machine, and when the bottle came out, he handed it to Joe.

Joe would stay out drinking all night on Saturdays, and it got to the point where Ben wouldn't play him on Sundays. So whenever Joe would get in on Sunday morning, he would go right to Ben's room and pound on the door and yell, "You son of a bitch! You'd better play me today!" If any of the rest of us missed curfew, we would be fined, but Ben knew it was useless to try to fine Joe. He said once that if he fined Joe every time he missed curfew, they'd have to hold back his salary and Joe would still owe the team money at the end of the year. Ben arranged for Jim Frey to room with Joe to try to keep him out of jail. He stayed out of jail all year, but he didn't stay out of trouble. One night about fifteen of the white players were eating at a café in Columbus, and when they were finished, they went back to the motel and sat around the pool. All except Joe. After a while a car pulled up and a guy got out and said, "Where's that guy with that big letter jacket with the Indian head on it? He walked out on a seven-dollar check." Everybody knew who he was talking about—Joe had been a great athlete in high school in Massachusetts, and he always wore that letter jacket.

Joe's drinking probably kept him out of the big leagues, because he was a natural hitter. I was only with him in 1953, but I understand that his drinking got worse before it got better. He used to arm-wrestle in bars, and that would lead to bets, and the bets would lead to fights. Joe was liable to do anything when he was drunk. He went to a black club with Barbara and Horace and me one night in Jacksonville, and after a while he started making passes at Barbara. I said something to him, and then Horace grabbed him and said, "Look, I got you in here and I'll get you out of here. But after that, you're on your own." When Horace and Joe were together in the Sally League the next year, Joe had some problems at a bar in Columbia. He thought the owner had taken some of his money, so he went back to the hotel, got his switchblade, and said he was going to return with his money or the guy's heart in his hand. There was another squabble over money when Joe and Horace were playing together in South America, only that time a guy came looking for Joe with a hunting knife. Joe's drinking and fighting got so bad that he ended up in jail years later.

I finally hit bottom, and when I did, I'll tell you what brought me out of it. It was thinking about Henry. By this time, Henry was a superstar, going after Babe Ruth's record and everything, and it made me think of all that he went through in Jacksonville. I thought, if he can make it through all of that and do what he has done with his life, I sure as hell can do something with my life. That's when I joined Alcoholics Anonymous, and I haven't had a drink since.

I've only seen Henry a few times since we played together, but he always amazes me. A couple years after he broke the record, he was in Boston, and I went to see him with a Mafia guy who wanted to have a ball signed. We weren't there two minutes when Henry pulls me aside and says, "Who is that guy?" I said, "You mean you could tell?" He said, "The guy reeks. You're not involved with him, are you?" I still don't know how the hell he could tell so fast. He just knew. He has that instinct about people.

He had me figured out that first year. At the beginning of the season I was batting over .400 and leading the league, and Henry was hanging back in the low or mid-.300s. Then I started to drop and he closed the gap, and for a while we had a batting race going. I thought I had a real chance to win it, but Henry came up to me one day and kind of shook his head and said, "You'll never last. You drink too much beer. Your hands are getting slow." And he was so right. That's what I mean about Henry's instincts. I've never met anybody like him.—Joe Andrews

By the All-Star break, I was leading the league in various things. Five players from each team were selected to play in the All-Star Game, and I was one of them. But neither Felix nor

Horace made the team, which I thought was strange. In fact, there were a lot of curious things about the All-Star Game. The game was in Savannah, and there were rumors that the governor of Georgia, Herman Talmadge, was going to ban me from playing in it. On one hand, it didn't make sense that he would keep me out of the All-Star Game when blacks had been playing in Savannah all year. On the other hand, he was Herman Talmadge, the man who conducted a nationwide campaign to prohibit blacks and whites from being on the same television show. Also, since the All-Star Game was the big fiftieth anniversary celebration of the Sally League, it could have been that they wished to uphold a league tradition that had been in place for the first forty-nine years. Another possible reason for keeping me out of the game was that all the players were invited to a reception at a private club where blacks were not permitted. Despite all of that, though, I was still intending to play in the game until the day before, when I got in a rundown between third and home in a game against Savannah and was spiked on the toe by a 240-pound catcher. I don't believe it was intentional, but I was never quite certain.

When I got hurt, another player from Jacksonville had to be named to take my place. Felix was the obvious guy, since he and I were both infielders and he was having a great season, but, instead, they picked another infielder named Billy Porter, who wasn't near the player that Felix was. So there were no black players in the All-Star Game. I didn't attend, but I've always regretted that I didn't. I should have at least gone to be introduced—just to force the issue and see what would happen. As it turned out, Talmadge didn't know that I wasn't going to play, and after he had lunch and took his seat, he got up and excused himself about fifteen minutes before the start of the game, saying he had a previous engagement. He had been getting a lot of flak from voters about the black players—it was technically against the law in Georgia for us to be on the same field as whites—and this way, he could say that he had never seen a black man play in a ballgame in his state.

By the All-Star break, we had just about eliminated every other team from the pennant race, except Columbia. Columbia was a Cincinnati franchise and a veteran team with the best pitching in the league. There was a veteran named Barney Martin, who was up briefly with the Reds that year, another named Maury Fisher, who made it up in 1955 for a few days, and Corky Valentine. I'll never forget Corky Valentine. There were some ornery pitchers in that league, but nobody as nasty as Harold Lewis Valentine. He was even nasty when he wasn't pitching. The day before he was scheduled to pitch, he'd sit on the dugout steps and say, "Have fun tonight, boys, because tomorrow I'm gonna stick it in your ear." He meant it, too. I'm not saying he was a racist; I think Corky Valentine just hated everybody. He put Joe Andrews in the hospital when he hit him in the shin. Joe couldn't walk, but he was crawling out to the mound to try to get at Valentine. I was lucky, I guess—or quick—because he never hit me, although I'm sure he tried. But I hit him. I hit him good. Valentine made it up to the big leagues the next year, when I did, and I hit the tenth home run of my career off him. I didn't spare the rod on Corky Valentine. The scary thing, though, is that he eventually became a policeman somewhere in Georgia. That's enough to make you drive fifty-five.

Even though I hit him pretty well, Valentine was always tough on us. Columbia was tough on us. But we never minded playing there—at least, Horace and Felix and I didn't. Horace had a lady friend there who was a mortician, and she always managed to find a couple of nice young girls for me and Felix. My favorite town to visit, though—at least, for a while—was Columbus. I met a girl there who lived across the Alabama border in Phenix City, and we had a pretty good thing going until it occurred to me that it would be prudent to call it off. Phenix City was wide open, with drinking and gambling in the streets, and I walked through all of that to get to this girl's house. It wasn't so bad until I was walking home one night and a bunch of white guys started calling me names and chasing me. They chased me all the way across the Chattahoochee River into Georgia. That was the last time I saw that girl. Later on, she came looking for me in Jacksonville, but by then I'd made up my mind to marry Barbara.

None of that affected my performance on the field, though,

because I never let anything take my mind off my job as a ball-player. I led the Sally League in hitting for most of the second half of the season. I only had one short slump the whole year, but came out of it fine. When Joe Andrews asked me what I did to break my slump, I told him I called Stan Musial. I was liable to tell Joe anything, but I guess he believed me, because it started going around that I was friends with Musial. I'd never spoken to a major leaguer in my life, much less Stan Musial. But if some-body had told me that four years later I would beat out Musial for Most Valuable Player in the National League, I wouldn't have thought they were crazy. Even then, I figured I ought to lead any league I played in. I might have been a shy and quiet kid, but I was a confident shy and quiet kid.

> *I was sitting behind Henry and Horace on the bus one night, and they were talking about hitting. At that time, Henry could turn around any fastball in the world, but he had trouble with slow stuff. Garner was trying to talk to him about off-speed pitches, and he was telling him what Jackie Robinson had said to him about hitting slow stuff. Jackie Robinson was the idol of most of the black players back then, and what he said was gospel. But that didn't matter to Henry. He cut Horace off before he could finish and said, "I don't care what Jackie Robinson says. I'm Henry Aaron, and I'll do it my way."—Jim Frey*

If I ever doubted myself that year, all I had to do to get my confidence back was count my watches or the bonus money in my billfold. Our owner, Sam Wolfson, gave out prizes to players who had big games. You'd check your locker after a road trip, and there was liable to be an envelope stuffed with five- and ten- and maybe twenty-dollar bills. I used that money to buy my par-ents the first television on our side of Toulminville. People came knocking on our door from all over the neighborhood to watch that TV. There was also a jeweler in Jacksonville who gave out watches if you hit the first home run of a game or a series, and I was giving away watches to all my friends. Other stores gave us slacks and sport jackets. I came up in the world that summer—although I wouldn't have carried it quite as far as the Columbia newspaper, *The State*, which wrote: "You will have a difficult time convincing Henry Aaron, a solid medium-size hunk of merchandise, that America is anything other than the land of opportunity. The communists will be unhappy to hear that this 19-year-old colored boy from Mobile, Alabama, is getting along nicely—and with a bright future ahead."

I didn't know anything about communists and I was still a foreigner in the land of opportunity, but by the end of the summer I was pretty sure I had a future in baseball. I was also pretty sure it wouldn't be as a second baseman. If I was a bad shortstop in Eau Claire, I was a worse second baseman in Jacksonville. Somehow, I managed to make thirty-six errors, which nearly gave me a clean sweep of all the individual titles in the Sally League. The only one I missed was home runs. I hit twenty-two, but Savannah had a guy named Tommy Giordano who hit twenty-four, a lot of them over the 270-foot left-field fence on the football field where they played. I think Giordano's eyes went bad later, and that kept him out of the big leagues, although he is an executive now with the Cleveland Indians.

My batting average at the end of the year was .362, which was about twenty points ahead of Everett Joyner of Columbus. I had 125 RBIs, and nobody else in the league had more than 100. But I was a butcher at second base. Especially on double plays. I threw the ball as hard as I could, underhanded, and the shortstop couldn't see it until it was about to hit him in the nose. Felix used to say a guy could get killed trying to turn double plays with me. We all knew that my best position was some other position.

One guy who didn't seem to be worried about my problems at second base, though, was Ben Geraghty. I guess Ben could sense that I was the type of kid who needed to be encouraged, because he was always telling me that I was going to make it big. He told some writers that I'd make people forget Jackie Robinson. I knew that was nonsense, but Ben's faith meant a lot to me. He wasn't saying anything that he didn't believe, either, because he bragged on me to the Braves, too.

One day Lou Perini [the Braves' owner] called me into his office and said, "We keep hearing about this Aaron kid down in Jack-

*sonville. When is he going to be ready for Milwaukee?" I said
that as a hitter, he might be ready next year. But as a second
baseman, it might take a couple more. So we sent Billy Southworth down there to grade his arm and see if maybe he could
play the outfield. Aaron was still at second base, but it so happened that in the next game, there was a little bloop into short
right field, and Henry had to chase it down and turn and gun
the ball to home plate. He threw a strike—overhand—and got
his man easily. Southworth came back and reported that Aaron
had one of the best arms he'd ever seen.''—John Mullen*

I did have a strong arm, but it was a long way from being the
best on our ball club. I've never seen anybody throw like Horace
Garner—unless it was Roberto Clemente. Horace would put on
throwing exhibitions around the Sally League. The fans would
come early to watch him stand at home plate and heave balls
over the center-field fence. Horace might have been a little uncertain in the outfield, but he could run and throw and hit with
anybody. His problem was that he was a little old. He was
twenty-seven the year we were together in Jacksonville, and I
guess the Braves figured he was past the stage of being a prospect.
But Horace had a lot of good baseball left. He stayed in the
Braves' minor-league system for eight years, and in those years
the teams he was on won seven pennants. He won batting titles,
home run titles, everything. But he never got a shot at the big
leagues. One year, the Braves told him they might call him up at
the end of the year, but just before he was supposed to go up, he
hurt his knee. He still played after that, but his chance was gone.
When I think about it now, it doesn't seem right that I have all
these awards and records and I'm in the Hall of Fame, and Horace
is driving a school bus in Cedar Rapids, Iowa, where ony a few
people even know that he was a ballplayer.

*When I played with Horace in the Three-I League, they had a
contest one day for throwing and running. We kept telling Horace to get into it, but he'd just had a tooth pulled and he had a
sore arm. He woudn't do it. Rocky Colavito was in the league,
and he threw one that short-hopped the center-field fence in*

Cedar Rapids, about 405 feet. We knew Horace could beat that, but he still wouldn't do it. Then we told him they were giving away a barbeque grill for first prize, and all of a sudden Horace was real interested. He grabbed the ball and threw it out of the ballpark. Then they had the sprints, and there was some guy in the league who had been a track man at Duke. When they ran the 100-yard dash, this guy got up to the line and dug in like he was in the Olympics or something, and Horace walked up there with his hat on backwards and his sweatshirt in his back pocket and beat the guy by ten yards.—Joe Andrews

Horace and Felix and I and several others on our team put up big numbers that year, but somehow Columbia stayed right on our heels all season. The rest of the league was at least twenty-five games behind, but we couldn't seem to shake Corky Valentine and company. Finally, we clinched the pennant in Savannah. The night we did, Horace and Felix and I drove in a bunch of runs, and when we came out of the clubhouse, there was a white man standing there waiting for us. We could tell he wanted to talk to us, but he didn't quite know what to say. He was kind of shuffling around, trying to find the right words. Finally, he blurted it out. He said, "I just wanted to let you niggers know you played a helluva game."

The team arranged a celebration party that night at a restaurant in Savannah. The only problem was that Felix and Horace and I weren't allowed in the restaurant. We had to stay in the kitchen while the rest of the team partied out in front. After a while, Spec Richardson, our general manager, gave us fifty dollars and told us to have our own party. We took fifteen dollars apiece for ourselves and bought some beer with the other five. When we got back to Jacksonville, there was another party for the team at a country club. Somehow, Mr. Wolfson arranged to get us in, even though black people were never included at affairs like that in the South. It was such a significant occasion that a writer from a black magazine came out to cover it, but he was stopped at the door.

The Braves also honored the players with a special night during the last homestand of the season. Since I led the league in most things, they asked me to stand on the field for a little ceremony. It was a pretty good feeling when Mr. Wolfson said, "Henry Aaron is like a son to me." That wasn't the sort of thing a wealthy white man usually said about a black kid in the South. Then they took up a collection and brought it to me in a grocery sack full of dollar bills. I had my hat in one hand and a trophy in the other, and when I tried to grab the sack, it spilled. It was a windy night, and money was blowing all over the field. So I put down my hat and trophy and got on my knees to start picking it up. Mr. Wolfson got down on his knees right next to me. I don't know who the other dignitaries were—maybe the mayor and some of the merchants who sponsored us—but they were all scurrying around the field with me trying to chase down dollar bills, which must have been a sight that those people in Jacksonville never thought they'd see. Anyway, when we got the money all gathered up, I split it among my teammates.

We were riding pretty high going into the Sally League playoffs. Mr. Wolfson was so proud of us that he bought the players sport jackets with "Braves" lettered on them. We felt like big leaguers. I don't know if guys in Class A ball can be too cocky, but in our first series, against Savannah, we didn't play like we had been playing all season. We struggled through and finally won the series when Felix and I hit home runs that enabled us to pull out the last two games. That set us up against Columbia in the finals, best of seven.

The first game was at Columbia, and we won easily. Then we went to Jacksonville for three games. The Braves beamed some old World War II searchlights into the sky to attract people to the ballpark, and we drew over five thousand each night. When we left Jacksonville, we were ahead three games to one. It seemed to us that the series should have ended in Jacksonville, since we had won the regular season pennant, but for some odd reason, the last three games were scheduled for Columbia. For some other odd reason, Columbia won all three of them. I crashed into Felix trying to field a ball in the fourth inning of the seventh game, and they scored four times that inning to beat us, 4-2. The only consolation was that Barney Martin was the one who beat us—Corky Valentine had nothing to do with it.

We were disappointed to lose the playoffs, but Horace and Felix and I didn't lose sight of what we accomplished that summer. We had played a season of great baseball in the Deep South, under circumstances that nobody had experienced before and—because of us—never would again. We had shown the people of Georgia and Alabama and South Carolina and Florida that we were good ballplayers and decent human beings, and that all it took to get along together was to get a little more used to each other. We had shown them that the South wouldn't fall off the map if we played in their ballparks. At the end of the season, we still heard a few choice names being shouted at us from the stands, but not as often or as loudly as in the beginning. Little by little—one by one—the fans accepted us. Not all of them, but enough to make a difference. That was the most gratifying part of the summer. It showed us that things were changing a little, and we were part of the reason why. And we weren't the only ones who noticed it. Dick Butler, the league president, said that we had successfully broken the color barrier in Southern baseball. A columnist for the Jacksonville *Journal* wrote that "I sincerely believe Aaron may have started Jacksonville down the road to racial understanding." I'm not sure I've ever done anything more important.

> *I wouldn't live that summer over again for a million dollars. But I wouldn't trade the experience for a million dollars, either.*
> —Horace Garner

After the playoffs, the only thing remaining was a banquet in Jacksonville, where I received the award for Most Valuable Player in the league. But I had something else on my mind that night. During the ceremony, I walked over to the telephone, called Barbara, and asked her to marry me. She said I had to ask her father, and I said to put him on the phone. Mr. Lucas had been something of a ballplayer himself, and he had doubts whether a black kid had much of a chance to make a decent living in baseball. Little did he know that one of his own sons, Bill, would also sign with the Braves a couple of years later. Bill never quite made it to the major leagues as a player, but he did even better. He got a job in the Braves' front office and ultimately became the highest-ranking black executive in baseball. In 1953, that seemed about as likely as me breaking Babe Ruth's home run record.

Mr. Lucas was a pullman porter, and he was porter on the train that carried his daughter to meet her new family in Mobile. This time, Mama and everybody else was at the train station, and when we got off, I noticed they were all staring at Barbara. Finally, Barbara said, "Why are you all looking at me that way? Is there something wrong with me?" One of my sisters said, "It's your eyes, girl! We've never seen a colored person with green eyes!" After we got home, neighbors kept coming by the house to look at the girl with green eyes. Because of her eyes, I called her Half-Breed.

We lived with my parents after we got married, but we didn't stay there. Felix—who also married a girl from Jacksonville—was going to Puerto Rico to play winter ball for the Caguas team, and he wanted Barbara and me to come along. Horace stayed behind in Jacksonville to tend bar at Manuel's Tavern, but I needed what Felix needed—a little money and all the ballplaying I could get. The Puerto Rican League was loaded with major-league pitchers, and it would be a good chance for me and the Braves to find out how ready I really was as a hitter. It was also a good chance to find a position I could play.

I started out at second base in Puerto Rico. Not only was I fielding poorly, as usual, but I was hitting about .125 after a couple of weeks. They were ready to send me home, but Felix went to the owner and talked him into letting me stay. That turned out to be one of the best things anybody ever did for me. If I had gone back to Mobile, I almost surely would have been drafted into the army. Although the Korean War had ended that summer, there was some pressure for the draft board to call me home and induct me anyway, because both of the Bolling boys were in the service and it didn't seem fair for me to still be playing ball. But when the Caguas team said I could stay with them, the Braves stepped in and got the draft board off my back. There were reports that I might be playing baseball with the Atlanta Crackers of the Southern League the next summer, and the integration of the Southern League was a serious enough matter that it persuaded the draft board to leave me alone for the time being.

The other benefit of staying in Puerto Rico was that I finally got out of the infield. I was playing so badly at second base that something had to be done. Out of desperation—and because the Braves thought it was a good idea—our manager, Mickey Owen, decided to see if I could handle fly balls.

I said, "Henry, how about trying the outfield?" He said, "Okay. I'm gonna be going into the army anyway. I'll do whatever you want until the draft board calls." I sent him out there and hit him some fly balls. He just turned and ran and caught them. I thought, well, he can catch the ball, but can he throw it? I'd never seen him throw any way but underhanded. So I hit him some ground balls and told him to charge and throw them to second base. He threw the ball overhand, right to second base. Then I told him to cut loose and throw one to third. So he cut loose and that ball came across the infield as good as you ever saw. That was it. He was an outfielder.—Mickey Owen

When I moved to the outfield, Owen was able to put Charlie Neal at second base. Felix and Neal, who later played with the Dodgers, were a much better double-play combination than Felix and me. In fact, with me out of there, we practically had a major-league infield. Rance Pless, who was my teammate at Jacksonville and would later spend a few months in the big leagues, was the third baseman, and the first baseman was Vic Power, who was in the Yankee organization and should have been their first black player. Power was a terror in the minor leagues and about as good around first base as anybody ever was, but he was colorful, and the Yankees wanted a solemn, dignified player to be their first black. So they brought up Elston Howard and traded Power to the Athletics, which enabled him to break into the American League and stay there for twelve good years.

Our center fielder was Jungle Jim Rivera of the White Sox, who was a good hitter and the meanest ballplayer I'd seen this side of Corky Valentine. One of the first days I was there, we were being beaten about 8-0 when Rivera got on base in the ninth inning. In Puerto Rico, it's considered a disgrace if you get shut out, so Rivera stole third and then stole home to break up the shutout. When we got in the clubhouse after the game, Owen screamed at him for bush-league baseball, and Rivera went wild. He jumped on Owen and was choking him until Felix and Power and Brooks Lawrence pulled him off.

The other outfielder was a local legend named Tetelo Vargas. He was almost fifty years old by that time, but he was known as the fastest player Puerto Rico had ever seen, and he was still fast enough to play a pretty fair left field. There's a stadium named for him down there.

The only problem on our team was catching. We had a local fellow who started out as the catcher, but the American pitchers objected because he wouldn't call for anything but fastballs. He couldn't speak any English, either. The pitchers would motion him out to the mound and explain that they wanted to throw a curveball, and he would nod his head and smile and go back and give the fastball sign again. So Owen had to take over himself. It had been a couple of years since Owen had caught in the big leagues, but with him behind the plate, at least Brooks Lawrence could throw his slider.

In addition to Lawrence, who won nineteen games for the Reds one year, we had a pitcher from the Braves' organization named Bob Buhl. Buhl was a paratrooper from Michigan, and if he wasn't as mean as Rivera, he was every bit as tough. One night Buhl and I were at a club together, and as we were walking home a gang of kids started following us. They were talking tough, and Buhl was talking back to them. When we came to a public park, they stepped up and surrounded Buhl. There must have been eight or nine guys against Buhl, and it was the damndest fight I ever saw. I started to jump in and help, but as soon as I made a move I felt the tip of a knife in my side. I was told to stay out of it, because they didn't want to hurt me. It turned out that Buhl didn't need me anyway. He wiped out every one of those guys. All I had to do was put his arm over my shoulder and walk him back home.

Another time, some kids followed Charlie Neal and me when we were walking home and threw a bottle at us. Usually, though, when Charlie and I were together, we'd fight each other. We were good friends, but we were always scrapping over something. If we weren't fighting, we were ready to fight.

Between fights, we played some good ball in Puerto Rico. Our team was in first place most of the winter against competition that was virtually at the major-league level. The Santurce team, which I was ready to join before Felix got me on with Caguas, had a bunch of guys who were or would be in the big leagues— Bob Thurman, Valmy Thomas, Ruben Gomez, Jack Harshman, and an outfielder named Willard Brown, who was such a hero in Puerto Rico that they called him That Man. The most famous player in the league, though, was a former Negro League outfielder for Ponce named Francisco Coimbre.

It was great experience to play with all of those guys, but what mattered most to me was the pitching. I saw major-league pitching almost every day, and after a while—after I moved to the outfield—I began to hit it. When it came time for the All-Star Game, I was hitting well enough to be selected. It was my third All-Star Game at three different positions in three different leagues in two years. And unlike most All-Star Games, I did all right in this one. They had a track meet before the game, and I won the sixty-yard dash. After the game, I was named MVP.

The All-Star Game was held in Caguas. In the Caguas ballpark, it was 400 feet to the bleachers, and then there was a big stone wall behind the bleachers. There were only three balls hit over those bleachers all year long. Stan Lopata, the big catcher for the Phillies, hit one. Aaron hit the other two in the All-Star Game.

He could hit a ball out of any park, but what I liked was the way he hit to all fields. One of the first days he was there, I saw him rifle a ball past the first baseman, like a bullet, and I said to myself, My God, he looks like Rogers Hornsby. I asked him if he had tried to hit the ball to right field, and he said he didn't know if he did or not. I said, well, whatever you did, keep at it. I can remember exactly what I said to him. I said, "Don't let anybody change you, because you're going to be a good hitter and probably a great hitter if you take care of yourself." I could just see Hornsby in him, the way he would take that whip swing and drive the ball all over the park. Both of them would get that big end of the bat around so fast. And they were both hitchers. They'd get their hands started before the swing, like a sprinter getting a running start. Aaron was even the same size as Hornsby. I believe if he hadn't started thinking about home runs later on, he would have had some years when he batted .400, just like Hornsby.—Mickey Owen

After my bad start, I was leading the Puerto Rican League in hitting until the last two weeks of the season. I dropped off a little and finished third at .322, but I did win the home run title —actually, I tied with Jungle Jim Rivera—with nine. Every time you hit a home run down there, they gave you a carton of Chesterfield cigarettes. Those were the strongest cigarettes in the world. I smoked back then—I'm not proud of the fact that I smoked for a long time—but a pack of those Chesterfields would last me three or four days. For leading the league, I was supposed to get more cigarettes, along with money and other prizes, but Rivera took all the loot for himself before I could claim any of it. I didn't make a fuss over it because I didn't want a problem with Rivera, and, besides, I had to get back to the States. I left before the postseason tournaments, but our Caguas team went on to win the Caribbean World Series that year over teams from Cuba, Panama, and Venezuela.

One of the reasons I wanted to get home was to show my parents—and Barbara's—their new granddaughter. Our first child, Gaile, was born in Puerto Rico and spent her first couple of months in the little house we rented there. Caguas was kind of a country town, and one of my lasting memories of Puerto Rico is hearing a bell ringing in our backyard and looking out to find a cow eating Gaile's diapers off the clothesline.

When we got back to Mobile to spend a few weeks before spring training, I kept reading that I was headed for the Braves' Triple-A team at Toledo. But I told Barbara I wasn't going to Toledo. I felt that I could make the big club in Milwaukee, and if that didn't happen—despite my confidence, I didn't really think it would—I had reason to believe the Braves would keep Felix and Horace and me together and have us do it all over again in Atlanta. At least, that's what they told the draft board.

It makes me shudder now to think about integrating another league in the South. But I did plenty of things back then that I can't imagine doing now—that I *wouldn't* do now. I was ready for Atlanta. Why not? I'd made it through the Sally League without even getting hit by a pitch. I was a good ducker. The Southern League couldn't hurt me too bad, I figured. Besides, Mobile was in it. I would get to go home a few times during the season and play at Hartwell Field in front of my family and white people. That didn't sound bad.

In fact, I was more willing to go to Atlanta in 1954 than I was when the Braves moved there twelve years later, after I had been around the block a few more times.

5

America met Henry Aaron and civil rights all in the same year.

It was in 1954 that a Baptist minister in Montgomery named Ralph Abernathy was introduced to another Baptist minister in Montgomery named Martin Luther King, and they began to talk. It was also in 1954 that the United States Supreme Court voted unanimously in favor of a black Kansas man named Oliver Brown who believed that his eight-year-old daughter should not have to walk twenty-one blocks to attend grade school when there was a perfectly good one two blocks from his house. Known historically as Brown vs. Board of Education of Topeka, the case struck down the "separate but equal" standards that prevailed around the country and is generally regarded as the thunderous first step in America's modern struggle for racial integration. In effect, there was no civil rights movement before 1954—except in baseball.

By Henry Aaron's rookie year, baseball was seven years into the process of desegregation. But the game had a history of civil rights that predated Jackie Robinson. Baseball's role reached back to the times when discrimination was an Irish concern, a German concern, an Italian concern. Since it first took shape in the grass of Hoboken, New Jersey, the diamond has been the Ellis Island of playing fields, offering its basepaths and batter's boxes for the hungriest and readiest of able young men. America's emerging ethnic group, whatever it has been at the time, has consistently dominated the game at its highest level. In the earliest days, when the Irish were muscling their way out of bigotry's shackles in cities like New York and Boston and Philadelphia, it was the urban Irish who played cutting-edge baseball—men with names like Kelly, Keefe, O'Rourke, Delahanty, and McGraw. In the early part of the twentieth century, Hall of Famers Wagner, Ruth, Gehrig, Heilmann, Hubbell, and Manush carried the banner for struggling German Americans. For the first- and second-generation Italian immigrants of the middle years, the vanguard was manned by the likes of DiMaggio, Lombardi, and Berra.

Baseball's open arms did not extend to blacks, of course. A couple of brothers named Moses and Welday Walker had flirtations in 1884 with Toledo, when it played in the American Association, which was then a major league, but Cap Anson and his unyielding brethren saw to it that the likes of the Walkers would not sully their ballfields again—and for more than sixty years. During that time, there were a few aborted attempts to modify or circumvent the unofficial ban on blacks. McGraw, to whom prejudice was a familiar scoundrel, tried to sign a black second baseman named Charlie Grant in 1901 and pass him off as an Indian, but the plot was exposed and quashed. In the 1930s, there was talk that several of the great players from the Pittsburgh Crawfords of the Negro National League—Satchel Paige, Josh Gibson, Buck Leonard, and Oscar Charleston—would move across town to bolster the floundering Pirates, but nothing ever came of it. In 1942, Bill Veeck arranged to buy the Philadelphia Phillies, intending to rebuild the team with black players, but on his way to Philadelphia he made the mistake of stopping to share his plans with the baseball commissioner, Judge Kenesaw Mountain Landis. When he arrived in Philadelphia the next morning, Veeck found that the team had been sold overnight to the National League. In 1945, a tryout with the Boston Red Sox was arranged for Robinson and two other black players, Sam Jethroe and Marvin Williams. They were in the process of clouting the ball to various reaches of the park when a voice from the executive offices at the top of the stadium called down, "Get those niggers off the field!" The speaker was never publicly identified, but the three black players left the premises and did not hear from Boston again. The Red Sox, in fact, were the last major-league team to integrate, remaining solidly white until Pumpsie Green joined them in 1959.

It was later in 1945 that Branch Rickey of Brooklyn confronted baseball with the notion of signing Jackie Robinson for the Dodgers' Montreal farm team. The owners of the other fifteen major-league franchises received Rickey's suggestion with unanimous disapproval, and Robinson was brought into the game only because Commissioner Happy Chandler overruled the owners. When he did, America's black population had a rallying point. In effect, Jackie Robinson—along with Joe Louis—was Martin Luther King's warm-up act.

When Robinson made his entry into the National League in 1947, it was such an event in the black communities that black clergymen throughout the country gathered their congregations to caution them against zealous overreaction. So delicate was the nature of "The Great Experiment," it was feared that conspicuous celebration over Robinson's triumphs, or conspicuous umbrage toward the inevitable discriminations against him, would be disastrous to both Robinson's cause and the black cause at large. But the people had their example in front of them. Robinson himself set the mood of baseball's long-awaited and controversial integration by exercising a degree of restraint that went well beyond normal human standards.

His enemies were cruel and ubiquitous. There was all but mutiny on the Dodgers before the 1947 season, a band of Southern players preparing to sign a petition declaring that they would never appear on the same field as a black man. The Cardinals threatened to strike if the Dodgers brought Robinson to St. Louis. Whenever Robinson ran onto the diamond in a Brooklyn uniform, he became the target of beanballs, spikes, tobacco juice, and unconscionable verbal abuse: "Hey, nigger, why don't you go back to the cotton field where you belong? . . . Hey, nigger, which of those white boys' wives are you dating tonight? . . . Hey, porter, carry my bags . . . Hey, boy, shine my shoes." He received at least ten death threats through the mail.

Larry Doby was accorded the same sort of treatment when he integrated the American League for Bill Veeck's Cleveland Indians later in 1947. All of the pioneer black players had to go through it—Roy Campanella and Don Newcombe of the Dodgers, Monte Irvin and Hank Thompson of the Giants, Satchel Paige and Luke Easter of the Indians, Sam Jethroe of the Braves. And then, in 1951, there came Willie Mays. Late in 1953, there came Ernie Banks. In 1954, there came Henry Aaron. After Aaron, Roberto Clemente in 1955, Frank Robinson in 1956, then Orlando Cepeda, Willie McCovey, Billy Williams, Maury Wills, Bob Gibson, Lou Brock, Richie Allen, Willie Stargell . . . Within a decade of the day Jackie Robinson broke the color line, black ballplayers were on the verge of dominating the National League.

Once again, baseball's social composition was turning over with the times. In 1955, a fourteen-year-old black boy from Chicago named Emmett Till was hanged in Mississippi for whistling at a white woman. Late that year and the next, King and Abernathy led a boycott of the Jim Crow city buses that Aaron had poignantly observed in sweltering Montgomery, Alabama. Civil rights had become a movement. Like the Irish and Germans and Italians before them, blacks were emerging in America and its national pastime all at once.

◆　　◆　　◆

When I look back at the clippings, I suppose I was something of a phenom that first spring. One of the stories in the Milwaukee *Sentinel* said, "Not since Mickey Mantle was moved up to the Yankees has there been a player with as big a buildup as Aaron, a lithe 19-year-old Negro." Well, first of all, I was twenty. And secondly, I wasn't reading that stuff. I was in Bradenton, Florida, trying to make the club and convince everybody that I wasn't a lazy kid just off the cotton field, which is what they all seemed to think.

In those days, there was no problem with saying it, either— as if nobody would mind but the coloreds, who didn't really matter anyway. It wasn't regarded as bigotry for a white person to make lighthearted reference to a black person's laziness or ignorance—it was just being a good ol' boy. I remember the manager, Charlie Grimm, calling me "Stepanfetchit" in the newspaper. It was in the headline of the Milwaukee *Journal*: "Aaron Has Nickname of Stepanfetchit, Because He Just Keeps Shuffling Along." I remember Joe Adcock, our first baseman from Louisiana, calling me Slow Motion Henry and saying I looked like a pretty good hitter but smart pitching would probably fool me.

I also remember the name over my locker being spelled

"Arron." And so I don't remember feeling like a phenom in the spring of 1954. Instead, I remember telling Barbara to keep the suitcases ready because I didn't expect to be with the big club for long. The Braves had Bill Bruton in center field and Andy Pafko in right, and over the winter they had made a big trade with the Giants to get my boyhood hero of 1951, Bobby Thomson. I figured the fourth outfielder would be Jim Pendleton, who was ten years older than I was and had batted .299 for the Braves in 1953. What I hadn't figured on was that Pendleton would be a holdout and report to camp overweight—something I would understand better when he became my roommate. I also hadn't counted on Bobby Thomson breaking his ankle.

I watched it happen. We were playing the Yankees at Al Lang Field in St. Petersburg, and I had already played, showered, and dressed. I was standing in a little alleyway behind third base drinking a soda when Thomson's leg folded under him as he slid into second base. They put him on a stretcher and carried him right past where I was standing. It was a horrible thing to watch, and it never occurred to me that it was my chance to play left field for the Braves. Bob Buhl, my buddy from Puerto Rico, rode with me on the bus back to Bradenton that day, and he was the first one who mentioned that I might get a chance to be the left fielder. He also mentioned it to Charlie Grimm. Buhl was like my press agent that spring. He must have been impressed with what he saw of me in Puerto Rico, because he went around telling everybody what a great young hitter I was. Grimm must have believed him. The next day I was starting in left field against the Red Sox in Sarasota.

That was my second break in two days, because the pitcher for Boston was Ike Delock—the guy against whom I hit that long home run in Jacksonville the year before. Sure enough, it happened again. I cracked one over a row of trailers that bordered the outfield fence—hit it so hard that Ted Williams came running out from the clubhouse wanting to know who it was that could make a bat sound that way when it struck a baseball.

Later on, I read in the newspapers that Grimm handed me the left-field job that day, but all I knew was that I still had a minor-league contract. I wasn't sure of anything until we left Bradenton to come north and the Braves gave me a major-league contract. After that, it would be about twenty-three years until I was out of the starting lineup.

Our opener was in Cincinnati, but that year as well as one or two others, the Braves and Dodgers barnstormed together on our way north, stopping off to play games in cities like Mobile, New Orleans, Birmingham, Memphis, Louisville, and Indianapolis. Before I even saw Milwaukee, I had a chance to play in front of my family in Mobile, wearing a Braves uniform—number 5— and sharing the field with Jackie Robinson. I hoped my father remembered what I told him when I was fourteen—that I would be in the big leagues while Jackie was still there. I had a single and a double that day.

The black players from the Braves and Dodgers stayed at the same hotels in the South—different ones than the white players, of course—and in the evenings I always managed to find my way to Jackie's room. He and Newcombe and Campanella and Joe Black and Jim Gilliam would sit around the room playing cards and talking about the National League and nightlife and everything I wanted to hear about. They even had strategy sessions on how to cope with the racial situation—what to do if a guy spit at them, for instance, or whether to join in if there was a fight on the field, that sort of thing. Those hotel rooms were my college. I would just sit in the corner thumbing through a magazine or watching TV, taking it all in.

Being around the Dodgers made me realize that I could never be just another major-league player. I was a black player, and that meant I would be separate most of the time from most of the players on the team. It meant that I'd better be good, or I'd be gone. It meant that some players and some fans would hate me no matter what I did. And it meant that I had a choice. Either I could forget that I was black and just smile and go along with the program until my time was up, or I could never forget that I was black. After hearing Jackie Robinson and the other Dodgers, there was only one way to make that choice.

If there's a single reason why the black players of the 1950s and 1960s were so much better than the white players—in the National League, that is, because there weren't many black players in the American League—I believe it's because we had to be. And we knew we had to be. There was too much at stake for us to screw it up. Black people had been crying out for opportunity in this country for two centuries, and finally we had it. Our mission—and that's the only thing to call it—was to do something with the chance we had.

Of course, no matter what you thought about missions and opportunities, you still had to hit a fastball on the outside corner. I was a big oh-for-five in my first major-league game, which also happened to be the first game in which players were required to bring their gloves off the field at the end of an inning. Before 1954, they would just toss them in the grass on their way to the dugout and pick them up as they ran out to their positions the next inning. As it turned out, we might as well have left our gloves in the dugout that day, because nobody was catching anything anyway. It seemed like everybody in both lineups was hitting the ball all over the park—except the guy batting fifth for the Braves, which was me. Bud Podbielan started for the Reds and Joe Nuxhall took over in the second inning, but I don't believe I could have hit Bud Abbott and Joey Heatherton. I was a spectator. There's always a parade on Opening Day in Cincinnati, and the crowd at Crosley Field was so big that they roped off the outfield and had people packed in on the warning track. I spent the afternoon chasing balls into the crowd—Jim Greengrass of the Reds hit four ground-rule doubles—and getting a little National League education. The first thing I learned was that Eddie Mathews was our money guy. He hit two home runs. The second thing I learned was what happens after a guy hits two home runs. I was on deck in the eighth inning when Andy Pafko, our cleanup hitter, came up against Nuxhall after Mathews's second homer, and I had a good view of Nuxhall's fastball crashing against Pafko's helmet. They took Pafko to the hospital, and the Reds won the game 9-8. It was a pretty ugly beginning.

I didn't hit for a few days. My problem was that Ike Delock was in the American League, but before long I found a pitcher to my liking—Vic Raschi, a righthander for the Cardinals. Raschi had won twenty games a few times for the Yankees, and I was fortunate to be facing him near the end of his career. I got my first major-league hit against Raschi, a double in a game we won in Milwaukee. Eight days later, he pitched against us again in St. Louis, and I hit my first major-league home run.

Once I got acclimated, I found that playing in the big leagues wasn't nearly as hard as getting there. My career was just beginning, but I felt like the struggle was over. There were no more Macons, no more Montgomerys, no more bologna sandwiches on dark buses. All I had to do was get to the ballpark and find a place to have dinner afterwards.

Of course, that wasn't quite as simple as it sounds. In cities like Cincinnati and St. Louis, the black players couldn't use the dining rooms in the hotels where the team stayed, and sometimes —especially in Cincinnati—it was difficult to find any restaurant that would serve us. Bruton and I tried to eat at a place called The Cat and the Fiddle in Cincinnati and sat there holding the menus until we realized that they would close before they would send a waiter to our table. We walked around town for a while and never did find a place that would let us buy a meal.

When we had an off day in Cincinnati once, I was with an old friend who had married an Italian girl while he was in the service. His wife's sister was along, and we were riding around in Covington, Kentucky, when a policeman pulled us over. He asked me if I was married to the white girl sitting next to me, and I said no. My friend said he was married to the white girl sitting next to him, so the cop let him go on. But he made me get out of the car right there. He said, "Boy, you get out of town. We don't have that kind of thing around here." When he left, I went into the woods to hide, because I figured he'd come back. A little while later, sure enough, there were police cars all over the streets. Somehow, I managed to keep out of sight and make it back to the hotel.

In St. Louis, my rookie year was the first year black players were permitted to stay with the rest of the team at the Chase Hotel. Before that, they stayed at a black hotel where it was so hot they had to soak the bed sheets. Even after we moved to the Chase, we weren't allowed to eat in the restaurant—Curt Roberts, a black player with the Pirates, sat in there for forty-five minutes once without being served—and we always had rooms facing a brick wall or the alley where they threw the garbage.

I went into the army for two years to serve in the Korean War, and when I got back to the Dodgers in 1954, we were still staying at the Adams Hotel in St. Louis. It was a hotel for blacks, with no air conditioning or any of the comforts the white players had at the Chase. I said to Jackie, "Look, I just got back from serving my country for two years, and I'll be damned if I'm going to put up with this." He said, "Let's go check it out." So we got in a cab and went over to the Chase and found the manager of the hotel. He sat us down in the dining room, and Jackie said, "You know why we're here, don't you?" He said yes. Jackie said, "All right, then, tell us why we can't stay here." And this is what the man said. He said, "The only reason you men can't stay here is that we don't want you using the swimming pool." Jackie almost fell off his chair. He said, "Mister, I don't even know how to swim." Well, that wasn't true, because Jackie could do anything. But we didn't give a damn about swimming at the hotel. I said I didn't swim during the season because I didn't want to hurt my arm. So we stayed at the Chase from then on. All the teams did. None of us ever got a room on the side of the pool, though. That bigot didn't want us looking at those pretty women in their bikinis. But what he didn't know was that I had women in my room all the time. Black women, white women, all kinds. That bigot should have come to my room one night and seen what was going on.—Don Newcombe

I roomed with Jim Pendleton at first—whenever he stayed at the hotel. Pendleton would drop off his clothes and you might never see him again. He was a nice-looking guy and he had women in nearly every town. He was also the only guy I ever saw who would take his paycheck right to the tavern and leave it there. If the check was $1,200, he might ask for $200 back for spending money and let them keep the rest for a line of credit until the next paycheck. About the only time I could count on seeing Pendleton was when he wanted to get something to eat. After a ballgame, he'd say, "Little Brother, let's go get some dinner." I figured we'd go find a good steak, but he'd head straight for White Castle every time. John Quinn, our general manager, caught us coming out of White Castle one night in Philadelphia, and the next day I was rooming with Bill Bruton.

Bruton was a serious guy and a family man—just the opposite of Pendleton. Bruton was actually a couple years older than it was reported, and he was the one who took charge of any special arrangements the black players had to make—finding restaurants, arranging cabs to the ballpark, that sort of thing. We especially needed somebody like that when we were barnstorming our way north, and when we were in Florida for spring training. At least, *I* needed somebody like that. I was lucky to have a guy like Bruton on my side. All of the black players called me Little Brother, but Bruton was really my Big Brother. He had me over to his house the first night we were in Milwaukee, and I followed him around most of that first year. He was a good man to follow around, because Bruton was a hero in Milwaukee. He had hit a home run to win the first game the Braves ever played there in 1953, and that made him special to the people of Wisconsin—who were the warmest, friendliest fans in the world.

Over the years, it was often said that playing in Milwaukee hurt my career—that I would have been a much bigger star and made more money on the East Coast or the West Coast or in a bigger city like Chicago or New York. That may be so, but I think I would have been a lost child in New York. On the other hand, Milwaukee was perfect for me. Any player would have been fortunate to play in front of those fans. Baseball has never seen fans like Milwaukee's in the 1950s and never will again. I was told that in the first game there in 1953—the game Bruton won— Warren Spahn was pitching to the second batter of the first inning, and all of a sudden people started standing and applauding all over the ballpark. They were just happy to have baseball. They could hardly believe it was happening, because nobody had any idea they were getting a team until the day it was announced, a few weeks before the season started. Those people were like kids at Christmas. They were the happiest fans in America, and they stayed that way all through the fifties. You could pop up with the bases loaded, and they would cheer you for trying. The people of Milwaukee just couldn't do enough for you if you were a Brave. We'd go into a store to buy a suit, and they wouldn't let us pay for it. They gave us free cigars, candy, eggs, jewelry, dry cleaning, haircuts. Andy Pafko got a Cadillac. Spahn got a tractor. Bruton got a down payment on a new house.

Milwaukee was the smallest city in the major leagues, but it had plenty of help from the smaller towns around it. The Braves belonged to all of Wisconsin, as well as parts of Minnesota, Iowa, Michigan, and North and South Dakota. It gave County Stadium a football atmosphere. The people would arrive by the carload, get there hours before game time, and have tailgate parties in the parking lot, drinking out of their Braves cups and waving their Braves pennants. They'd bring beer and cheese and sandwiches for the picnic, then carry whatever was left into the ballpark. On weekends, the train would pull up full of fans from Minnesota and drop them off in the rail yard right outside the ballpark. Those people had been on the train for most of the day, and they'd come running off carrying cases of beer. I'm not sure half of them ever made it into the ballpark. On Sundays, there might be 200 school buses parked outside the stadium. I used to take the streetcar to the park and walk right along with the fans as they came streaming down the hills and over the bridges from Story Parkway. It was something to see. In my rookie year, the Braves' initial print order for tickets was the largest ticket order in the history of the printing business. We drew 2.1 million people and broke the National League attendance record in August.

I'd like to think that I had something to do with it, but I'm afraid that wasn't the case—at least, not in 1954. I had a decent rookie year, but I wasn't the one the fans came to watch—which was why I could walk to the ballpark without being recognized. Mathews, on the other hand, hit forty homers that year and was such a hot young star that in August he appeared on the cover of the first *Sports Illustrated* ever published. Spahn was already a superstar by the time the team arrived in Milwaukee, and in 1954 he won twenty-one games, which was about his average. Bruton led the league in stolen bases. Those were the guys the fans wanted to see. And the stars they had been reading about for so many years but thought they would never see in person—Stan Musial and Jackie Robinson and Duke Snider and Ted Kluszewski and Willie Mays.

Mays was at the top of his game when I broke into baseball, and from the very beginning, he was the guy I was measured against. It went on for as long as we played in the same league—twenty years—and then some. Usually, I suffered from the comparison. Willie set the tone for this right off the bat. While I was a quiet rookie in Milwaukee, he was taking the league by storm. In 1954, Willie became the hottest player in the game, leading the National League in batting, hitting forty-one home runs, and making that unforgettable catch and throw against Vic Wertz as the Giants won the World Series. There were Willie Mays comic books, Say Hey baseball caps, and a dozen songs about Willie. It wasn't New York that made Mays what he was, though, and it wasn't Leo Durocher. It was his amazing ability. And it wasn't just me who suffered from comparisons to Willie. That year, he became the standard for all other players.

Meanwhile, I was just a guy filling in for Bobby Thomson. To give you an idea of how important I was in 1954, on the Braves' highlight film from that year, it showed me hitting a foul ball. That was it. "The annals of sports," it said, "will never be able to record how much Bobby's absence meant to the Braves." Thomson was a big hitter and would have meant a lot to the team—especially batting behind Mathews in the lineup—but I didn't think I dragged us down all that much. I was hitting in the cleanup spot by July, and we had a better year than most people expected, finishing third behind the Giants and Dodgers—who, by the way, made a little history of their own that year. On July 17, in a game against us, Brooklyn sent out a starting lineup that included Jackie Robinson, Roy Campanella, Junior Gilliam, Sandy Amoros, and Don Newcombe. It was the first time a major-league lineup had more black players than white—and if you think that wasn't a big deal, you don't know anything about the 1950s.

By the end of the season, I knew I belonged in the big leagues, but I was a little disappointed in myself. It was probably because I figured I ought to lead any league I played in. My batting average was up and down all year—I had trouble hitting the change-up —but Charlie Grimm stuck with me and I reached .280 when I went five-for-five in a doubleheader at Cincinnati. In the second game, I was sliding into third for a triple when I broke my ankle the same way Thomson broke his in Florida. When they carried me off the field, Thomson came in to run for me. It was September 5, and I was finished for the season.

I suppose I might have made a run at Rookie of the Year if I had played the rest of the games, but I would have had a hard time catching Wally Moon of the Cardinals, who hit .304. As it was, I got one vote—which was one more than Brooks Lawrence, who won 15 games after joining the Cardinals in June. Ernie Banks hit nineteen home runs and got four votes.

Ernie had actually joined the Cubs late in the 1953 season, and although I didn't know it at the time, Horace Garner and Felix Mantilla and I were indirectly responsible. Apparently, the Cubs had asked their Macon farm club to accept a black player or two in 1953, when we were with Jacksonville in the Sally League. The general manager at Macon didn't think the town was ready for that. But the first time Horace and Felix and I played in Macon, the colored section was filled up and they had to rope off more of the white section to get all of the black people in. They had the biggest crowds of the season when we were there, and suddenly the general manager decided that maybe a black player or two wouldn't be such a bad idea. He got back in touch with the Cubs about it, and the Cubs told him to go find his own black player. So Macon scouted around and decided to go after Banks, who was playing for the Kansas City Monarchs of the Negro American League. But Banks wouldn't sign with the Cubs' organization unless it sent him right to Chicago, and that's what happened. Ernie never played a day in the minor leagues.

By the time Ernie and I came up, there was a pretty good crop of Negro League veterans in the big leagues, including Jackie, Willie, Campanella, Newcombe, Monte Irvin, Larry Doby, Minnie Minoso, and others. A lot of them played together on barnstorming teams in the fall, and I would have liked to join them in 1954, but I was in no shape to play ball. My leg was in a cast most of the winter, so I didn't do much but play with my baby daughter and drive my new Pontiac convertible around Mobile. I didn't know much about budgeting. I kept asking the Braves for advances on my salary, and they kept sending me money.

I probably couldn't have barnstormed if I didn't have the cast on my leg anyway, because there was a good chance I would have been away on military duty. When I made the major leagues, I became too visible for the draft board to ignore. I admit I wasn't crazy about the thought of being in the army—when you grow up as a black kid in a Jim Crow city, you somehow don't feel a great urgency to serve your country—but Donald Davidson, the Braves' traveling secretary, took me down to the draft board to register one morning during my rookie year, and we got in line behind about 200 other guys. I told Donald we could leave because it looked like they had enough. I don't think he appreciated my humor. Anyway, the Braves talked to the draft board and the plan was that I would be drafted after the season. When I broke my ankle, I was reclassified.

After I got my cast off, I had my brother, Tommie, throw me change-ups at Carver Park the rest of the winter. Tommie was just fifteen, and we never imagined that we'd be on the same team in the big leagues some day. He eventually made it as first baseman, but his change-up was good enough to get me ready for 1955.

I still needed some hard work to get in shape after having the cast on all winter, so, at John Quinn's request, I reported early to Bradenton. After I was there a day or so, I got a telegram from the commissioner, Ford Frick, telling me I was fined for reporting early. He had a rule that all players had to report on the same day, and several players on the Braves received the same telegram. Mr. Quinn wasn't around when mine arrived, so I put it in my locker to give to him later. After a while, Charlie Grimm came in and wanted to know where my telegram was. I forgot I'd put it in my locker. That's all there was to it. But the way the story got around was that I had thrown it away, and when somebody told me it was from Ford Frick, I said, "Who's that?"

Because I was black, and because I never moved faster than I had to, and because I didn't speak Ivy League English, I came into the league with an image of a backward country kid who could swing the bat and was lucky he didn't have to think too much. Along the way, there were plenty of stories that played along with the image. A lot of them came from Charlie Grimm. Charlie never meant anybody any harm; he was just an entertainer—when he wasn't telling tales, he was picking the banjo—but his stories about me contributed to an image that I'm still trying to shake. After a while, the stories about me all seemed to adopt a common theme—that I was just a simple colored boy. The Ford Frick story is one example. Another is when I hit a triple against Curt Simmons in spring training my rookie year. Afterwards, somebody asked me if I knew who the pitcher was, and I said no. So it came out in the paper that I didn't know Curt Simmons or Robin Roberts or any of the pitchers that everybody knew. What it didn't say in the paper was that I knew what they all threw, and how hard, and where their release points were. I might not have known names and words the way sportswriters did, but I had a mental capacity at home plate that nobody seemed to appreciate. There's no such thing as a good hitter who is a dumb hitter. To me, it's dumb to think that there is. There are simply different kinds of intelligence, and I found out that if you don't express yours in the same way that the critics express theirs, then they assume that you're dumb. For years, the newspaper and magazine stories described me with words like "uncomplicated," "slow-talking," "shuffling," "lethargic." They said that hitting was just something that came naturally to me. Maybe it was. But part of that natural ability was the natural ability to think in the batter's box.

I thought about baseball constantly, and I made it a point to learn what I could from older players. I picked up a lot of information just by listening to Mathews and Del Crandall and Spahn and Lew Burdette on the train. The train was about the only place where I got a chance to sit and talk with the white players—or at least, to sit nearby and listen to them talk, since I wasn't much on conversation. If we had traveled by plane instead of train in my early days, I would have hardly gotten to know the white players and to benefit from their knowledge and background. Black players never roomed with white players and seldom went out to dinner with them. I guess it was a carryover from spring training, when the blacks and whites had separate living arrangements.

> *The train gave us all a chance to be together. The only big room in the train was the lounge area of the men's room, so we would gather in there with a couple cases of beer and stay up into the wee hours. We could sit with the black players on the train, but they couldn't eat in the dining car. We'd have to bring food back to them.*
>
> *It was rough on the black players. We all knew the situation was ridiculous—especially spring training. As I look back on it now, I realize I should have done more about it than I did—we all should have. But we were young, and we just accepted the way it was. I wish I'd have been more indignant for our black players, but I had no idea how to approach something like that. None of us were outspoken about any of it. There were no black leaders in the country at the time, nobody making a real issue of it.—Eddie Mathews*

When we were in Bradenton, the white players stayed at the big, pink Manatee River Hotel and the black players lived in an apartment over a garage owned by a black schoolteacher named Lulu Gibson. That is, most of us lived in the apartment—the penthouse, as we called it. Being the elder statesman among us, Bill Bruton had "big house" privileges, which meant he had a room in the main house with Mr. and Mrs. Gibson and her sister from North Carolina, who came to help with the cooking every year. The rest of us shared two bedrooms and a hallway in the penthouse. It was crowded, but it was clean, and you couldn't beat the meals. We'd wake up every morning to bacon and biscuits and gravy.

One year, as soon as we arrived in Bradenton, the Ku Klux Klan marched right down Ninth Street, where Mrs. Gibson's house was. I don't know if their little demonstration was intended for us, but we got the message. Bradenton was very much a Southern town back then. The blacks still had separate sections at the ballpark—Barbara wouldn't come to the games, because she refused to sit apart from the white wives—and separate drinking fountains and restaurants. After a game once, I went with some of my teammates to the Dairy Queen across the street from the ballpark. When I stepped up to the window to order an ice-cream cone, the lady inside told me to go around to the colored window in back. I forgot all about that incident until a few years ago, when I got a letter from a man who had been living in Bradenton then. He said he and his wife were good friends with the couple that ran the Dairy Queen, and his wife worked for them occasionally. She was the one who had to serve me that day at the colored window, and it bothered her so much that she broke off the friendship with the other couple, quit the job, and went home and cried for a couple of days.

Some of the newspapers in Florida wouldn't even print pictures of the black players. In a lot of ways, Bradenton was worse than Alabama. We were advised not to drive cars at night, and you never knew what would happen if you tried to catch a cab. Sometimes, white drivers would refuse to take you anywhere, and on other occasions, policemen stopped cabs and ordered black players to get out. We were liable to be arrested just for being on the street.

> When I was with the Reds in Tampa, my first day there I was with one of my white Spanish teammates. He went into a white movie house to buy some ice cream, and I couldn't go in, so I waited for him outside. While I was waiting, a couple of policemen walked up and arrested me. I couldn't speak a word of English, but they put me in a police car and started to take me away. I was making like I'm hitting a ball so they would understand I was a baseball player. So they took me back to the camp and said, "You stay here." I practiced those words over and over, and when I got inside, I asked somebody what "You stay

*here" meant. Then I understood I wasn't supposed to leave the
camp.*—Tony Gonzalez

There was a story about Vic Power being arrested for crossing
the street on a red light in St. Petersburg. He explained to the
police captain that he was just beginning to figure out what to do
in Florida. He had learned that whites drank at one fountain and
blacks at another, and whites went in one bathroom and blacks
went in another. So when he was standing on the corner and the
light turned green and all the white people crossed the street, he
figured that meant he was supposed to cross on red. I don't know
if that's true or not, but I do know that the Jim Crow laws were
especially frightening for the Latin players. One rookie from the
Dominican Republic never left our apartment in Bradenton except to go to the ballpark.

Even the whites felt the discrimination occasionally—when
they were with us, that is. On a bus trip for an exhibition game
one time, we stopped at a fast-food place and the guy behind the
counter told the black players to go around to the back entrance.
Charlie Grimm didn't want to hear it. He ordered everybody to
get back on the bus until we found a restaurant that would accept
all of us.

It wasn't that long ago, but young people today can't imagine
what 1955 was like. There hadn't even been a bus boycott in
Montgomery yet. Ronald Reagan was host of "General Electric
Theater." Blacks were still coloreds, and the white world was
afraid of us. Baseball was afraid of us, too—even in Brooklyn,
where they had won four pennants since Jackie Robinson arrived. In the spring of 1955, when the Dodgers were thinking
about having eight black players on their roster, Dick Young of
the New York *Daily News* wrote, "I honestly don't believe baseball is ready for that step right now." Why not? What would
happen? When would there be a right time? Baseball had been
integrated for eight years, and some people still couldn't accept
it. We had an exhibition game scheduled for Birmingham that
spring, and it was canceled because the city didn't want blacks
and whites playing together.

We never knew exactly what it was that white people were afraid of. The way we saw it, we were the ones who had reason to be afraid. We were the ones who could be arrested without a moment's notice. Or spiked, or beaned, or beaten, or shot, or even hanged.

My first spring with the Dodgers in Vero Beach, I had an argument with a white Cuban named Fermin Guerra. He had been my manager that winter in Cuba and he had sent me home early and I was still angry about it. Guerra was a catcher with the Philadelphia Athletics, and when we played them in Vero Beach I resumed the argument. Here was a black man arguing with a white man in front of all these people. We were standing by a picket fence, and one guy in the crowd grabbed a picket off that fence, threw it to Guerra and told him to kill me with it. Sam Lacy, a writer for the Baltimore Afro-American, grabbed me and got me out of there, and it's a good thing he did. Who knows what that crowd would have done? After that, they almost had to spirit me out of town. There was talk that I was going to be lynched, and nobody took it lightly. At five in the morning, Branch Rickey, Jackie Robinson, Roy Campanella, Sam Jethroe, Buzzy Bavasi, the sheriff, the chief of police, the mayor and I all convened at Mr. Rickey's home to devise a plan on how to handle this thing. They decided that the only way to allow me to stay was if I didn't leave the camp. But they were prepared to get me out of town if they had to. The whole time we were talking, they had an airplane waiting at the end of the runway.—Don Newcombe

There was never any racial violence or open hatred on the Braves, but the black players knew where all the white players were coming from. For instance, Pendleton had been beaned by Lew Burdette when they were both in the American Association, and with the Braves they were teammates. Burdette was from West Virginia, and he had a reputation as a player who would throw at blacks and call them names on the field. He'd had a few run-ins with Jackie and Campanella. But there was nothing phony about Burdette. You knew where he stood, and everything was out in the open. And if any pitcher on another team ever threw at one of our black players, we could count on Burdette to protect us when he got to the mound. You couldn't say the same thing for all our pitchers.

I had no problems with Burdette, but I did have an occasional confrontation with Joe Adcock. One time I was sitting in a toilet stall in the clubhouse, and Adcock was in the next stall. He didn't know I was there, and he was talking to somebody about scouting some black player and said something about finding a nigger in Harlem. We both flushed the toilet at the same time and walked out and found ourselves looking at each other. I said, "Yeah, it's me." He said, "Hank, I'm sorry, I'm sorry." But I always knew he was like that. It didn't bother me. I just spoke up because I wanted him to respect me. I wanted him to know that I heard him and I knew what he was all about. After I said that, I just walked out, because I didn't intend to get into a personal battle. Besides, if I did, Adcock was liable to beat the crap out of me.

I understood the guys like Burdette and Adcock, who were up front. The fellow that I had the hardest time reading was Warren Spahn. Spahn wasn't a Southerner, and he was a little more sophisticated in the way he expressed his feelings. Spahn would say things in a loose, locker-room kind of way, and you were never quite sure how to take him. Being the veteran superstar on the team, and the leader, I think he just felt like he could get away with things. He'd make jokes like, "What's black and catches flies? The Braves outfield." He didn't mean any harm, and sometimes he would offend people without even realizing it—although he probably should have. Like the time in Birmingham, when he made a joke comparing me to a cockroach.

We were playing the Dodgers on our way north after spring training, and we were sitting around the clubhouse in Birmingham waiting for it to stop raining. Henry and I used to have some running jokes with our trainer, Charlie Lacks. We'd go back and forth insulting each other. I'd call Henry "Stepanfetchit," things like that. Well, when we were sitting in the club-

house that day, this black bug went over one of the joints in the concrete and fell over on its back. It was just laying there, so I said, "Hey, Doc, come turn Hank over." I was referring to the fact that it was just laying there motionless more than I was to the color, because we used to tease Hank about how slowly he moved. Hank didn't say anything about it at the time. Well, on the day we opened the season, Adcock and I were having a little disagreement by our lockers, and Hank popped up and said, "You're always causing trouble, Spahn." I said, "What do you mean?" He said, "You know what you said in Birmingham." I had to think about what I'd said. When I thought about it, I realized Hank thought I was making an inference about his color, which he had a right to think. I said, "Believe me, Hank, that was not my intention." We talked it out. Maybe we became better friends after that.

You know, when I came into baseball in the forties, we'd call an Italian a Dago, and a German like me was a Flathead or a Hardhead. But when Jackie Robinson came into the league, he had immunity. You couldn't say anything toward the color of a man's skin. I think Jackie took advantage of that. Jackie got arrogant after a while. Then Campanella came along, and some of the others, and by the time Hank got there, the groundwork was broken. With all the blacks coming in, it was the beginning of something really different. We, the players, had nothing to do with the fact that they had to stay in different hotels in some places. The black players knew about these things when they came into baseball. I don't say it was right, but they knew these situations existed. I'll say this—I was terribly happy I was a white guy, and probably envious that I didn't have the talents of a black guy.—Warren Spahn

The trouble I had with Spahn was that it didn't seem like he wanted to understand what was going on. When Dr. King was leading all the marches, Spahn came up to me in the clubhouse one day and said, "Henry, just what is it that you people want?" I said, "All we want is the things you've had all along." We got along fine after that. From then on, I think he knew where I was coming from and I knew where he was coming from.

And I'll say this about Spahn. They can talk about Koufax

and Feller and whoever they want, but you have to go a long way to beat this guy's record. He was a pitcher who hated to lose, and we could count on him to win twenty games year after year after year after year. He led the league in wins more times than any pitcher who ever lived, and that's about the best thing you can say about a pitcher. It was a privilege to play behind him.

It so happened, however, that 1955 was the only season in a stretch of nine that Spahn didn't win twenty games—in fact, he only missed four times over a period of seventeen years. On the other hand, 1955 was the first time I hit more than twenty home runs, which was something I did for twenty straight seasons. It was also the first time I hit .300, which I would do ten times over the course of eleven seasons. It was the first time I scored 100 runs, which I did for thirteen years in a row, and drove in 100, which I did eleven times.

And it was the first time I wore number 44 on my back. Before the season, I went to Donald Davidson, our traveling secretary, and said I wanted a number with two digits. Donald told me I was crazy. He enjoyed insulting me and would use any excuse to do it. That's just the way Donald was. He was only four feet tall, but he talked like he was Dick Butkus. Of course, that only encouraged guys like Spahn and Burdette, and they pulled some wicked stunts on Donald. I didn't pick on him too much—occasionally, I would lift him up while we were walking, or set him on a table—but he seemed to take delight in tearing me apart. Once, he called me on the phone in my hotel room and started cussing me up and down. I asked him why he was doing it, and he said he was mad and I was the only one on the team he could yell at and get away with it. The fact is, Donald was one of my best friends in baseball. I think because of the prejudices we both faced, we understood each other. Once, he and I sat down for breakfast at our hotel in Pittsburgh and the waitress wouldn't wait on me. Donald never scheduled us into that hotel again.

Anyway, when I told him I wanted to wear a bigger number, Donald told me I was too damn skinny to carry around two numbers. He also said that Musial and DiMaggio and Ruth and Gehrig and all the great players had single numbers, and he thought I should have one, too. But I still wanted a bigger number—preferably a double number. Finally, Donald gave me 44. As it turned out, I hit forty-four home runs four different times in my career, which made Donald complain that he hadn't given me 66.

Donald also took credit for naming me "Hammerin' Hank," although that might have originally come out of New York. At the Polo Grounds in 1955, I hit a ball off the facing of the second deck, and one of the New York newspaper guys wrote, "Hammering Hank nearly tore through the balcony facade." But Donald was the one who spread the name around. In fact, I'm proud of the role he played in my career, because, until he died in 1990, Donald was a baseball institution for more than fifty years, going back to the Boston Braves, and also one of the best-liked men in the game. He certainly meant a lot to me and my career. Since he always traveled with the Braves, either as traveling secretary or public relations director, Donald saw every home run I hit in the National League except for one that he missed when he had the flu.

I was a better player as number 44. The difference between the quiet .280 hitter of 1954 and Hammerin' Hank of 1955 was the fact that I had learned to read the pitchers a little better and wait on the change-up. Actually, I improved as the year went on. Early in the season, I was struggling on one of our road trips, and Barbara told me not to come home until I had my average up to .300. I got it up there in time to make my first All-Star team.

The All-Star Game was in Milwaukee that year. I didn't start, but Leo Durocher put me in late and I got to bat twice because the game went into extra innings. Actually, I put it into extra innings by driving in the tying run. I was two-for-two, but the hero of the game was Stan Musial. Musial was one of my favorite ballplayers, because he treated everybody the same—black or white, superstar or scrub—and he genuinely loved the game. I understand he was one of the few Cardinals who refused to go along when they were talking about boycotting Jackie Robinson in 1947, and he got into an argument with his teammates over it. In the mid-sixties, when he and I were part of a group of players who toured Vietnam, Musial became the first white man I ever roomed with. We had been good friends for quite a while, because whenever the Braves played the Cardinals, he and I would always manage to meet up at the batting cage and talk about hitting. I wasn't aware of it at the time, but I'm told other players used to get quiet and listen when Musial and I were talking. I can assure you, though, I listened harder than anybody, because Musial was probably the hitter I most respected. And it all went back to the twelfth inning of the 1955 All-Star Game. Musial led off the inning, but before he went up to bat, he turned to me and a few other guys and said, "I don't get paid for overtime. I'm gonna end this thing." And he walked up and hit a home run. I'll never forget that.

Maybe one of the reasons I took to Musial so well was that he felt the same way I did about hitting. Basically, his method was to study the pitchers and swing the bat, and that was the way I felt about it. I admire the way Ted Williams made a science of hitting—I read his book backwards and forwards—but that wasn't my style. Williams concentrated on the things he had to do himself. I concentrated on the pitcher. I didn't stay up nights worrying about my weight distribution, or the location of my hands, or the turn of my hips; I stayed up thinking about the pitcher I was going to face the next day. I used to play every pitcher in my mind before I went to the ballpark. I started getting ready for every game the minute I woke up.

A lot of people thought I was an undisciplined hitter, because I swung at a lot of bad pitches—especially early in my career. But there were a couple of things they didn't take into account. One was that I only swung at a bad pitch when it was a good pitch for me—the kind of pitch I was waiting for. The other thing was that I didn't want to put my fate in the hands of the umpire. I wouldn't go as far as to say that black players had a different strike zone than white players, but I didn't want to test the umpires. When you've grown up black in the South—at least, in my times—you're conditioned not to rely on the white man's justice. If the pitch was close, I wasn't taking any chances.

Actually, I think the umpires liked me, because I made their job easy. I would swing at anything in the area code, and I never argued. In fact, I was so casual at the plate that Robin Roberts said I was the only hitter he ever saw who could take a nap between pitches. But I wasn't napping. It was just that my body didn't need to be busy when my mind had work to do.

By 1955, I had begun to figure out major-league pitching, and one of things I figured out was that I'd have to do a lot more figuring before I'd be in the class of Stan Musial or Eddie Mathews or Willie Mays. Mathews hit forty-one home runs again—there must have been something magical about our numbers, because that was his—and Mays led the league with fifty-one. My modest .314 and twenty-seven home runs didn't attract much attention in that kind of company.

My progress as a player pretty much paralleled the Braves' as a team. We improved enough to finish second in 1955, but we were no challenge to the Dodgers. Don Newcombe was the best pitcher in the league that season, and with Jackie and Campy and Snider, they were never out of first place. The '55 Dodgers were one of the best teams I ever saw. Even though we were chasing them in the standings, I have to admit that I was a fan of the Dodgers. I even kept a scrapbook on them that year.

I got a chance to know Newcombe and Mays better when I joined up with Willie's barnstorming team that winter. Jackie Robinson had started the tradition of a black barnstorming team, and Roy Campanella took it over for a while, then Mays. We had a pretty good outfield on our club—Mays, myself, Monte Irvin, and Larry Doby. We also had Ernie Banks at shortstop and Campanella catching and George Crowe and Hank Thompson and Junior Gilliam, and for pitchers we had Newcombe and Joe Black and Sam Jones and Brooks Lawrence. We didn't lose. I mean, we didn't *ever* lose. We played a group of Negro League all-stars that toured with us, but I don't think it would have mattered who we played. That might have been the best team ever assembled. I know I never saw a better one. And there were a lot of people who could judge for themselves, because we drew big crowds wherever we went. We would start right after the season in New York, then head south and play for thirty days until we got to San Francisco. The players on our team would get 90 percent of the gate, and we'd divide it evenly between us. We could make $3,000 or $4,000 for a month of baseball—which was about half of what most of us made over the whole season.

We made the tour in cars, and I usually rode in Willie's big Cadillac. Once, we were driving through some little town in Mississippi and Willie got pulled over for exceeding the speed limit by five miles an hour. One of the guys in the car said, "Don't worry, I'll take care of this." He got out and talked to the policeman for a while. I don't remember who it was, but he must not have been from the South. When he was finished, the policeman told us to turn around and go back fifteen miles to pay the fine at the courthouse. Another time, when we were in Birmingham, which was Willie's hometown, Willie and I were in a men's store and he pulled out a roll of $100 bills to pay for some clothes. When he did that, the people in the store started to call the police. Then Willie told them he was Willie Mays, and that changed everything. It was okay to be black as long as you were Willie Mays.

Over the years, sportswriters tried to build up a big competition between Willie and me, but I don't think either of us felt it the way everybody said we did. In a way, all the black players felt competition among themselves, and it had a lot to do with barnstorming together. The competition was the result of friendship. I knew I'd be with Willie and Brooks Lawrence again the next winter, and I didn't want Willie to have the satisfaction of outhitting me during the season or Lawrence to tell me about all the times he struck me out. In fact, one of the pitchers from the tour, Sam Jones, became my biggest enemy in baseball.

Actually, it started during the season in 1955. Sam Jones was a tall righthander who always had a toothpick in this mouth—when he was pitching, when he was sleeping, all the time—and he threw about the nastiest curve ball I've ever seen. One day in Chicago, he struck me out three times with that curve ball. Of course, we always played day games at Wrigley Field, so that night Ernie Banks picked me up at the hotel to go out to dinner. Sam Jones was with him, and he kept talking on and on about those three times he struck me out. Well, I got tired of hearing him talk about it, so I told him he would never do that again. I said he might get me out three times in a game, but he would never strike me out three times again. I said he'd never again strike me out two times in a game. Sam was a fierce competitor, and it made him mad when I talked back to him like that. Well, the next time he pitched against us, I hit a line drive that practically took his head off. After that, he started throwing at me. Sam didn't mind throwing at you a bit, because he was mean to begin with. On our barnstorming trips, he even fought with Mays, and Mays was the one who brought him along. When he was drinking corn, Sam was mad all the time and he'd fight with anybody. He was always wanting to fight me when the Braves played the Cubs or the Cardinals or the Giants, whoever he was pitching for at the time. He'd throw at me, and then he'd tell me to meet him under the stands after the game. I tried not to pay any attention to him. Everything was going along fine as far as I was concerned, because I usually hit better after I'd been knocked down. I had to. In those days, if the pitchers found out you could be intimidated, you were finished.

One game Don Drysdale threw at Hank a time or two, and Hank went down. He complained about it after the game, which was rare, because Hank never complained about much. We had a staff meeting the next day, and I can remember John Quinn saying, "Well, we've got a great young hitter in Hank. Now we'll find out if he can stay in the league. It will depend on how he gets back after being knocked down like that."

Later on, of course, Hank made a career out of hitting Drysdale. I used to drive all around the state with Hank going to speaking engagements, and one time in the car I asked him why he never talked about hitting—about the way he hit Drysdale and everybody else. I'll never forget what he said. He said, "If you can do it, you don't have to talk about it." That's just the way he was. Most of the time, I don't think Hank even knew his batting average. One time I walked up to him and said, "What are you hitting, 44?" He said, "I do the hittin'. You do the figurin'." I don't know if he meant it or not, but I think he did. There was usually just one thing Hank knew about his hitting—

how many base hits he had. He always counted his base hits.
—Bob Allen, former Braves publicity director

Eventually, I made the pitchers think twice before throwing at me. Early in my career I was a bad-ball hitter anyway, and sometimes I could get good wood on a ball that was headed for my chin. When Gene Mauch was managing the Phillies, he once fined John Boozer fifty dollars for coming in too close to me. I chopped the ball over the fence for a home run, but I don't think that was the reason for the fine. I understand Mauch had a rule on his team that no pitcher could throw at me.

I only wish Walter Alston had had a rule like that with the Dodgers, because they had the orneriest staff in the league. Newcombe was mean, and Drysdale was mean, and Stan Williams was so mean that it probably kept him from being as good a pitcher as he should have been. I heard Williams kept pictures of guys like me and Frank Robinson in his locker so he could throw at us in the clubhouse. He hit me in the head once on a three-and-oh pitch. When I got to first base, Gil Hodges said, "Go get him." I said, "My mama didn't raise no fools." I hit a home run the next time up. Another time Vernon Law and Elroy Face of the Pirates hit me in the head on consecutive days. They thought I was stealing signs for Adcock when I was on base—which doesn't make much sense, because why would they put me on base if they thought I was stealing signs?

It was common for black players to be thrown at. In those days, it was common for all players to be thrown at. The situation finally lightened up a little after an incident between us and the Cubs on Memorial Day in 1956. Russ Meyer was pitching for Chicago, and three of us had already hit consecutive home runs in the game. Bruton had one of the home runs, and when he came up to bat again, Meyer buzzed him with the first pitch, then hit him with the second. Bruton rushed to the mound, and Charlie Grimm had to come out of the dugout to tackle him. It was starting to get out of hand. After that, the National League passed a rule that fined and penalized pitchers for headhunting.

But that didn't scare Don Drysdale. Of all the guys who threw inside, Drysdale did it the most effectively. God, Drysdale was rough. He would as soon knock you down as strike you out, and he was big and threw hard and came from the side—it seemed like he let the ball go about a foot from your ear. Drysdale was so rough on me that I thought he was going to put me out of the league—not by hitting me, just by making me look bad. I batted so poorly against Drysdale at first that Fred Haney, our manager at the time, was going to bench me one day when he pitched. Back then, sitting on the bench for a day wasn't like it is now. Now, with the guaranteed contracts and diluted rosters, guys are happy to get the day off. But back then, nobody wanted to come out of the lineup, because there was always somebody eager to take your place. I said, "Mr. Haney, you just let me play against him today. I can't sit on the bench. I've got to play." Drysdale got me the first couple of times that day—struck me out and made me look bad—and then I got a couple of hits. The last one was a bloop double that won the ballgame. From that day on, I hit Drysdale. In fact, when it was all over, I'd hit more home runs against Drysdale—seventeen—than any other pitcher. We had a great rivalry going, and there was nothing bitter about it. Later, when Claude Osteen was pitching for the Dodgers—I hit thirteen home runs against Osteen—Drysdale used to call him before the Dodgers played the Braves and give him a little pep talk . . . tell him to bear down and give me a few more home runs so the Big D could get his name off the books. There are some people who thought Drysdale didn't deserve to be elected into the Hall of Fame because he barely won 200 games, but I don't agree. Anybody who batted against him knows he was one of the dominant pitchers of his day.

As intimidating as Drysdale was, and as much as we battled each other, I don't think he ever hit me. And I never thought it was anything racial with Drysdale. He knocked down Johnny Logan once at Ebbets Field, and that started the biggest baseball fight I ever saw. Fortunately, we had Logan, Mathews, and Carl Sawatski on our side. Mathews was a Hall of Fame fighter, as he later proved when he punched out Frank Robinson. Whenever a melee broke out, you could count on Mathews to take on everybody. Logan was a battler, too, but his role was starting the fights; Mathews would finish them. They both went to the mound that time against the Dodgers, along with Sawatski, and all I can remember is that Drysdale was on the bottom of the pile.

I never got involved when a fight broke out. I would fight at the drop of a hat off the field—it seems like ballplayers are around drunks a lot, and fights happen—but something kept me away from that kind of stuff at the ballpark. I believe it was the same thing that kept me from getting hurt by beanballs. When I was on the field, the Lord would just take those troubles away. I think I was being prepared for something I didn't even know about. It's easy now to look back and see what it was, but I played baseball for a long, long time before anybody—including myself —had any clues that I would make history by hitting home runs. What a lot of people did think, though—including myself—was that I had a chance to bat .400, which hadn't been done since Ted Williams in 1941, and still hasn't.

I never dreamed he would hit a bunch of home runs, because that wasn't the type of hitter he was. Henry was the type of hitter who would use the whole field. He did most of his hitting to right field and right-center. He could run like a deer, had great hands, and we were all amazed at how quick he was. He could do some remarkable things on the ball field. There are two incidents I'll never forget. One, we were playing in St. Louis, and there was a ball hit to right field. It had rained before the game, and the ground was still wet. Henry slipped as he turned to reach the ball, and his gloved hand went to the ground and he stepped on it. With his back to home plate and trying to keep his balance as he was stepping on his glove, he threw up his right hand and damn if the ball didn't hit in it, and he caught it. Another time, we were playing the Dodgers, and they had the bases loaded and two outs. Hank was playing center field at the time, and he came running in to catch a ball at his fingertips. He couldn't quite reach it to grab it completely, and the ball bounced and hit him in the thigh as he was running full speed. He never missed a stride, and just pulled the ball in as easy as anything for the third out. If he misses that ball, three runs score. When he did that, I thought, hey, I'm glad this guy is on my side, because he's going to do something extraordinary in baseball. And I thought I knew what it was. I always felt that some year Hank Aaron would hit .400.—Warren Spahn

I was named the Braves' Most Valuable Player for 1955, and it got me a salary of $17,000, although, when the contract first arrived in the mail, it called for $13,500. I had played second base for a month or so that year when Danny O'Connell was hurt, and when the contract came, I mailed it back to John Quinn with a note saying that he must have sent me Danny O'Connell's contract by mistake. We didn't have agents in those days, and you had to develop your own negotiating style. My style was to keep it in good spirits without being a pushover. And my strategy was to sign before Spahn took all the money.

I was making more money than I ever imagined I would, but after our barnstorming tour that winter, I took a job with the recreation department in Mobile, working with kids at Carver Park. As a result, I was in good shape when I reported to Bradenton in the spring of 1956. The first time I stepped into the cage, I hit a few line drives, then stepped out and said, "Ol' Hank is ready." The writers picked up on things like that, and they portrayed me as sort of a down-home character, which I suppose I was. I didn't have the charisma that Willie Mays and Ernie Banks had, but I tried to have a little fun with the game. The press liked it when I told my old Sally League manager, Ben Geraghty, that I'd started using two bats in the big leagues—a short one for inside pitches and a long one for outside pitches. The only thing was, I'm not sure if they knew I was kidding.

I understood that the writers would take some liberties—in those days, part of their job was to create images for ballplayers, and it was flattering to know that you were enough of a celebrity to have your own image—but occasionally there would be an article that would make me boil inside. In 1956, Furman Bisher of the *Atlanta Journal*—a man I would get to know very well in my career—visited Milwaukee to do a story on me for *The Saturday Evening Post*. He came to the little apartment where I lived in an alley in a black section of the city—the place was so small we didn't even have room for a couch—and apparently he left with exactly what he was looking for. I guess the general purpose of the article was to tell about what a fine young ballplayer I was, but to me, there was an underlying theme. The way I read it, it was as if the article was saying, "Folks, this is a good ballplayer, but at the same time, we're talking about a dumb country nigger here, you understand?" The message came across in the way Bisher described me—"satchel posterior and shuffling gait"— and the way he quoted me. I'm the first to admit that I didn't speak like Winston Churchill, and still don't, but there's a big difference between the spoken word and the written word. I just didn't think it was necessary for Bisher to use quotes the way he did. For instance, in a discussion of Satchel Paige, he quoted me as saying, "I didn't know he come from Mobile, and I never seen him till yet." On hitting .400: "Nobody is hit .400 since Ted Williams." I'm not saying he quoted me incorrectly. I'm just saying he used the quotes in such a way as to confirm all the stereotypes. Several of the quotes started with "Man, . . ." And the quotes I most objected to were ones that he didn't get from me, because he was writing about things that had happened in the past. He told the story about the commissioner's telegram and wrote that when I was informed it was from Ford Frick, I said, "Who's dat?" The story had been reported several times before, and none of the other versions used the word "dat." Bisher was just writing it the way a shuffling colored boy would say it. As far as I was concerned the title of the article pretty much set the tone: "Born to Play Ball," with the subhead, "Hank Aaron doesn't go in for 'scientific hitting' . . . just grabs a bat and blasts away." As I read it again now, though, there's one thing in the article that I have to chuckle about. It said, "While he had a total of forty home runs in his first two big-league seasons, it is unlikely that Aaron will break any records in this department."

It was true that I wasn't a home run hitter then, but if all I did was grab a bat and blast away, it's doubtful I would have batted .328 in 1956 and led the National League. After a bad start, I went on a twenty-five-game hitting streak to take over the league and then held it most of the season. My streak was stopped by a journeyman pitcher for the Cardinals named Herm Wehmeier, who was my worst nightmare that year, and also the Braves'.

We were in the pennant race all summer, and in midseason we took over first place by winning eleven in a row after Fred Haney replaced Charlie Grimm as our manager. The whole state became excited about the Braves. There were Braves hairdos and Braves cocktails and Braves banners stretched across the streets. Everybody thought we'd make it to the World Series, including the players. But the Reds and Dodgers wouldn't go away. The Reds set a league record for home runs, with Frank Robinson— who was a rookie—Ted Kluszewski, Wally Post, Gus Bell, and Ed Bailey all hitting at least twenty-eight. Their problem was pitching. The only winner Cincinnati had was my old barnstorming buddy, Brooks Lawrence. Lawrence won nineteen games, but down the stretch, when any game might have meant the pennant, he didn't pitch. Later, he told me the reason was that his manager, Birdie Tebbetts, didn't want a black man winning twenty games.

The Dodgers didn't have that problem, though, and Don Newcombe won twenty-seven. Still, we led them by a game going into the last weekend of the season, with the Reds still alive, too. To this day, I believe we should have won the pennant that year, but we choked. On Friday, the Dodgers were rained out with Pittsburgh and we lost in St. Louis, 5-4. We were still a half-game ahead, though, and the key day was Saturday, when Brooklyn played the Pirates twice at Ebbets Field and we sent Spahn to the mound against Wehmeier. I managed to drive in a run in the first inning with a double, and Spahn pitched a great game, but we couldn't do anything more with Wehmeier, and it was 1-1 after nine innings. It stayed that way until the bottom of the twelfth— with Spahn and Wehmeier still in the game—when Musial doubled, Ken Boyer was walked intentionally, and with two outs Rip Repulski hit a sharp ground ball toward Mathews at third that took a funny bounce and rolled into left field to end the game. Meanwhile, the Dodgers were sweeping the Pirates. We won Sunday, but it was too late because Brooklyn won, too, finishing a game ahead of us and two ahead of Cincinnati.

Beyond a doubt, that Saturday game in St. Louis was the most heartbreaking moment I had in twenty-one years of baseball. But it was also one of the things that proved the integrity of baseball. The Cardinals were in fourth place, going nowhere, and they played us to the bitter end and beat us two out of three. The thing about it was that the Cardinals would have actually made more money if we had won the pennant, because the teams split the earnings and the Dodgers had a smaller ballpark. We had every reason to win, but it was like it wasn't meant to be. There were some unreal things in that game. Crandall hit a ball that looked like a home run, and it died. Mathews hit a ball to the left-field fence and the center fielder, Bobby Del Greco, should have been playing him to pull, but he wasn't and he ran over to rob Mathews. Del Greco made a couple of great catches on Mathews that day. He was climbing the fences and running all over the ballpark. We couldn't believe it.—Warren Spahn

Del Greco was traded to the Cubs the next year, and he dropped the first fly ball hit to him. I guess that convinced us that 1956 just wasn't our year, and, looking back on it, maybe I know why. It was Jackie Robinson's last season in the big leagues, and it was only fitting that he got to go out in a World Series.

Jackie used to preach to black players that the job was never done, but at least it had reached the stage where the rest of us could carry on after his retirement. He had always made it a point to get to know new black players as they came into the league and to make them realize they had a responsibility that went beyond playing ball. He made a special point of talking to the players he thought would be stars, because he knew that their voices would be heard over the others'. I was honored that he pulled me aside a few times.

On top of everything else that he was, Jackie was a ballplayer's ballplayer, and he would also counsel us on the fine points of playing the game. He was a third baseman at the end of his career, and I'll never forget a little piece of advice he gave me in 1956. One night against the Dodgers, I kept faking like I was going to bunt, and Jackie never came in close to play the bunt. I asked him about it later, and he said that any time I wanted to bunt in

Ebbets Field, that was all right with the Dodgers. I appreciated what he was telling me. He was saying that he respected me at the plate and also that I ought to respect myself a little more. That did a lot for my confidence—especially coming from the man whose judgments I valued more than anybody's.

Jackie's best friend on the Dodgers, Don Newcombe, was voted Most Valuable Player in the National League in 1956. Newk had a fantastic season, but I have to say that I've never thought pitchers should be eligible to win the MVP award for the simple reason that everyday players can't win the Cy Young Award. It so happened that 1956 was the first year of the Cy Young, and Newcombe won both awards. In fact, three of the top four vote getters that year were pitchers. With the season Newcombe had, I could understand him winning, but it was hard for me to accept finishing third behind Sal Maglie of the Dodgers, who was 13-5 with a 2.89 earned run average. I had been the second youngest player ever to win the batting title in the National League and led the league in hits and total bases as well. It was some consolation that *The Sporting News* named me National League Player of the Year.

Of course, that didn't cut much ice when you were out of uniform—especially in the South. After the season, I drove back to Mobile with Barbara, and we pulled into a service station in Mississippi to get some gas. I asked the attendant if I could use the bathroom, and he said they didn't have a colored bathroom. When I heard that, I yanked the nozzle out of the car and drove away. Actually, I'm surprised they didn't arrest me. Another time, I was driving through a town in Mississippi on my way home, and a policeman started following me as soon as I got inside the city limits. He followed me all the way through until I was out of town.

It seemed a little friendlier in Mobile, because I was with my family most of the time—Gaile lived there with Mama—and because we knew where to go and where not to go. I suppose it didn't hurt that I was a baseball player, either. But even so, we had to keep our place. An editorial in the Mobile *Press* that year said Mobile could be proud of Aaron because he didn't "take advantage of his peculiar position as a famous Negro player to further any bitterness over race or other questions.''

That wasn't something *I* could be proud of, though. In fact, with Jackie Robinson out of baseball, it was something that would have to change.

6

There is a scene from the television show "Happy Days" in which an alien named Mork, from Ork, played by Robin Williams, visits Richie Cunningham (Ron Howard) in Milwaukee with the intention of taking an Earth person back to his planet. Richie, not realizing that Mork wants him, assumes that the designated Earthling will be somebody important and frantically tries to guess who. "The President?" he asks, then, realizing his folly, answers himself: "No, the President's not in Milwaukee." Pause. Light bulb. "Are you gonna take Hank Aaron?"

"No," says Mork. "He's too famous. We'd have to trade the entire planet for him."

Long before it was the name of a television show, Happy Days typified Milwaukee in the fifties. There was a delirious innocence there and then, a milk-shake, day-at-the-lake, roll-in-the-hay, Chevrolet, bee-bop, bobby-sock, rat-fink, skating rink, lover's-lane, feel-no-pain sort of attitude that reigned all across the home of the brave but really poured over the home of the Braves, who were very much a part of it all.

As small as the city was by baseball standards, Milwaukee kept setting attendance records. It called itself Baseball's Main Street, and the attending phenomenon was widely referred to as The Miracle of Milwaukee. It was a two-part miracle—the city and the team. When the Braves moved from Boston, they had brought a tradition of wretched attendance and matching baseball. But they also brought Warren Spahn and Eddie Mathews, and behind those Hall of Famers, they began to build—Del Crandall, Joe Adcock, Johnny Logan, Bill Bruton, Lew Burdette, Bob Buhl, Gene Conley, and then, the muted, graceful, coiled outfielder who was the crowning piece.

Hank Aaron was not as famous in the 1950s as Mork from Ork made him sound—that came later—but by the latter part of the decade he was the best hitter in the game. Newsweek confirmed it without fanfare—as if it occurred by default—in its issue of June 15, 1959: "With the established batting masters, [Ted] Williams and Stan Musial, entering the twilight, Aaron suddenly has become the best hitter in baseball." Perhaps it was not so sudden as it was unexpected, because all the while he was becoming the best hitter, nothing about Aaron cried out for attention—except for the emphatic whip of his wrists, perhaps, or the hum of his low-slung line drives. The wrists were compared to those of Floyd Patterson, the heavyweight champion—they were bigger around—and the line drives to those of Williams, Musial, and Hornsby. More than once, a shortstop would spring to catch a head-buzzing projectile after it left Aaron's Louisville Slugger (Del Crandall model), only to feel foolish as it crashed or cleared the left-field wall more than two hundred feet away.

Milwaukee was particularly partial to the baseball heroes who came with the team and happened also to be white—Spahn, Mathews, and Crandall, principally—but its grandmotherly embrace took in Aaron, as well. The song "Dance with Me, Henry" played well there, and the ringing echo from Aaron's bat was hot Milwaukee music. The black community was especially wild over the slim young slugger. When he won Milwaukee's first pennant with a heroic home run, there were personal messages of congratulations in the local newspapers from such establishments as Mayme's Ebony Lounge and Shanty Town, "with club foxes, Nellie, Barbara, Mary, and Rose."

It was 1957 when it all came together in Milwaukee—when the crowds peaked, the World Series was won, and an introspective twenty-three-year-old black man from Alabama felt so good about it all that he bought a big house in a white neighborhood twenty miles outside the old German city. It was also 1957 when "Leave It to Beaver" premiered on Friday nights, President Eisenhower signed the Civil Rights Act, and a couple of new products came out called the Frisbee and the Edsel.

◆   ◆   ◆

If anything good came out of blowing the pennant in 1956, it was 1957. We didn't want it to happen again, and Fred Haney intended to make sure it didn't. Haney seemed to think that all we needed was some toughening up, so when we reported to Bradenton, it was boot camp. We ran sprints and did push-ups and sit-ups—things that *athletes* do when they're in training. It was sort of a new concept for baseball, and to us it made Haney seem more like a drill sergeant than a field manager. We called him Little Napoleon.

I never quite figured Haney out. On one hand, he was a military man, very concerned with fitness and motivation. One of his friends was Pat O'Brien, the actor who played Knute Rockne, and in the heat of the pennant race he would bring in O'Brien and have him give us his "Win one for the Gipper" speech. On the other hand, I sometimes thought that after he got us in shape, Haney didn't do much managing at all—that he more or less let the team run itself. Maybe that was his philosophy. But I didn't go along with most of his methods and never really warmed up to him. It might have been due to the time he blessed me out in front of the whole team for arriving late one day after I got a flat tire on the highway. I would have felt differently about it a few years later, because I think it's helpful for the young guys to see that the veterans are no better than they are. But at the time, I was still learning my way in the major leagues, and what I needed more than anything was confidence. I wasn't going to get it by being humiliated.

Nonetheless, I have to admit that I had some of my best years when Haney was the manager, starting with 1957. I was the type of player who responded well to praise, and now and then Haney would provide it, whether he intended to or not. During the spring of 1957, he commented to some newspapermen that he thought I'd soon be taking my place with the great right-handed hitters of the game. Comments like that excited me. The year before, Charlie Grimm had said in spring training that he thought I'd win a batting title, and damn if I didn't.

When I arrived at spring training in 1957, I realized that a batting championship changed a lot of things. First of all, Mrs. Gibson informed me that I had finally earned the privilege of staying in the "big house." I was moving up in the world. Also, since I had proved I could hit for average, the writers started asking me about home runs. My response was that I'd leave the home run championship to stronger guys like Willie Mays and that the most important personal goal to me was the batting title. I honestly didn't consider myself a home run hitter, but at the same time, I did think I had a chance to win a home run title. That's not double-talk: I just figured that if you hit the ball hard enough often enough, the home runs would start to pile up. What I really had in mind was a Triple Crown.

I had two good chances to win the Triple Crown, and 1957 was the first. The Braves got off to a fast start that year, and most days I found myself in the middle of the action. I hit a home run against Hal Jeffcoat as Burdette shut out the Reds, 1-0, in the opener; had five singles a few days later against the Pirates; drove in four runs the next day; had a home run and four hits a couple days after that; drove in both runs as we beat the Dodgers, 2-1. Then, late in June, I went on a home run streak, hitting seven in eight days. All of a sudden, people started thinking of me as a home run hitter.

It seemed like he made a conscious change in his batting style after he led the league in hitting. It was quite obvious to me that he didn't hit the ball to right field as he had before. I noticed it because this was a guy who I thought was going to hit for a higher average than anybody in history.

He was so quick with the bat, it was amazing. I've never seen any other batter who could take a swing in the batting cage, pop the ball straight up into the cage, and snatch it in his bare hand as it came down. I used to marvel at that. As far as his baseball instincts, we were all amazed. There's no question in my mind that he could have stolen sixty or seventy bases a season if that had been our style. There wasn't anything he couldn't do. To me, Henry was the best ballplayer I ever saw. I think Willie Mays was his only rival, but I don't want to get into comparisons with Mays because I don't want to bring Mays into it too much when talking about Henry. The thing was, people always talked about Henry in terms of his hitting, because he didn't have the flair that Willie did. But defensively, he was a very, very good ballplayer.

If there was a competition with Henry, I think it was with

Eddie Mathews. It was good competition. Mathews had a way of bringing Henry out. I think he had a great deal to do with bringing Henry into the real world of kidding, understanding the value of humor, maybe a little sarcasm. It seemed to me that Eddie Mathews was a very important person in Henry's life.
—Del Crandall

Maybe subconsciously, I was affected by the fact that the home run hitters like Mathews and Mays got more publicity than I did—and more money—but I felt like I was swinging the bat the same way I'd always swung it. I think the extra home runs were just the result of a guy getting a little older, a little stronger, figuring out the pitchers a little better. On the other hand, maybe my teammates knew me better than I did, because I seem to be the only one who saw it that way.

As the years went on, I thought he started competing with Mathews for home runs. I thought it became a personal thing.
—Bill Bruton

I always felt there were two competitions in Henry's life. One, he wanted to hit more home runs than Mathews. I think that's why he started to pull the ball more. He gave up part of the plate when he did that, and his average went down a little. The other competition was that I think he wanted to be a better all-around player than Willie Mays. I never heard Henry say any of this. It's just what I perceived to be the case.—Warren Spahn

Hank and Mathews got along very well because there was something about the way they both approached their careers that was similar. They had the same drive to get to the top. Hank would hurt inside when he couldn't drive in the winning run, and Mathews was the same way. I believe they respected each other more than any two people on the team. They had a rivalry going, but it was out of respect for the other's ability. Henry would hit a home run, and where somebody else would say he got lucky, Mathews would say, "What a shot." Mathews would hit a home run, and Hank would say, "Helluva shot." Their relationship was like fourteen-karat gold.—Wes Covington

Hank and I had a friendly rivalry. He pushed me and I pushed him. He'd win the home run title one year, I might win it the next. Rivalries were important to us. We always looked for rivalries to keep us going. If we were in St. Louis, for instance, I might say to myself that I want to beat Ken Boyer this series in every department.

Maybe we felt that way because guys like Hank and I didn't get the publicity we should have, due to the fact that we were playing in Milwaukee. Goddamn Winfield gets more publicity just arguing with Steinbrenner than we got our whole careers. Willie Mays, in my opinion, wasn't as good a player as Hank Aaron, but whenever Willie did something, the New York press and the skies lit up. I just felt that Hank was a touch better than Willie. Hank was a complete ballplayer. He never threw to the wrong base, never missed the cutoff man. Willie never hit the cutoff man. Christ, we had a standing rule with the Braves, keep running on Willie, because when he throws home you can go to second in a fox trot. Henry didn't steal bases like Willie, but goddamn, he could steal bases. He could run like hell, and he didn't even look like he was running. I'll bet you in a footrace, Hank would have beaten Willie. But he didn't run like Willie. Willie was like Clemente—when he ran it looked like he was coming apart at the seams. It was hard to explain with Henry, but he could hit full speed in three steps and look like he wasn't even running.—Eddie Mathews

By June, it looked like I had a good chance at the Triple Crown and we had established ourselves as favorites in the pennant race. We only had one weakness—second base. All through the 1950s, second base was our problem spot. But in mid-June of 1957 we made a trade with the Giants for Red Schoendienst, giving up our second baseman, Danny O'Connell; Ray Crone, a pitcher who had been with me in Jacksonville; and Bobby Thomson, who was returning to the scene of his glory. Schoendienst was getting a little old, but he was a master second baseman and he still had plenty of hits left in him from both sides of the plate. He made our team complete, and after the trade it looked as though nothing would stop us—except maybe injuries. Joe Adcock broke his leg about a week after Schoendienst arrived, and

Frank Torre had to take over first base. Adcock's spot on the roster was assumed by a journeyman named Nippy Jones. We had so many outfielders hurt that we brought up two rookies— my old Eau Claire teammate, Wes Covington, a strong lefthanded hitter who had the look of a star, and a twenty-seven-year-old rookie named Bob Hazle. Johnny Logan was hurt, too, and that put my old pal, Felix Mantilla, into the lineup at shortstop.

It was good to be reunited with Felix, who was the godfather of my daughter, Gaile, and became my roommate as soon as he joined the team. Felix and Bill Bruton were my best friends in baseball, which made it especially horrible for me to watch when they crashed together full speed while chasing a pop fly early in July. They both hurt their knees, but Bruton's injury was worse. Before then, he had been an outstanding leadoff man and base-runner and one of the finest center fielders in the game, but I don't think he was ever quite the same again after that collision.

I had been out of the lineup a few days myself with a sprained ankle. I was supposed to be out for two weeks, and Barbara and I used the time to move into our new house in the country suburb of Mequon. But when Bruton got hurt, I had to get back onto the field. It was a five-team pennant race, and we were already losing ground. We had fallen into second place and couldn't very well make a run with four starters down. So I moved into center field. I felt like Raggedy Andy out there after watching Bruton play the position like a wizard for three years, but we got by. After the season, Haney said that going back into the lineup before my ankle was healed probably cost me the Triple Crown, because I lost a lot of points on my average. But it was worth it.

The first day back, I hit a two-run homer off Clem Labine to beat the Dodgers in the ninth inning. The next day, I hit a three-run homer off Newcombe and later won the game with a two-run double against Ed Roebuck. We were back in first place within a week, then went back and forth for a while with the Cardinals, barely staying ahead of Brooklyn, Cincinnati, and Philadelphia.

Finally, early in August, we caught fire, putting together a ten-game winning streak at the same time as St. Louis went on a nine-game losing streak. All of a sudden, we had an eight-and-a-half game lead with forty left to play. We also had the hottest new star in the game—Bob "Hurricane" Hazle. The way Hurricane Hazle was ripping through the league, it looked like we were destined to blow everybody away. But after what happened in 1956, we were taking nothing for granted. We had shown that we were capable of choking, and deep down everybody was afraid it might happen again. The newspapers referred to the pennant as the "you-know-what," so they wouldn't jinx us. Lou Perini, the owner, said, "We can't flub it this year. We just can't."

Sure enough, we started to swoon. The Cardinals began to chip away at our lead, and then they swept us in a big Sunday doubleheader at County Stadium early in September. We were ahead in the first game, 6-1, but they caught us and beat us when Musial hit a two-run homer in the tenth inning. Vinegar Bend Mizell shut us out in the second game. Our lead was down to two-and-a-half games. We hung on and got it back up to four, then five when Adcock, back from his injury, won a game with two home runs. That was how it stood when the Cardinals came to Milwaukee for a do-or-die series starting September 23. We could clinch the pennant with one more victory, but after the way the Cardinals had handled us the last time, and after what had happened the year before, the whole city was on edge.

We should have put the first game away early, but we just couldn't make it happen. We had the bases loaded inning after inning and kept hitting into double plays or losing runners at home plate. It was shaping up as a long, cold night. The temperature was in the forties, and the stands were packed with people in overcoats or sitting under blankets. The Cardinals had a bonfire going in their bullpen. The relief pitchers had to stay warm, because the game went into extra innings tied 2-2. We had Gene Conley pitching in relief of Burdette, and in the eleventh the Cardinals went with a righthander named Billy Muffett, a curveball pitcher who hadn't given up a home run all year. I came up with one out and Johnny Logan on first, looking for a pitch I could drive hard enough to bring Logan around. I got the breaking ball I was waiting for and hit it deep to center field. Wally Moon went to the fence and jumped for the ball. I knew—everybody knew—that if he didn't come down with it, we would win the pennant. He didn't. It landed in a grove of trees they called Perini's Pines. I galloped around the bases, and when I touched home plate, the whole team was there to pick me up and carry me off the field. People threw scorecards and streamers and confetti in the air. I had always dreamed about a moment like Bobby Thomson had in 1951, and this was it.

The next few hours were a blur, but I can remember all the players standing around a big table in the clubhouse after the game stuffing themselves with ribs and chicken and shrimp. I told the writers that for the first time in my life, I was excited. What I meant was that for the first time I felt like I could let down my guard and really act excited. I've never had another feeling like that. When I broke Babe Ruth's home run record, I was more relieved than excited. But this was as good as I knew how to feel.

The morning after, there was a picture in the paper of me on the shoulders of my teammates. Most of them, naturally, were white. On the same front page was a picture of a riot in Little Rock, Arkansas. It seemed that Little Rock, like much of the South, wasn't leaping into the spirit of Brown vs. Board of Education. The Wisconsin *CIO News* noticed the irony of both those pictures on the same page, just as I had. It wrote, "Milwaukee's dusky Hank Aaron blasted the Braves into the World Series only a few hours after an insane mob of white supremacists took the Stars and Stripes in Little Rock and tramped it on the ground in front of Central High School . . . The cheers that are lifted to Negro ballplayers only dramatize the stupidity of the jeers that are directed at those few Negro kids trying to get a good education for themselves in Little Rock."

I don't suppose it mattered much to those kids in Little Rock, but the next night I won my first home run title when I hit my forty-fourth, beating out Ernie Banks by one. It was a grand slam, but the best part was that it came against Sam Jones. That gave me two thirds of the Triple Crown I wanted so badly, because I also won the RBI title with 132. In batting average, though, I fell well short of Musial, .351 to .322.

I was disappointed that I wasn't a Triple Crown man, but the

World Series was not without one. Just my luck: I finally got out of Mays's shadow, and there was Mickey Mantle. In those days, the press was preoccupied with personal duels, and even though there were plenty of great confrontations between us and the Yankees—the lefthanded power of Eddie Mathews and Yogi Berra, the pitching matchups of Warren Spahn versus Whitey Ford and Lew Burdette versus Bob Turley—a lot of people seemed to think the Series would come down to me and Mantle. In a way, they might have been right, because Mantle was out of the picture before the Series was half over. In the third game, he was on second base when Bob Buhl turned and threw to pick him off. The throw was a little wild, and Schoendienst had to dive to catch it. When he did, he came down on Mantle's shoulder. Mantle homered later in the game, but by the next day his shoulder was so stiff he couldn't play. It was an injury that bothered him the rest of his career.

That was the first World Series game ever played in Milwaukee, after we had split two games in New York, Ford beating Spahn and Burdette beating Bobby Shantz in low-scoring games. Milwaukee was all decked out for the occasion, but the Yankees weren't impressed. They called Milwaukee "bush" and jumped on us for three runs in the first inning. They were threatening to break it open early when I ran in from center field—Bruton was still hurt—and slid along the ground to grab a line drive by Gil McDougald before it touched the grass. There were a lot of photographs of the catch, and they made it look like the ball hit the ground before I caught it. I can't explain the photographs, but I'm sure I caught that ball, and the umpires agreed. At any rate, it was the first time I ever got any attention for my defense. But it didn't make much difference in the game, because the Yankees pulled away and were ahead 7-1 when I hit a two-run homer in the fifth against Bob Turley. It wasn't a tape-measure shot, but might have been the hardest ball I hit my whole career. Again, though, it hardly mattered, because the Yankees scored five times in the seventh and clobbered us to take a two-to-one lead in games.

The next afternoon, I hit a three-run homer in the fourth off

Tom Sturdivant to put us ahead 4-1. It was a windy day, and the way I heard the story, Casey Stengel came out to the mound and Sturdivant asked if he should walk me intentionally. Stengel said to pitch to me because Babe Ruth couldn't hit one out in that wind. After the inning, Sturdivant slammed his glove down in the dugout and reminded Stengel of what he had said. Casey replied, "He ain't Babe Ruth." At least, that's what I'm told.

Stengel stories are kind of like mine—you never know what to believe. For instance, there was a story about Yogi Berra telling me during the Series that I was holding my bat wrong because I couldn't read the trademark, to which I said, "I'm not up here to read, I'm up here to hit." Actually, I did say that once, but it was to a rookie catcher in spring training, not to Yogi Berra in the World Series.

Anyway, our lead in the fourth game didn't hold up, because the Yankees tied it in the ninth on Elston Howard's three-run homer. Then they went ahead in the tenth on a single by Tony Kubek—who was playing in front of his home folks in Milwaukee—and a triple by Hank Bauer. At that point, we were in imminent danger of going down three games to one, and I don't think anybody in America would have imagined that the guy who would turn the Series around would be Nippy Jones. Nippy was a first baseman who had been out of the big leagues for five years before we brought him up to fill in when Adcock was hurt, and he had never really made his mark—until this day. When he did, the mark was on his shoe. Tommy Byrne had thrown a pitch at his feet, and all of a sudden Nippy started arguing ferociously with the umpire, Augie Donatelli, claiming the ball had hit him. Like most arguments, it was going nowhere—until Nippy reached down, picked up the ball, and showed Donatelli the scuff mark from his shoe. That put him on base, and Logan followed with a double to tie the game. Then Mathews delivered probably the biggest hit of his career, a game-winning homer that won the game and tied the Series.

After that, we felt like we couldn't be beaten. But in reality, we probably would have been if not for Burdette, who beat Whitey Ford in game five, 1-0. Then the Series moved to New York, which isn't the most gracious place to try to win a World Series. I can still picture getting stuck in a traffic jam on our way to Yankee Stadium. As we were sitting on the bus, we saw a guy push his car to the side of the street because it had overheated. As soon as he walked away to go for help, four guys ran up and stripped the car in plain view of everybody. Before the owner could turn around and get back, the four guys were running down the street with the radio, tires, everything they could remove. It was something you don't see in Alabama.

Turley was pitching the sixth game for the Yankees, and as we batted in the third inning a torrent of leaflets suddenly poured down from the upper deck—propaganda from Cuban activists. In the seventh inning, I tied the game 2-2 with a home run. But Bauer beat us with one in the bottom of the inning. That set up the seventh game, with Spahn scheduled to pitch for us against Don Larsen, who had become famous with his perfect game against the Dodgers in the 1956 Series. But Spahn came down with the flu, and Haney had to ask Burdette to pitch on two days' rest. The way he was going, I think Burdette could have pitched if he'd been up all night working in one of those coal mines back in West Virginia. Burdette had been traded by the Yankees before he ever got a chance to really pitch for them, and he hadn't forgotten it. Covington made some big defensive plays for him in left field—he had been doing it the whole Series—and Burdette took care of the rest, shutting out the Yankees again for his third win of the series, 5-0. Happy days had arrived. During the celebration downtown, fans carried around a huge banner that said, "Bushville Wins!" The Milwaukee Braves were world champions.

I batted .393 for the Series with three home runs, but Burdette was naturally the Most Valuable Player. My honor came a few weeks later when I was named MVP of the National League, winning by a narrow margin over Musial, with Schoendienst a close third. I knew I had the statistics to win, but I hadn't counted on it because Musial and Schoendienst were very popular players, as well as great ones, and both of them were sentimental choices since they were getting along in years. Schoendienst had never won an MVP, and on top of that, he was the toast of Milwaukee in 1957, owing to his German roots and his immediate impact on the Braves. The Milwaukee *Sentinel* carried a full-page spread on Schoendienst, calling him "a Moses come to lead [the Braves] out of the wilderness of bitter disappointment and frustration."

Given all of that, I was thrilled to be selected and proud to be recognized. For me, it was one thing to perform well—I always knew I could do that—but it was another thing to be appreciated for it. All of those things made 1957 the best year of my baseball life, and it went along with the best year of baseball that any city ever had. It doesn't get any better than Milwaukee in 1957.

But even for a twenty-three-year-old MVP, there was more to life than baseball, and I went through a vast range of emotions that year. There was plenty to celebrate—namely, the world championship, the MVP award, our new home, and most of all, our growing family. Our oldest boy, Henry Junior—Hankie—was born before the season. Our daughter, Gaile, who was three, was still living with Mama in Mobile and we didn't think it was the right time to bring her up to Milwaukee, but with our new home in the country, we kept Hankie with us and started to establish a family life in Mequon. It wasn't as simple as it sounds, though. Mequon was semi-rural, and nearly all white. Most of the neighbors were hospitable, but there were occasional instances that reminded us we were different. I remember walking into a neighbor's yard and the dog growling at me, and the neighbor saying, "Oh, I'm sorry, he's not used to colored people." Silently, I wished that dogs were the only ones around there not used to colored people. And then there was the man who called all the neighborhood women and made filthy suggestions to them, identifying himself as me. As a ballplayer, I'd learned to expect a certain degree of racism, but it was starting to touch my family. My youngest sister, Alfredia, came up to stay with us and go to grade school in Milwaukee that fall, and she was treated so badly that she had to leave and go back to Mobile.

I wanted to move to Milwaukee so much that I put half my clothes in a trunk and sent them up to Henry's house. Mother said, "Where are all your clothes?" When I told her, she figured she might as well send me along, too.

I guess I never thought about what it would be like in school. I was the only black kid in the whole school, and there was a lot of racial tension over it. At first, I never talked about it with Henry and Barbara. Once, at the breakfast table, they asked me how I liked school and I broke out crying. It was just little cruel things they would do—not just the kids, but the teachers and staff. I had to take a TB test once, and I remember the nurse saying, "It'll be hard to tell on this one." Another time, we were studying Africa, and a boy in my class brought a stalk of sugarcane and put it next to my desk and said, "Here, this will take you back home." Parents would pick up their kids at school so they wouldn't have to walk home with me. And I was the only girl in school who wasn't allowed to wear pants in the winter; I had to sit there and be cold. Finally, Henry and Barbara took me into the principal's office to talk about what was happening. The principal looked Henry right in the face and said, "There wouldn't be a problem if you hadn't brought her to this school."
—Alfredia Aaron Scott

That winter, nine months after Hankie was born, Barbara gave birth to our third and fourth children, twin boys we named Gary and Lary. They were born prematurely, and Gary never made it out of the hospital. Lary was very weak, and after a few months the reports from the doctors weren't encouraging. We took him to Mobile to stay with Mama. As soon as he got there, she bathed him and bundled him up and then fed him, and it was the best he had ever eaten in his life. Then he went to sleep, and from that moment on, he started to improve. I have no doubt that Mama saved that boy's life. He stayed with her while he was growing up. Mama still thought about my brother Alfred dying of pneumonia, and she did all she could to keep Lary out of the weather. He wore a stocking cap all the time, and she even had him ride his bicycle in the house. Lary had problems with epilepsy, but with Mama feeding him greens and keeping him warm and giving him his medication, he grew up strong.

It was around the time the twins were born—in fact, while Lary was still in the hospital—that a Catholic priest sought me out and introduced himself as Mike Sablica. Father Sablica was very interested in civil rights and had even gone back to school for a doctorate degree with the idea that it would give him more credibility and allow him to have his positions heard and reported. We were able to benefit from each other's experience and started to spend a lot of time together, mostly playing handball at Marquette University and talking about discrimination over coffee at the student union. Through my relationship with Father Sablica, I began to broaden my scope a little bit.

> *In the middle of the Braves' pennant drive one year, I got a call from their general manager, John Quinn, who wanted to talk to me about Hank. He said that Hank was basically an uncomplicated person, and he didn't want me throwing him off his game. He told me that I would be disturbing him if I kept giving him all these diverse thoughts. Of course, I just ignored him.*
>
> *At the time, Hank was aware of social problems, but he was not articulating this awareness. He expressed himself to me, but he didn't do it publicly because he didn't want to be known as a troublemaker. I thought it would be beneficial for him to become a Catholic. In those days, I had a lot of black converts at my church, St. Boniface. I would naively tell them that the Catholic Church was their only hope to get their civil rights. I became particularly interested in the possibility of Hank becoming a Catholic the first time I rode in his car and saw a copy of a pamphlet called "The Life of Christ" in his glove compartment. It happened to be the pamphlet from which Branch Rickey read to Jackie Robinson when he was talking to him about breaking the color line in baseball. I asked Hank if he had read any of the pamphlet, and he said he read some of it every day.—Father Michael Sablica*

Eventually, Gaile and Hankie and Barbara and I were baptized Catholic in Milwaukee. But it was a few years before our family would all come together, and until it did, we found ourselves shuttling between Milwaukee and Mobile in the offseason.

When we made the trip to Mobile after the World Series in 1957, we did it in style for a change, arriving on the L&N Hummingbird. Mobile had arranged a Hank Aaron Day, and I decided the only proper way to get there was aboard the Hummingbird, which to me was like leaving town in an old beat-up Volkswagen and returning in a Rolls-Royce. A band met us at the train station, playing "Take Me Out to the Ball Game" and "On Mobile Bay." Then they put us in a limo, and we rode in a motorcade to the Colored Elks Club. The mayor, Joseph Langan, gave me a key to the city. I don't know it for a fact, but I expect that I was the first black person to get a key to Mobile. It might seem like nothing more than a token, but believe me, that was a proud day for all the black people of Mobile—a kid from Toulminville being honored by the mayor himself.

We were brought back to earth real fast, though. I had been invited to speak at one of the white service clubs in Mobile, and I asked if I could bring my wife along. They explained it was a stag affair, so I said, fine, how about if I bring my father? Daddy had never been to anything like that, and I thought it would be a real treat for him. But when I asked, the man just squirmed and hemmed and hawed, and finally he said they just couldn't allow it. It was one thing for a black World Series hero to speak to their club, but it was another thing to have his black daddy sitting with all the good white men in the audience. Naturally, I canceled the engagement. I was beginning to see the other side of Mobile. I don't know whether it was related, but a few days later, seven KKK crosses were burned around the city.

We also spent some time in Jacksonville during the offseason, visiting Barbara's family. Her brother, Bill, had begun to play in the Braves' system, and I got to know him better. Felix was there, too, staying with his wife's family, and he and I drove together from Jacksonville to Bradenton for spring training in 1958. I had a new Malibu, and we were getting close to Bradenton when some white kids in a big Buick pulled up behind us on the highway. They kept tapping my bumper, so I thought maybe they wanted to get around me. I pulled over to one side, and they pulled ahead of me and slowed to about fifteen miles an hour. I went around them, and when they tried to pass me again, they

ripped into the front of my car at sixty miles an hour. Felix and I
went into a ditch, then bounced out and swerved into the highway, with cars speeding all around us. When we got to camp, I
told some people on the team about it, and they said, "Don't
mention it to the newspapermen. If you do, the NAACP will get
hold of it, and there you go." I couldn't believe it. I said, "I almost
lost my life, and you want me to keep it a secret?" We went ahead
and talked to the Milwaukee writers, and it was in the newspaper.

I was beginning to lose my timidity and speak up about the
racism in baseball. In particular, I talked about the segregation at
spring training and exclusion of black managers. For the most
part, though, the black newspapers and magazines—publications
like *Jet* and *Ebony*—were the only ones that cared to print that
kind of thing. When I was in the spotlight with the home run
chase, writers often asked why I was so outspoken all of a sudden
when I hadn't said a thing about race relations for twenty years.
The fact is, I was saying things all along. But until I became the
guy with a chance to break Babe Ruth's record, the mainstream
media just didn't care what I had to say—with a few exceptions.
For instance, there was a note about my attitude in *The New York
Times Magazine* in 1958: "One subject on which Henry Aaron
feels deeply and toward which he displays no indolence is race
relations."

According to most of the stories about me, though, I displayed plenty of indolence. *Time* published an article that referred to me in the headline as "The Talented Shuffler." It said,
"Thinking, Aaron likes to imply, is dangerous. But by now everyone knows that Aaron is not as dumb as he looks when he shuf-
fles around the field . . ." Another article called me "a child of
nature."

I never got along particularly well with the New York press—
especially Dick Young of the *Daily News*—but for a few years
there, at least I didn't have to deal with it very often. Between the
time the Giants and Dodgers both left for the West Coast in 1958
and the Mets were established in 1962, there was no National
League team in New York. We did manage to get back there once
in 1958, however—in October.

We won the pennant by eight games that year—the same margin we won by in 1957—but somehow there wasn't quite the atmosphere that we'd enjoyed the season before. Maybe it was just that we expected the same magic all over again and that was impossible, because 1957 was a once-in-a-lifetime experience. Maybe it was because Hurricane Hazle had run out of miracles and was traded to Detroit. Maybe it was because Schoendienst was sick part of the year and in and out of the lineup. For whatever reason, we just didn't seem like quite the same team despite the fact that we were every bit as good in '58 as we had been in '57. Wes Covington had become a dangerous hitter, and the addition of his bat to Mathews's and Adcock's and Crandall's and mine gave us a terrific amount of power in the middle of the lineup. In a game against Ron Kline of the Pirates that year, we tied a record when I hit a home run and then Mathews hit one on the next pitch and Covington hit one on the pitch after that. We were thin in pitching—Buhl and big Gene Conley were both hurt that year—but Spahn and Burdette each won their twenty. As Burdette liked to say, they had a good room.

We clinched the pennant early, in a mid-September game against the Reds when we were down 5-4 and I hit a two-run homer in the seventh inning. The Yankees didn't have much trouble getting to the World Series again, either. The two of us were far and away the class of our leagues, and we knew that if we could beat them twice in a row we would clearly establish ourselves as the best team in baseball.

This time around, Mantle was healthy, but we rolled through the early games and took a three-to-one lead. When Spahn won the opener and then shut out the Yankees with a two-hitter in game four, it looked as though he would do what Burdette had done the year before. But then Bob Turley shut us out in the fifth game and we had to go back to Milwaukee. That didn't seem so bad, though. We didn't think we could lose two straight in Milwaukee. Maybe that's why we did.

Spahn held the Yankees to two runs for nine innings of the sixth game, but we only got two against Whitey Ford, Art Ditmar, and Ryne Duren. Then Gil McDougald hit a home run in the tenth and they got a bunch of singles for another run. We came back with one, but left the bases loaded and lost 4-3. The next day, the Yankees scored four runs after two were out in the eighth inning and beat us, 6-2.

I had nine hits in the Series, and after getting eleven the year before, it made me think about putting together a long history of hitting in the World Series. Little did I know that I would never be in one again.

Little did I know, also, that I would never win another MVP award after 1957. I was just learning the game, and I was certain I would have better years. I probably did, but 1958 wasn't one of them. It wasn't bad, though. I had thirty home runs, batted .326, and won my first Gold Glove award, which was enough to place me third in the MVP voting behind Ernie Banks—who led the league in home runs and RBIs—and Willie Mays.

It was company that I enjoyed being in. The three of us, along with Frank Robinson and Roberto Clemente and several others, were starting to develop a little National League fraternity of black players. To start with, our names always seemed to run together in the league leaders, but we had a lot more in common than that. We were a small group in a big league, and we understood that we had to stick together. Whenever we were in a new town, we would meet up with the black players from the other team. If we were in New York, or later San Francisco, we looked up Mays. In Chicago, it was Ernie. In Pittsburgh, we would all gather at the Crawford Grill, which had been an old Negro League hangout.

Pittsburgh was also Mal Goode's town. Mal was a local media guy who had a radio show and worked with the Pittsburgh Courier, and he was like our godfather. All the black players went to Mal's house when they were in Pittsburgh. If we had a day game on Saturday, we'd all meet at Mal's afterwards and he and his wife would serve up a big dinner that we'd eat out on the lawn. It was a black neighborhood, and people would come off the streets and sit around and eat with us. We felt at home there. We'd tell Mal our problems, and he'd tell us about Jackie Robinson and Joe Louis. Now and then he'd take us to an NAACP meeting. Later on, Mal became one of the first black network correspondents, covering the United Nations for ABC-TV. But he never lost touch with his ballplayers. Mal probably had more Hall of Famers at his house than anybody alive. He took care of us.

> I'll tell you what stands out most about Aaron. I don't know where he got the idea, coming from Mobile, Alabama, but Henry Aaron believed innately that he was as good as anybody. He'd let you know right now if there was any indication that somebody was trying to discriminate against him. If you went to a counter and somebody was slow giving service, he was sensitive about it. He'd say, "When you gonna wait on me?" Mays was timid about that sort of thing, but not Henry Aaron.—Mal Goode

Part of the reason the black players stuck together was to protect ourselves against falling in with the wrong kind of crowd. There are hustlers in every city who hang around ball clubs because they figure the players have money and are on the road a lot and live fast. And it's true that a lot of ballplayers take advantage of these opportunities. But black players couldn't afford to do that in the 1950s. We were still guests at the party, and we had to mind our manners every minute.

That wasn't too difficult for me, because I lived about as fast as I talked. A big night for me was watching late movies. When the Braves were playing at home, I was a homebody—Barbara would always leave the game after the eighth inning and go back to Mequon to get dinner ready, because she knew I'd be coming through the door one hour after the game was over. The temptations were on the road. It was important to know who you could trust, and more important to know who you couldn't. For that purpose, the doormen and bellhops in the hotels were always a big help, because they knew the guys who hung around the hotel. The players helped each other, too.

> When Hank would come to Chicago, I'd say, stay away from so-and-so. Then he'd come around our hotel when we were in Milwaukee and he might say, that guy's all right but don't trust

*that other guy. We looked out for each other, passed along in-
formation. We did the same thing with Mays and the others.
Some of it went back to the friendships we made barnstorming,
but where we really were able to stay up with each other was
meeting every year at the All-Star Game.*—Ernie Banks

For us, the All-Star Game was like old home week. Willie and
Ernie and I met each other every July for almost fifteen years. The
All-Star Game meant a lot to us, because the big difference between the National League and the American League was that we
had black players. In 1959, there were eight black players on the
National League team—Mays, Banks, Frank Robinson, Vada Pinson, Junior Gilliam, Sam Jones, Charlie Neal, and myself—and
the only one on their side was Vic Power. Many years, their only
black All-Star was Elston Howard. So it was a matter of pride
with us. And we always knew we would win. We won eight in a
row and twelve out of thirteen at one stretch during that period.
When people talk nowadays about the National League's domination of the All-Star Game, they usually say that the National
League always seemed to take the game more seriously. But they
don't say why. Willie and Ernie and I know why.

Ernie won the MVP award again in 1959 by leading the
league in RBIs and finishing one behind Mathews in home runs.
It was a tremendous feat, and as far as I'm concerned, there has
never been another ballplayer like Ernie Banks—a guy who
could play shortstop as gracefully as he did and also hit home
runs the way he did. Nor has there ever been another ballplayer
with Ernie's disposition. It might seem odd that we became good
friends, because, in addition to being rivals, we were opposite
personalities. He was as outgoing as I wasn't. Ernie was so upbeat
and happy all the time that a lot of people thought he was a
phony. Well, if Ernie's a phony, he must be a hell of an actor,
because he's been fooling me for almost forty years.

Ernie had to have a great year to beat me out for the MVP
award in 1959, because I was never a better hitter. I finished April
that year batting .508 and in the middle of a twenty-two-game
hitting streak. There was a night in the middle of May when I hit

two home runs and lost four points on my average. About that time, the Milwaukee *Sentinel* predicted that I would break Bill Terry's league record of 254 hits. There was also a lot of talk that I might bat .400, and the way I was going, I didn't think it was impossible. I've never been in a groove quite like I was at the beginning of 1959. At Connie Mack Stadium in Philadelphia one day, I hit twelve straight balls onto the roof in batting practice and got a standing ovation—which is about as common in Philadelphia as mango trees along the interstate. I was seeing the ball so well that I stopped going to movies for a while, because I didn't want anything to affect my eyes.

I was still over .450 late in May when, on a cold night in County Stadium, we came up against a little lefthander for the Pittsburgh Pirates named Harvey Haddix. Burdette was pitching for us, and he went into the game leading the league in wins. He kept shutting down the Pirates, but we couldn't do anything with Haddix. He had us off balance all night, and his control was perfect. In fact, he was perfect. After nine innings, we hadn't had a base runner. Meanwhile, the Pirates were banging out hits practically every inning, but they couldn't cross the plate—which was Burdette's style. The game was still 0-0 three innings later, and we had sent thirty-six men to the plate. Harvey Haddix had pitched a perfect game for twelve innings, a feat that has never been matched and probably never will be.

Both pitchers went out for the thirteenth inning—if a pitcher went thirteen innings nowadays, his agent would throw a fit—and Burdette kept Pittsburgh off the board again, despite the fact that the Pirates had twelve hits in the game. Felix Mantilla led off the bottom of the thirteenth for us and hit a routine grounder to Don Hoak at third base. But Hoak's throw was low, and finally the perfect game was over. Haddix still had his no-hitter going, though, and Haney was so desperate for a run—just for a chance at a run—that he had Mathews put down a sacrifice bunt, which is not something you see very often from a guy leading the league in home runs. I was up next, and Haddix walked me intentionally to bring up Joe Adcock. Adcock was a powerful pull hitter, but this time he hit one deep to right center. I saw it wasn't going to be caught, and I saw Felix cross the plate to end the game, so I stepped on second and then turned back to the dugout. What I hadn't realized was that the ball cleared the fence. Adcock kept running, but when he passed me on the bases, he was out. I had cost him a home run, but thank goodness, my dumb mistake was lost in the attention given to the incredible and heartbreaking game that Haddix had pitched. I'm sure Adcock wanted to strangle me, but he never said much about it. He didn't have to.

About a month later, we came up against Johnny Antonelli at Seals Stadium in San Francisco. I'd hit two home runs off Antonelli the previous time we faced him, and when I batted in the first inning this time, he happened to mention to me that I could afford to lose some teeth. I said, yes, but can you? He threw one near my head, and on the next pitch I hit one a little bit over his, into the top deck. I hit two more home runs that day, the only time in my career that I hit three in a game.

Not long after, the players voted for the All-Star team, and I became the first player ever elected unanimously—which meant that Antonelli and Sam Jones both must have voted for me. We played two All Star Games that year and split them. The first was at Pittsburgh, and it was one of the few All-Star Games in which I really did something. I drove in the tying run, and then scored the winning run as Mays tripled me home in the eighth.

Mays had a young teammate, Orlando Cepeda, who had joined us at the All-Star Game that year and would be there for years to come. He also had a rookie teammate, Willie McCovey, who would soon become a regular at our little midseason get-togethers. McCovey was from Mobile, and because of it, he wore number 44, like me. But McCovey wasn't the only newcomer from Mobile in the league that year. We were playing at Wrigley Field in Chicago one day when I heard somebody call me "Henry." The only people who didn't call me Hank were from back home. Sure enough, Billy Williams had made the big leagues. Before long, we would be having a Mobile reunion at every All-Star Game. We were all proud of the fact that our hometown produced so many good ballplayers. Billy even talked about changing his number from 26 to 44 and getting all Mobile players to wear 44, but it never came off.

With McCovey joining Mays, Cepeda, and another power hitter named Willie Kirkland in the Giants' same lineup, and with
my two pals, Sam Jones and Johnny Antonelli, winning forty
games between them, San Francisco took the lead in the pennant
race and held it for most of the summer. Our problem was
the same one we always seemed to have—second base. But we
weren't concerned about second base as much as we were about
Red Schoendienst. Red had been ill the year before, and in the
offseason we found out it was tuberculosis. He missed almost all
of 1959.

We hung in the race, though, with Spahn and Burdette each
winning twenty-one games and Buhl another fifteen. Mathews
led the league with forty-six home runs, I hit thirty-nine, and
Adcock hit twenty-five. Adcock actually hit twenty-seven, but he
only got credit for twenty-five. I cost him one in the Haddix game,
but the one that hurt worse was at the Los Angeles Coliseum
against the Dodgers late in September. At the time, there were
less than two weeks left in the season and we were one game
behind the Giants and one ahead of the Dodgers. Adcock had put
us in front with a home run over the short left-field screen in the
first inning, and in the fifth he lofted another high fly off Johnny
Podres that struck a supporting pole and fell in between the fence
and some mesh that was behind it. At first, it was ruled a home
run, but then the umpire, Frank Dascoli, said that a ball caught
in the screen was a ground-rule double, and that's how he ruled
it. We ended up losing the game in extra innings, and that one
run was the difference—not only in the game, but in the pennant.

The Dodgers had a one-game lead going into the last weekend
of the season, but they lost to the Cubs on Saturday and we beat
the Phillies to pull into a tie. We both won Sunday, setting up a
three-game playoff for the pennant. As far as we were concerned,
the hard part was over, because we had survived the pennant
race and we were sure—everybody in Milwaukee was sure—that
we were the superior team. These weren't the same Jackie
Robinson–Roy Campanella–Don Newcombe–Duke Snider Dodgers that had blown the league away in 1955. Their big hitters,
Snider and Gil Hodges, were getting old, and Drysdale and Sandy
Koufax were still young. We had been trying to catch the Giants

most of the year, and with them finally behind us, we felt like we were home free. After two straight pennants, it had taken us a while to get serious about winning another one—Haney, especially. It seemed as though he didn't start managing until we made a run at it in September, when we won seven straight to get back in it and then finished the season on a roll. To do it that way—to be behind all season, then turn it on at the end and tie for first place—made it seem as though we could claim the pennant whenever the spirit moved us. But we couldn't. Or else the spirit never moved us.

The first playoff game was in Milwaukee, and even though it was miserable weather, it was surprising to see only 19,000 people at County Stadium. I suppose that should have told us something about our future in Milwaukee. Two years before, we were the biggest thing to hit the city since sauerkraut, and here we were in a playoff for the pennant and couldn't draw 20,000. It wasn't that the people stopped caring about the Braves; I think they just started taking us for granted a little bit. I can't really blame them for that, because in a way, we took ourselves for granted.

Our confidence seemed justified when we scored two runs against Danny McDevitt in the first inning of the first game. But Walter Alston brought in Larry Sherry, and we were done for the day. Meanwhile, they scored twice to tie us and then won the game when John Roseboro homered in the sixth.

The second game was in Los Angeles, and we took the lead again. Frank Torre drove in me and Mathews in the first inning, and Mathews homered later to give us a 4-2 lead behind Burdette. It was 5-2 when the Dodgers started to rally in the bottom of the ninth. Haney brought in Don McMahon after they got three straight hits to load the bases, and when Norm Larker drove in a couple of runs with a single, Haney called Spahn out of the bullpen. Carl Furillo tied the game with a sacrifice fly, and Haney switched to Joey Jay. With two outs and a couple of men on base, Gilliam hit a ball toward the right-field corner and deep. I got there just before it hit the fence and managed to hang onto the ball as I bumped the wall at a pretty good clip. After that, Jay and

I was an eighteen-year-old shortstop for the Indianapolis Clowns in 1952—for about two months, anyway. Fortunately, they took a picture of me before I signed with the Boston Braves. (Mrs. Ed Hamman)

INDIANAPOLIS Clowns

Hank Aaron

I joined the Eau Claire Bears in June of 1952. Eau Claire was in the Northern League, Class C, and I earned $350 a month. It was also in the middle of Wisconsin, which felt like a foreign country to an eighteen-year-old black kid from Alabama. My brother had to talk me out of returning home to Mobile. I'm on the left, second row. On the far right of that row is Julie Bowers. Wes Covington is in the last row, third from right. John Goryl, a future major leaguer, is second from the left in the front row, and our manager, Bill Adair, is in the middle of the second row.
(*Eau Claire Leader-Telegram*)

I had a lot of heart-to-heart talks with Ben Geraghty, the manager of the Jacksonville Braves in 1953. Many of them had to do with breaking the color line in the Sally League, which I did along with teammates Felix Mantilla and Horace Garner and two black players for Savannah. It was rough going, but Felix and Horace and I had a great friend and ally in Ben. To this day, I believe that he was the best manager I ever played for. (Aaron collection)

After the Sally League season in 1953, I joined the Caguas team of the Puerto Rican winter league. Some of my teammates (from left) were Rance Pless, Dale Long, and Bob Buhl. It was in Puerto Rico that I became an outfielder.
(Photo courtesy *Periodico El Mundo*, San Juan, Puerto Rico)

I hadn't expected to be with the Braves to open the 1954 season. But when Bobby Thomson broke his ankle, I became the starting leftfielder. This was the lineup for our opening game in Cincinnati: Bill Bruton, Danny O'Connell, Eddie Mathews, Andy Pafko, me, Joe Adcock, Johnny Logan, and Del Crandall. (*Milwaukee Journal* photo)

This was the big time for me. Spahn and Mathews were already stars by 1954, and I was a timid rookie. You can tell this picture was taken during my rookie season, because it was the only year that I wore number 5 before switching to 44. (National Baseball Hall of Fame)

This is almost certainly the best team I ever played on, and it might have been as good as any team ever assembled. It was the barnstorming team that Willie Mays put together after the 1955 season. We had five Hall of Famers in the lineup—Mays, Roy Campanella, Ernie Banks, Monte Irvin, and me—and good pitching, besides. Needless to say, we didn't lose. Ever. From left, front row,

Junior Gilliam, Hank Thompson, Mays, Sam Jones, Gene Baker, Banks, Irvin.
Back row, Don Newcombe, Joe Black, George Crowe, myself, Brooks
Lawrence, Charlie White, Connie Johnson, Larry Doby, and Louis Louden.
Campanella was not present for the picture.
(Brooks Lawrence collection)

While the rest of the Braves stayed at the Manatee River Hotel during spring training, the black players boarded with a Bradenton schoolteacher named Lulu Gibson and her husband (pictured). Most of us shared a couple of small rooms in the garage behind the house. I earned my way into the "big house" after I won the batting title in 1956. (*Milwaukee Journal* photo)

Between us, Ted Williams and I won the Triple Crown in 1957. He led the American League in batting, and I led the National League in home runs and RBIs. (National Baseball Hall of Fame)

With the year the Braves and I had in 1957, photographers were coming out to our house to take pictures of the growing Aaron family. Our second child, Hankie, pictured here, was born early in the year. Our oldest, Gaile, was living with my parents in Mobile. (UPI/Bettmann Archives)

There is no better feeling than being carried off the field by your teammates. This was after my eleventh-inning home run that beat the Cardinals and clinched the 1957 pennant. Ever since I'd heard the radio description of Bobby Thomson's miracle home run to win the pennant for the Giants in 1951, I'd dreamed of a moment like this. (*Milwaukee Journal* photo)

Milwaukee went bonkers after we won the pennant. In fact, the city was so excited that the Yankees and the New York writers referred to Milwaukee as "Bushville" before the World Series. We were happy to bring the championship to Bushville. (National Baseball Hall of Fame)

The 1957 Series was my first trip to New York and Yankee Stadium. A lot of the buildup focused on me and Mickey Mantle, but Mantle was injured in the third game and wasn't the same the rest of the Series, which we won in seven.

(National Baseball Hall of Fame)

I'm supposed to be getting the news that I had been named the National League's Most Valuable Player for the 1957 season. The truth is, I wouldn't have put on a coat and tie just to answer the telephone.

(National Baseball Hall of Fame)

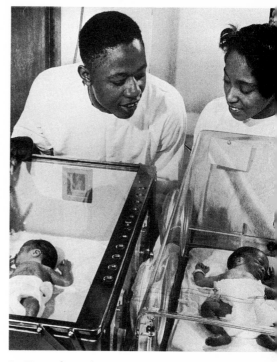

Barbara, Hankie, and I arrived in Mobile in style after the 1957 season—on the fancy L & N train they called the "Hummingbird." My hometown had a special day for me after the Braves won the World Series.

(National Baseball Hall of Fame)

In December of 1957—just nine months after Hankie was born—Barbara gave birth to premature twin boys, Lary (left) and Gary. Gary never made it out of the hospital. (*Milwaukee Journal* photo)

We were still celebrating in 1958, after winning our second National League pennant in a row. From left, manager Fred Haney, owner Lou Perini, Spahn, Don McMahon, and me. We led the Yankees three games to one in the World Series, but they came back to beat us, winning the last two games in Milwaukee. I was never in another World Series. (*The Sporting News*)

My brother Tommie became my team-mate and roommate in 1962. Three times that year he and I hit home runs in the same game. (*The Sporting News*)

Until I remarried and adopted my youngest daughter, Ceci, Dorinda was the baby of the family. She was born on my birthday in 1962. (Aaron collection)

I've been a Cleveland Browns fan for a long time, but when I was in Milwaukee I followed the Green Bay Packers like everybody else in town. Here, teammate Denis Menke and I visit with Vince Lombardi. We used to stand near the Packers' bench and listen to Lombardi scream at his players. (*The Sporting News*)

It was a sad time for all of us when the Braves left Milwaukee after the 1965 season, ending an unforgettable relationship that lasted thirteen years. Mathews and I walk up the tunnel to the clubhouse after the last game the Braves ever played at County Stadium. (*The Sporting News*)

Judging by this photograph, I'd have to say that success has gone to Bill Cosby's cheeks. A trip to Los Angeles was always a chance to catch up with the celebrities—and also Roy Campanella, the great Dodger catcher and integration pioneer who was paralyzed in an automobile accident. Campy is still employed by the Dodgers. (The two women are American Airlines stewardesses.) (Aaron collection)

The Aaron family at home in Atlanta in 1968—from left, Lary (sitting on the bar), Hankie, Gaile, Barbara, and Dorinda. (*The Sporting News*)

On May 17, 1970, in the second game of a doubleheader at Crosley Field in Cincinnati, I singled against Wayne Simpson of the Reds for my 3,000th hit. I was the eighth man in baseball history to reach 3,000 hits, and the first since my friend Stan Musial, left. On the right is Braves owner Bill Bartholomay. (National Baseball Hall of Fame)

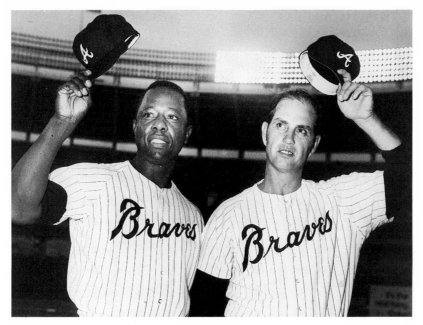

When we returned to Atlanta after my 3,000th hit, I was honored along with Hoyt Wilhelm, who had become the first man to pitch in 1,000 major-league games. The amazing thing about Wilhelm was that he didn't make the big leagues until he was almost 29. In 1969, at the age of 46, he was a key man in our successful drive for the division title. (Photo by Bob Johnson)

Roberto Clemente, Willie Mays, and I played in a lot of All-Star games together. I got along well with both Mays and Clemente, despite reports that we had nasty rivalries. (UPI/Bettmann Archives)

I was proud that this picture was used for the cover of Donald Davidson's book, *Caught Short*. Donald was the long-time traveling secretary of the Braves, but he was more than that. He was an advisor, a guardian, and one of the best friends I ever had. He saw more of my home runs than anybody but me. When this picture was taken, Eddie Mathews had become the manager of the Braves.
(Aaron collecton)

In the early seventies—long before he was famous—Jesse Jackson used to come by the clubhouse to visit with the black players whenever we played in Chicago. He often invited several of us to his house for dinner. Over the years we've kept in touch and been advisors to each other in causes pertaining to civil rights and baseball.
(Field Enterprises)

I'm not sure what the occasion was for this picture, but it must have been something big, because Daddy was wearing a tie. From the left, it's Daddy, Dorinda, Lary, Mama, Gaile, Alfredia, and Barbara. (Aaron collection)

My mother and father still live in the house where I was raised in the Toulminville section of Mobile. Mama wanted me to be a teacher, but she started to have doubts after Daddy caught me skipping school in the pool hall. (Ken Regan/Camera 5)

My secretary, Carla Koplin, handled 930,000 pieces of mail in 1973. According to the U.S. Postal Service, that was about 870,000 more than anybody else. In the beginning many of the letters were hateful and racist. The worst of those were handed over to the FBI. After I spoke out about the hate mail, the vast majority of letters were supportive.
(Aaron collection)

There was a lot said and written about how well I was handling the pressure of the chase. But I'd be lying if I said I wasn't tense in those days. The only way I could get away from the cameras and reporters and autograph hounds was to sit in my apartment with the door locked.
(National Baseball Hall of Fame)

Darrell Evans (center), Davey Johnson, and I made history in 1973 by becoming the first three men on one team to hit forty homers each in a season. But I failed to make history in my pursuit of Ruth, finishing the season one short of the record. (Newsday)

Billye and I were married in Jamaica late in 1973, but we had our reception in Atlanta.
(National Baseball Hall of Fame)

I'm about two steps away from tying Ruth. Dusty Baker is ready to slap my hand and Ralph Garr has his arms open for me. Johnny Bench, however, is not about to shake my hand. Number 714 came against Jack Billingham in my first time at bat in 1974. (Aaron collection)

It seemed like everywhere I went, I was greeted by men who would be President—Gerald Ford in Cincinnati and Jimmy Carter in Atlanta. Here I pose also with Johnny Bench, Bowie Kuhn, and Pete Rose.
(National Baseball Hall of Fame)

The big moment—number 715—came on April 8, 1974, against Al Downing of the Dodgers, before the biggest crowd in Braves history. Due to the crowd and the ceremony and my own burning desire to get it done, I felt like I had to break the record that night—and that I would. (Aaron collection)

As I came around second base on the record-breaking home run, a couple of University of Georgia students named Britt Gaston and Cliff Courtney were suddenly running at my side. But I was in my own world at that time, and, strange as it sounds, I honestly don't remember them being there.
(UPI/Bettmann Newsphotos)

I'll never forget the hug from Mama, though. Lord, that woman can hug. The ball is being held by one of our pitchers, Tom House, who caught it in the bullpen and ran it all the way in to me. Sammy Davis Jr. offered me $25,000 for the ball. I keep it in a bank vault.
(UPI/Bettmann Archives)

When the press asked me how I felt that night, I said, "Thank God it's over." I was also thankful that we had won the game, unlike the day in Cincinnati when I tied the record.
(Atlanta Braves)

Of all the public appearances I
made after breaking the record, none was more rewarding
than the time I spoke to a
crowd of thousands at a park
in Harlem. It made me think
back to the day in Mobile
when I skipped school to hear
Jackie Robinson.
(New York Daily News)

In 1974 I had the honor of
being the first athlete to address Congress on Flag Day.
The Speaker of the House
behind me is Carl Albert.
(National Baseball Hall of Fame)

After the 1974 season, Billye and I visited Japan, where I competed in a home run hitting contest with the Japanese all-time leader, Sadaharu Oh. In recent years Oh and I have teamed up in business and charitable ventures. (Aaron collection)

After I married Billye, I adopted her daughter, Ceci. She was in the first grade—taught by Mrs. Webb—when I visited her class at Lovett Elementary in Atlanta. (Aaron collection)

I'll never forget my return to County Stadium. It was great to be back with the best fans in baseball. (*Milwaukee Sentinel* photo)

My brother Tommie was a very successful manager in the Braves' minor-league system. When I was named director of player development for the Braves, I recommended that Tommie be promoted to manager of the AAA club at Richmond. He did a good job there and probably would have become a major-league manager if his life had not been taken by leukemia. (Manny Rubio)

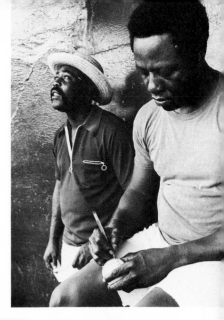

My day at the Hall of Fame came in 1982. I shared it with Travis Jackson, Happy Chandler, and Frank Robinson. Chandler has never gotten enough credit as the commissioner who went out on a limb to overrule the other owners and allow Branch Rickey to sign Jackie Robinson. Frank was close to my heart because we were both in the brotherhood of black players who came into the National League in the fifties, and in 1975 he became the first black manager.
(National Baseball Hall of Fame)

I've had my disputes with the Hall of Fame over the years, but everything is forgotten when I stand in front of my plaque.
(National Baseball Hall of Fame)

(Carl Davaz, *Topeka Capital-Journal*)

Stan Williams of the Dodgers held the game scoreless through the first two extra innings, and Bob Rush took over for us in the bottom of the twelfth. With two outs and two on, Furillo hit a high, tricky bouncer to Felix, who was playing shortstop because Johnny Logan had been injured earlier in the game. Felix came up with the ball, but he had to throw off-balance and pulled Torre off the bag at first. The season was over, and so was our little run as the best team in the National League.

Every team has ifs and buts, but that doesn't make it any easier. It still bothers me that we were only able to win two pennants and one World Series with the team we had. We should have won at least four pennants in a row. The fact is, we had them won and blew them. If we had done what was there for us to do, we would be remembered as one of the best teams since World War II—right there with the Big Red Machine and the A's of the seventies and the Dodgers and Yankees of the fifties. But we didn't do it, and in the record book we're just a team that won a World Series. Damn it, we were better than that.

I wish I knew what kept us from winning more, because there is no question that we had the talent—three Hall of Famers, and that was just the start. Del Crandall was as good a catcher as I ever saw. Bruton was a great center fielder. Adcock and Covington were dangerous hitters. Logan was a money player. No other team could match Spahn, Burdette, and Buhl. Or Mathews and me. Besides that, half our guys would fight their mothers to win a ballgame. We were rugged. And we were loose. We weren't a team that believed in love and togetherness and all that modern nonsense, but we got along in our own way. We enjoyed the game, and we enjoyed ourselves.

Of course, some of the guys enjoyed themselves more than others. Spahn and Burdette seemed to do most of the enjoying, usually at other people's expense, but they mostly picked on guys who enjoyed giving it back—like Covington. They called Covington "Kingfish," because he talked such a good game. In return, Covington would make fun of the way Spahn and Burdette dressed, which was without any kind of style whatsoever. Covington was just the opposite. On the train to Brooklyn one time, he was getting on Spahn and Burdette about their clothes and they were teasing him about a fancy new straw hat that he had. When we got to Ebbets Field, Covington put his hat in his locker, but after he left and came back, it wasn't there. Somebody told him that Spahn and Burdette had taken it out to the field. When he got out there, they were setting fire to it on home plate.

Of course, that wasn't as bad as the things Spahn and Burdette did to Donald Davidson. It seemed like they were always at war with Donald, irritating him with little tricks like messing with the special car Donald had—lowering the pedals so he couldn't reach them. They also warned Donald that if he ever came onto the field, they'd take off his pants. Now and then Donald would walk out toward the batting cage, but he always kept one eye on Spahn and Burdette and the other eye on the gate. Once, though, he ventured too far, and they got him. They carried him out to center field, with Donald kicking and cursing all the way, and walked away with his pants. The crowd wasn't in the park yet, but when people started arriving, Donald was still out there screaming for somebody to bring him his pants. Finally, Fred Haney got them for him.

Another time, Spahn and Burdette left Donald in the whirlpool during a ballgame. When the game was over, they got to the clubhouse and found their shoes nailed to the floor and their clothes in the shower. They had nothing to wear home. But it was hard for Donald to have the last laugh, because he was at a severe disadvantage and Spahn and Burdette would take any opportunity to abuse it. In Cincinnati, the three of them once got into the hotel elevator at the same time and Donald asked Spahn or Burdette to push twenty-six, since the button was too high for him to reach. They just ignored him and got off on their own floor, which was about fifteen or so, leaving Donald fuming as the elevator door closed on him. He had to go all the way back down to the lobby, where he marched right over to the desk and cussed out the clerk, demanding that they never again put him in a room higher than the third floor.

Once when Mathews was in a slump, he walked into the clubhouse, saw Donald, and said, "I know why I haven't been hitting. I haven't been messing with you." So he picked Donald up and placed him in the trash can. It was a big can, and Donald couldn't get out. The players were all coming in about that time, and one by one they would walk by and say, "Hey, Donald, how you doing?"

Mathews liked to have a good time and was probably the hardest-living guy on the team. He would have fit right in on the Yankees, with Mantle and Whitey Ford and Billy Martin. As it was, he had some pretty good flings with Buhl and some of the other guys on the Braves. I didn't go out with Mathews very often, because you never knew what might happen. At a restaurant in Cincinnati once, we waited a long time to be served—it probably had something to do with me and another black player being there—and when Eddie started to make noise about it, some lady cracked him upside the head with a bottle.

Trouble didn't tail me like it did Eddie, but it located me now and then. I was walking out of the Hillsborough Hotel in Tampa to catch a cab one night, and there was a loudmouth out there giving a hard time to the ballplayers and women and everybody else. I told him to shut up, and he said something back that I didn't like, and I popped him. On our team, it seemed like you had to hit somebody sometime to earn your stripes. But none of us could top the time Gene Conley punched out a Doberman pinscher. I was away at the All-Star Game at the time, but the team was staying over in Los Angeles and a bunch of the players were invited out to some Hollywood producer's house. Things got a little carried away, and somehow a young actress ended up in the swimming pool. I think she was the girlfriend of the producer, and he told the players to get the hell out of there. Apparently, they didn't get out fast enough, and that was when he sent the Doberman after them. The way I heard it, Conley just turned around and flattened that dog.

We were winning pennants all the while these things were going on, so there wasn't too much that Haney could do about it. But some of the guys used to drive him crazy. In Los Angeles one time, Spahn and Burdette rented a helicopter and went sightseeing. Haney had a fit when he found out that he had forty wins up there buzzing Hollywood. Another time, the Braves' radio guy, Joe Dorsey, was interviewing somebody in the dugout for the pre-game show, and as he was talking, Spahn and Burdette removed his pants.

But the guy who really kept us loose was Johnny Logan. Logan was funny when he tried to be and when he didn't try to be. One Friday night, we were flying at about 30,000 feet when the stewardess came up to Logan and asked him if he wanted steak or fish. Logan, who was Catholic, thought for a minute, looked out at the heavens, and said, "I'd better take the fish. We're getting pretty close to headquarters." Logan always had something to say, but he was like me in a way—he wasn't always sure of the right words to use. The difference was that I was self-conscious and would keep my mouth shut, but nothing stopped Logan. He would say things like, "Hey hey there, pal, I know your face, but I can't replace you." He was asked to say a few words once at a banquet honoring Mathews, Spahn, Musial, and me as future Hall of Famers, and he brought the house down when he stood up and said, "It's really a thrill to be sitting next to Stan Musial, one of the most immoral players of all time."

It seemed like we spent most of those years laughing or fighting. And winning. And having our hearts broken. They were happy days that should have been a little happier and lasted a little longer. At the time, it never occurred to us that they would be over when the fifties ended. We were too good and too cocky to believe that. When we were letting the pennant get away in 1959, we never realized that it would be our last good chance.

I suppose it was a little consolation to me that I took home my second batting title in 1959 with an average of .355. I might have had another shot at the Triple Crown except that a fan in Philadelphia threw a bottle at me around midseason and I twisted my ankle when I saw it whizzing by. But I still led the league with 223 hits, and at age twenty-five, I was the second youngest player to reach 1,000, after Ty Cobb. Pete Rose did it when he was twenty-seven. Although it was still way off in the future, my career goal at the time was to get 3,000 hits. I was still putting more emphasis on base hits than home runs, and I think my 1959 season answered anybody who thought I was swinging for the fences. It was interesting, though, that the two players who finished ahead of me in home runs—Mathews and Banks—were the two players who finished ahead of me in the MVP voting. Ernie also beat me in RBIs, 143 to 123.

All things considered, I believe 1959 might have been my best year of hitting, mostly because of one statistic that I think is probably the most important—total bases. The reason I put so much stock in total bases is that it combines the ability to get on base with the power to move baserunners around. You can't excel in total bases unless you are an all-around hitter, and the best all-around hitter will produce the most total bases. I had 400 in 1959, the only time I ever had 400 and the most since Stan Musial in 1948. Some of the guys who never had 400 total bases in a season are Ted Williams, Mickey Mantle, Ernie Banks, and Willie Mays. In fact, the only players to do it since Musial are me in 1959 and Jim Rice in 1978.

Intent as I was on being an all-around hitter, though, I kept being seduced by the money and glamour of home runs. If anything finally changed me, it might have been Home Run Derby, a made-for-television competition held in Los Angeles after the 1959 season. Players were squared off one-on-one, and the object was to see who could hit the most balls over the fence in nine innings, with anything that wasn't a home run counting as an out. A hitter kept coming back for more shows as long as he won, and every show was a chance to earn more money. I hadn't expected to do well because I wasn't accustomed to swinging for home runs, but somehow I kept winning until I was finally knocked out by Dick Stuart. I ended up hitting more home runs and winning more money than anybody. I took home about $30,000, which was almost two years' worth of salaries, and used it to buy my parents a grocery store in Toulminville. We also bought a color television for our house in Mequon. After that, there was enough left over to purchase some property around Mobile. The ability to buy property—not to mention a color TV —was a new and great feeling, and it only confirmed what I had been observing all along: home run hitters made the money. I noticed that they never had a show called Singles Derby.

7

By 1960, the few black players of the National League had become a hurricane that threatened to rip off the roofs that sheltered the heads of comfortable white players. Henry Aaron, Willie Mays, Ernie Banks, et al., had proved there was nothing to fear from their habits and skin color and had proved, at the same time, that their talent was positively ferocious.

In their first full decade, black players had comprised less than 8 percent of the major-league rosters and yet managed virtually to dominate an entire league. Of the ten Most Valuable Players the National League recognized in the 1950s, eight were black—Roy Campanella three times, Ernie Banks twice, and Willie Mays, Don Newcombe, and Henry Aaron once. For the decade, black players batted .280 as compared to .261 for whites, showing, more than anything, that marginal white players were allowed to hang around while marginal black players were not. For every twenty home runs that a black player hit, a white player hit thirteen in the same number of at-bats. For every ten bases a black player stole after those times at bat, a white player stole four.

And yet, the black players were just warming up. It was in the 1960s that their mastery of the National League approached the level of total. But for two discriminations that remained— those toward black pitchers and black journeymen—the domination might have been so thorough as to nearly split the two leagues down racial lines.

In the sixties, black players still made up but 23 percent of the major-league player pool—Latins comprised another 14 percent—but in the league in which they were more prevalent, the National, they held a working monopoly on achievement. Of the ten National League batting leaders of the sixties, seven were black or Latin. Of the ten National League home run leaders of the sixties, ten were black or Latin. A white player did not even finish second in home runs during the 1960s. Totaling the top five places each year in each category, thirty-seven of fifty batting leaders and forty-one of fifty home run leaders were black or Latin—giving a staggering 78 percent domination to the groups in the distinct minority.

At the same time, black and Latin players won the Most Valuable Player award in the National League on seven occasions in the 1960s, demonstrating that racial prejudice did not overtly infiltrate the voting. Magnetic personalities such as Mays, Banks, Clemente, and Cepeda seemed, in fact, to benefit from their colorful public images.

And yet, it remains difficult to reconcile the fact that Hank Aaron, the man who holds the all-time records for home runs and runs batted in and retired as the National League career leader in hits and runs, won exactly one Most Valuable Player award in twenty-three seasons. While it is true that Aaron's excellence was not expelled in blinding bursts of energy but rather played out, patiently and inexorably, over a whole generation, nonetheless he had seasons that deserved better. Even in the year he won the MVP award, 1957, it was hard to rationalize how he could prevail by a mere nine votes over Stan Musial and eighteen over teammate Red Schoendienst when he led the league in home runs, RBIs, runs, and total bases, finished third in batting (Musial was first), second in hits (two behind Schoendienst), switched outfield positions to bail his team out of an emergency, and hit the home run that clinched the pennant.

The close vote that year might have been attributed to the popularity of Musial and Schoendienst, but the undervaluation of Aaron's accomplishments was beginning to take on a puzzling pattern. Perhaps it was Aaron's lack of charisma, his reticence, the unassuming way he carried himself; perhaps it was playing in Milwaukee; perhaps it was his walk. It was odd that Joe DiMaggio was also quiet and deliberate, and yet in DiMaggio's case these traits were perceived as dignity and grace, which translated into American heroism. In Aaron's case, the same qualities translated into comparative invisibility.

Yet, it is too simple to blame this discrepancy on race, and there are too many inconsistencies. Perhaps, in a complicated and convoluted way, it had as much to do with racial stereotyping as with racial discrimination. Perhaps, in Aaron's time, it was necessary for a black player to fit into one of the prevailing stereotypes. Among the black stereotypes of the 1950s was the entertainer—the musician, the dancer. Perhaps, in tacit American stereotyping, fast-stepping Willie Mays was the dancer. The people applauded Willie Mays, the dancer. And perhaps, in that same subliminal stereotyping, slow-moving Hank Aaron was the plantation hand, the cotton picker. People passed by Hank Aaron, the cotton picker, on their way into town.

Season after season, Aaron's work went unrewarded by those who dispensed the spoils. In 1959, he finished third in the MVP voting despite leading the league in batting, hits, and total bases as the Braves finished in a dead heat for the pennant. Ernie Banks was a worthy winner, yet it is curious that Aaron could place behind teammate Eddie Mathews, who compared favorably with Aaron in power numbers and batted forty-nine points lower. In 1960, Dick Groat, shortstop of the pennant-winning Pirates and league batting champion, was named MVP. Aaron, who scored more runs than Groat, exceeded him in total bases by more than 100 and in RBIs by 76—he led the league—finished eleventh. In 1961, he batted .327, hit 34 home runs, and had 120 RBIs—and finished eighth.

The voting of 1963 may have been the most inscrutable of all with regard to Aaron. While the Braves finished sixth with a winning record, Aaron had one of the best years of his career, batting .319 with league-leading totals of 44 home runs, 130 RBIs, 121 runs, and 370 total bases. He even finished second to Maury Wills in stolen bases. At the same time, Sandy Koufax, who won the award, had a sensational season, going 25-5 for the pennant-winning Dodgers. The argument is not with Koufax, unless one believes—as Aaron does—that pitchers should not be eligible for MVP awards. How, though, could Dick Groat of second-place St. Louis beat Aaron by sixty-five votes when they both batted .319, both had 201 hits, and Aaron dwarfed Groat in every other offensive category—by 36 runs, 57 RBIs, 38 homers, and 28 stolen bases? What's going on here?

It is notable that a player with a background and personality similar to Aaron's, fellow Mobilian Billy Williams, encountered the same sort of neglect in MVP voting. In 1965, Williams batted .315 (fourth in the league) for the Cubs with 34 home runs (third), 203 hits (third), 39 doubles (second), 108 RBIs (fourth), and 115 runs (fourth), and placed an incredulous fourteenth. The next year, Aaron set a major-league record for home runs by the end of June, led the league with 44 homers and 127 RBIs, and was eighth in the MVP balloting. Roberto Clemente was the recipient that year, but Aaron's Atlanta teammate, leadoff batter Felipe Alou, exceeded Clemente in every major category except RBIs and placed fifth. It was evident that players who shared Aaron's conditions also shared his problem.

On and on it went. When it came time to name the Player of the Decade for the 1960s, the Associated Press selected Koufax, who had been MVP once, second in the voting twice, and in the top twenty on two other occasions. Aaron finished fourth in the voting, behind Mays, who tailed off significantly the last three years of the sixties, and Mickey Mantle, whose last big season was 1964. On the other hand, Aaron was among the top fifteen in the MVP voting for each of the ten years considered—for fifteen straight years, in fact, starting with his second season, 1955. He was in the top twenty for an incredible nineteen years in a row—this, despite the obvious inconsistencies in the voting.

For all the times he was slighted by the baseball writers, Aaron nonetheless exceeds Mays as the highest-ranked player since World War II in terms of MVP finishes—based on a point system of appearances in the top twenty, with twenty points for a first-place finish and one for twentieth, and so on. Considering only top-ten seasons, Aaron and Mays are at a dead heat at the top of the list, followed by Mantle, Musial, Ted Williams, Yogi Berra, Frank Robinson, Mike Schmidt, Pete Rose, and Al Kaline. Musial and Williams would be one-two if the period were expanded to include their full careers.

Aaron's remarkably regular presence among the leaders of the league was a symbol for his times. He came into the National League at a point when black players were beginning to preside over it, and he, along with Mays, Banks, and a few gifted others, *wore the mantle into the next generation. They shared it from year to year, but only among themselves.*

◆ ◆ ◆

I consider myself a second-generation black player. By 1960, the first generation had passed almost entirely. Don Newcombe was in his last season, and all the other pioneers—Jackie, Campanella, Joe Black, Larry Doby, Monte Irvin—were out of the game. But with the integration of the Red Sox in 1959, every major-league roster included at least one black player. The stars of the second generation were in their primes, and the third was coming on. It included my home boys from Mobile, Willie McCovey and Billy Williams, and the likes of Orlando Cepeda, Bill White, Bob Gibson, Curt Flood, Vada Pinson, John Roseboro, Willie Stargell, Juan Marichal, Leon Wagner, Maury Wills, Tommy Davis, Willie Davis, Lou Brock, and Richie Allen.

Most of them came through the minor leagues in the 1950s, and almost all of them had their own horror stories. Frank Robinson said that no man should have to put up with the abuse black players endured in the Sally League, where he followed me. The hatred in the Carolina League used to send Curt Flood back to his room in tears. When he was with San Antonio, Billy Williams became so fed up with eating in restaurant kitchens that he left his team and went back home to Mobile until his family and old friends made him understand the importance of sticking with it. Northerners like Billy White and John Roseboro were scared to death of being sent to the South. Roseboro said that every time he thought of Mississippi, he pictured Emmett Till hanging from a tree. In Little Rock, a policeman pulled a gun on Richie Allen as he was running home with a bottle of soda he bought from a machine. Willie Stargell was walking on the sidewalk in Plainview, Texas, when a white man jumped into his path, put a shotgun to his temple, and said, "Nigger, if you play in that game tonight, I'll blow your brains out."

We shared these stories with each other, and as the years

went by, we began to talk more and more about changing things. By the early sixties, we represented the best players in the National League, and we thought the least we deserved was the right to stay in the big-league hotels during spring training. That was one concern with which Jackie Robinson had never been deeply involved, because the Dodgers had their own training complex in Vero Beach. It was something the rest of us would have to work out.

On the Braves, Bill Bruton spoke for the black players when it came to political and racial matters. Bill was not an agitator, though, and Bradenton was a tough town to crack. We realized that desegregation would be a slow process, but we were all committed to it. As the black player with the longest service on the team next to Bruton, I was sort of Bill's second in command—we were also partners in an investment company in Milwaukee, and we campaigned together for JFK in 1960—and when he was traded to Detroit after the 1960 season, his responsibilities fell on me. I wasn't any more of an activist than Bruton, but I could stand my ground and let guys like Wes Covington stir things up. Slowly, we started to make a little headway. As *Jet* magazine reported in 1961: "First team to hit the Jim Crow ball head-on in the segregation-minded Sarasota Spring resort area was the Milwaukee Braves—under the pressure of Hank Aaron, Wes Covington and recently traded Andre Rodgers ... After meeting with Aaron and Covington, Brave General Manager John McHale ordered all race signs dropped at the Bradenton park, and has assured his sepia stars that all living facilities will be integrated next spring."

The segregation of the hotels was the hardest thing to break down. There wasn't a white man in Florida—or in baseball, for that matter—who was going to change things just out of his sense of decency. It had to happen through pressure. And one of the movers behind it was the man who would one day become president of the National League.

The hotel situation in Florida wasn't a big issue with black players in the fifties, because most of the guys were from the

South and they accepted it. But there were other, little things that worked on us. The St. Petersburg Yacht Club used to invite eight or nine Cardinal players to a breakfast every spring, and one day I made the comment to Joe Reichler, who was a baseball writer for UPI, that none of the black players were ever invited. He wrote an article about the segregation in spring training, and I think that started the ball rolling. After the article, the Yacht Club invited me to breakfast at something like one o'clock in the morning. I told them thank you, but that was a little early for me. The Yankees were involved in the same thing, and Elston Howard ended up going to the breakfast.

After Reichler's article, there was a lot of pressure in St. Louis to do something about the segregation. There was even talk about boycotting Augie Busch's beer. The result was that the Cardinals were the first team to rectify the situation of segregated hotels. Their solution was to segregate everybody, not just the black players. They leased a motel in St. Petersburg and just took the whole thing over.—Bill White

Once the Cardinals integrated, it was only a matter of time before the rest of the teams got the message. Not long after, our vice-president, Birdie Tebbetts, called me into his office and asked if I was happy with the way things were. I said, "Hell, no, I'm not happy. It's about time you all realized that we're a team and we need to stay together." The Braves had been saying for a few years that they would like to bring us all into the same hotel, but the tricky part was finding a hotel to go along. The Bradenton hotels stuck together on segregation, because they knew that if one of them gave in, the others would have no choice. Their position was spelled out at a meeting of the hotel association in which they all agreed that none of them would take blacks. But as soon as the meeting was over, Tebbetts got a call from a man who had a place called the Twilight Motel in a little town named Palmetto, which was next to Bradenton. Since he wasn't situated in the city, he was willing to take the whole team. The white players weren't too thrilled to move out of the sprawling Manatee River Hotel into a two-bit motel in the next town—and for that matter, the black players knew we'd leaving behind some first-rate chicken and biscuits—but it had to be done.

I ran into Mrs. Gibson on the street a few weeks later, and she was crushed. She figured I was behind the move—I suppose I was—and it made her feel as if I'd walked out on her. She said, "Don't you love me? Don't you like being in our home?" I said, "Mrs. Gibson, that's not it at all. I love your home, but it's time now for baseball to understand that we have to have a choice of where we want to stay, and you have to understand that, too. It's very important that we make that statement." But Mrs. Gibson didn't see it that way. She said, "I don't think you like us anymore." That was the last time I saw her.

I wish I could say that we were a better team with segregation behind us, but the fact is that while we were coming together off the field, we were coming apart on it. The Braves were never the same after we lost the 1959 playoff to the Dodgers. Haney left for Los Angeles, where his heart was, to run the expansion Angels. He was replaced by Charlie Dressen, a tough, old-school baseball man who had been managing in the big leagues for parts of twenty-five years. John McHale took over as general manager for John Quinn, who went to the Phillies. Birdie Tebbetts had already come over from Cincinnati as an executive vice president. We had new philosophies and old players. Del Crandall and Johnny Logan were getting near the end of the line, and sooner or later Warren Spahn was bound to slow down.

There was still enough of the old team left to finish second to the Pirates in 1960. Spahn and Burdette won their forty games, and Mathews and I hit 79 home runs and drove in 250 runs between us. It was Crandall's last good year. He likes to brag that it was the only year he outhit me—.294 to .292. But Schoendienst was never the same after his tuberculosis, and we had familiar old problems at second base. Dressen even played me there a couple of games and was thinking about making it permanent. When he heard that, Buzzie Bavasi, the general manager of the Dodgers, said he was going to sign Big Daddy Lipscomb—the 300-pound tackle for the Baltimore Colts—as a pinch runner.

Dressen knew as much baseball as any manager in the game, but he wasn't the right man for our club. We were a veteran team, and guys like Spahn and Burdette didn't need to be told how to do their jobs. They let Dressen know about it, and, in turn, Dressen stuck the needle in them every chance he got. At one point, when Burdette was wondering aloud why he had such a hard time pitching at the Los Angeles Coliseum, Dressen said it was because he didn't have a "drop ball" like Johnny Podres of the Dodgers. After he heard that, Burdette went out and whipped Podres in the Coliseum and hit two home runs off him. Then he walked up to Dressen in the dugout and said, "That's what I think of his goddamn drop ball!"

I have to say, though, that Dressen was more than fair with the black players. In Florida, he often told the bus driver to keep going until we found a restaurant that would accept the whole team. For that reason, I suppose I should have been more supportive of Dressen, but the fact is, I didn't do him any favors. Dressen never had cause to fine me like he did a lot of the other players, but I'm sure he was tempted now and then to slug me. Mathews and I used to sit in the clubhouse playing a card game called casino, and Dressen would come by every few minutes to order us out to the field. We'd just stay there dealing hands until about two minutes before game time, with Dressen getting angrier every minute. But we were choirboys compared to Spahn and Burdette. They were Dressen's undoing. After a game one night, they started a fire in the back of our bus. When that happened, it was obvious that Dressen had lost control of the club. He didn't make it through the 1961 season. Birdie Tebbetts came down from the front office to manage the last twenty-five games.

We had a new second baseman in 1961, a white player from Mobile named Frank Bolling. Frank and I were only two years apart in age, and we had grown up within a few miles of each other, yet we'd never met until he came over to the Braves in a trade with Detroit and put his stuff into the next locker. Frank solved our problem at second base. The only hitch was that we had to give up Bill Bruton to get him. Bruton was the first of the original Milwaukee heroes to go.

As much as we missed Bruton, we all realized that the old Braves would be breaking up. On the other hand, what really hurt was losing the young Braves. A week after he traded Bruton, McHale acquired a shortstop, Roy McMillan of Cincinnati, for

Juan Pizarro and Joey Jay, our two best young pitchers. McMillan was the premier fielding shortstop in the league, and at the time it was made, the trade was hailed as the one that would get the Braves back on top. So I can't fault McHale. Nonetheless, I've always felt that we would have won some more championships if we had held on to Pizarro and Jay. We needed young pitchers to take over someday for Spahn, Burdette, and Buhl, and we never came up with them. Jay and Pizarro should have been the guys. Jay won twenty-one games in each of his first two seasons with the Reds, and I'm not sure I ever saw a pitcher with more ability than Pizarro had when he came to us out of Puerto Rico at the age of nineteen.

> *I don't think our managers and front office ever understood Pizarro. He was always in shape and ready to pitch, but he was moody. Managers would say things to him about being moody, and it would just make him angry. Then they would tell him to do something, and he would do something else. But it was hard to blame him for acting the way he did. One time, he pitched a one-hitter in Pittsburgh, but when his turn came up at Philadel-phia in the next series, he didn't pitch because I was playing second base. A lot of teams had an unwritten rule that you could have five white guys and four black guys on the field, but you crossed the line when you had five black and four white guys. I remember one game against the Giants, they had eight black players on the field against us—Jim Davenport was the only white guy—and one of the white players on our team said, "Who we playing, the Harlem Globetrotters?" Fred Haney wouldn't put five black players on the field unless it was an emergency and there was nothing else he could do. If somebody was hurt and I had to fill in at shortstop or second base, that gave us four black guys, and Pizarro wouldn't pitch. That was what happened in Philadelphia. I don't know if the decision came from Haney or from the front office, but Pizarro had to go to the bullpen, and he didn't pitch for another nine or ten days after his one-hitter. Finally, San Francisco was pounding on us one night, about 9-1, and Haney told Pizarro to warm up. Nat-urally, he got mad. They had a little cart that relief pitchers were supposed to ride when they came into the game, but Pi-*

*zarro wouldn't ride in the cart. Then he started throwing noth-
ing but fastballs, and the Giants were hitting him all over the
park. After the game, Haney asked him why he didn't ride the
cart, and Pizarro said because he didn't feel like it. Haney said
that the next time it happens, it'll cost you $100. Pizarro said,
make it $200. Haney said, I'll make it $400. So Pizarro went to
his coat pocket to get his checkbook.*

*Pizarro and I used to talk about how he and I were almost
never on the field at the same time, because we always had
Hank, Bruton, and Covington in the outfield, and that only left
room for one more black guy in the lineup. Neither of us ever
got a full-time job as long as we were with the Braves, even
though we both became starters as soon as we left. It was
strange, because as long as I was in Milwaukee, we always had
a problem at second base, and yet they never gave me the
chance to win the job. They would say that I'd get tired if I
played all the time, or I was having trouble making the double
play. They'd bring in a second baseman and he would come
and go, and another one would come and go, and by the time I
left, I had been there six years without ever playing more than
sixty games at second base.—Felix Mantilla*

If the Braves had given Felix Mantilla the chance to win a
position, it might have made all the difference in our team in the
long run. He could have solved our problem at second base, or
he could have been ready to take over at shortstop when Logan
was traded to Pittsburgh during the 1961 season. If Felix had
been our shortstop, we wouldn't have had to give up our two best
young pitchers to get one. As it was, Felix went to the Mets in
the expansion draft and became their third baseman. Then he
went to the Red Sox, hit thirty home runs, and became their
second baseman.

Logan had been our regular shortstop for nine years when
they traded him for Gino Cimoli. He was just about finished by
then, but he had been the soul of our team and we missed him.
A few weeks after Logan left, the Braves waived Wes Covington,
who signed with the Phillies and hit the ball hard for another five
years, bad knees and all. When the Braves swapped Buhl to the

Cubs early in 1962 for a pitcher named Jack Curtis, all my old buddies were gone. After the season, Adcock was traded with Curtis to the Indians for an outfielder named Ty Cline and a couple of others. Finally, Burdette went to St. Louis in 1963. That left Spahn and Mathews as the only original Milwaukee Braves remaining and those two and me as the only veterans of our championship teams.

The problem was that while the old Braves were being sent away, we weren't replacing them with good young players from our farm system. The major exception was Joe Torre, who came up in 1961 as a pudgy catcher from the same home in Brooklyn that had given us Frank Torre, a valuable reserve first baseman during the fifties. Joe was a much better hitter than his older brother, and he was a perfect successor to Crandall. Lee Maye and Mack Jones also gave us some good years in the outfield, but for the most part the Braves were unsuccessful at replacing the guys who had carried us through the happy days—especially the pitchers.

It caught up with us in 1961, when we fell to fourth place despite a strong lineup. I had 34 homers and 120 RBIs, Adcock and Mathews were right there with me, and Frank Thomas, a left fielder we traded for, wasn't far behind. In a game at Cincinnati that year, the four of us set a major-league record by hitting consecutive home runs. The problem was we lost, 10-8, which was symbolic of our team. We had become power-heavy and pitching-poor.

The Braves had so many home run hitters through the Milwaukee years that some people thought of our park as a bandbox, but that wasn't the case at all. I liked hitting in County Stadium—it was a fair park, and you could see the ball well—but for as long as we were in Milwaukee, I hit more home runs on the road than I did at home, 213-185. Most of the Braves did. Years later, when I was chasing Ruth's record, my detractors frequently pointed out that I had the advantage of playing in the launching pad of Atlanta Stadium. There's no denying that Atlanta Stadium is a home run park, and I certainly benefited from it, but I never once read that County Stadium cost me home runs.

The fact is, it wasn't until late in 1971—my eighteenth season—that my home runs at home finally exceeded my home runs on the road.

The reason the Braves hit so many home runs in Milwaukee was that we had home run hitters, including two guys—Mathews and me—who hit more than any pair of teammates in baseball history. And the reason we won so many games was that we had two guys—Spahn and Burdette—who for ten seasons won more than any pair of teammates in baseball history. From 1953 to 1963, they averaged about thirty-six wins a season. Spahn led the league in victories for five straight years, from 1957 to 1961, and in 1961, at the age of forty, he pitched his second no-hitter. He also won his three hundredth game that year—all with the Braves. I had the privilege of catching the last out in Spahn's three hundredth victory. I acted like I didn't know what was happening and pretended to throw the ball into the crowd. Crandall ran out to the mound to congratulate Spahn, but when Spahn saw me turn toward the stands, he left Crandall and went sprinting out to right field to stop me.

Spahn and Burdette did their usual number in 1961, but Buhl had an off year and we had nobody to pick up the slack. Spahn and Burdette had been so good for so long that people didn't realize how much Buhl meant to us. He was a nasty pitcher and a fierce competitor, and besides that, he was one of the few guys on the team who could put Spahn in his place. Buhl and Mathews always sat together on the old DC-9s we flew on, and one night they were getting settled into their seats when Spahn walked by. Spahn had this way of coming up on people from behind and slapping them upside their head, which he could usually get away with because he was Warren Spahn. But Buhl didn't care about that. When Spahn slapped him this time, Buhl wasn't in the mood for it, and he turned around and busted Spahn as hard as he could, just leveled him. It was sort of embarrassing for us, watching this Hall of Famer get laid out in the aisle. But I guess Spahn stopped slapping people after that.

Buhl still had more than fifty wins left in his arm after 1961, but the Braves gave up on him. We were never serious pennant contenders after he was traded. In 1962, with Buhl gone and Burdette slipping, we dropped another place to fifth. Mathews and Adcock were starting to fall off a little, and as a result I felt more responsibility to hit more home runs. I finished the season batting .323 with 128 RBIs and 45 homers, which was my highest total until 1971. Among them was the longest ball I ever hit. It came against Jay Hook of the Mets at the Polo Grounds, and it landed to the left of the clubhouse in the center-field bleachers, about 470 feet from home plate. Babe Ruth had hit one into the bleachers in the 1920s, but they were moved back after that. Since they had been moved, the only other player to hit one where I did was Adcock, who did it in 1953. Ironically, though, Lou Brock, who was a wiry rookie for the Cubs in 1962, had hit one to the right of the clubhouse just one night before my home run.

My extra power at the plate brought with it a little more economic power. My salary was up to about $50,000 by this time, which wasn't in league with Mays and Mantle and Spahn but was more than I needed for my family's lifestyle. We stayed at home a lot, watching Westerns on our new color TV or barbequing in the pit that was built into the patio. The patio was shaped like a baseball field, with a fence around it, benches for the bullpen, and the barbeque pit in dead-center. We were pleased with our house. In the den we had a huge fireplace and an autographed picture of JFK, which he sent to me after I campaigned for him.

It was a roomy house, and we made good use of the space. Our baby daughter, Dorinda, was born on my birthday in 1962. By that time, we had also brought Gaile up from Mobile to stay with us and go to school in Milwaukee, which put the whole family under the same roof except for Lary, who was still living with Mama. We had been baptized Catholic, and although I didn't remain a Catholic for very long, the kids went to Catholic schools as long as they were in Milwaukee.

My father always thought we could get a better education if we went to schools that had white students. For a while, I was the only black in the Catholic school system of Mequon. All of our friends were white. They would sleep over at our house, and we would sleep over at theirs. It was no big deal. I really don't remember racial things occurring there. One time, though, when I was in about second grade, I noticed that my boots were slit up the side as I put them on to go home after school. I didn't think anything of it, but my father and mother met me at the door and said, "What's wrong with your boots?" They were thinking about racism. The next day they were at my school talking to the principal.

My father really believed in education. He would always tell us, "I'm Hank Aaron, and you're not." He knew we would eventually have to make our own way. Not only that, but he knew that his life as a ballplayer wouldn't last forever. He always said that he could break something and never play again, and the only thing to fall back on would be our education. He always said you could fall off the same ladder you climbed up on.

We had everything we could want—I guess you might say that we were privileged, especially compared to other black kids— but at the same time, my parents also saw to it that we learned what the other side was like. Before the baseball season started, when everybody was down in spring training, we stayed with a lady named Mittie and her husband in the heart of the city. And I mean, the heart of the city. When we were with Mittie, we went to a Catholic school that had other blacks. It was a whole different experience for us, being with black kids. When we were with Mittie, we learned how to do without.—Gaile Aaron

With all of the kids around, our house became a pretty lively place. It seemed like it was always full with friends or relatives. Somebody from my family in Mobile or Barbara's family in Jacksonville was usually there, and during the season we'd have as many as twenty people staying at the house.

In 1962, my brother Tommie stayed with us, too, although he wasn't just visiting. He had finally joined me on the Braves—and just in time, because with Felix gone, I needed a roommate on the road. Tommie had been an outstanding minor-league hitter, and the Braves expected big things from him. I think they expected too much, really. When they traded Adcock, the spotlight was on Tommie to take over at first base. I believe he could have done it if I hadn't been on the same team, but with me around, it was difficult for Tommie to be his own ballplayer. He spent his entire seven-year career with the Braves, but he never batted higher than .250 or hit more than eight home runs, which is the number he hit as a rookie. Of those eight, three came during games in which I also homered. We were a couple of proud Aarons on those days. In fact, we had a house full of proud Aarons.

If Tommie never reached his potential as a ballplayer, I can say without bias that he was as good a man as there was in the game—and also a great roommate, except for one morning at the Chase Hotel in St. Louis. I think Tommie had been fiddling with the air conditioner—I don't know what happened, really; they might have been working on the unit in the room below us—but I was just sitting on the bed eating my breakfast when all of a sudden the thing exploded. Flames broke out and smoke filled the room so fast that we didn't even have time to get dressed. It ruined everything in the room. The people who ran the Chase probably figured that's what happens when you start letting in the coloreds.

With Tommie around and Aarons running all over the house, we were beginning to feel at home in Mequon. It was pleasant out there, with dairy cows in the pastures and foxes running through the meadows. Mequon was a world away from the urban life of Milwaukee, where a black person couldn't venture beyond 12th Street without putting his life in jeopardy. The only thing I didn't like about it was driving those country roads in the winter. Once, a guy passed me in the snow and slid in front of a truck coming the other way. I ran to check on the driver of the car and found him decapitated. Things like that made us think about spending our winters in the South.

We never imagined the way in which it would come about, though. We never considered the possibility of the Braves leaving town. But The Miracle of Milwaukee, like hula hoops and duck-tail haircuts, had been left behind in the fifties, and year by year, our attendance decreased until it was well under a million by the early 1960s—about a third of what it had been in the happy days of the mid-fifties. I'm sure it was a combination of many things:

The novelty had worn off, and the fans were no longer awed by the National League. Most of them were thrifty German and Polish descendants who earned working-class wages at the breweries and machine shops, and they probably had been spending too much money on baseball. The dollars were well spent when they were rewarded with championships, but we weren't the team we had been in the fifties. The ballpark wasn't the same place, either. There was a squabble over the right to bring beer into the stadium, and Milwaukeeans certainly don't need anybody to tell them when and how to drink their beer. On top of the local problems, the Braves' regional impact was dramatically reduced when the Washington Senators moved to Minnesota in 1961. And it was probably not a coincidence that our decline coincided with the spectacular rise of the Green Bay Packers.

I was, and still am, a fan of the Cleveland Browns—I loved to watch Jimmy Brown run and admired the way he carried himself—but like everybody else in Wisconsin, I soaked up the Packers. Bud Selig—the same one who now owns the Milwaukee Brewers—was a college kid at the time, and we became friends by going to Green Bay games. Bud's father had a Ford dealership that advertised with the Braves, and Bud was friendly with a lot of the players. We would get sideline passes and listen to Vince Lombardi rant and rave by the Packers' bench. We saw him throw his clipboard at Jim Ringo, and we heard him tell some of his offensive linemen that if they didn't stop worrying about getting revenge on some dirty linebacker and start opening some holes, they could leave their uniforms on the clubhouse floor and forget they were ever Packers.

Lombardi was on the Braves' board, but not even he could save us. And we couldn't play well enough to save ourselves. In 1963, we finished in sixth place, the first time since coming to Milwaukee that we had been out of the first division. Our lineup was strong enough to keep us over .500—we were actually only four games out of third place—but Burdette was all but through and Bobby Bragan, the new manager, had to get by somehow with a one-man pitching rotation. The amazing Spahn won twenty-three games at the age of forty-two. Despite the fact that the team was falling apart around him, old Hooks was as good as ever in 1963.

I was, too, for that matter. I was a different player that year. The Braves had become a plodding team, and Bragan figured it would help us—and me—if I stole more bases. I ended up second in the league, behind Maury Wills, with thirty-one steals in thirty-six tries. I had always had some success stealing bases, but by running more, it seemed to change the perception that I was a lethargic player. It broke down some of the prejudice toward me, and for that I can thank Bobby Bragan, who did as much for me as any manager since Ben Geraghty. At one point when Bragan was managing the Braves, there was a rumor that the Mets would pay half a million dollars to buy my contract, and Bragan made the comment that he wouldn't trade me for a million. (It's interesting that teams were willing to talk about that kind of money for a ballplayer in those days, yet they would never pay that kind of money to the ballplayer.)

Bragan worked well with all of our black players, which was quite a commentary on the progress that baseball had made in race relations since 1947. A hard-core Alabaman from Birmingham, Bragan had been a reserve catcher for the Dodgers when Jackie Robinson was breaking in, and he, along with Dixie Walker—whom Bragan brought to the Braves as his batting coach—and several other Southern players, had raised some serious objections to the notion of a black man on the same team. Bragan's feelings were well known. He was one of Jackie's first hurdles.

> *I was one of seven boys and two girls growing up in Birmingham. We had a black fellow named Frank who used to come and do our yard on Saturdays, and when he got through he would come in and play the piano. He taught all the Bragan boys how to chord the piano, and I'm still playing. Frank was our friend, but he was still the yard man. Where I came from, blacks had a certain place, and feelings about segregation were deep-seated. It was out of the question to sit down at dinner with a black person, or invite one to your house. That's just the way it was.*

In spring training of 1947, when it looked like Jackie was going to be with us, Branch Rickey called in several of us Southerners and said that he understood we were against Jackie being on the team. I told him that I couldn't speak for the others, but I would just as soon be traded. Rickey didn't trade me, but he appreciated the fact that I leveled with him. Dixie Walker put it in writing that he wanted to be traded, and he was. But I stayed, and Mr. Rickey and I became good friends after that. As far as I'm concerned, Branch Rickey was the greatest man to ever appear on the sports stage. My biggest thrill in more than fifty years of baseball is getting to be one of Mr. Rickey's boys. Anyway, I'd say that about three weeks after Jackie joined us, I was as quick to sit with him in the dining car as I was with anybody. He got everybody's respect in a hurry, because he was good people. Years later, Jackie and I sat next to each other at Mr. Rickey's funeral in St. Louis.

I'm grateful to Jackie for the conversion he made in me. If it hadn't been for Jackie, I wouldn't have been as good with Maury Wills or Rico Carty or Henry Aaron. I made Wills into a switch-hitter at Spokane in 1959, when he was twenty-seven years old and going nowhere because of the fear of the right-hander's curve ball, but I would have never done a thing like that if it hadn't been for my experience with Jackie. Of course, I didn't have to do anything like that with Henry. Henry Aaron was ideal. All you had to do with him was write his name into the lineup. He always gives me credit for making him a complete player, but all I did was this. When I first met Henry in spring training, I called him over and said, "Henry, Willie Mays is making $125,000 and you're making $75,000, and do you know what the only difference is? He runs. From now on, you've got the green light to run any time you want." He stole thirty-one bases that year, and the next year he was making six figures. That's the only contribution I made to Henry Aaron in three-and-a-half years as his manager. And he kept me in business all the time.—Bobby Bragan

It turned out that 1963 was the closest I ever came to the Triple Crown. I hit forty-four home runs and tied for the league lead with the other number 44, Willie McCovey. My 130 RBIs led the league, and my .319 average was only seven points behind Tommy Davis of the Dodgers. I also finished first in runs with 121 and led the league in total bases for the sixth time in my ten seasons. That year, in fact, the top National League five hitters in total bases—me, Mays, Vada Pinson, Orlando Cepeda, and Bill White—were all black. The top five in stolen bases—Wills, me, Pinson, Frank Robinson, and Willie Davis—were all black. Ken Boyer of the Cardinals was the only white player among the top five in RBIs, Frank Howard of the Dodgers was the only white player among the top five in home runs, and Dick Groat—who beat me out for second place in the MVP voting behind Sandy Koufax—was the only white player among the top ten in batting average.

The early to mid sixties were probably the peak years of the black ballplayers. I suppose it had to do with trends and choices and Jackie Robinson. There were some great black basketball players—Bill Russell, Elgin Baylor, Oscar Robertson—and some great black football players—Jim Brown, Bobby Mitchell, Big Daddy Lipscomb—but baseball was the sport that was attracting the most black athletes. We were the Jackie Robinson generation. By 1963, black players were leading the National League in so many things that it made you wonder what the quality of baseball was like before Jackie joined it—and what the quality of Negro League baseball was like before Jackie left it.

The same year, Commissioner Ford Frick made a statement that expressed his view of integration: "Baseball evolved in slavery days. Colored people did not have a chance to play it then, and so were late in developing proficiency. It was more than fifty years after the introduction of baseball before colored people in the United States had a chance to play it. Consequently, it was another fifty years before they, by natural process, arrived at the stage where they were important in the organized baseball picture. And as quickly as they attained that importance, organized baseball began to show an interest in them." What I don't understand is, if it took us fifty years to pick up a bat and another fifty years to learn how to swing it, by what miracle did we come to dominate the National League after only ten or fifteen more? The way I saw it, the commissioner's remarks were an insult to Satchel Paige and Josh Gibson and every black ballplayer who came before Jackie.

I'm not sure what prompted Frick's statement, but racial issues in general were at a head that summer. In the hometown of Bobby Bragan and Willie Mays, Sheriff Bull Connor commanded Birmingham firemen to turn their hoses on civil rights demonstraters. Late in August, Martin Luther King led a quarter of a million people on the March on Washington and delivered his greatest speech, "I Have A Dream." Eighteen days later, a bomb went off at the Sixteenth Street Baptist Church in Birmingham and killed four little girls who had arrived for Sunday school. I remember hitting a home run in St. Louis that day.

I can't say it was because of the bombs and the Bull Connors that black players tore up the National League in 1963, but I can't say it wasn't, either. The national climate called attention to our color, and we knew we were being watched. There weren't many places in America where blacks and whites worked alongside each other, there were fewer places where the black man could make more money, and there were no places more visible than the big-league ball fields. We had targets on our backs and two things on our side: each other to lean on and our Louisville Sluggers to swing. So we leaned hard and swung from the heels, and there was hell to pay if you hung a curve ball.

Outside the park, I got involved in the civil rights movement in the little ways that I could, endorsing sympathetic candidates and reading James Baldwin and Dr. King. Baldwin wrote about the waiting and more waiting that American black people had done for generations, which made me think about my parents waiting and waiting back in Mobile. I agreed with him that the waiting period was over. I also agreed with Dr. King about passive resistance, but I wasn't sure that I was capable of it. I wasn't able to participate in civil rights marches because of baseball, but I'm not sure I would have been much good in one, anyway. I don't think I could have been passive in that situation. Getting kicked by a second baseman was part of baseball, as I saw it, but getting kicked by a policeman might have been more than I could tolerate.

My kinship with the movement had to come through baseball, which was why it was so important to me to see our team
under one roof in Bradenton. As it turned out, though, we stayed
together at the Twilight Motel for only one year, because in 1963
the Braves moved their spring training operation across Florida
to West Palm Beach. Mr. Perini was in the process of building up
an entire side of the city—I remember him taking me around in
his car and telling me what he was going to do with all that
swampland—and a major part of the development was a new
spring facility for the Braves. Before the 1963 season, he sold the
Braves to a group of Chicago businessmen, but part of the deal
was that the team would train on his swampland.

As happy as the black players were to be out of Bradenton,
the racial climate wasn't a whole lot different in West Palm
Beach. The ballpark still had a colored section, and black fans
had to walk through a hole in the outfield fence to get in. But
President Kennedy had a summer home in Palm Beach—I had
the privilege of meeting him when he was down there—and he
had been very visible in support of Martin Luther King, so it
wouldn't have looked very good for the hotels to discriminate
right in front of the President's nose. The whole team stayed at
the Howard Johnson.

Moving in with the team made things much easier for the
black players. It meant that we didn't have to worry about catching cabs and getting our bags to the bus and all of the things that
the white players took for granted. It meant that we could concentrate more on playing the game. In effect, it eliminated a major
competitive disadvantage that the black players had been oper-
ating under, because you can't overestimate the value of mental
preparation in baseball.

The mental aspects of hitting were especially vital to me. I
was strictly a guess hitter, which meant that I had to have a full
knowledge of every pitcher I came up against and develop a
strategy for hitting him. My method was to identify the pitches
that a certain pitcher had and then eliminate all but one or two
and wait for them. Usually, I would wait for his best pitch, because I knew he would use it sooner or later. For instance, Bob
Gibson was a fastball pitcher, so—depending on the situation—I

might eliminate the slider, curve, and change-up and just wait for a fastball. With a pitcher as good as Gibson, though, it wasn't enough just to guess the pitch. That much was obvious. The trick was to guess location. So I might wait for a fastball low and inside. If I got it, I hit it. If I didn't get it, I had to try to adjust. One thing I had in my favor was that I had strong hands and wrists, which enabled me to adjust quickly if I guessed wrong. Another advantage I had—and all good hitters have—was my eyesight. Sometimes, I could read the pitcher's grip on the ball before he ever released it and be able to tell what pitch he was throwing. On the other hand, the pitchers I had the most trouble with were the ones who had a peculiar release point or varied it. I always had difficulty with Curt Simmons, because he would put the ball behind his back and then pound his leg with his glove, and you never knew where the ball was coming from. To me, hitting was a matter of knowing where the ball was going to be and when.

A few years ago, I was at a baseball banquet sitting next to Keith Hernandez and Mike Schmidt, and Hernandez asked me how I'd gone about hitting sidearm pitchers. I had a lot of luck with sidearm pitchers—Drysdale was one—because I knew where the ball was coming from. I explained that hitting a side-armer is the same as hitting a pitcher with a conventional release point—you just pick out the spot where the ball will be coming from and watch it. I told Hernandez to find a spot on the pitcher's body to focus on and then watch the ball, watch the ball. I don't know what the problem was—maybe the coaches today are so concerned with mechanics that they don't teach hitters to watch the pitchers—but Hernandez and Schmidt both looked at me like I was crazy. They said, "What are you talking about?" I couldn't believe they didn't understand what I was telling them. I said, "Man, if you guys are that goddamn dumb, I don't know how you ever hit the ball." The thing is, I know those guys were smart hitters. That's what confounds me. I guess it shows that every good hitter has his own method. If nothing else, it convinced me that I would never make a batting coach—at least not these days.

Because of the way I waited for the pitcher's pitch, I often hit good pitchers the best. The good pitcher was the one who threw the ball where he was supposed to throw it. If Marichal wanted to throw a fastball low and inside, he threw it low and inside, and if I was expecting a fastball low and inside, I was right on it. A lot of times I would hit a home run off a good pitch and when I got back to the dugout my teammates would say, "Man, that was a wicked pitch, how did you hit that thing?" Hell, it was what I was looking for. I never expected a pitcher to make a bad pitch. I respected the pitcher. Actually, I hated pitchers. I never talked to the other team's pitchers on the field before the game, because I didn't want to like them. But I respected the job they did, and I expected them to make good pitches. As a result, I might pop up a hanging curve ball, because I was looking for a good curve ball. That was why I liked hitting against the Dodgers so much. Guys like Koufax and Drysdale and Podres knew exactly what they were going to do with the ball, and if I could just think along with them, I was ready. I guess the respect was mutual, because Koufax and Drysdale were the ones who gave me the nickname Bad Henry.

In large part, my success against good pitchers was a matter of confidence. Without trying to boast, I can say that never once in my big-league career did I feel overmatched by a pitcher. I used to tell the writers that I felt I had an advantage at the plate because I had my bat—actually, Del Crandall's bat—and all the pitcher had was that little ball. They chuckled when I said that, but I meant it. I always thought that if I lost that mental edge, I would lose my special ability as a hitter. And my mental edge was knowing that I could hit a good pitcher's best pitch.

I have to admit, though, that some pitchers worked me over pretty good with a certain pitch before I started getting even. The thing I had on my side was patience. Patience—which is really the art of waiting—is something you pick up pretty naturally when you grow up black in Alabama. When you wait all your life for respect and equality and a seat in the front of the bus, it's nothing to wait a little while for a slider inside. Johnny Podres had a great change-up that gave me fits, and one game I made up my mind that I would wait as long as I had to until I got a change-

up from him. The first time, he threw me a fastball and I took it
for a strike, then he threw me two more and I took them for
strikes. The same thing happened again the next time. He struck
me out twice and I never even swung the bat. The third time, I
was still waiting for the change-up, and when he finally threw it,
I hit it over the left-field fence. As I recall, it seems like it might
have won the game.

> *Forget statistics. It's just the conviction of most managers that
> Aaron wins more games than any guy since maybe Hornsby in
> his prime. One night last August, for example, we concentrated
> on stopping him. I mean, we gave it the works. We gave him
> nothing but very bad pitches. We jammed him and dusted him.
> We worked every trick to pick him off base. We got rough on
> him when he slid. So he winds up with two singles and a home
> run, stole a base, robbed us of a triple with a helluva catch,
> accounted for four runs and beat us from here to Toledo. More
> times than anyone else, he's made me wish I wasn't a manager.*
> —Walter Alston, Sport, 1963

I must have been one of the few guys who hurt the Dodgers,
because by 1963 they had clearly become the class of the National League. Koufax was devastating. He wouldn't test your
manhood the way Drysdale would—Koufax was too nice a guy
to throw at anybody—but he would challenge you physically
with his speed and confidence. One day he pitched against us
with a blister on his hand, and we knew we would see nothing
but fastballs. He beat us something like 2-1 in thirteen innings.
With the pitching the Dodgers had, they could afford to play one-
run baseball, and with Tommy Davis driving in Maury Wills
night after night, they mastered it. It had been a long time since
baseball had seen a player like Wills, but we would be seeing a
lot more like him. When the Cardinals caught up with the
Dodgers in 1964, it was largely because they had their own ver-
sion of Wills in Lou Brock.

The National League was turning over in those years, and it
was turning over on the Braves. We didn't have the speed that

the Dodgers and Cardinals had, and when Spahn finally lost it, we couldn't match Koufax or Gibson. It happened all of a sudden with Spahn. We should have been expecting it, because he was forty-three years old, but he had been so good for so long that we couldn't feature him doing anything but winning. He finally hit the wall in 1964. He still looked like himself, with the fancy windup and the big leg kick, but there was nothing left on the ball. He went from 23-7 to 6-13. The sad part about it was that we might have won the pennant in 1964 if he'd been even a shadow of the old Spahn, because, after years of searching for young pitchers, we found Tony Cloninger and Denny Lemaster. We finished fifth, but only five games behind the Cardinals. That was the season the Phillies led the race all the way, then collapsed in the last few weeks. St. Louis got hot and finally beat out the Phillies and Reds on the last day of the season, but the pennant was sitting there for anybody to claim. I shouldn't imply that our failure fell on Spahn's shoulders, though, because I didn't have one of my better years, either. I hit .328 but only had twenty-four home runs. A little more power from me might well have made the difference, because we were starting to put together another potent lineup. Four other guys on the Braves hit at least twenty homers that year—Mathews, Torre, a bonus-baby shortstop named Denis Menke, and a young outfielder named Rico Carty.

Carty was a strapping, rugged guy from the Dominican Republic who called himself "the beeg boy." He didn't speak much English and needed someone to take him under his wing when he came up, so I roomed with him his rookie year. His numbers of 1964 almost matched mine, and it looked as though we'd be fielding a pretty fair outfield for years to come. Between Rico and me in center field was Lee Maye, a slashing left-handed hitter who always wanted to fight somebody. We used to ask Lee where he buried his dead. But deep down, Maye was a lover, and he kept us entertained by singing Motown music. He'd done some singing with the Platters before they started making records.

With the exception of Spahn, Mathews, and me, we had become a team of kids—due in part, no doubt, to the fact that young players come cheaper than veterans. The Braves were hurting financially. Crowds at County Stadium had dropped off so severely that it looked as though the city couldn't support us anymore. All indications were that we would be moving to Atlanta in 1965. John McHale even moved his office there after the season.

But Milwaukee wasn't going to give up that easily. The city and county fought the move, led by a local politician named Eugene Grobschmidt, the chairman of the county board. It became a legal battle, Milwaukee versus the Braves. For the players —and for the fans—it was horrible to see our team and our city going at each other in court, like a messy, bitter divorce. We loved Milwaukee, and none of us wanted to move, but it was hard for us to tell the good guys from the bad guys. Grobschmidt, the county's front man, was pushy and unpolished. The man representing the Braves was a mannerly, deep-voiced fellow whose path I would cross again in the future, an eastern attorney named Bowie Kuhn.

Grobschmidt managed to get a court injunction that kept the team in Milwaukee for the 1965 season, but everybody knew the move was inevitable. You could feel it all over town. As their personal crusade against Atlanta, local restaurants and bars even stopped serving Coca-Cola, which is headquartered in Atlanta. There was no other way—no positive way, at least—for the people to vent their emotions, because they weren't about to support a team that they thought was deserting them. They stayed away from the ballpark in droves. The local banks took our pocket schedules off their counters. It was really an awkward, peculiar time. On the official level, Milwaukee was trying to keep us around, but the people there wanted nothing to do with us. And it certainly didn't help the situation when the Braves sold Spahn to the Mets.

When they got rid of me, I'm sure the plan was to go to Atlanta with virtually a rookie club. They could save a lot of money for the move that way—Hank and Mathews were about the only veterans who made the move. It was a terrible thing for it all to

end that way, because we had something special in Milwaukee. I tell you, any ballplayer missed something if he didn't play in Milwaukee during those thirteen years. It was something else. If you wanted a doctor or lawyer, you had to call the ballpark.
—Warren Spahn

We actually had a contending team in 1965, although nobody in Milwaukee seemed to care. Nobody seemed to care, either, about the record Mathews and I set that year—the most home runs by teammates. First, we broke the National League record of 745 held by Duke Snider and Gil Hodges. I missed the first three weeks of the season because of an operation on my ankle, and right after I got back in the lineup, Mathews hit the homer that tied the record. Then, in the second game of a doubleheader against the Phillies, I connected for a long one off Bo Belinsky to break it. A lot of two-man records are phony, because one man carries most of the load, but at the time we passed Snider and Hodges, Eddie had 378 homers and I had 368.

Nobody bothered to look up the major-league record at the time, because they figured we were still far behind Ruth and Lou Gehrig. But later in the year, after Mathews and I passed 800 homers, Bob Wolf of the *Milwaukee Journal* did some checking and found that we had already passed Ruth and Gehrig. Their record had been listed incorrectly at 870. When it was broken down in terms of how many they actually hit when they were teammates, the real figure was 793. Before we were done, Eddie and I had 863 home runs together. Eddie has said that our record is his proudest accomplishment. It makes me proud that he thinks so. I was lucky to have Eddie for a teammate all those years. There's no doubt that he made me a better player.

There were times when Eddie hit behind me in the lineup and times when I hit behind Eddie. He was hitting ahead of me against the Mets one night in 1965 when we found ourselves up against the man we'd been playing behind for more than a decade. For about as long as I had known them, Spahn and Eddie had argued back and forth about what would happen if they ever faced each other in a game. This was the time to find out. The bases were loaded, so there was no room to fool around. Eddie didn't. He walked up, dug in, and hit a grand slam. It was a big shot for the Braves, but there wasn't a lot of backslapping. We all felt for Spahn. He was forty-four years old, and he just didn't have it anymore. When I came up next, I couldn't bring myself to go after him. I won't say that I ever deliberately made an out, but I will say that I didn't have the heart to get a base hit that night against Warren Spahn. I just had too much respect for the man as a pitcher. I think I popped up.

On the other hand, the pitcher that I desperately wanted to hit was Curt Simmons of the Cardinals. Simmons used to drive me crazy with his herky-jerky delivery and his floating change of pace. One night in St. Louis I decided to just wait for the change-up, and when I finally got it I double-hitched my swing, took a big step up to meet the ball, and knocked it onto the pavilion roof in right field. I was on my way to first base when Bob Uecker, who was catching at the time, started jumping around and screaming at the home-plate umpire, Chris Pelekoudas. Before I knew it, Pelekoudas was calling me out for stepping out of the batter's box. Of course, Bragan went berserk and was thrown out of the game. Somehow, I managed to stay in the game, but to this day, I believe that was a home run. I'm sure Pelekoudas never doubted that he was right, and I won't swear to you that I didn't step over the line of the batter's box, but it was nothing that I or other hitters hadn't done before. Really, I blame the whole thing on that damn Uecker.

I hit thirty-two homers that year anyway, but the sensation of our team was Tony Cloninger, who won twenty-four games and looked like he was going to be a superstar. He and a twenty-one-year-old lefthander named Wade Blasingame kept us close to the top of the league for most of the year, and we were within half a game of the Dodgers as late as the last week of August. But even a hot pennant race didn't seem to interest the people of Milwaukee. They were still too proud and bitter to come to the ballpark, and Grobschmidt only made it worse. At one point, he accused Bragan of deliberately losing games to drive the fans away. That was about the worst thing he could say to a baseball man like

Bobby. They had an ugly exchange in the newspapers, then went to breakfast together and straightened it out. But that didn't bring the fans back. Our final attendance for the year was 550,000—a quarter of what it had been just eight years before. There were only a few thousand people in the park when I hit a home run off the Phillies' Ray Culp a couple of days before the season ended. It was the last home run that Milwaukee would see for a while. We finished the season in fifth place and never returned.

People in Milwaukee still haven't gotten over the tragedy of the Braves leaving. I know I haven't. What the Braves and Milwaukee did together for baseball was legendary. The sociological ramifications of a baseball team in a city is a subject that fascinates me, and I don't think there was ever a team that did more for a city than the Braves did for Milwaukee. And it worked both ways. It's hard to say exactly why it stopped working, but I can say that the Braves were not aggressive marketers. And by saying that, I'm being kind. Very, very kind.—Milwaukee Brewers president Bud Selig

We were getting great attendance for a lot of years, but even then, our ticket, concession, and parking prices were very low. When we were drawing two million people, it was equivalent to attendance revenues of about one million. When the attendance dropped off, it became a situation we had to deal with. We would have kept the team in Milwaukee if somebody had stepped forward to buy it. We never wanted to move the Braves, and we certainly didn't buy them with the thought of moving them. Most of us lived on the north side of Chicago, and we wanted to be able to go to the games. That was our main purpose. We had tried to buy the White Sox for that reason. We had a minority interest in them before we bought the Braves, but couldn't buy the rest from Chuck Comiskey's sisters. The thing is, we were baseball fans, and we wanted a team nearby that we could enjoy. We weren't looking to move to Atlanta or anywhere.—former Braves owner Bill Bartholomay

When the Braves moved from Boston to Milwaukee in 1953, it was the first time since the early part of the century that a major-league team had left one city for another. But as long as the Red Sox and Ted Williams were around, the Braves were going to be a distant number two in Boston, so they did the natural thing. They moved to a town where they were second to nothing, except maybe beer. It was perfect. The fans of Milwaukee couldn't believe how lucky they were, and, as players, we felt even luckier. We thought we were playing in the best town in the world. Then, thirteen years after John Quinn passed out those caps with M's on them, we became the first team ever to leave a city without baseball. It seemed unthinkable that it could happen in Milwaukee. Not with those fans. Not with our team.

To this day, whenever I'm in Milwaukee, which is often, I'm reminded that the people there still haven't gotten over the Braves leaving. If it helps, they should know that the players haven't either.

8

They called it "the city too busy to hate." It was, at
any rate, a busy town, and in the context of other American cities of the same latitude, comparatively chummy. Despite
its sense of brotherhood, however, the issue of race was so pre-
ponderant in Atlanta as to dominate its very slogan by implication alone. The object of the hate that the city was allegedly too
busy to manifest was, of course, its black members, who were
numerous enough to someday elect mayors.

Atlanta's black community was the brightest and busiest in
all of America. By the mid-1960s, Atlanta had become the center
of black action and thought, a development that was fostered, in
large part, by the presence of the Southern Christian Leadership
Conference, over which Martin Luther King presided, and more
historically by the cluster of colleges that made up Atlanta University. W. E. B. Du Bois had taught and philosophized there,
setting the tone for the rally of ideas that necessarily preceded
King and the modern movement. Du Bois was one of the first to
challenge the conventional wisdom of Booker T. Washington,
who in 1895 advised an attentive black audience at the Cotton
States Exposition in Atlanta, "When your head is in the lion's
mouth, use your hand to pet him."

The scholarship of the black professors did not exempt them
from the sweeping illiteracy laws of the 1940s that denied Georgia blacks the right to vote. But by 1961, all of Atlanta's polling
places and public institutions had been integrated and the city
was moving forward on every conceivable front, earnestly pressing its mission as the capital of the New South. In many ways,
Atlanta had become a virtual city-state within Georgia, as at-
tested by the fact that in a mayoral vote it rejected the notorious
arch-segregationist and future governor, Lester Maddox, in favor
of the more temperate and distinguished Ivan Allen—albeit by a
slim margin. Allen represented an acute departure from the old-
boy stereotype that for so long had willfully administered the

South in partnership with ubiquitous companion Jim Crow. Atlanta's new white-haired mayor actually testified in Washington
on behalf of civil rights and boldly stood his ground in the eye of
a race riot just blocks away from the ballpark that he was instru-
mental in building.

Atlanta Stadium was a vital part of Allen's agenda and remains a salient feature of his legacy. It was constructed before
the Braves were a rumor, and it was the magnet that drew Atlanta into the big leagues. Once it had a stadium, Atlanta was
all the things that Milwaukee wasn't anymore—most promi-
nently, an aspiring city that was the focal point of a thousand
satellite towns. There was no Minneapolis that would steal Alabama from the Braves, no Chicago that would take away Tennessee. The radios of the South had been set for countless summers
on the Cincinnati Reds and St. Louis Cardinals, teams that
played in cities too far away to compete with Atlanta's commut-
ers. On top of it all, Coca-Cola provided an awesome advertising
base.

The only thing Atlanta lacked was baseball tradition, although it claimed Ty Cobb by territorial rights and was proud of
its minor-league Crackers. It knew ballplayers. It just didn't know
black ballplayers, having never, ever, seen one make it to first
base in the Southern League. Such was the local custom.

The bottom line was that the white men who owned the
Braves couldn't stay away from Atlanta, and the black men who
played for the Braves could have managed it rather easily. They
knew about Dr. King and the New South, but they knew what
they knew, too: For all the Dr. Kings and catchy slogans, Atlanta
was still Georgia, rednecks still had each other, and when push
came to shove, a black man was still the wrong damn color.
Hank Aaron, for one, had played ball in Georgia before.

◆   ◆   ◆

The first time I took batting practice in Atlanta-Fulton
County Stadium, I knew that my career was headed in a new

direction. Atlanta was the highest city in the major leagues, as well as the hottest, and if you could get the ball into the air, there was a good chance that it wouldn't come down in the playing field. Even in the last years in Milwaukee, I was still a line-drive hitter who liked to use the whole ballpark, but in Atlanta the way to use the ballpark was to take advantage of the atmosphere. I changed my batting style immediately, no longer trying to pounce on the ball and whip it in any direction but turning and pulling it toward the seats in left field.

Of course, I wasn't the only one who picked this up, nor was I the first to put one over the fence. We played an exhibition game against Detroit before the season started, and my brother Tommie had the honor of breaking the home run seal on the stadium. Then, in the first official game, Joe Torre knocked two balls out of the park.

I don't know if I had ever wanted to hit a home run as badly as I did that night. As much as I'd loved Milwaukee, and as warm as the fans of Milwaukee had been to me, I wanted things to be a little different in the new city. This time, I was a charter member of the local team, and I saw an opportunity to secure an important place in the community. I also knew that, as a black player, I would be on trial in Atlanta, and I needed a decisive way to win over the white people before they thought of a reason to hate me. And I believed that the way to do all of that was with home runs. What's more, Eddie Mathews was no longer the hitter that he had been, and I felt responsible for taking up the slack. There was every reason for me to turn my attention to home runs in 1966. With the new park and the new city and my own maturity—I was thirty-two years old and no longer the skinny kid who was all wrists and forearms—it was time to give up the idea of hitting .400 and put the ball in the air. It was like starting over, and on Opening Night I wanted to start over with style. I wanted to hit a home run for Atlanta and for myself and, ultimately, for Tony Cloninger.

It didn't take long to realize also that we were playing for an entire section of the country. The biggest cheer on Opening Night came when they flashed a message on the scoreboard: "April 12,

1861: First Shots Fired on Fort Sumter . . . April 12, 1966: The South Rises Again." I'd never played in front of so many Southerners before—50,000 in the stands on a cold night. Except for a few crackers, the crowd was polite and well dressed, and it reminded the veterans—that is, Mathews and me—of what County Stadium in Milwaukee used to be like. On top of that, Cloninger was doing a great imitation of Warren Spahn. He held the Pirates to one run through nine innings, the problem being that we had nothing more than a solo homer by Torre. Beagan kept asking Cloninger if he wanted to come out of the game, but Cloninger was a tough guy from North Carolina and he wasn't leaving under his own power. He kept pitching and pitching until the thirteenth inning, when Willie Stargell hit a ball that floated over my head and dropped into the seats. There was a man on base, and Torre's second homer in the bottom of the inning only made the final score 3-2. I felt helpless watching that ball go over my head. I was supposed to be the guy at home plate and Stargell was supposed to be the guy watching the game-winning homer go over his head. The only memorable thing I did that night was to steal the first base in Atlanta Stadium.

Before long, though, I found myself hitting home runs as I'd never hit them before. Early in the season at Philadelphia, against Bo Belinsky, I hit one onto the roof of Connie Mack Stadium for the four hundredth of my career. It came right around the time that Willie Mays was overtaking Mel Ott's National League record of 511 home runs, which led the writers to ask me if I thought I'd ever get to 500. I couldn't imagine why I wouldn't. The fact was, the only player to hit more home runs than me by the age of thirty-two was Mathews. Publicly, I still said that my main goal was 3,000 hits, but the way the home runs were coming, I had a pretty good idea that I'd be up there with Willie before too many years went by—especially playing in this new ballpark. By the first day of summer, my home run total was at twenty-four, which tied a major-league record. My batting average was down from previous years, but I felt I had successfully made the transition into a power hitter.

I was not as successful, though, at making the transition into a popular player. Part of it, no doubt, was the fact that I was black, but I have to admit I didn't help myself much in terms of public relations. Before the Braves moved, I had talked openly about not wanting to come to Atlanta, and Barbara felt the same way. It wasn't Atlanta that we objected to, though; it was the whole idea of leaving Milwaukee and moving our family back to the South.

We changed our minds about Atlanta when we visited and found neighborhoods that were suitable, although segregated. We also figured it would be easier to talk Mama into letting Lary live with us if we weren't so far away from Mobile. I'm not sure Mama intended to let him go, but after we got settled in Atlanta I brought Lary to the house and just never took him back.

We moved into a ranch house on two acres in southwest Atlanta, which had one of the nicest black communities in the country. But we couldn't be completely comfortable. Atlanta wouldn't let us. It was made perfectly clear to us from the very beginning that we weren't in Milwaukee anymore. There was often a hate letter or two in the mail, and I was always concerned about Barbara and the kids being abused when they went to the ballpark. If nothing else, they would hear me being called some of the same names that had burned my ears thirteen years before in the Sally League.

> We'd sit in the stands and hear Aaron being called "nigger" and "jigaboo." One time a guy sitting behind me was yelling about "nigger" this and "nigger" that. I didn't say anything, but I went out to get a hamburger and made sure I put some extra mustard on it. The next time that guy said "nigger," I turned around and put that hamburger right in his face.—Barbara Aaron

One day Barbara was pulling into the Braves' parking lot with her sister-in-law, Rubye Lucas, and the police guard wouldn't let her through the gate. I don't know why, other than the fact she was black. She used that gate all the time, but this must have been a new policeman who didn't know who she was—or didn't care. He used some very abusive language, which Barbara wasn't about to take. She tried to drive on through the gate, and when she did that, the officer pulled his pistol. The incident got a lot of publicity, and Barbara was charged with failing to obey a police officer. But when the real story started coming out and Ivan Allen interceded, the charges were dropped.

The ironic part of it all was that Barbara's brother and Rubye's husband, Bill Lucas, had been working so hard to keep racial incidents from occurring at the ballpark. After playing in the Braves' minor-league system and then spending a hitch in the army, Bill—actually, the family called him Joe—had worked for the team in Waycross, overseeing the barracks. His boss was Dick Cecil, who, when the Braves moved to Atlanta, was put in charge of handling the transition. One of the first things Cecil did when he arrived in Atlanta was hire Bill to be a liaison with the black community.

When we were setting the whole thing up, we looked at the situation in Atlanta and said, let's face it, we're moving into a community that's more than 40 percent black. What's more, they had built the stadium in an area that had been designated as urban renewal, and there were a lot of hard feelings about it in the black community. We came in on a negative note in the black community, and we had to spend a lot of time there convincing the people that we wanted to be good citizens. I needed Luke to help me do that. He and I did it all, working quite a bit with the mayor, Ivan Allen. We put in a recreation area that the Braves paid for, started a Good Neighbor program, all sorts of things. It was a very interesting time in Atlanta. One of the first things we attended was a Peace Prize banquet honoring Dr. King. He and Andy Young loved sports and were out at the ballpark quite a bit. We worked with a lot of the black leaders in the city, and we made a conscious decision to integrate our personnel across the board. From the start, the percentage of our ushers and ticket takers was almost 60-40 black. We decided that if Atlanta was going to be big-league, we had to be big-league in every way.—Dick Cecil

The Braves were successful in maintaining good relations with the black community. But even so, the percentage of black fans at the ballpark—like all the ballparks in the major leagues—was very low. And as much as I wanted the city on my side, I just couldn't bring myself to be buddy-buddy with a crowd of white Southerners—especially after what I'd seen in our first few months in Atlanta. If people thought I was aloof, I suppose they were right. I never refused an autograph, but I never went out of my way to sign one, either. It quickly became obvious that I wasn't destined to be Atlanta's fair-haired boy. When the games were over, I dressed as quickly as I could and hurried home, which meant that I didn't sit around the clubhouse telling stories for the writers. I wasn't their favorite anyway, and I would have felt phony trying to be. The most influential columnist in town was Furman Bisher, and I knew where he stood from *the Saturday Evening Post* article he had written about me ten years before. With that as the precedent, I figured that the less was written about me, the better I would look.

Besides, the fans had Mack Jones and Rico Carty. Jones was popular because he was a native of Atlanta and had his own radio show, and Carty because he craved it. Rico was always signing autographs and throwing baseballs to the kids and playing up to the reporters. The players saw a different side of Carty, but Atlanta loved him. And everything else aside, there's no denying he was a gifted hitter, although personally I had much more respect for the other Dominican on our team, Felipe Alou. Alou came from a large family and was one of three brothers who played in the big leagues—Matty and Jesus were the others. Somehow, he had gotten interested in scuba diving, and I can still see Joe Torre walking around our clubhouse in Felipe's scuba gear. All three of the Alous came up with the Giants, and Felipe had some good seasons with them, but nothing like the one he had for us in 1966, when he led the league in hits, runs, and total bases.

Three of us—Alou, Torre, and I—hit more than thirty home runs in 1966, but it was the same old story for the Braves. We finished above .500 for the fourteenth straight year—since the first season in Milwaukee—but didn't have the pitching to contend seriously for the pennant. Cloninger seemed to have lost something, and at times it seemed that maybe they ought to make him an outfielder. In a game against the Giants that year, he hit two grand slams—something I never saw another player do, much less a pitcher.

The way all of us were banging the ball out of the park, it wasn't long at all before Atlanta became known as the home run capital of baseball. That was true enough—the ball carried there like nowhere else—but playing in Atlanta wasn't exactly a Sunday picnic. It was so hot and humid that a player could wear himself down by the Fourth of July. A few years later, when the league was split into divisions and the Braves were put into the West, we had to travel much farther and longer than other teams. To hold out over the long season, a player in Atlanta had to learn to take things slowly and pace himself. I suppose I was the role model in that respect.

I think the heat got to all of us that first summer, though. I tailed off and finished with forty-four home runs again, which was still enough to lead the league. I also led with 127 RBIs, but only batted .279. It was the first time in six years I had failed to hit .300, and I guess it made me a little testy, because late that year I got myself thrown out of a game for the first and only time in my career. Bob Veale, an enormous and very fast lefthander, was pitching for the Pirates, and Tony Venzon called me out on two pitches that didn't resemble strikes, in my estimation. After strike three, I just laid down my bat by home plate and said, "If you're going to take the bat out of my hands, here it is." It was the eleventh inning, and I think the game was over after one more out, so I didn't miss any playing time.

Normally I didn't say much on the field, but I opened my mouth one other time in 1966, with more gratifying results: I finally got even with Bob Uecker for the home run he took from me in 1965. It was after I hit a little pop fly down the first-base line against the Phillies. Uecker, Larry Jackson, and Harvey Kuenn all converged on it, and as I ran by, I screamed, "I got it!" I guess they figured it was one of them screaming, and all three of them backed off. It was one of my better singles.

Off the field, I was beginning to speak out more often. I had made comments in the past about the importance of having some black managers: There was an article in *Sport* magazine to that effect in 1965, in which I named Jackie Robinson and Bill White as the best candidates to be the first black manager and several others also qualified—Bill Bruton, Junior Gilliam, Ernie Banks, Willie Mays, and myself. In previous years, I had also stated my objection to the fact that black players—Negroes was the term we used then—were seldom allowed to remain in the major leagues as fringe players. But these complaints were fairly common. It wasn't until 1966 that I crossed the line and became an agitator.

One afternoon in Chicago, a reporter from *Jet* magazine approached me at Wrigley Field and asked if he could have an interview for a story on me. I don't remember what I was angry about, but something must have been under my skin because I told him to come back after the game for a real story. We went out afterwards, and I proceeded to run down the whole list of ways in which baseball discriminated against black players—in salary, longevity, managing, the front office, everything. The reporter's name was Roscoe Harrison, and when he returned to his office with notes from the interview, the editors ripped up the cover they had already prepared and replaced it with the one that said: "Hank Aaron Blasts Racism In Baseball." A few days later, Monte Irvin was appointed to a newly created position in the commissioner's office.

It seemed like I was in a foul mood for most of 1966. I didn't like it when Bobby Bragan was fired midway through the season, replaced by Billy Hitchcock, and I was very unhappy when Paul Richards took over as general manager. Richards got on my bad side right away, when he walked in and announced that everybody on the team was trade bait, including Hank Aaron. I was prejudiced against him from then on, and it only got worse when he traded Eddie Mathews in the offseason. What made the Mathews trade so intolerable was that he didn't even tell Eddie about it. To me, that was vintage Richards. He was the kind of guy who would call you into his office and talk to you as he looked out the window, as if you weren't really there. I couldn't believe it when I saw in the newspaper on New Year's Eve that he'd traded Mathews to Houston. Eddie found out about the deal from a reporter. He was devastated, and so was I. This was a guy who had played more games at third base than anybody in the history of baseball and who shared a record for most home runs with one team. He was the only Brave to play in Boston, Milwaukee, and Atlanta. As far as I was concerned, he was Mr. Brave. I'm not a man who forgives easily, and I haven't forgiven Paul Richards for trading Eddie Mathews the way he did. After that, I felt like he might as well trade me, too. It might be my personal prejudice talking, but I've always believed that it took the Braves a long time to recover from Paul Richards.

It was an eventful offseason that year. Before Eddie was traded, I had gone on a tour of Vietnam with Joe Torre, Stan Musial, Harmon Killebrew, Brooks Robinson, and announcer Mel Allen. It was an eye-opening experience for somebody like me, who had never given a lot of thought to war. We watched as an American helicopter sank two Vietcong sampans. Later on, I thought my own life was in danger when we visited an officer's club. While we were there a WAC came over to me and started talking, and after a few minutes, we sat down on the couch to talk some more. No sooner did we sit down than a foreign soldier—I think he must have been Australian, because I heard they were the meanest guys over there—came up to me and told me to get the hell away from the white woman. I knew it was a mistake to mess with the guy, but at that moment I didn't care. I said, "Look, I didn't come all the way over here to die, but if I have to, I will." The other guys broke it up, which was fortunate for me, I'm sure.

But not all my memories of that trip are violent. It was rewarding to do something for the servicemen, and I was also able to develop a deeper friendship with my roommate, Stan Musial, who, for my money, was the greatest gentleman in the game. I used to tease Musial all the time about being a millionaire, and he would just laugh and deny it. Finally, when I ran into him at a baseball function a few years ago, he came up to me, shook my hand, and said, "Hank, Hank, I finally made it!"

After we got back from Vietnam, we were all invited to visit

Lyndon Johnson at the White House. He was the first of three Presidents I would meet there. It made me feel like I was finally in tall cotton, which was soon to get taller: A few months later, I signed my first $100,000 contract. Bill Bartholomay handled the negotiations himself and increased my salary by $30,000 over 1966, putting me in the company of Mays, Mantle, Koufax, Drysdale, and Frank Robinson, who, in his first year in the American League, had won the Triple Crown for the world champion Orioles. It seemed to me that hitting home runs paid off.

I didn't see it as clearly then as I do now, but I was changing fast, and it started when we moved to Atlanta. Atlanta changed me as a hitter and a person at the same time. It was as if I had spent the first twelve years of my career in fantasy land, and the real world made me hungrier and angrier than I had been as a young Milwaukee Brave. I wasn't content anymore to let other guys have all the fame and fortune. I wasn't even happy at home anymore. Barbara and I had drifted apart. There were things I wanted to accomplish in my profession, and she had her own agenda. I started spending more time away from the house, going out to bars with my teammates, drinking a little more, losing my innocence. In a strange way, it seemed that returning to the South took some of the boy from Mobile out of me and replaced it with a man who was weary of the way things were. I was tired of being invisible. I was the equal of any ballplayer in the world, damnit, and if nobody was going to give me my due, it was time to grab for it. It was still a long, long way away, but looking back, I suppose that first year or two in Atlanta was when I made up my mind that if I ever got close to Babe Ruth's record for home runs, it would be mine.

At that point, nobody had mentioned me in connection with the record. For years, everybody thought Mantle was the one who had a chance at it, and when Mays broke Ott's National League record, they started talking about Willie. Furman Bisher was the first one in Atlanta to write that I might have a chance to get there, but the very first time my name came up in connection with the record might have been when Oliver Kuechle, sports editor of the Milwaukee *Journal,* dropped it into a column in

June 1967, around the time I had a streak in which I hit home runs four days in a row against the Cardinals and Reds.

There were not very many good days in 1967, however—starting with the first, when we played Houston and Mathews beat us with a triple. That was a hard thing to digest—Eddie Mathews beating the Braves. When that happened, we didn't seem like the Braves anymore. It may or may not be a coincidence, but the year we traded Mathews was the first year we finished under .500 since the Braves moved to Milwaukee in 1953.

What made it worse was that in the absence of a guy like Eddie, who was a ballplayer's ballplayer and would do anything to win, we had a guy like Rico Carty, who was his own ballplayer and would do anything to boost his batting average. Carty was a big guy with plenty of power, but if he came up in the ninth inning with us down by a run, he'd be choking up on the bat trying to punch the ball into right field for a hit. Some of the guys on the team called him El-Chokee. One night in Houston, Don Wilson beat us with a no-hitter, which made me mad at Wilson, mad at myself—I had made the last out—and mad at Carty, who had loafed after a ball in left field and made Felipe Alou sprint all the way over from center to cover for him. On the plane to Los Angeles that night, Carty was playing cards two rows behind me when I heard him called me a "black slick." I stood up and asked him what he said, and he repeated it. The strange thing about Carty was that he was as dark-skinned as any of us, but he didn't consider himself black and would go around calling the black players "nigger" and other things. I wasn't in the mood for it that night, and a second later we were swinging at each other. Carty had been a boxer in the Dominican, and I don't know if he ducked or I just missed, but my fist went right by his head and put a hole in the luggage rack of the plane. Our teammates finally broke it up—I think there were three guys holding me—but then Carty rushed at me again with something in his hand. About that time, Billy Hitchcock came running back from the front of the plane. Hitchcock always smoked a pipe on the plane, and Pat Jarvis told me that he looked like a steam engine chugging back there to see what was going on. Nobody was hurt in the fight, but Jarvis had his shirt ripped trying to get between us, and the plane was rocking back and forth at 30,000 feet. The pilot got on the loudspeaker and told us to stay in our seats or he would have to land in Albuquerque, or wherever it was. It was a very regrettable incident.

I was fighting and feuding most of that season. The feud was with our announcer, Milo Hamilton. It started at a luncheon when the Pirates were in town and Milo introduced Roberto Clemente as the man who beat out Hank Aaron as the National League's All-Star right fielder. The fact of the matter was that Clemente, Mays, and I had been voted in as the starting outfielders, and I received the most votes. Clemente was truly a brilliant right fielder, and the manager, Walter Alston, asked me if I would move to left for the game. I was happy to do it, but I didn't appreciate Milo's insinuation that Clemente was the premier right fielder in the league. That was my turf. I also thought Milo's remarks were completely inappropriate considering that we both worked for the same employer, and I let him know about it. The next day, I went four-for-four against the Pirates with two two-run homers and threw out Clemente trying to go from first to third on a single. In the postgame interviews, I said, "When you're number two, you've got to try harder." A few days later I confronted Milo in our hotel in New York, and we nearly came to blows. The whole thing went on for a couple of years, and at one point *Newsweek* even wrote about it, calling it "a concentrated study in public feuding." Other people would tell me about things that Milo said on the air that I didn't appreciate, and I kept getting angrier. In one game in Atlanta, I singled to right field and watched Clemente pick up the ball. He had a habit of dropping his arm before he threw the ball back to the infield, and I waited for him to do that, then broke for second. I slid in before his throw got to the bag, and as I dusted myself off, I looked up to the radio booth and flipped Milo the bird. The situation had gotten out of hand. Finally, Bartholomay called a meeting for us to patch things up, but when Milo showed up with a lawyer, I walked out. Eventually, it blew over, because Milo and I had to do a lot of appearances together during the Ruth chase. I regret the whole episode, and I realize now that I should have let it ride from the beginning. Milo and I have become friends. I was deeply touched when he walked down the left-field line with me before a game one day in West Palm Beach and said he wanted me to be the first to know that he had leukemia. Fortunately, it was a mild form that he was able to survive.

One of the most important qualities I had as a player was the ability to play on despite what was happening in my personal life. I've noticed the same trait in other players who are driven like I was—Pete Rose, for instance. There were times during his career when Rose would have controversy coming at him from every side, and he would just keep hitting as if nothing affected him. Baseball is a game that requires concentration, and a ballplayer has to be able to block out all the extracurriculars. That's what I had to do all through the years of Carty and Milo and hard times at home. My motto was always to keep swinging. Whether I was in a slump or feeling badly or having troubles off the field, the only thing to do was keep swinging. Despite all the problems of 1967—there was also a fire at our house that year, which killed our poodle and destroyed many of my trophies—I managed to lead the league in home runs and runs scored and bring my average back over .300. It was a season I was proud of, except for the fact that the Braves had fallen deep into the second division.

Tony Cloninger's arm was all but shot at the age of twenty-six, the only consolation being that we turned to a knuckleball pitcher named Phil Niekro who led the league in ERA. The problem with Niekro was finding somebody to catch him, and for that, Richards acquired—would you believe it?—Bob Uecker. Actually, Uecker had been with us for a while in Milwaukee, and despite our little rivalry on the field, I enjoyed him. With Uecker around, at least we could lose laughing. He would make a joke about anything—even plane crashes: We would be coming in to land, and Uecker would pick up the microphone in the back of the plane and say something like, "This is the captain speaking. Please keep your seat belts fastened until the plane has hit the side of the terminal building and come to a complete stop."

When Uecker started making appearances on the "Tonight" show, I heard the same jokes he'd told in the plane and clubhouse twenty years earlier.

The same year Uecker joined us, Richards also traded for the Yankees' third baseman, Clete Boyer. I suppose that's one deal I have to give Richards credit for, because Clete Boyer was one of a kind. I never saw much of Brooks Robinson, except on television during the World Series, but I don't believe a man was ever born who could outplay Clete Boyer at third base. He was no Mathews at the bat, but his glove was pure magic. Boyer also brought a Yankee attitude to the Braves. He was a true Yankee in the tradition of Mickey Mantle and Whitey Ford and Billy Martin. They trained him well. I was amazed that Clete could play the way he did and lead the kind of lifestyle he led. He could be out on the town all night long, grab a couple of hours' sleep, and come to the park and make the greatest plays you've ever seen. As a fielder, he was practically perfect. He'd be out there taking ground balls before the game, and his rear end would be rubbing the ground. Nothing could get by that man. He was also one of the best friends I ever had in baseball, and I think he helped me loosen up a little bit, which was something I needed. We played together, drank together, and eventually got divorced together.

With teammates like Boyer and Uecker and Pat Jarvis—an old rodeo rider from Illinois whom we called Bulldog—I started running around with the white players for the first time in my career. Actually, I was in over my head a little bit, because those guys were major-league barhoppers. Boyer and Torre had their own bar called Pig Alley, which was pretty lively. The newspapers called us the Playboys of Peachtree, but I couldn't identify with that too closely. At heart, I was just a homebody in search of new perspectives.

As it turned out, perspective kicked me in the head in the spring of 1968, when I was walking down a street in Savannah with Bill Bartholomay. The date was April 4, and we had stopped in Savannah for an exhibition game on our way to Atlanta. It was a casual time, and I didn't have much on my mind until a policeman walked up and told us that Martin Luther King had been gunned down at a motel in Memphis. I had a hard time sleeping that night. Laying there half awake in the dark, I kept staring at a pair of pants I'd left hanging on the doorknob and imagining that it was Dr. King coming through the door. I had to get up and call Barbara to straighten myself out. Then I had to get my thoughts together to play another baseball season in the South.

Dr. King's funeral was in Atlanta the day before Opening Day, and there was some discussion about whether the Braves should reschedule the game. Bartholomay talked to Daddy King, Dr. King's father, who told him that Martin would want the game to go on. Daddy King even came to the game himself.

I was proud to hear later about something Dr. King had said just a month before he was killed, when he visited at Don Newcombe's house. According to Don, Dr. King sat down at the dinner table and said, "Don, you and Jackie and Roy will never know how easy you made it to do my job." I'm sure that hearing those words made it all seem worthwhile to Don, a thousand times over.

My little contributions could never compare with those of Jackie and Don and the other pioneers, but I believed that I had a role to play in the movement, too. Ivan Allen once made a statement that made me feel the way Don must have felt that night with Dr. King. He said, "There was a lot of subtle apprehension about how the South's first major-league sports franchise and its black players would go over. Hank played a major role in smoothing the transition and confirming the end of segregation in the South through his thoughtful consideration and exemplary conduct. He taught us how to do it. The first time he knocked one over that left-field fence, everyone forgot what his color was."

I'm not so sure that everyone forgot my color, but I'd like to think that I had a small hand in bringing Atlanta into the modern era. If Rico Carty was the first black player the South learned to love, I'd like to think I might have been the first one it learned to respect.

At any rate, I was the first black player—the first player, period—to have my own night in Atlanta Stadium. It came in August of 1968, after my five hundredth home run. I was so nervous that it reminded me of the night in Jacksonville when I dropped dollar bills all over the field. This time, I dropped my hat, and when Bill Bartholomay and I both bent down to pick it up, we bumped and knocked over the microphone.

The five hundredth home run came against Mike McCormick of the Giants, which meant that Willie Mays was on the field at the time. Willie elected not to have his picture taken with me that day, saying it wasn't appropriate for him to fraternize with a player whose team had just beaten the Giants. For years, Willie had been king, and I'm sure he wasn't crazy about me elbowing into his territory. Most fans and critics still considered Willie to be a better player than me. It seemed like the only ones who took up my cause were my teammates. Guys like Uecker and Boyer used to argue with the visiting writers who didn't think I belonged in the class with Mays. It made me feel a little awkward to sit by my locker and hear them going on like that, but don't think I didn't appreciate it.

Actually, the 1968 season wasn't the best time to present my case. It was the first time since my rookie year that I didn't drive in or score 100 runs. I was so frustrated that at one point I tried using a pep pill—a greenie—that one of my teammates gave me. When that thing took hold, I thought I was having a heart attack. It was a stupid thing to do, and besides that, I shouldn't have been so concerned about my hitting in the first place. Nobody was hitting in 1968. That was the year of the pitcher—Drysdale's streak of scoreless innings and Bob Gibson's 1.12 earned run average.

With the premature retirement of Koufax, Gibson had become the dominant pitcher in the league. Gibson was every bit as mean as Drysdale, and he threw harder. When they raised the mound in 1968 and Gibson brought in that hard slider—God almighty! He had also been the hero of the 1967 World Series, in which the Cardinals beat the Red Sox, and it was interesting to see that Carl Yastrzemski, Boston's rightfielder, who won the Triple Crown that year, got rich on endorsements after the season while Gibson made enough extra money for about three loads of laundry.

Gibson is probably the best black pitcher in major-league history, but I have serious doubts whether he was the best black pitcher who ever made it to the majors. That might sound confusing, but you have to consider the case of the old man who became my teammate in 1968. Bill Bartholomay happened to read where Satchel Paige, who had pitched for the Indians and Browns after his long career in the Negro Leagues, was a little short of qualifying for his major-league pension, so he signed Satch and placed him on our roster at the age of sixty-two—or however old Satch was; I'm not sure he even knew. Satch never pitched in a game that year because the Braves were afraid he might get hurt, but personally I don't think they had anything to worry about. That old man knew more about taking care of himself than anyone I ever met, and on top of that, he could still throw. He threw on the sidelines, and although this might seem hard to believe, I'm certain that Satch threw harder than some of the guys on our staff that year. And his control was impeccable. He used to tell us all his old stories about using a chewing-gum wrapper for home plate and about pulling his infielders off the field and telling his outfielders to sit down. All of us would gather by his locker, or sit around him by the dugout, and let Satch spin his yarns. We weren't sure what to believe and what not to believe, but that's probably the way it should have been, because nobody will ever know how good Satchel might have been if he had spent his whole career in the big leagues. My guess is that he might have won 300 games with his outfielders sitting down.

Because he was from Mobile, and because he was the living symbol of Negro League baseball, I felt a special kinship with Satchel. I had the privilege of being his chaperone when he was with us, which meant that I sat next to him on the plane and he spent a lot of time at our house. Satch loved to have the rookies fetch and carry for him. Dusty Baker and Ralph Garr came up at the end of that season, and Satch would make them carry his fishing poles onto the airplane. He would call Baker "Daffy." Baker would say, "My name's Dusty," and Satch would say, "I know, Daffy, I know." The only things Satch took seriously were fishing and pitching. When the veteran writers came into the clubhouse, Satch would ask them how Koufax's and Gibson's fastballs compared with Bob Feller's and Dizzy Dean's. The thing was, Satch knew he threw as hard or harder than Feller and Dean, because he had pitched against them and beaten them many times on barnstorming tours. After spending time with Satchel, I firmly believe that he may have been the greatest pitcher of all time. Of course, I have no way to compare him to guys like Walter Johnson and Christy Mathewson and Lefty Grove, and I can't even compare him to Koufax and Gibson and Marichal, but there was something about the man that made me believe in him. He was brilliant. A lot of people might not understand how a man who talked and carried on the way Satchel did could be brilliant, but coming from the same background, I understood him. Believe me, Satchel Paige had life figured out.

Of course, that doesn't mean he wasn't an old fool sometimes. Satch had a lot of fun with the players and vice versa. Once, Uecker called from the clubhouse to the switchboard, got patched into an outside line, and made the other clubhouse telephone ring for Satchel. Then he put on a German accent and said he was the manager of the Dinkler Hotel, where Satch was staying, and that Satch had to move out of his room so another guest could move in. Satch got furious and said he was going to come down there right away and kick his ass. Then he hung up the phone and we all watched him take off his uniform, get dressed, and storm out of the clubhouse to kick that German's ass.

Satch was still with us when we reported to West Palm Beach the next spring, and when I looked around the field at the guys next to me, I felt almost as old as him. Torre had been traded to St. Louis for Orlando Cepeda, and aside from me, the player with the longest tenure on the team was Rico Carty, who came up in 1964—ten years after me. I had played through an entire generation of Braves. It put the idea of retiring into my head for the first time—until, one day in spring training, an old baseball writer named Lee Allen started talking to me about all the things I had a chance to accomplish in my career. Early in the 1969 season, I would pass Mel Ott in home runs to take fourth place on the all-time list behind Ruth, Mays, and Mantle, who had played his last season. I had a good chance to go to bat more times than anybody in the history of the game. And I had an excellent chance at 3,000 hits, which was the goal I had always set for myself. Allen explained to me that the fun would really start when I reached 3,000 hits, because from that point on I would be able to create my own niche in baseball history. I may not have felt the same way about it if I had been a white player, but to somebody like me—having come along in a period when black players were only beginning to assume their rightful place in baseball—the chance to make history sounded like something worth pursuing with all of my resources.

I knew that the next few years would make all the difference in my final record as a player. At thirty-five years old, I was nearing the traditional age of retirement. If I played out my career in typical fashion, I would finish high on many of the all-time lists—hits, home runs, total bases, RBIs. Going into the 1969 season, my .314 lifetime average was the highest of all active players. I knew, and the record would show, that I had been one of the best ballplayers to come along. My credentials would put me in the company of Ruth and Mays and all the others. But I also knew that in the final analysis—in the books and sports columns and barbershops—I wouldn't be in their class. To be in their class, my numbers had to be better than theirs. I didn't agree with it, and I didn't accept it, but it was reality and I had to deal with it.

Somehow, though, I didn't feel like I had to deal with it alone. Whatever forces seemed to be working against me in my career— whether it was bigotry or neglect or whatever—I always felt that a higher power was working for me. I might not have known what my destiny was, but I knew that I had one, and something was helping me attain it. Whatever that something was, it helped bring me through Jacksonville and the early years in Milwaukee, and it was still on the job in 1969.

That was the year Cepeda came over to us from the Cardinals. We missed Torre, but it was one of those rare deals that worked out wonderfully for both teams. Both of them were big-time hitters, but Cepeda was a rah-rah guy who gave us that little push we needed. He was also a great clutch hitter and a major power threat behind me in the batting order, which enabled me to hit forty-four home runs once again that year.

I was still a .300 hitter—in fact, I hit .300 on the button in 1969—but I had become such a dead pull hitter that teams were starting to put on a defensive shift when I batted. The Reds' manager, Dave Bristol, positioned three infielders on the left side, and they took three hits away from me in two games. Another time, he used four outfielders against me. But I wasn't going to change my style. The fact is, the shift didn't bother me as much as the bone chips and calcium deposits in my back, which were so painful that I had to take sleeping pills at night. But we were in a pennant race for the first time in years, and I wasn't going on the disabled list.

The things I'll always remember most about The Hammer was his ability to play with pain. Many times, he'd limp into the clubhouse like he could barely make it to his locker. Then he'd sit down with his newspaper and not even look up as everybody else came in and got dressed and fooled around. I believe he was thinking away the pain. He'd sit there for the longest time, and his eyes wouldn't even move. Then it would be time for the game to start, and he'd get up like there was not a thing wrong with him. He'd pound the ball and run the bases like a kid. Then, when the game was over, he'd come limping back into the clubhouse like he was on his last legs.

Hank believed strongly that it was a ballplayer's duty to go out on that field. He preached that to guys like me and Garr. He'd say, "Now, you got to play a hundred and fifty games a year, so pick your spots. You can miss two games a month. Just two a month. So pick the days you're gonna be hurt, or you're gonna rest, or you're gonna have a drink or two. The rest of the time, be out on that field."—Dusty Baker

Even with the pain in my back, it was great fun to win again. And it was nice to be playing behind an ace pitcher again, which is what Phil Niekro had become with that knuckleball of his— despite the fact that Uecker was gone. Uke and Boyer had been in a bar fight at the Cock and Bull in West Palm Beach, and the

Braves released him on the spot. I had to give Uecker fifty bucks to get back to Atlanta. Uecker always joked that he had the same career average as Don Carter, the bowler—200—and that's exactly what it was when the Braves sent him packing for the last time.

Niekro managed to win twenty-three games in 1969 without him, though, and because of the new league format, we were in pennant contention all year. That was the first season in which the leagues were divided into divisions. We were in the West, and while we jockeyed with the Giants and Reds and Dodgers, the Cubs were running away with the race in the East. I enjoyed playing the Cubs because of Billy Williams and Ernie Banks and Wrigley Field, but we had some nasty games with them in 1969. Leo Durocher, their manager, thought Claude Raymond was throwing at Banks one day, and he ordered Dick Selma to throw at me. Selma threw the first two pitches at my leg, which caused me to step out of the box and yell at him. I thought it was bush to throw at me, because I was the third batter up in the inning. I believe that if you're going to throw at a batter in retaliation, it should be the first man up. I didn't appreciate being singled out as a target.

Later that year at Wrigley Field, a thin lefthander named Ken Holtzman had a no-hitter going against us when I came to bat late in the game. I got hold of a slider pretty good and lifted it up toward the left-field bleachers. Billy Williams backed up to the wall to watch the ball go over, and all of a sudden the wind caught it and started bringing it back. The wind was blowing in hard from the lake that day, and it carried the ball over to the part of the fence that curves out when it gets near the foul line. Billy drifted around the curve of the fence, jumped up, and picked the ball right out of the ivy. He told me later that it was already five or six rows into the bleachers before it started coming back toward the field. That play saved Holtzman's no-hitter.

I saw Billy again at the All-Star Game that year. He deserved to be a starter, and if he had been, half of the eight National League regulars would have come from Mobile. Cleon Jones of the Mets started with me in the outfield, and Willie McCovey was at first base. McCovey hit two home runs that day, and forty-five for the season, beating me out of the home run title by one.

Mays was on the team, too, of course, and I was with him in one of our hotel rooms after the announcement was made that Joe DiMaggio had been named the Greatest Living Player. Willie was extremely upset about that, which I'm sure he had a right to be. But at least he was named to the Greatest Living Team. The other outfielders were DiMaggio and Ted Williams, which meant that Mantle, Musial, and I were left off. Given the company I was in, I didn't think it would be in good taste for me to raise any objections—nor did I have any.

After the All-Star break, we continued to battle it out with the Giants, Reds, and Dodgers, and well into the summer it was still very unclear who would meet the Cubs in the first league playoff series. All the while, though, we never gave a second thought to the possibility of anybody other than the Cubs winning the East —especially the Mets. They had only been a game out of last place the year before and had never even been close to the first division. Nobody could believe it when they blew by the Cubs down the stretch. They played like a team possessed, and, in fact, had an easier time winning their division than we did.

We didn't actually move into first place until September 17, when I hit a twelfth-inning home run to beat the Dodgers. Then we were in and out of the lead until a wild game in Houston. Norm Miller of the Astros was on third with the tying run in a crucial situation late in the game, with Cecil Upshaw pitching for us and Bob Didier catching. Upshaw threw a pitch that Didier had to reach for, and when he did, his finger guard came off and went flying back toward the screen. Miller thought it was the ball and came tearing in for home plate. When he got there, Didier just stepped out as easy as you please and tagged him. After that, we swept the Astros and went on to win nine in a row to sew up the division. Hoyt Wilhelm, our forty-six-year-old relief pitcher, got four saves in the final week, and we clinched against Cincinnati on the final Saturday.

As you might expect, there was some celebrating that night—a little too much. A bunch of us went to Niekro's bar, The Knuckler, and stayed well into the morning hours. I had about $400 in cash that I didn't want to carry around, so I put it in a sack and taped it to the battery of my car. The only problem was that Pat Jarvis borrowed my car and took it home with him; but the money was still there the next day. I don't recall how I got home, but it was very late and the door was locked and I didn't have a key and somehow I gashed my hand trying to get in through a window. When I showed up the next day with stitches, it was announced that I had cut my hand on our fence when our dog got caught in it.

> When I saw him come in with that hand all cut up, I was scared to death. I thought, oh no, Hank's messed up now and he's not gonna be able to play in the playoffs. I asked him about it and he said, "What you gonna do, Ralph?" I said, "Man, it's impossible to play ball like that." He said, "Don't worry, Ralph. It'll work out all right." I didn't believe it, though. Then he calls in the team doctor, goes into the back room and takes a couple shots of novocaine in his hand, puts on a black glove, and goes out and hits .357 against Seaver and Koosman and Gentry. From that day on, I said no man alive could ever compare with Hank Aaron. That was the thing that made me realize he wasn't like the rest of us.—Ralph Garr

I didn't think we were in very good shape to win the playoffs, and it wasn't because of my hand. I frankly didn't think we had the attitude to win. When we sat down before the playoffs to talk about splitting up the prize money, it was evident to me that a lot of guys on the team had a defeatist attitude. They were talking about how to split up the shares if we lost the playoffs. I said we ought to divide it as if we were going to the World Series. But they wanted to be covered in case we lost, and so they voted not to give a share to Donald Davidson. Clete Boyer and I tried to explain that the traveling secretary usually got a full share, but they wouldn't listen. Later on, Bill Bartholomay gave Donald a full share, anyway. But after that meeting, I knew we were not the team we needed to be going into the playoffs—not against the Mets.

The Mets had won 100 games, and although a lot of people thought they did it with mirrors, they did it with pitching—namely, Tom Seaver and Jerry Koosman. Seaver, who won twenty-five games in 1969, had quickly joined Gibson at the top of the heap of National League pitchers and was one whom I had a lot of respect for. The feeling must have been mutual, because when he came up in 1967, he said that I had been his favorite player as a kid, which might have been because he was from Southern California, where Jim Murray, the popular columnist for the *Los Angeles Times*, had always written very kindly about me. The first time Seaver pitched against me, he had to walk behind the mound and compose himself. Then he threw me a low fastball and I grounded into a double play. The next time, he tried another low fastball and I hit it out of the park. He was a quick study, however, and we had some good duels.

Seaver and Niekro started the first playoff game in Atlanta, but it seemed as though the hitters were more keyed up than the pitchers. It was already 4-4 when I hit a solo homer in the seventh to give us the lead. We couldn't keep the Mets down, though. They scored five in the eighth against Niekro, with my home boy, Cleon Jones, right in the middle of it. Cleon had hit .340 during the season, and he was even better in the playoffs. He and another outfielder from Mobile, Tommie Agee, tore us up the whole series.

Agee hit a home run in the second game and the Mets ran up an 8-0 lead before we started coming back. I homered in the fifth, and we scored five runs to cut the lead to 9-6, but we were finished and the Mets got two more. The third game was in New York. I homered in the first to give us a 2-0 lead against Gary Gentry, but the Mets just kept coming and coming. Nolan Ryan pitched seven good innings of relief, Agee hit another homer, and they swept the series by beating us, 7-4.

When we had lost the pennant to the Dodgers in 1956 and 1959, I had felt each time that it shouldn't have happened. But the Mets jumped all over us in the '69 playoffs, and when they were through, we knew we'd been up against more than we could handle. We didn't necessarily believe that they were the better team, but we knew that nothing was going to stop them. After they made short work of Baltimore in the World Series, one of my teammates, Tony Gonzalez, said that we ought to send the Mets to Vietnam and let them win the war.

It was ironic that losing the pennant would do so much for my reputation as a player, but for some strange reason, it did. I noticed that people started to view me a little more sympathetically—and respectfully—after that playoff series. I still don't know why, exactly. I expect that the exposure of playing in New York had something to do with it, and the fact that I hit a home run in every game with a bad hand. But I can't believe it was as simple as that. Maybe people saw me as the old man going up against destiny and giving it one more good shot. Maybe it was the fact that Mantle had retired and Mays was on the way down. I don't know. Maybe it was just my time.

9

At first, it was all about base hits. Hank Aaron kept up with his progress by counting his base hits. It was easy: Two hits were better than one and two hundred were better than a hundred and seventy-five and the number to shoot for—the number that made Hank Aaron keep swinging all those years— was 3,000. Stan Musial was the last 3,000-hit man. Ted Williams would have been except for the war, but that was the thing about 3,000 hits—it was attainable only to those who brooked no inter- ference. It wasn't enough to be a great hitter. A 3,000 man was one well favored by the baseball fates, immune from injury, slump, bad luck, aging, and the real world. Joe DiMaggio wasn't one. Babe Ruth wasn't. Mickey Mantle wasn't. If a man had 3,000 hits, he had done what only great ones could do and some of the greatest ones couldn't. A man had to keep swinging to get 3,000 hits, and that was what Hank Aaron was all about. Three thou- sand hits would mean that he had kept on, survived, endured, persevered, pressed ahead, succeeded, excelled, and finally, conclusively, made it.

Though the idea was never broached in the journals, there was a time when Hank Aaron seemed capable of 4,000 hits. In the first stages of his career he seemed, in fact, more capable of 4,000 hits than Pete Rose, who eventually broke Ty Cobb's record of 4,191. Aaron was younger than Rose when he reached 1,000, 2,000, and 3,000 hits, and his batting abilities were retained vir- tually as long. It is not at all inconceivable that if Aaron had not moved to Atlanta and taken on an attending home run mental- ity, he may have reached Cobb before Rose did. Aaron finished with a higher lifetime batting average than Rose, while playing but one season fewer. The principal difference in their hit- making capacities was attributable to Aaron's power—he came to bat fewer times because of his position in the middle of the batting order as opposed to Rose's at the top. Three places in the batting order can make a difference of more than fifty at-bats in the course of a season and roughly 1,200 over the twenty-three seasons that Aaron ultimately played. At Aaron's .305 lifetime batting average, those 1,200 at-bats would have translated into more than 360 hits. Add to that the additional hits he would have gained by swinging for singles instead of home runs, and his final total of 3,771 hits could easily be inflated to more than 4,200.

Once he reached Cobb's home state, however, Aaron was no longer a serious threat to the Georgia Peach. The move to Atlanta trained his sights on the long ball, which brought Babe Ruth into focus, and as his hits left the premises with increasing frequency, Aaron took on the luminous bearing of a home run hitter. He was characterized no longer by the screaming doubles to right-center, but by the purposeful drives that seemed always to know where the wall was. There was nothing Ruthian about Aaron, none of the epic Yankee clout that defined the Babe and later Mantle. Instead, there were economic fly balls that, like the man who struck them, just kept going and going until they reached their rightful place.

As the balls continued to drop over the fences day after day, year after year, there developed a sense of anticipation when Aaron moved up from the on-deck circle. The Aaron home run became a familiar routine, the way he carried his bat in one hand, his helmet in the other, stopped outside the batter's box, balanced the bat on his thigh, affixed his helmet with two hands, stared at the pitcher, twisted his spikes into the deep part of the box, waved his bat over the plate in two or three loose, rhythmic, rising parabolas, cocked his right arm, took a pitch or two, stepped out, stepped in again, waited, watched, saw something, recoiled, stepped forward, turned his hips, snapped his hands, raised his eyes, dropped his bat, and commenced to circle the bases in that loping, effortless stride, head straight, shoulders back, elbows swinging high behind him, a gait intended to show up nobody and still make the point. Babe Ruth stood and watched his skybound blows and took the bases in his funny short-legged trot, waving to the crowd as he went. By no accounts, least of all his own, was Aaron another Ruth. He didn't *have the ham in him, the show-stopping histrionics. But he had the home runs.*

◆   ◆   ◆

When I joined it in 1970, the 3,000-hit club was exactly half of what it is as I write this. There were just eight members: Ty Cobb, Stan Musial, Eddie Collins, Tris Speaker, Honus Wagner, Napoleon Lajoie, Cap Anson, and Paul Waner, who had been my first batting coach with the Braves. None of them was black, and only Musial had played after World War II. Three thousand hits was a big deal and my first brush with fanfare. It even got me on the cover of *Sports Illustrated* for the second time in two years— after fifteen years without ever being on it.

The hit came in Cincinnati, in our last trip ever to Crosley Field. Crosley was a quirky ballpark with a terrace that ran up to the outfield wall and a big laundry building over the left-field fence. Like most of the old stadiums, it was a hitter's park and one that I would miss. The old parks had dirty, smelly club-houses, and the players were generally glad to get into the new, spacious, clean ones, but I think we left something behind when we moved on, in the same way that air travel took away some-thing that train rides added to the game. Teams weren't quite as close anymore. Players became a little more pampered and a little more selfish.

After the Reds moved into Riverfront Stadium that year, Wrigley Field in Chicago was the only ballpark remaining from the time I broke into the National League. Crosley Field, Forbes Field in Pittsburgh, Connie Mack Stadium in Philadelphia, and Sportsman's Park in St. Louis were all replaced by circular, AstroTurf parks, and the Dodgers, Giants, and Braves had moved away from Ebbets Field, the Polo Grounds, and County Stadium. It was hard to believe the change that had transpired in the time it took me to accumulate 3,000 hits.

More than anything else, 3,000 hits is a testament to a player's staying power, and I was glad to reach it in one of the parks where I had memories. Crosley Field was the place where I had played my first major-league game and where I had broken my ankle as a rookie. It seemed like something out of the ordinary happened every time we went to Cincinnati. This time, it was a Sunday doubleheader before the biggest crowd Crosley Field had seen in more than twenty years. Among the spectators was my pal Stan Musial, who hopped over the fence and came running onto the field when I beat out my three thousandth hit, which was a slow dribbler against Wayne Simpson, a hotshot rookie who was five years old when I got hit number one. Before I joined the 3,000 club, Stan the Man had been the only member still living, and he was eager to have some company. I was proud to be joining a man I admired so much and pleased to carry on his tradition. Musial's hit number 3,001 was a home run, and so was mine.

When we got back to Atlanta, the Braves had a day for me to celebrate the occasion. Hoyt Wilhelm was honored at the same time for being the first man to pitch in a thousand games. I was a little nervous about having a day, considering my history of doing something clumsy every time I stood out by the microphone, but this time I didn't drop anything. I walked away with a French poodle, a year's supply of Coca-Cola, and a golf cart with number 44 painted on it. The prize that meant the most to me, naturally, was the ball I hit for number 3,000, which I gave to the Hall of Fame when the people there asked for it. When it arrived, they stashed it away in a back room. I told them that I would just as soon keep it myself if they weren't going to display it, and they replied that they never displayed mementos from active players. Then I found out that they had immediately showcased the ball from Don Drysdale's consecutive scoreless inning record in 1968. It was the first of a series of problems I had with the Hall of Fame.

As eager as I had been to put my three thousandth hit behind me, I started off 1970 stroking the long ball. In our home opener, batting against Frank Reberger of the Giants, I hit the first home run that ever landed in the left-field upper deck of Atlanta Stadium. The Braves painted a gold hammer on the seat that marked the spot. I had eight homers in April and started May with a deep one against Joe Decker of the Cubs. I also hit a smash against Decker that I was afraid broke his wrist. It bounced off his arm and they had to take him out of the game, but I think it really hurt Ernie Banks more than it hurt Decker. Before the game, Ernie had been telling me about this young pitcher who was really going to show me something: "Joe Deck-a," Ernie said. "Watch out for Joe Deck-a!" I informed Ernie that he had been warning the wrong guy.

Cepeda, Carty, and I were banging the ball pretty hard in 1970. Rico led the league in hitting at .366, and all three of us drove in more than 100 runs. But there was no chemistry on the team anymore. Niekro had a bad year, and we couldn't win if he couldn't. We fell all the way from the top of the division to fifth place, with a losing record. I contributed directly to one of those defeats when we played our first series at Riverfront Stadium in Cincinnati. I had hit the first home run in the new park, but a couple of nights later I made up for it. The game was tied with two outs in the bottom of the ninth when Pat Corrales hit a high fly that I chased to the fence. I bobbled the ball when I stabbed at it, and when I reached for it again, I knocked it up and over the fence for the game-losing home run.

I also messed up my knee that season, sliding into home plate against the Giants. I wouldn't permit an operation on it, but I had to have it drained half a dozen times during the year. I managed to hit thirty-eight home runs anyway, which was just about enough to keep me thinking of Babe Ruth, although I was still about the only one who made the connection. Most of the Ruth talk still centered around Willie Mays, who had fallen far off the pace and then come to life again with twenty-eight homers in 1970. Willie was such a magical player that some people thought he could catch a second wind and make a run at Ruth.

Not long after I got my three thousandth hit that year, Willie got his. It was the first time I had ever reached a milestone ahead of him, and, frankly, it felt good. But Willie was still more than forty homers ahead of me, and that's where the attention was focused. It was still mostly on Willie, and I'd be lying to say it didn't bother me a little bit, because the same thing had been going on for fifteen years. I had to work at not being envious of Willie. I always told myself that my time would come. I considered Mays a rival, certainly, but a friendly rival. At the same time, I would never accept the position as second best. I looked at Willie as my guideline. There were certain things that I couldn't do as well as he could, but I felt if I could do some things a little better, I should and maybe would be classified as the same type of ballplayer. I've never seen a better all-around ballplayer than Willie Mays, but I will say this: Willie was not as good a hitter as I was. No way.

By 1970, I was putting most of my energy into the home run chase, and the results were taking over my life. As I drew closer to Willie and Ruth, I fell farther away from Barbara. We were two people headed in different directions. As a result, I felt more comfortable at the ballpark than I did at home, and the more she objected to my lifestyle, the more I wanted to be away. I felt lonely and angry, and, to a degree, I was taking my domestic problems out on the pitchers. The only way I knew to feel better was to pound the ball into the seats. Or go hunting.

Even when things were hunky-dory around the house, I always managed to get away for a hunting trip in the offseason. In my Milwaukee days, I used to go duck and pheasant hunting every year in Doland, South Dakota. While I was there, I made it a habit to visit a home for retarded children, where I would teach the kids how to hit and throw a baseball. One boy was a special favorite of mine, and I'd often work with him, trying to get him to throw a ball to me. He finally did it one day, and when he did, he was so happy he walked up to me, grabbed the ball out of my hand, and rammed it into my forehead.

I almost always headed northwest for my hunting trips. The first time I shot a deer was in the hills of Montana. I took aim at this four-pointer, and the guide told me not to shoot him. I asked why, and he said if I killed that deer, it would fall into the canyon and we'd never get it out. Well, I shot him, and he dropped 500 feet to the bottom of the ravine. I turned to the guide and said, "How you gonna get him out?" He said he wasn't going to. I told him I wasn't going to leave my deer at the bottom of the ravine, so we hired a rancher with a helicopter and he pulled him out.

In my Atlanta days I took hunting trips with Steve Carlton, Tim McCarver, and the future sheriff of DeKalb County, Georgia, Bulldog Pat Jarvis. One year, Joe Hoerner went with us, and when we stopped over in Denver, he and McCarver went into the VIP room and practically emptied the liquor cabinet. By the time we got to Casper, Wyoming, we were so rowdy that the stewardess warned us to put the bottles away and finally the pilot just landed the plane down and made us get off. Actually, he told me I could stay on because I didn't have anything to do with it, but where was I going? We had to rent another plane to fly to Montana. It was a tiny thing, and as soon as we got up in the sky, there was ice all over the windows. The pilot didn't seem to notice. He was jabbering and pointing out the sights and showing us where Jesse James used to ride; but at that point I didn't give a damn about Jesse James. When we finally landed, we rode over to a place that belonged to a friend of Carlton. I didn't know much about the guy, but he was an oil man and he had stacks of money in the house. Anyway, we took some guns and drove along in a pickup truck shooting elk as they ran alongside. After that, I didn't have much stomach for shooting things. The last time I shot a deer was a two-pointer at Ted Turner's ranch in South Carolina. It made me feel empty inside.

Jerry Koosman met us in Montana, and from there we went up to the Canadian Rockies. It was a long way from civilization, and we had to get up at three in the morning to ride packhorses through the mountains. That didn't sound like a very good time to an old crawdad catcher from Mobile, and I told Jarvis that I'd gladly use part of my big salary to bring in a helicopter to get me out of there. So the five of them—four crazy pitchers and a crazy catcher—went off on their packhorses while I spent the week frying fish in the camp.

It seemed like almost everything in my life turned into a disaster in those days—including my marriage. That was around the time that Barbara filed for divorce. I knew that our marriage had been difficult since the move to Atlanta, but somehow I never really believed she would go through with a divorce. We managed to get it done quietly, and it was settled in February 1971. I moved into the Landmark Apartments in downtown Atlanta, but I found myself over at the house a lot because Barbara had custody of our four children and I couldn't stay away from them.

The divorce only made things harder for the kids, who were all in school at the time and didn't have it easy to begin with, having a public figure for a father. They were natural targets for other kids, and it would have been easy for us to spoil them to compensate for it—especially after the hardship of the divorce. But I thought it was important that they learn to make their own way. One time Hankie wrecked a car, and instead of giving him the money to fix it I got him a job with the Braves' ground crew. I figured the best thing I could provide my kids was opportunity, because that's what the struggle was all about.

After the divorce, I drove the kids to school when I could—Hankie and Lary went to a private high school that was a long way from the house—and saw them almost every day when I was in Atlanta. But that didn't take away the pain. I was miserable. I just wasn't cut out to be single, and I felt lost. A friend offered to set me up on a date with Aretha Franklin, but I wasn't interested in dating. At that point, I wasn't interested in much of anything but hitting home runs.

For a while there, Hank was as sad and lonesome as any man I ever saw. It made me sad just to see him that way. Before the divorce, when Ralph Garr and I first came up to the Braves, Hank and Barbara more or less adopted us. We'd be over at their house for dinner almost every night. Then, all of a sudden, Hank was alone.

Of course, he had women following him around all the time, and that was where I came in. My assignment was to tell them to get lost. As you might expect, after a while I'd get tired of telling them to get lost, and now and then I'd pull one of them aside and get to know her a little.

Ralph and I felt privileged to be around Hank so much, but he always took the young players under his wing—especially the black players. He wouldn't go around offering advice, but if you asked him something, he'd give you the answer. He taught us how to take care of ourselves—things like how to eat properly. Hank would always eat a big lunch early in the afternoon and after that, just eat light the rest of the day. Ralph and I started doing the same thing. In the offseason, we would all go to the gym, and Hank would be running lap after lap around the track while Ralph and I played basketball. Hank would look at us and shake his head and say, "Get up here and run." He even told us how to act on the field. He'd say, "Now, don't be hotdogging around the bases. If you don't show up the pitcher, he might not have a vendetta going against you the next time you bat. When you hit a home run, just run the bases. Then you can go into the tunnel and get happy."

Hank was a great help to us, but at the same time he was smart to keep us around, because you could never be too sad if Ralph Garr was nearby. Ralph would keep you laughing, and Hank liked to have his laughs. One time I wasn't feeling too well and Hank told me to take some pill. I took the pill and went to the bathroom, and I was scared to death when I saw that my urine was red. I thought The Hammer would never stop laughing that time.

Ralph and I would always sit with him on the plane, and he would tell us stories about the old days and then close his eyes and nod off to sleep. When he nodded off, we would get up as quietly as we could to go to the back of the plane with the other guys and have some fun, but as soon as we started to get up, The Hammer would clamp down on both of our wrists with a grip that was like a vise. He'd say, "I want you guys to stay here." So we stayed.

We were all friends, but at the same time Hank was like a father to Ralph and me. I met Hank when I was eighteen years old and just getting out of high school. At the time, I was trying to decide whether to go to college or sign with the Braves, and when the Braves were in Los Angeles they sent Hank over to talk to me. I asked Hank if I should sign, and he said, "If you have confidence that you can make it, then sign." My mother made Hank promise to take care of me like a son, and he promised.—Dusty Baker

Dusty and Ralph and home runs kept me going in 1971. Late in April, I hit my six hundredth home run, which pleased me doubly because it came against Gaylord Perry of the Giants. I didn't appreciate the fact that Perry threw a spitball. I regarded a spitball as cheating, and because of it I have serious doubts as to whether Perry belongs in the Hall of Fame. Anyway, the only problem with number six hundred was that we lost the game— and what's more, the winning run was driven in by Willie Mays on his fourth hit of the day. I had to wonder if I would ever get out of that man's shadow.

But it didn't take long after that. Willie only had eighteen homers in him that year, at age forty, and as my total kept mounting, it became increasingly obvious that if anybody was going to challenge Ruth's record, it would be me. I think the press and the fans were reluctant to concede this point, because they had always imagined that a challenger to Ruth would be a charismatic player like Willie or Mickey Mantle—somebody they knew was coming. I had sort of tiptoed along all those years. All of a sudden they looked up and saw me treading on sacred ground, only a hundred homers away, and they wondered how it was possible. What's *Aaron* doing here?

It was somewhere along in 1971 that everybody realized this might be serious. I was thirty-seven years old and hitting home runs at a faster, more regular clip than I'd ever hit them before. There wasn't a single month in 1971 that I hit fewer than seven home runs or more than nine. I missed a lot of games because of my knee, and when I was in the lineup it was usually at first base, but I was focused in, and I just couldn't seem to keep the ball in the park. It might be the only time in my career that I surprised myself. I knew I could still hit, but I didn't expect forty-seven homers that year—the highest total of my career—not to mention 118 RBIs and a .327 batting average in fewer than 500 at-bats. When the season was over, I had little doubt that I would surpass Ruth if I stayed healthy. I had hit the ball as well at thirty-seven as I had at twenty-seven, and the playing field had gotten smaller.

I reveled in the Ruth chase, which I found to be a great way to release my pent-up emotions. But it didn't make me a happy man. When I wasn't around Dusty and Ralph, I was usually moping about something or other. On top of my personal troubles, I

was still having problems with Paul Richards, who released Clete
Boyer during the 1971 season. As far as I could tell, the best
reason was that Richards didn't like him. After it happened, Clete
was quoted in a New York newspaper as saying there was no
room in baseball for a man like Paul Richards. When Richards
confronted him about it, Clete said he was not misquoted. Richards said he was embarrassed to have been paying so much
money to a lousy player, which made Clete so angry that he gave
the Braves back two months' worth of severance pay. Bowie
Kuhn, the commissioner, made the Braves return the money.

After Clete was released, I went to Lum Harris, our manager,
and suggested that he give Darrell Evans a chance at third base.
Evans was a young left-handed hitter with a good home run
swing, and I thought he'd be very effective playing in Atlanta.
We also had a powerful young catcher named Earl Williams who
hit thirty-three home runs as a rookie. With those guys coming
up, it was obviously time to rebuild, because we weren't going
anywhere that season. Cepeda was hurt most of the year, and
Carty missed all of it with a knee injury.

Carty also took a bad beating that year from some off-duty
Atlanta policemen. He and his brother-in-law were driving along
North Avenue in Atlanta when they got into an argument with
some white men who drew up alongside them in another car.
There was a police car behind them, so Carty pulled over and
complained to the officers. As he did, the other guys got out of
their car and started pummeling Rico right in front of the cops. It
turned out the policemen knew the white men because they were
also on the force. When the news got out, three policemen were
fired and the police chief called the incident the worst case of
misconduct he had ever seen in his department.

Rico and I weren't buddies, but it hit close to home when I
saw a black ballplayer—any black person, for that matter—
treated so viciously in Atlanta. It hit closer to home when Tommie was sent back to the minor leagues at the end of the 1971
season, never to return to the majors. I was feeling more and more
alone.

The feeling was intensified when I signed a huge contract

before the 1972 season. Nowadays it wouldn't buy a utility infielder, but back then nobody had ever heard of a contract like the one the Braves gave me. It was a two-year deal that made me the first player ever to earn $200,000 in a season. I was grateful to the Braves for the gesture, and thrilled to have the money, but I didn't anticipate the outcry it would bring from the fans of Atlanta. I don't know what it is about baseball fans, but many of them just can't stand to see players making big money. I can appreciate the argument that playing ball is far less important than physics or medicine or public service, but I can't understand why athletes are the only ones who seem to get jabbed with the sharp side of this attitude. Maybe it's because an athlete—especially a baseball player—is going to fail a high percentage of the time, and the good fan takes it hard when he does. But, frankly, I don't have a problem with ballplayers making the kind of money they do. For one thing, there are only about six or seven hundred people in the world who play major-league baseball, and they are selected from one of the biggest pools of applicants of any industry—maybe the biggest, when you consider that half the boys in America want to be big-league ballplayers. On top of that, ballplayers are entertainers, and the top entertainers in every field make ridiculous amounts of money. You don't hear people booing Michael Jackson because he makes a million dollars for a night's work; they don't throw things at Bill Cosby if he tells a bad joke; nobody calls the talk shows to complain about Stephen King's royalties if they don't like his latest book. If people buy your product, the money is yours. That's the system. But for some reason, people seem to think that baseball is above the system, or at least independent of it. I've seen it happen over and over with players who signed record-breaking contracts: The fans threw batteries at Dave Parker and ran him out of Pittsburgh when he was earning baseball's biggest salary. People in Cincinnati were outraged when Eric Davis signed for three million. Darryl Strawberry has been taunted in every ballpark in the National League.

I can't believe it's a coincidence that the players who take the most abuse because of their salaries are black players. As hard as it is for some fans to accept the fact that a ballplayer can make more money than they will earn in a lifetime, they find it repulsive that a black ballplayer who maybe never even went to college can be so rich. The Atlanta fans weren't shy about letting me know what they thought of a $200,000 nigger striking out with men on base.

Unfortunately, that was something I did with some regularity in 1972. My batting average was way down from the year before; it seemed like the only hits I could manage were home runs. Early in June, I hit number 649, a grand slam against Wayne Twitchell of the Phillies that tied Gil Hodges for the National League grand-slam record—which my friend Willie McCovey later broke—and moved me past Mays into second place on the all-time list. By that time, Willie was back in New York, where his career had started, traded to the Mets for a pitcher named Charlie Williams and some money. Willie was hot for a while when he returned to New York, but there was no real hope anymore that he could catch Ruth. If there had been, the Giants would have never let him go.

It might have been easier for Willie to give up the chase if I hadn't come along. But he had been the king for so long that it was hard for him to step off the throne. On top of that, I'm sure it ate away at Willie to watch somebody else go after a record that he thought should have been his. I think Willie resented the fact that he'd spent two years in the service and I hadn't. I couldn't blame him for that. He may well have been the one to break the record if he hadn't had to go in the army. From my point of view, though, those are all ifs, ands, and buts, and that's how I have to regard them.

The sportswriters often said that Willie and I were jealous of each other, but I don't believe either of us was. However, we were both very, very proud, and there were times when that might have been misunderstood as jealousy. The writers were always looking for signs that Willie and I didn't get along. I appeared once on Ralph Kiner's talk show in New York, and there was a report that Willie declined an invitation to come on at the same time, but I never heard that from Willie and I don't believe it's true. A writer in Houston once tried for forty-five minutes to get me to say something bad about Willie. The worst thing I could say was that he wasn't a Brave. I often daydreamed about how things might have turned out if the Braves had been the ones to sign Willie, as they thought they were going to do, or if I had signed with the Giants, as I nearly did. As it turned out, though, he was lucky to have McCovey in the same batting order, and I was lucky to have Eddie Mathews.

Midway through the 1972 season, I set a record that went together with the one Eddie and I had established for home runs by teammates. This one was Ruth's record for home runs hit by a player with one team. It happened in Cincinnati again, and against Wayne Simpson again. The home run was number 660—which, incidentally, was the number Mays retired with in 1973. My record didn't get a lot of public attention, but it meant a lot to me because it reflected a contribution to a team that no other player could match.

As many home runs as I hit for the Braves, I never hit a single one for the National League in more than twenty All-Star Games until I finally connected against Vida Blue in Detroit in 1971. The next year, the game was held in Atlanta, and I got another one. It came in the sixth inning against Gaylord Perry to give us a 2-1 lead. After the home run, our manager, Danny Murtaugh of the Pirates, let me go out to right field for the seventh inning and then sent in a substitute, which allowed the home crowd to give me a standing ovation, the longest and loudest I had ever heard in Atlanta. It was one of the best moments I had there—one of the rare occasions in my career when I felt a little magical. Maybe it seemed that way to the fans and critics, too, because people were really starting to believe I had what it took to catch Ruth. It was as if I had been running a marathon along lonely back roads all these years and that night I burst into the crowded stadium.

Along the way, I passed milestones that seemed to mean more to me than anybody else. As I've said before, total bases is a better way to measure a hitter than home runs, but very little was made of the fact that I broke Musial's all-time record for total bases in September of 1972, when I hit two home runs in a game against the Phillies in Atlanta. If there is any one record that I think best represents what I was all about as a hitter, that's the one, because, as far as I was concerned, the object of batting was to hit the ball and get as many bases as possible. It also tells me something that the record had been Musial's, because I consider myself to be much more like Musial than Ruth, both as a hitter and as a person.

As my records and home runs piled up, I became a celebrity in spite of myself. The Braves gave me a personal secretary to help me answer my mail and schedule interviews. LeRoy Neiman stood in the doorway of the clubhouse one day and painted my portrait from across the room. Hardly a day went by that I wasn't talking to some magazine or TV network. After so many years of being ignored, the attention made me uncomfortable. The older players on the Braves laughed it off, but I was concerned that the younger players would resent the old man with his entourage. To avoid that, I tried to make a special point of sharing things with the young guys.

Every spring, Hank used to give me his glove from the year before. He also let me drive his rental car around West Palm Beach, which was a privilege. Hank was such a good friend that I just wanted to do things for him. But I could never do as much as he did for me just by taking me under his wing. He gave me the best advice I ever got in the big leagues. He said, "Whatever God gave you, that's what will keep you here. So whatever you did in the minor leagues to get here, that's what you do when you're here. The coaches will tell you how they want you to hit, and when you're in the batting cage, do what they say to do. But when you get up to that plate and it's just you and the pitcher, do what got you here. Take advice from everybody, but do what you have to do." That advice kept me in the big leagues for ten years.

Hank was just so smart about playing ball. A lot of people seem to think black players have ability and that's all there is to it, but it's just not true. I learned how to think on the ball field from Hank Aaron. He was a scientific ballplayer, the most knowledgeable baseball man I ever met. And if you talk to other players on our team—guys like Dusty Baker and Clete Boyer and Darrell Evans—they'll all tell you the same thing. —Ralph Garr

I had emerged from the doldrums by the end of the 1972 season, and one of the reasons was that I was reunited with Eddie Mathews. Eddie was brought back to Atlanta to replace Lum Harris as manager, which was one of the best things that could have happened to me at that moment. Dusty and Ralph were great friends, but they were new friends. So many of my old friends and teammates had been sent away that I felt cut off from my past and out of place, almost like my class had graduated and I was still sitting at my desk as the new kids arrived in the fall. But having Eddie around me made me feel like I was in this thing together with somebody. Hundreds of times throughout my career, Eddie's face was the first one I had seen, and his hand was the first one I had shaken, after circling the bases and touching home plate.

The Braves had become an uninspired team by 1972, and Eddie wasn't the only necessary change. Around the same time, Paul Richards was reassigned from general manager to super-scout, which called for a toast. My only reservation was that I didn't know much about Richards's replacement, Eddie Robinson. All I'd heard about Robinson was that he wouldn't shake Larry Doby's hand when Doby joined the Cleveland Indians as the first black player in the American League. But, like Bobby Bragan and so many others, Robinson had changed a lot since the 1940s. At any rate, by that time I think I would have welcomed Lester Maddox if he were replacing Paul Richards.

It was a period of new faces in my life, the most important and prettiest of which belonged to a gracious television personality named Billye Williams. Billye was co-hostess of a morning talk show in Atlanta called "Today in Georgia," and she first contacted me about a series of profiles she was doing on Braves players.

My husband had died following surgery in 1970, and it was a very difficult time for me. At one point during that period, the producer of the show, Bill Imboden, suggested that I needed to lighten up and it might be good therapy if I did a series on some of the Braves' ballplayers, which we called "Billye at the Bat." I had actually met Henry very briefly in 1969, when he was interviewed for the show by my co-host, Charlie Welch, but I didn't really know him. Anyway, he was the first one booked for "Billye at the Bat," and naturally it was a big thing for us. We ran promos on it for a week.

The show came on at nine, and at nine o'clock on the day he was scheduled, there was no Henry. At nine forty-five, he was still not there. It was very embarrassing to me and the show, and we had to rebook him. This time, we made sure we didn't go overboard with the promos. He was living at the Landmark Apartments at the time, and it happened to be on my way to work, so on the day that he was rescheduled to appear on the show, I stopped by to see if he was up. The Braves had played extra innings the night before, and I knew that he might still be sleeping. So I kind of leaned on the doorbell until he answered. When he finally came to the door, I offered to wait for him to go to the studio. But he assured me he would come as soon as he was dressed, which he did. —Billye Aaron

After the interview with Billye, I asked her out to dinner, but she said she wasn't ready yet to go out in public. At any rate, I told her I would help her arrange to get other players on the show, and we started to talk on the telephone quite a bit. That sort of became the way we dated. We both needed somebody to talk to, because I was having trouble dealing with my divorce and she was coping with the death of her husband.

Billye had been married to Dr. Sam Williams, a pastor at Friendship Baptist Church, a philosophy professor at Morehouse College, and one of the giants of the civil rights movement in Atlanta. Dr. Williams had been known as the voice of reason in Atlanta and acted as intermediary between the black activists and the white community. But there was nothing halfway about his own convictions, and he was extremely influential. One of his students at Morehouse had been Martin Luther King, and King gave him credit for many of his ideas. He also debated

Stokely Carmichael and was constantly in touch with nearly all of the leaders of the movement.

In addition to being refined and charming and a wonderful mother—she had a beautiful little girl named Ceci—Billye had all the education that I lacked. She had been an English teacher at the Atlanta University center, which was where she met Dr. Williams. She helped bring me into the world of books and ideas and made me more conversant in the things I believed in. At the same time, I made her a baseball fan, although she would have me believe that she went to the games for the hot dogs and peanuts.

My thinking was expanded by being around Billye, but she never tried to change or influence me. It happened naturally, just as it did when I was around the Reverend Jesse Jackson. Sometime in the early 1970s, Jesse had started coming around the ballpark whenever we were in Chicago. After we became friends, I would take Baker and Garr over to Jesse's house for dinner and small talk about baseball or civil rights or religion or whatever we felt like talking about. Jesse saw that we were in a position to make a difference in the movement, and that I was especially. He knew that as I approached Ruth, there would be reporters and cameras and film crews all across the country. If I wanted to use it, I would have a forum greater than almost any politician or statesman in America. Jesse never tried to get me to say anything I didn't believe in, but he let me know that if there was something I did believe in, I had a rare opportunity to make my point.

The first substantial contribution I made to black society was a bowling tournament I put together after the 1972 season for Sickle Cell Anemia. We had Ernie Banks, Reggie Jackson, Tom Seaver, Frank Robinson, Jim Palmer, Willie Stargell, Eddie Mathews, Lew Burdette, Gale Sayers of football—more stars than I can remember—and we raised a lot of money. It made me proud to think that I could attract all those great people and made me feel good to see them giving up their time for a worthy cause. In a way, it was my first tangible dividend for hitting home runs.

I also proved that year that I could lose money as easily as I could earn and raise it. After the press reported my salary, I was suddenly besieged by people who wanted to help me invest my money. I decided to trust a couple of insurance guys who formed an investment company called Menke-Riback, and turned almost everything over to them. My paychecks went directly to them, and they had power of attorney to sign checks and vouchers in my name. Their biggest investment for me was a large office complex northeast of Atlanta, the only problem being that we didn't have the tenants to fill it. The buildings were auctioned off about a year later, and I ended up losing over a million dollars in the deal. I had borrowed against my deferred compensation payments from the Braves, so it not only wiped out everything I had but also cut way into what I had coming. My secretary, Carla Koplin, kept telling me I should have Menke-Riback checked out, but I didn't want to be bothered with it. Finally, she arranged to have an auditor called in. The next day, they had cleared out of their offices—which were in a downtown penthouse. We never found anything illegal, but they charged me enormous fees for everything from writing letters to answering the telephone. I had to hire a lawyer to get me out of the deal and cut my losses. After that, I made up my mind that I would never sign another piece of paper or enter into a deal or even shake anybody's hand without consulting my lawyer first.

My history of bad business deals actually dated back to Milwaukee. I didn't lose anything with the Aaron-Bruton Investment Company, but one time I agreed to let a fellow use my name for a restaurant and tavern on North 12th Street. I didn't check into it sufficiently and realized too late that it was more of a neighborhood tavern than a restaurant and it might not be the nicest thing to have my name associated with. The Braves agreed—very strongly—and I had to hire a lawyer to negotiate me out of that one, too.

In Atlanta, I once got involved in a barbecue restaurant that was going to set up outlets all over the South. The problem was that it was run by white people to be put into black neighborhoods, and what the guys didn't understand was that you can't sell chopped barbecue in black neighborhoods; it has to be ribs. That venture was doomed from the beginning. Just recently, I was visiting the Cleveland Browns' camp when their coach, Bud Carson, told me that he lost money investing in my restaurant when he was an assistant coach at Georgia Tech. He said he only invested in the place because it had my name attached to it. That was a good reason *not* to invest in it. There was also the time when I played tennis with a nice-looking black guy in West Palm Beach who described himself as a broker in sugar futures and persuaded me to invest $20,000 with him, which was money down the drain.

It got to the point where I almost had to break the record to get back on my feet financially. I hit thirty-four homers in 1972, which left me only forty-one shy of Ruth. It seemed unlikely that I would hit forty-one or forty-two homers in 1973, at the age of thirty-nine, but I was only one year removed from hitting forty-seven, and I was powerfully motivated on several fronts. The most basic motivation was the pure ambition to break such an important and long-standing barrier. Along with that would come the recognition that I thought was long overdue me: I would be out of the shadows. I can't deny that I was also very interested in the financial benefits that the record would surely bring. Then there was the sense of doing something for my race. I felt stronger and stronger about that as the years went on—as I read about people like Martin Luther King and listened to people like Jesse Jackson, and as I saw what went on around me in baseball, and in Atlanta. The hate mail drove me, too. In 1972, when people finally realized that I was climbing up Ruth's back, the "Dear Nigger" letters started showing up with alarming regularity. They told me that no nigger had any right to go where I was going. There's no way to measure the effect that those letters had on me, but I like to think that every one of them added another home run to my total.

There was one last thing that hardened my resolve after the 1972 season. Late in October, Jackie Robinson died. It was just a couple of weeks after he had been in Cincinnati for the World Series. His hair was white, he walked with a cane, and he was going blind with diabetes, but he was still a spellbinding presence. Jackie gave a talk while he was in Cincinnati and said that until the time came when there was a black man calling the shots from the dugout or from a swivel chair in the front office, baseball would have its head buried in the sand. I wasn't there, but I understand that after his talk, Jackie wandered into the Oakland clubhouse, thinking that some of the black players might want to come up and talk to him, maybe even say thank you. But none of them did, and after a while, Jackie just walked out with his cane and went back to his hotel room. It was the last time he was seen in public.

A lot of the black players from the early days were at his funeral, but I was shocked at how few of the active players showed up. It made me more determined than ever to keep Jackie's dream alive, and the best way I could do that was to become the all-time home run champion in the history of the game that had kept out black people for more than sixty years. I owed it to Jackie. I just wish he could have seen me do it. God, he would have been proud.

10

There were a few things, if only a very few, that Hank Aaron and Babe Ruth had in common. They were obviously linked by home runs, although there was little resemblance in the geometry and physiological dynamics that the two of them applied to send balls into the seats. They both played with the Braves, although Aaron devoted twenty-one years to the team and Ruth but twenty-eight games. Their fathers both ran neighborhood taverns, although George Herman Ruth, Sr., was the bartender, not the proprietor, and Herbert Aaron sold more booze out of the stash hidden behind the loose board over his front door. They both left high school early to embark on their careers, although Ruth went into organized ball and Aaron the Negro League. And as they tried to make their ways in the game, both players were referred to publicly and frequently as "nigger," although Aaron was black and Ruth wouldn't have been allowed to play big-league ball if he had been. Ruth did, however, sport certain facial features that some regarded as Negroid, and when some bold antagonist such as an opposing player would speak up with this observation, as many did, the Babe would fly into a rage, becoming so palpably angry that he was liable to do something like wave at the center-field bleachers and then hit the ball there, which was the sort of thing that went into the legend of baseball's most romantic, colorful, conspicuous, influential, historic, epic, and legendary figure. The man was so distinct that he became an adjective. He was Ruthian.

There would never be such a thing as an Aaronian clout. There would never be another baseball player who could foster the language and legacy that Ruth did, because there cannot be. It was his lot to be the symbol and savior of the game, its slugger, its prototypical Yankee, its beloved Bambino. Some guys are pitchers, some are second basemen, some are real estate developers, some are night managers at Burger King, and Babe Ruth is the most romantic, colorful, conspicuous, influential, historic, epic, and legendary figure in baseball. It's just what he is. In the History of Baseball, he is lesson number one.

Ruth is one of two players whose legacy to baseball was both indispensable and inimitable, with Jackie Robinson being the other. Unlike Robinson, though, there was nothing sociological about Ruth's contribution. In fact, there was little that was even logical about what he did. He was a ponderous-looking man, practically an oaf, a graceless, bawdy, overindulgent fellow whose peculiar speciality was something that had not previously been contemplated; at least, not in Ruthian terms. In the days before Ruth, a home run was something to be sampled, an hors d'oeuvre at which a few notable players nibbled. But the Babe came along and cleaned off the tray. Then he had some beer, belched, and wolfed down some more. He was a study in conspicuous consumption, an unfettered basher whose disrespect for the home run paradoxically raised it to a level of reverence. They say he invented the home run, and to pass off that statement as hyperbole is to be tediously technical. In the same way, he invented the Yankees.

It seemed that the grandest things of baseball were the manifestations of Ruth. He was the potbelly of the world's fattest batting order, the swaggering Sultan of Swat. To many baseball fans, Ruth meant everything. He was the Babe, babe. There would never be another.

This was the message that was shoved into Henry Aaron's face as his home run total approached 700. It was all too true . . . and all too irrelevant, because Hank Aaron never desired to be Babe Ruth or to take his place. He had no interest in bringing down anybody's hero. All of that was somebody else's business. The fact is, Aaron had very little feeling at all about Babe Ruth. Ruth was practically finished with the Yankees when Aaron was born in 1934, and as a child Aaron had no particular affinity for him or any other white ballplayer. They were of another world. Even when he began appearing in the same sentences, Aaron knew instinctively that he was nothing like Ruth. On a personal level, they were as different as their batting styles. Aaron was a man who ate in his room and called home every night, Ruth a

social glutton who held curfew in contempt and wore out waiters' shoes. Ruth told dirty jokes to the social matrons of New
York; Aaron was uncomfortable hearing them from his closest
teammates. Ruth was a backslapper who accumulated friends he
couldn't even name, Aaron a loner who observed people with
canny suspicion.

On the more pertinent level, Ruth was a swashbuckling home
run king of bigger-than-life proportions, Aaron a humble man
who happened to hit balls over fences. The two had very little to
do with each other, in any capacity, except for the number 714,
which happened to be the amount of home runs Ruth hit before
he retired in 1935. It was a total that so exceeded the sum of any
other player's home runs as to seem eternally unapproachable,
which was a sensible assumption in light of the fact that, indeed,
no one would threaten Ruth's transcendent status among home
run hitters. By definition, it was impossible for that to happen,
because Ruth would always be the original, the great man whose
example engendered descendants of the home run who would
compete with each other in a way the Babe never had to.

Aaron was the survivor of that competition. And a survivor
is generally what he was, a player who simply kept swinging
longer and more effectively than all the others. It puzzled him
that few could see or respect that. And it angered him that he
could not go about his private quest without being compared,
criticized, cross-examined, and cussed out in the context of a
broad-nosed white man he cared little about.

◆　　◆　　◆

It was a tragic winter. On New Year's Day, word came that
Roberto Clemente had been killed in an airplane crash after taking off from Puerto Rico in bad weather. He had been on a mercy
mission, flying supplies to earthquake victims in Nicaragua. I was
shaken when I heard the news. For several days, I kept believing
that they would find Roberto and he would be all right. And the
whole time, I kept thinking about how trivial our little rivalry
seemed about who was the best right fielder.

Roberto was six months younger than I was, and he was still at the top of his game when he was taken from us. Incredibly, he had finished the 1972 season with exactly 3,000 hits. It wouldn't have been right for him to have even one fewer, which made me realize that we should take nothing for granted in life or in baseball. Clemente's death also made me realize how precious my opportunity was—the privilege of setting a new record for home runs.

With all that had happened in the previous year, I was probably never as eager and ready for a season to begin as I was in 1973. Willie Mays was behind me, Mathews and Billye were alongside, and Babe Ruth was straight ahead. A ballplayer needs something extra to keep him going at the age of thirty-nine, and no player ever had as much to play for as I had that year. I was on the verge of doing something that would give me a place in baseball history, and I couldn't wait to do it. I had been waiting and waiting all my life for something or other; now it was up to me. Unless you grew up black in the South, I don't think you can imagine the surge of freedom and power I felt just knowing that I controlled my own destiny.

My high lasted for about a month, maybe less. Ironically, the thing that brought me down was hitting home runs. It wasn't that I couldn't hit them; the problem was that I couldn't hit anything else. Seven of my first nine hits in 1973 were home runs, and for several weeks my batting average was down around .200. That was all the critics needed to see. It was plain to them that I was no longer a complete hitter, I was concerned only with the record, and I had lost all interest in the good of the team. They made that clear in their letters to me.

Dear Henry:

First I would like to say you are regarded by many as a good baseball player and a good hitter. To even remotely suggest that you are a great player or hitter, a person would have to be judged insane.

I went into the season wanting to break the record that summer, but it wasn't long before I changed my goal. I still wanted the record, but I didn't want to do it batting .240. I wanted to hit .300, and if the record came along the way, great. If not, it would come the next year. There was no time pressure. Only two things could keep me from breaking the record—a serious injury or a terrible batting average. If I couldn't get my average up to a respectable level, there was a chance I would stop short, because I'd never been a one-dimensional hitter and I didn't want to be one at the moment history came knocking. So, as far as I was concerned, everything was fine and dandy as long as I stayed healthy and the base hits fell in.

Not everybody shared that opinion, however.

Dear Nigger,

Everybody loved Babe Ruth. You will be the most hated man in this country if you break his career home run record.

Dear Nigger,

In my humble way of thinking, you are doing more to hurt Baseball than any other that ever played the game. You may break the record and you may replace Babe Ruth in the hearts of the liberal sportswriters, the liberal newspapers, TV and radio, as well as in the hearts of the long-haired Hippies. But you will never replace the Babe in the hearts of clear-thinking members of our Society. So, roll on in your undeserved glory, Black Boy.

Friend Hank,

If you should "break" Babe Ruth's record of 714 home runs, remember the Babe averaged a home run for every eleven times at bat. For several years he was pitching. If the Babe had been playing every day possible, his home runs would be close to 900.

I believe you are a man of high morals and wouldn't want to be the holder of a title that could be later classified as being tainted. Think it over Hank.

Dear Black Boy,

Listen Black Boy, We don't want no nigger Babe Ruth.

Dear Super Spook,

First of all, I don't care for the color of shit. You are pretty damn repugnant trying to break the Babe's record. You boogies will think that you invented baseball or something.

Dear Mr. Nigger,

I hope you don't break the Babe's record. How do I tell my kids that a nigger did it?

In May, when our crowds were so pitiful that you could practically hear somebody crack open a peanut, there was a small group of rednecks who sat in the right-field stands and heckled me for three straight nights. At first, it was the same stuff I was used to hearing, mostly about all the money I was making for striking out and hitting into double plays, but as they became drunker and louder they became more obscene and personal, and I became angrier and angrier. They were using Sally League language, and I wasn't going to let anybody take me back to the Sally League. Finally, in the ninth inning of the third night, I walked over to the stands and told them I was going to come up there and kick their asses if they didn't shut up. But before I could do anything I would later regret, the security police arrived and escorted them out of the park. I really can't say what might have happened if security hadn't come. All I know is that I was fed up.

I didn't expect the fans to give me a standing ovation every time I stepped on the field, but I thought a few of them might come over to my side as I approached Ruth. At the very least, I felt I had earned the right not to be verbally abused and racially ravaged in my home ballpark. I felt I had earned the right to be treated like a human being in the city that was supposed to be too busy to hate. The way I saw it, the only thing Atlanta was too busy for was baseball. It didn't seem to give a damn about the Braves, and it seemed like the only thing that mattered about the home run record was that a nigger was about to step out of line and break it. I was angry enough that I made a public statement in which I charged that America was still a racist country and all that Atlanta had to offer was hatred and resentment. I knew, of course, that there were plenty of good people and at least a few good baseball fans in Atlanta, but I was mad at the whole South. Later, I backed off a little and said that the only thing wrong with Atlanta was that it had Georgia sticking out of it. The fact is, I like and admire Atlanta now, and in many ways I'm proud to live there, but I sure didn't feel that way in 1973.

And believe me, the feeling was mutual. All year long, Atlanta overwhelmed me with its indifference. Early in the season, we averaged less than 8,000 fans at home and more than three times as many on the road. I would get standing ovations in New York and Los Angeles and Chicago and St. Louis, and I couldn't make it through the hotel lobbies for all the people wanting autographs; but it seemed like Atlanta frankly didn't give a damn. It was true that we didn't have a contending team, but we had the kind of team that fans usually like to watch. We led the league in home runs.

Three of us were among the home run leaders from the beginning of the season—myself, Darrell Evans, who had become our regular third baseman, and Davey Johnson, a second baseman we got from Baltimore in a trade involving Earl Williams. Johnson was a good glove man who had never been a home run hitter until he came to Atlanta. In Baltimore, most of the players used heavy bats because that was what Frank Robinson used, but I convinced Davey that he should use a lighter bat in the National League because there were more fastball pitchers. He started popping those fastballs into that hot Atlanta air, and the results amazed everybody, especially Davey. At one point, an old lady in tennis shoes stopped me at our hotel in Los Angeles and asked if I were the home run king, and I told her, no ma'am, Davey Johnson was up in his room sleeping.

It was all I could do to stay close to Darrell and Davey in home runs, because I was only playing about two thirds of the time. My knees and back were feeling every bit of thirty-nine, and my throwing arm had weakened so much that I asked Mathews to move me from right field to left. He had already given up on the idea of me playing first base—he said he moved me back to the outfield to save my life. It was obvious that I wasn't the all-around player I'd been ten or five or even two years before, but I did have the best home run percentage in the National League. My batting average also climbed steadily starting in the middle of May. All things considered, I thought I was having a hell of a year.

Dear Nigger,

You can hit all dem home runs over dem short fences, but you can't take dat black off yo face.

Dirty old nigger man,

Had Ruth played and been at bat as many times as you, old nigger, he would have hit just short of 1100 home runs. I hope lightning strikes you for trying to blemish Ruth's record. Retire old man. I repeat I hope lightning strikes you old man four-flusher. The worst to you old black man.

Dear Hank Aaron,

How about some sickle cell anemia, Hank?

Dear Jungle Bunny,

You may beat Ruth's record but there will always be only one Babe. You will be just another Black fuck down from the trees. Go back to the Jungles.

Dear Brother Hank Aaron,

I hope you join Brother Dr. Martin Luther King in that Heaven he spoke of. Willie Mays was a much better player than you, anyway!

Dear Nigger,

You're a real SKUM. You should still be in the Nigger Leagues.

Dear Jungle Bunny,

You have the nerve to try to break the Babe's record. 1st of all you're black so you have no business even being here. Go back to Coonsland. You and your people always talk about be treated bad. Well look what the Krauts and the Romans did to the Jews and Christians, never giving them a chance. In America we gave you niggers everything and you want more. Personally I like you because I don't think your prejudice like them bigots but cause your black you're un-equal to me the King. In closing I hope you hit 713 and get a heart attack on the field but your a nice jig.

Dear Nigger Scum,

Niggers, Jews, Yankees, Hippies, Nigger Lovers are the scum of the Earth. Niggers are animals, not humans. Niggers do not have souls because they are animals, have strong backs and weak minds. The time has come to send the niggers back to Africa, there is an animal shortage over there. You niggers are no good, sorry, dirty as cockroaches and a dead nigger is a good nigger. The nigger loving Jews are sorry as niggers, and a disgrace to the White Race. These scum should be sent back to Israel.

Boy, I despise, hate and detest you scum. The world is better off to get rid of you scum—scum—scum—scum—scum.

As the hate mail piled up, I became more and more intent on breaking the record and shoving it in the ugly faces of those bigots. I'm sure it made me a better hitter. But it also made my life very, very difficult. A lot of the letters threatened me, and it got to the point that the FBI was reading and confiscating some of my mail before I ever saw it. My secretary, Carla Koplin, was going through almost 3,000 letters a day at one point. Most of the mail was supportive, and the encouraging words people wrote helped me fight through the hate. The good fans helped keep me going, and I was grateful to them, but in a different way, they could be as hard to deal with as the bad ones. In Los Angeles, the Braves arranged for the bus to pick us up in front of the dugout, because I could never make it through the autograph hounds to the parking lot. All over the league, I had to register at our hotels under fictitious names. I would reserve one room in my name, where the operator could put calls through and let them ring, and another in a name like Diefendorfer, where I actually stayed. The problem was that sometimes my children couldn't get through, and that worried me because they weren't safe.

My oldest daughter, Gaile, was a student at Fisk University in Nashville, and she was receiving strange, unsettling phone calls. Other students told her that a man had been asking them about her schedule and her habits. One morning, Billye and I were having breakfast at home when an FBI agent knocked on the door and told me there were reports that Gaile had been kidnapped. It turned out that she hadn't been, but an informer told the FBI that the kidnapping had been plotted and attempted. It was enough to scare the hell out of me, and, needless to say, it was a horrifying experience for Gaile.

> *My dorm mother came and got me one day and brought me to a room where four FBI men were waiting for me. That was when they told me they had received a report that I might be kidnapped. They told me what to do if it happened, and they told me how they planned to protect me. There were FBI agents all over the campus, disguised as yardmen and maintenance men. That whole year at Fisk, I was never by myself. It was pretty frightening, and I know my father was worried sick about it. He flew up to Nashville to visit me almost every time he had an off day.*—Gaile Aaron

We were able to keep closer tabs on the other kids, who were living with Barbara and going to private schools in Atlanta—Hankie and Lary at Marist High School and Dorinda just down the road at a Montessori elementary school. The schools were very strict about keeping strangers and visitors away from the kids, but we couldn't protect everybody all the time, and there were enough crackpots out there to make us constantly nervous. Once, when the newspaper ran a picture of Dorinda and me at a Braves father-kid game, somebody clipped it and sent it to me with the words, "Daddy, please think about us. Please, please!" Nobody close to me was off limits. People would even call my parents in Mobile and tell them that they would never see their boy again. My father would tell them to go to hell and then hang up.

I tried not to take the threats on my own life too seriously, but they were always in the back of my mind. As preposterous as it seemed that somebody would want to kill a ballplayer for breaking a record, I knew that an aroused bigot is capable of almost anything. There were too many chilling examples out there for me to ignore the situation entirely. Now and then, when the FBI would advise me of a threat on a particular night, I would tell my teammates not to get too close to me in the dugout. One night in Montreal, I was standing out in left field with my hands on my knees when a firecracker went off in the stands. It sounded like a gunshot, and I thought, uh-oh, this is it. I kept my eyes straight ahead and didn't move a muscle until I realized I was still in one piece and breathing.

A lot of the threats came through phone calls to the Braves. Donald Davidson was the man in charge of my contacts with the outside world, and he was a good man for the job because nothing fazed Donald. One time there was a rumor that I had been shot, and when a reporter reached Donald to inquire about it, he said, "I'm sure if Henry had been shot he would have called and told me."

But the danger was real enough that the Braves and the city of Atlanta arranged to have a policeman named Calvin Wardlaw escort me to and from the ballpark and make sure I was tucked in at night. I saw as much of Calvin that year as Billye or Mathews or anybody. Whenever we were together, he carried a binoculars case with his badge and a pistol inside. He never had to reach for the pistol, but I felt better having him around. One time, he accidentally left a package on the seat of my car that I wasn't supposed to see, and inside was some toilet paper with a picture of a gorilla and a note to me that said, "This is your mother." It didn't take much to figure out what kind of people we were dealing with, and as a result we were always on the lookout. Calvin and I almost never made eye contact when we spoke to each other in public, because I was always looking over his shoulder and he was always looking over mine. To this day, I'm still that way.

Dear Hank,

You are a very good ballplayer, but if you come close to Babe Ruth's 714 homers I have a contract out on you. Over 700 and you can consider yourself punctured with a .22 shell. If by the all star game you have come within 20 homers of Babe you will be shot on sight by one of my assassins on July 24, 1973.

Dear Hank Aaron,

Retire or die! The Atlanta Braves will be moving around the country and I'll move with them. You'll be in Montreal June 5–7. Will you die there? You'll be in Shea Stadium July 6–8, and in Philly July 9th to 11th. Then again you'll be in Montreal and St. Louis in August. You will die in one of those games. I'll shoot you in one of them. Will I sneak a rifle into the upper deck or a .45 in the bleachers? I don't know yet. But you know you will die unless you retire!

Dear Hank Aaron,

I got orders to do a bad job on you if and when you get 10 from B. Ruth record. A guy in Atlanta and a few in Miami Fla don't seem to care if they have to take care of your family too.

Hey nigger boy,

We at the KKK Staten island Division want you to know that no number of guards can keep you dirty son of a bitch nigger mother fucker alive.

Dear Nigger,

Beware of the white man's wrath [with picture of Klansman's hood].

Mr. Aaron,

We the Ku Klux Klan Knights of America are now going to make this something you better pay attention to. If you do not retire from the baseball seen (QUIT) your family will inherit a great bit of trouble. We can't make this sound any clearer (DEATH). We will be in touch later with something more CONVINCING.

Dear Nigger Henry,

It has come to my attention that you are going to break Babe Ruth's record. I don't think that you are going to break this record established by the great Babe Ruth if I can help it. Getting back to your blackness, I don't think that any coon should ever play baseball. Whites are far more superior than jungle bunnies. I will be going to the rest of your games and if you hit one more home run it will be your last. My gun is watching your every black move. This is no joke.

Dear Nigger,

You black animal, I hope you never live long enough to hit more home runs than the great Babe Ruth. Niggers are like animals and have a short life span. Martin Luther King was a trouble-maker, and he had a short life span.

Dear Hank Aaron,

I hope you get it between the eyes.

Dear Hank Aaron,

I hate you!!!! Your such a little creap! I hate you and your family. I'D LIKE TO KILL YOU!! BANG BANG YOUR DEAD.
    P.S. It mite happen.

I was the only one of the Braves' officers who actually lived in Atlanta, so I was technically in charge of Henry's situation that year. I met with him early on and said, "Look, a lot of this stuff is going to be coming." He asked me if we would just handle it for him. He didn't even want to know about the threats unless we thought there was one serious enough to get the FBI involved. You could tell that most of the letters were cranks. There was a guy from Fond du Lac, Wisconsin, who wrote him all the time with filthy racial remarks, and another one from Victorville, California. There was a lot of KKK stuff, much of it from the North. The FBI told us that if anybody was going to do something to Henry, they probably wouldn't write him first, but we had to take it seriously when there was a specific threat.

When we would get a letter like that, we would stick it in a plastic bag and turn it over to the FBI. There were a lot of crazies out there.

When I look back on that whole episode of Henry going after the Ruth record, that's the most amazing part of it to me. People had no idea what he was going through. Nowadays, a player will get one threat and he won't even go out on the field. Henry had them practically every day, and for a long time he didn't say a word about it.—Dick Cecil, former Braves vice president

I asked Carla to save the hate letters that she didn't have to turn over to the authorities. I didn't read most of them, but I wanted to have them as reminders. I kept feeling more and more strongly that I had to break the record not only for myself and for Jackie Robinson and for black people, but also to strike back at the vicious little people who wanted to keep me from doing it. All that hatred left a deep scar on me. I was just a man doing something that God had given me the power to do, and I was living like an outcast in my own country. I had nowhere to go except home and to the ballpark, home and to the ballpark. I was a prisoner in my own apartment. Outside my apartment, I could see a hotel sign that blinked on and off, and it got to where I could tell you how many times that sign blinked in a minute. That whole period, I lived like a guy in a fishbowl, swimming from side to side with nowhere to go, watching everybody watching me. I resented it, and I still resent it. It should have been the most enjoyable time in my life, and instead it was hell. I'm proud of the home run record, but I don't talk about it because it brings back too many unpleasant memories.

You find out who your real friends are during times like that. Ralph and Dusty always lifted my spirits, and Billye really came through for me, talking me through a lot of tough times, helping me keep things in perspective and showing me that there was still some love in the world. And I don't think a manager ever meant more to a player than Eddie Mathews meant to me during those times. He knew me and understood me as well as anybody in baseball, and he did all he could to take the pressure off me. Also, one of Eddie's coaches was my old teammate, Lew Burdette, who had a reputation as not being the biggest ally of the black ballplayer; but Lew was there for me when the going was rough, just like he had been when he was pitching and the other team was throwing at my head. One more fellow I couldn't have done without was a veteran catcher named Paul Casanova, a big Cuban who had a good grip on things and was a trusty companion for dinners and drinks and long flights. I needed somebody on the team to pour out my troubles to when I couldn't keep them inside any longer, and Cassy was the man.

> Hank kept almost everything to himself. You couldn't read him, because he wouldn't let anything show. It was the same as when he was batting. If he hit a home run or struck out, there was no difference. If he was in a slump, you knew it had to be killing him, but he would just walk to the dugout and sit down, or maybe go in the tunnel and have a cigarette and think about what he had to do the next time. He would never let the pitcher know how he felt. That was part of his strategy.
>
> One time that relief pitcher for St. Louis, "The Mad Hungarian," Al Hrabosky—the one who was always strutting around the mound and talking to the baseball—one night he struck out Hank in a big spot to win the game, and he was jumping up and down and making a big show. The next time we saw him, Hank hit one into the upper deck, and when he got to the dugout, he said, "Let's see the son of a bitch find that one and talk to it." But he wouldn't say anything like that to the pitcher. He would never do anything to show up a pitcher.
>
> I've never seen a man who could control his emotions like Hank did. We had bad teams in those years, and there was a lot of pressure with Hank going for the record, but he was the one taking the pressure off us and keeping us loose. One night in Montreal, we'd lost eight in a row and Hank came to bat in the ninth inning with two men on and us down by two runs, and he hit one that was headed way out of the park. Everybody in the dugout jumped up and started screaming because our losing streak was finally over, and all of a sudden the wind caught hold of the ball and brought it all the way back into the ballpark, and the left fielder caught it standing against the fence. We got on the bus to go to the airport, and nobody said anything for

thirty minutes. We felt terrible. Finally, Hank stood up in the back of the bus and said, "I'll bet any amount of money that damn Babe Ruth was up there blowing that ball back." It loosened everybody up, and we started playing better ball after that.

He almost never mentioned Babe Ruth, though. One time, he said to me, "Cassy, I'm not trying to break any record of Babe Ruth. I'm just trying to make one of my own." It was terrible the way people hated him for trying to break the record. The whole thing must have been eating him up. One day in Philadelphia we walked across the street from the hotel to eat breakfast and that was the first time he told me about the letters he had been getting. I couldn't believe what he was telling me. I said, "What?" He said, "Cassy, these people are crazy. I don't know what's going on, I really don't." But he was worried. As hard as he was to read, you could tell he was worried.—Paul Casanova

It was in Philadelphia in May that I finally mentioned to some sportswriters about the hate mail. One of them made a note of it at the bottom of a baseball story, but then the story was picked up in Atlanta and New York and the whole thing broke open. From that point on, the mail turned. I guess people were stunned by what they read, because thousands and thousands of them started writing me positive letters. One of the sports-talk radio shows in New York conducted a campaign to get people to support me. It was especially nice to see kind words coming out of New York, because that seemed to be where the greatest number of hate letters came from.

Dear Hank,

I understand you get a lot of crank letters concerning breaking Ruth's record. Enclosed is something [matches taped to the page] that will take care of those letters.

Dear Mr. Arron,

For years sports fans have been waiting for the right man to come along and break that record. You, Henry Arron, are that man. You are the MESSIAH that has finally arrived.

Dear Mr. Aaron,

I'm glad your catching up with Babe Ruth. By the way, can you tell me who Joe Shlabotnik is? I read Charlie Brown and his favorite ballplayer is Joe Shlabotnik.

Dear Mr. Aaron,

I am twelve years old, and I wanted to tell you that I have read many articles about the prejudice against you. I really think it's bad. I don't care what color you are. You could be green and it wouldn't matter. These nuts that keep comparing you in every way to Ruth are dumb. Maybe he's better. Maybe you are. How can you compare two people 30 or 40 years apart? You can't really. So many things are different. It's just some people can't stand to see someone a bit different from them ruin something someone else more like them set. I've never read where you said you're better than Ruth. That's because you never said it! What do those fans want you to do? Just quit hitting?

All over the National League, the fans started yelling encouragement to me. At the Astrodome, they even flashed a message on the scoreboard saying that despite the feelings of those who wrote the hateful letters, the good fans of Houston were behind me all the way. Meanwhile, the mail was flooding in. I received so much of it that the post office didn't even need an address. Letters would arrive in my mailbox with Hank Aaron written on the envelope—one of them just said "The Hammer"—and nothing else. At the end of the year, the U.S. Postal Service calculated my mail at 930,000 letters and gave me a little plaque for receiving the most of any nonpolitician in the country. Dinah Shore was second with 60,000. Several newspapers and magazines carried pictures of Carla surrounded by the sacks of letters that filled her office. After that, though, she started getting hate mail herself from people who couldn't accept the fact that a white woman would work for a black man in the South and assumed there must have been more between us.

The overwhelming majority of letters were supportive after the news of the hate mail got out, but to the bigots it was just another reason to rip me apart. If there was a recurring theme to the negative mail—other than the fact that I was just a nigger—it was the tired old argument that I was no Babe Ruth. The same points were brought up over and over and over—that I had batted so many more times than Ruth, that I played with a livelier ball, that Ruth had been a pitcher for part of his career, that pitchers were better in Ruth's time, that travel was tougher in Ruth's time, that Ruth had a higher batting average than me. I heard them all, and I respected them all; and I thought that none of them made a damn bit of difference because Babe Ruth was Babe Ruth and I was just a man trying to do my job. I never got into the arguments over Ruth versus me, or Ruth's time versus my time, because I knew that nothing would ever be solved. If people want to hear me say that Babe Ruth was the greatest home run hitter, fine, Babe Ruth was the greatest home run hitter.

But I do want to get my two cents in once and for all. I don't like to get involved in the common arguments that support me and modern players—the fact that I had to fly all over the country and play night games in bigger ballparks while facing fresh relief pitchers who threw sliders, which is the nastiest pitch of all and hadn't even been invented in Ruth's day—but there is one point that I do care about because it hits close to my heart. That's the fact that Ruth played in a time when there were no black players. To me, that's the most relevant point of all, because it stands apart from the changes that reflect the natural evolution of the game—things like new facilities and better equipment and modern innovations. This goes deeper than the other changes because it has to do with the people who play the game. It goes right to the foundation of the Babe Ruth legend, which is the fact that he towered over all the other hitters of his time. He did that, and there's no denying it. There has never been a more dominant hitter. But it should be understood that he dominated a very weakened field. If black players had been allowed to play in the major leagues at the time, it is highly unlikely that Ruth would have dominated in the manner that he did. Think about it. What would the National League have been like in my time without black players? Who would have been the greatest home run hitters if I had not been in the league, or Mays or Banks or Frank Robinson or Willie McCovey or Orlando Cepeda or Willie Stargell or Billy Williams or Richie Allen? I'll tell you. The white player who hit the most home runs in the National League in the 1960s was Ron Santo, who was almost fifty ahead of the next white player, Eddie Mathews. With no black players in the game, Ron Santo—who is not in the Hall of Fame—would have stood well above all the other home run hitters in the league during his time. By the same token, if I had played with only whites, as Ruth did, I would have outhomered every other player in the National League in the sixties by more than 120 (although Harmon Killebrew hit more than I did in the 1960s while playing in the nearly all white American League). In addition, it would have been significantly easier to hit in the National League if there hadn't been black pitchers like Bob Gibson, Juan Marichal, Ferguson Jenkins, and Bob Veale. By all of this, I certainly don't mean to imply that Babe Ruth was no better than Ron Santo, or that I was better than Ruth, or that Ruth was anything less than his legend. Like I said, I'm willing to call him the greatest home run hitter. I just want to show that comparisons go around in circles. They're like weeds—as soon as you deal with one, another one pops us. And I got damn tired of them.

There was no escaping them, though. One of the popular bumper stickers around Atlanta said, Aaron Is Ruth-less. On the radio sports shows, it seemed like every other caller was under a deep moral obligation to give his reasons why I couldn't carry Ruth's bat. And the newspaper writers were as bad as the fans when it came to making comparisons. It seemed that whatever town we were in, some writer was taking me to task for not being Babe Ruth. Without meaning to, they only aggravated an issue that did nobody any good. In general, arguments and comparisons are good for baseball. They show the diversity and depth of opinion that makes the game great. But this was a different case, because it wasn't harmless, as baseball arguments generally are. It wasn't just an argument over two players. It wasn't DiMaggio versus Williams or me versus Mays or even Mays versus Mantle.

This went a lot deeper than that. It was a case of people preserving their legend. It was a case of people defending their turf.

Dear Mr. Aaron,

I just can't bring myself to rooting for you, Mr. Aaron. I pray that you let the record books stand.

When a little kid thinks of baseball he thinks of home runs. And when a little kid turns the page in a record book and looks for home runs, and sees at the top of the list: Babe Ruth 714, he asks, "Who's Babe Ruth, dad?" After the father tells the child that Babe Ruth was such a dominant player a town had to build the biggest stadium to date in order to compensate for the hundreds of thousands of people who would flock to Yankee Stadium just to see him hit a baseball out of the park; that Babe Ruth was the one ingredient that led to the most powerful dynasty in the world of sports, the Yankee dynasty, which lasted four decades; that Babe Ruth had a lifetime batting average of .342; that Babe Ruth would do anything for a kid; and after that the father tells the child that in one of those World Series, Babe Ruth pointed to the spot in the centerfield stands where he was going to send the next pitch—and then went ahead and did it! After the father tells the child all of these god-like events by a warm, beautiful human being like Babe Ruth, the child's mind is now permanently set on admiration for this giant of a man named Babe Ruth. It is what is commonly known as a hero.

Therefore, how could *you*, Mr. Aaron, ruin, destroy, and shatter to pieces the one record which separates Babe Ruth from any other man to play the great game of baseball? How could you do it, Mr. Aaron? Are you ready to destroy that child's dreams? Because that's what you'll do, Mr. Aaron. If not for that child, then for the children of the future. And you know what that means to the future of America. So what it all boils down to is this: when my son turns the page in a record book and looks for home runs, and sees your name at the top of the list, he's not going to care one bit about Babe Ruth, Mr. Aaron, because Babe Ruth isn't going to be there. Is that what you want, Mr. Aaron? When you and I are dead and gone, do you want the world to know nothing about Babe Ruth because *you* took the one thing away from him that the world today still remembers him by? I hope and pray that you reconsider.

Now, of course, you know, Mr. Aaron, that this is not one of the thousands of hate letters you are receiving every day. Instead, this is a pleading letter. I would also like to point out that I wouldn't care if you were white as a sheet. The fact that you are black is totally irrelevant to the subject at hand. As a matter of fact, if my favorite player of all time, Mickey Mantle, were in your shoes, there is no doubt in my mind that this letter would be going right to him.

In closing, Mr. Aaron, I cannot wish you good luck. I can only remind you to think for the future, if, indeed, you do break the record. I dread the day it happens. I pray it never does. The decision is yours.

Mr. Hank Aaron,

One week ago I sent you a letter re Babe Ruth's Home Run Record. Since then I have talked to younger fellows about you and what they thought about the whole thing. This is what they said. "We don't think Aaron will live long enough to break the record. Somebody will get him one of those days or nights if he gets close. And if he does break the record by hitting more than the Babe's record he will be in danger of his life all the time." They also said what I said in my letter, nobody wants to see you or others harmed, but that does not rule out some nut who goes berserk and might reach you when you least expect it. Look what happened to George Wallace. Dr. King. And the cities you visit with your club, the race problem is so intense in all those places, you'd be smart by just coasting along without hitting homers. I'm sure the baseball public would be pleased with your decision. For your own safety let the Babe's record stand as a LEGEND. It would stand as a peaceful gesture and a contribution to Society on your part. It would make you a giant amongst blacks and whites.

My only answer to all of this was to do what I was there to do, which was hit. The home runs were coming at a rate that would put me very close to Ruth by the end of the season. Number 700 came in Atlanta late in July against Ken Brett of the

Phillies. It was a 400-footer that gave us the lead in the game, but we lost, which took the thrill out of the whole thing. After the game, I had my picture taken with a high school kid who won 700 silver dollars for catching the ball. I got the ball back, and this time I did not send it to the Hall of Fame because it had never acknowledged receiving the balls from my five hundredth and six hundredth home runs.

The Hall of Fame thing might seem trivial, but there was a larger pattern developing. Bowie Kuhn, the commissioner, had not been in Cincinnati when I got my three thousandth hit in 1972, and he didn't even send a telegram when I hit my seven hundredth home run. I spoke out about it, because I believed he would have shown more interest in the record if a white player had been involved and I also believed it was my duty to call attention to discrimination in baseball. The commissioner's response was that he had been waiting to congratulate me personally at the All-Star Game, which was a few days away. He also said he would be in the stands ready to jump out on the field when I hit my 714th and 715th home runs. I still wasn't satisfied, and Kuhn made a trip to St. Louis to talk to me about the situation. He said that it was his policy not to send telegrams for personal feats because there were so many of them that he might overlook somebody. I didn't think he had to worry about missing somebody who hit 700 home runs, though, since the only other person to do it had been dead for twenty-five years. Our little tiff got a lot of attention in the papers, which naturally prompted another round of letters.

Dear Nigar Aaron,

It's too bad that the commissioner of baseball didn't send you a telegram or come over and kiss you for hitting the 700 home run big deal why you dirty nigar you should thank God that the white man let you play period. The white people don't owe you filthy nigars nothing.

Dear Mr. Aaron,

How could a person be a star and great for so many years then become just another nigger?

Dear Hank,

When I was a doctor in Montgomery I used to attend Braves games in Atlanta and was a fan of yours. But after hearing you lately, I think you should give thanks to your God for the gifts he gave you and be thankful for every home run and be less critical of the things that you think should come your way and do not. Examine yourself and ask yourself the question if you just might be partly to blame for the situation you are in. Unless you have a change of heart I would not drive across the street to see you play or even to see you hit that 714th home run.

Hank Aaron,

> With all that fortune,
> and all that fame,
> You're a stinkin nigger
> Just the same.

Dear Hank,

On the day you hit your 700th home run, my sister in Dayton, Ohio, had a baby boy. Because of our great respect for you as a ballplayer and as a person we have chosen the name Aaron, in your honor.

I was affected in a lot of ways by reaching 700. There was something about getting there that made me feel I was almost at my destination, like I had been traveling the back roads for twenty years and suddenly I was on Ruth's street, turning onto his driveway. One of my teammates said he actually saw me smiling a little when I came around third base on number 700, which was something I probably hadn't done since the pennant-winning home run in 1957. I was excited about it, and I guess I had expected other people to be excited with me, which was why it was so disappointing not to receive a telegram from the commissioner. The whole situation took something out of me. I think I let up for a little while after that, and suddenly I stopped hitting home runs. It was ten days before I hit my 701st and more than two weeks after that before I hit number 702, which tied Stan Musial's all-time record of 1,377 extra-base hits.

I was beginning to wear down. It's always hard to keep up your energy level through the muggy summer in Atlanta, and on top of that I wasn't getting much rest. As much as I tried to fight off my anxieties and fears, they hounded me at night in lonely hotel rooms. I started coming to the ballpark a couple of hours early to catch some sleep on a cot in the trainer's room, knowing there would be no more peace the moment I poked my head into the clubhouse. The camaraderie of the clubhouse had always been an important part of my baseball life, and although I realized it wasn't their fault, the news people had taken that away from me. I missed my teammates.

Newsweek called me the most conspicuous figure in sports, and Lord knows I felt like it. When we had a day off once I went home to Mobile to fish in the bay, and three boats full of reporters and photographers cruised alongside mine. A camera crew from NBC followed me for weeks to shoot a prime-time television special. I saw Tom Brokaw more than Eddie Mathews. It was impossible to give personal time to every reporter, but I tried to do as many interviews as cordially as I could, and generally the press was appreciative of my cooperation. The last time a player had been through something like I was going through was when Roger Maris broke Ruth's single-season home run record in 1961. Maris was like me in some ways, a private person who didn't relish the limelight. He accommodated the interviews, but he was testy and became so unnerved by the whole ordeal that his hair fell out in clumps. I guess the writers were looking for the same sort of reaction from me, but I knew what was coming and was determined not to let it get the best of me. I coped by playing little games with the reporters. I knew they were watching every move I made to see when they could swoop down on me, so I'd come out of the clubhose and walk over the foul lines onto the playing field where the press couldn't follow me. Sometimes I would just walk all the way up the baseline to the outfield fence and then turn and walk along the warning track. I could feel all the eyes in the park trailing me every step of the way.

My teammates and the Braves also did what they could to keep the media off me as much as possible. At one point a horde of about a dozen Japanese reporters showed up unannounced for an interview, and for some reason I couldn't accommodate them. So our public relations director, Bob Hope, stepped in and said he would answer their questions if as if he were me. The Japanese writers were thrilled—some of them said it was the best interview they'd ever had.

The media swarm was heavy for my seven hundredth home run, but then it slacked off for a while until I got close to 714. The crowds slacked off at the same time—at least, in Atlanta. When school and football games begin late in August, you can forget about drawing crowds to baseball games in Georgia. It didn't matter if we were playing for a pennant or if somebody was trying to break the home run record. There were nights when high school football games would outdraw the Braves . . . and I mean *single* high school football games. On the night I hit my 711th home run, we had all of 1,362 people at the ballpark, the smallest crowd in Braves history. That was a pretty strong statement of what Atlanta thought about me and my record.

Henry didn't stir the emotions. He was aloof. He did things so much easier than other ballplayers that he didn't get people excited when they watched him. Also, there's no question that Henry spoke out on things that a lot of people didn't want to hear—especially in Georgia. He took a leadership position in regards to racial things in a time when blacks weren't supposed to speak out. Henry suffered a lot of that backlash. You've got to realize, too, that in Atlanta a lot of our crowds came from small towns around the South. Those people were accustomed to blacks behaving a certain way, and that wasn't Henry. Henry did not shuffle.—Dick Cecil

It was peculiar that while Atlanta was folding its arms and turning the other way as I approached Ruth, the chase was a national event in the rest of the country. Preachers in black churches gave sermons on me. *Time* and *Newsweek* raced to see who could get me on their cover first—*Newsweek* won. There were five or six ballads written about me and more than a dozen books. I was offered movie parts, and when the soap operas found out that I spent the afternoons watching them—"Days of Our Lives," "The Edge of Night," "All My Children," "The Secret Storm"—I was invited onto their sets. People wanted to put my name on pens and pins and cups . . . one guy even suggested a Hank Aaron Gear Shift Knob. It was enough to make me feel like a big deal—until we got back to Atlanta.

Occasionally, I would catch little glimpses of things in Atlanta that let me know a few people cared, at least. I came out of a game once late in 1973 after a collision at first base, and as I ducked into the dugout I noticed a lady in the box seats looking at me with a horrified expression and sobbing. A tombstone maker named E. M. Bailey who lived near the ballpark built a little statue of me for his front yard. Mr. Bailey was interviewed by one of the newspapers, and he said that it brought tears to his eyes to think of all the things that I had gone through, and black people had gone through, to reach the point where a man like me could break a record like Babe Ruth's.

The people who cared most about the record were black people, and for the most part they were not the ones who had money to spend at the ballpark. The fans who could afford to come wouldn't, and I believe they missed a lot that year. The only thing ordinary about our team was our record. Phil Niekro pitched a no-hitter in August, and Evans, Johnson, and I hit home runs at an unprecedented pace. All the while, I had a chance to catch Ruth by the end of the year, and my 712th came in Houston against Dave Roberts on our last road trip. When the Astros came to Atlanta for the final series of the season, I needed two homers in three games to tie the Babe.

I did nothing Friday, but on Saturday I hit a slow curve from Jerry Reuss for number 713. It was also my fortieth homer of the season, and since Evans and Johnson had gotten there ahead of me, it marked the first time that one team ever had three players with forty or more. There were a lot of reporters in town because I was so close to Ruth, and the Braves held a press conference for the three of us after the game.

> *Davey and I knew that the only way we would be in the Hall of Fame was if we all hit forty homers. Hank was the last one to do it, but of course he was the one all the attention was on. When we had the press conference, nobody asked Davey or me a single question. Finally Hank said, "Look, I wanted to share this with these guys. If nobody is interested in that, then the press conference is over." And he got up and walked out. End of press conference.* —Darrell Evans

Sunday was cool and wet, and the Houston pitcher was Dave Roberts, who didn't throw particularly hard but was the kind of guy who gave me a lot of trouble because he kept batters off balance. Roberts was quoted in the paper as saying that he had been thinking about me for days and it bothered him to be consumed with me while I probably never gave him a second thought. He was wrong about that. I always thought long and hard about the next pitcher I had to face, and before going out there against Roberts I thought longer and harder than usual. I wanted badly to tie the record so it wouldn't be hanging over my head all winter. I had other plans that winter—mainly, to get married. I knew that the record would come quickly in 1974 if I didn't get it on Sunday, but I hated the idea of coming so close and not making it. It sounded too much like failure to suit me.

At the same time, I knew that I'd had a successful season whatever happened Sunday, and I'd proven that I wasn't just hanging around to get the record. My 40 home runs had come in fewer than 400 times at bat, and I nearly drove in 100 runs. I also had an outside chance to reach .300. As far as I was concerned, that would be my biggest accomplishment for the season, because it was what I had set out to do early on. It had seemed impossible to hit .300 when I was still in the low .200s in June, but I kept chipping away and went into the final Sunday at .296. If I'd had to choose on Sunday between getting one more home run and hitting .300, it would have been a tough call. The best plan was to hit the ball where nobody could catch it, the best place being the other side of the left-field fence.

.I'd pulled a slider for a home run against Roberts the last time we faced him, so I knew not to look for a slider to pull. In fact, I could count on Roberts to give me nothing on the inside part of the plate or above the knees. As much as I wanted to tie the record, he was probably more concerned with a home run than I was, and it would be impossible for him to forget about it. Every time I came to bat for the last month or so of the season, the pitcher was reminded about the record because the umpire would put the game ball in his pocket and toss the pitcher a different one. The Braves put infrared code numbers on balls that were to be used when I batted, so that my home run souvenirs could be identified and collected. As a result, the main thing on every pitcher's mind when I stepped into the box was to keep that infrared ball in the park, because if it went out, it would have his brand on it, too. Roberts was trying to win the game on that last Sunday, but he was also trying to keep his name out of the record books—which meant that I had a better chance of batting .300 than I did of hitting my 714th home run.

I couldn't believe it the first time up when I got a pitch to pull. I was so surprised that I jumped at it and fouled it off. From that time on, I saw nothing but off-speed stuff around the edges of the plate. But I managed a single, and then another one. The second hit put me at .300, and Mathews might have been tempted to pull me out of the game right there if it had been any other day. As it was, Eddie didn't have to ask me.

Roberts was still on the corners when I came up for the third time. I'm not sure I've ever had a battle quite like the one I had with him that day. When I singled the third time, I was three-for-three, and yet I felt, and I'm sure he felt, that he was doing a hell of a job on me. Still, I knew I'd get one more shot, and my average was high enough that I didn't have to worry about falling under .300. I didn't have to worry about slow stuff on the corners anymore, either, because Roberts was gone by the time I batted in the bottom of the eighth. He pulled a muscle in his back—I'd

like to think it was because of nerves—and was replaced by Don
Wilson . . . which was the worst news I could get.

There was never another hard thrower who gave me as much
trouble as Don Wilson—not Gibson or Drysdale or Koufax or
anybody. He was the pitcher who put me in a bad mood by
throwing a no-hitter on the night I fought with Rico Carty. What
made Wilson so tough on me was that he had a cut fastball that
would sail right away from my bat every time. It made me mad
that I couldn't hit him, and what aggravated me even more was
that Ralph Garr knocked Wilson around like he was nothing.
Ralph just wore him out. When Wilson was scheduled to pitch
against us, I'd moan and make a fuss, and at the same time Ralph
would be saying, "Bring him on! Bring him on!" Then Wilson
would throw one up in Ralph's eyes, and Ralph would reach up
and smack it into center field. And I'd go out there and look like
a damn fool. Don Wilson was the last man in the world I wanted
to see in the eighth inning that Sunday. But I got to him this time.
Yeah, I got to him good—popped that ball all the way out to
second base, where Tommy Helms caught it. My season was
over. Babe Ruth would have to wait until the spring.

But there was one more thing yet to come in the 1973 season,
and it caught me off guard. When I got out to left field for the
ninth inning, the fans out there stood up and applauded. Then
the fans on third base stood up to applaud, and the fans behind home plate, and right field, and then the upper deck. There
were about 40,000 people at the game—the biggest crowd of the
season—and they stood and cheered me for a full five minutes.
There have been a lot of standing ovations for a lot of baseball
players, but this was one for the ages as far as I was concerned. I
couldn't believe that I was Hank Aaron and this was Atlanta,
Georgia. I thought I'd never see the day. And, God Almighty, all
I'd done was pop up to second base. I looked up at that crowd
and I took off my hat and held it up in the air, and then I turned
in a circle and looked at all those people standing and clapping
all over the stadium, and to tell you the truth, I didn't know how
to feel. I knew I felt good. I don't think I'd ever felt so good in my
life. But I wasn't ready for it. I didn't know how to respond to

something like that, because it had never come up before. In all my years of baseball, I thought I was prepared for just about everything, but there was nothing in those years that prepared me for five minutes of standing ovation in Atlanta, Georgia, after popping up to second base.

I was severely disappointed to have to wait six more months before I had a chance at the record, but the send-off in Atlanta did a lot for my spirits. So did Billye, who would become my wife in November. And so did a telegram from a man named Al DiScipio. I received so many telegrams in those days that Mr. DiScipio's sat in the pile for a few days, unopened, before Carla could get to it. I was grateful to have a secretary like Carla, because if I hadn't I might have missed a million-dollar contract. Al DiScipio was president of Magnavox, and his telegram was an offer to become the company's spokesman on tours and television commercials. I immediately contacted my lawyer, Irving Kaler, and he started negotiations with Magnavox that ended up in the biggest endorsement deal ever given to an athlete. At last, my ship had come in.

Of course, Mr. DiScipio's offer was not the only thing that came in the mail.

Hi Hank!

I am a black man 20 years old and want to say that I'm very happy that you didn't tie or break Babe Ruth's home record. I think you just froze at the pressure. When you face real pitchers you can only hit singles. There is 6 months until the '74 season begins. Until then, one can break a leg, his back, develop sickle cell anemia or drop dead. Babe Ruth's 714 record will never be tied or broken. Babe Ruth was a white man and the greatest of all. In fact, there are presently at least 20 better ball players than Hank Aaron. Tom Seaver, Rose, Bench, Koozman, Mercer, Munson, Staub, etc, etc.

Dear Hank,

I hope lightning will strike you before next season.

Billye had announced our engagement on "Today in Georgia," but we kept the wedding plans secretive and stole off to be married in a small ceremony in Jamaica. Billye was a godsend to me, and our marriage really put my life back in order. After being a lost soul for a couple of years, I finally had a home again. Not only that, but there was a child in it. Ceci was seven years old when her mother and I were married, and it wasn't long before I adopted her.

We tried to keep our wedding quiet, and gave *Jet* magazine exclusive photo rights, but it made the newspapers anyway. As a result, Billye and I didn't have much of a private honeymoon. Besides that, I was thinking about Jack Billingham half the time. We were scheduled to open the 1974 season in Cincinnati, and I knew Billingham would be pitching for the Reds. I thought all winter about what he would throw me on Opening Day, even lying on the beach in Jamaica with my bride.

There was plenty to keep me busy in the meantime, though. The offseason began when I went to Oakland and became the only active player to throw out the first ball at a World Series. After that, I was honored at banquets in Atlanta, Mobile, Milwaukee, Chicago, Boston, Washington, Denver, and New Hampshire. I appeared on "Hollywood Squares" and the Flip Wilson, Dean Martin, Merv Griffin, Mike Douglas, and Dinah Shore shows all within a couple of weeks. Billye and I put on aprons and cooked with Dinah Shore, and Flip Wilson pitched me an oversized mush ball that I swung at and missed.

While we were in Los Angeles, I went over to Sammy Davis Jr.'s house to talk about a movie he wanted me to be involved with. I got there at about ten in the morning, and Sammy was sitting at his kitchen counter drinking martinis. He was depressed in those days because he had been ostracized over his friendship with Richard Nixon. He pointed to his door and said, "Through that door used to walk Frank Sinatra, Dean Martin, all the greatest stars. Now nobody will speak to me." While I was there, Sammy got on the phone with somebody at the Rolls-Royce dealership and told him to come pick up his new Rolls because he didn't like the color. He must have had four or five big luxury cars outside. I'm thinking, damn, here's this guy with this huge house and all these fancy cars, and he thinks he's got problems. Then he took me upstairs and I looked in his closet and there must have been a thousand suits lined up one after another in there. I couldn't believe how those Hollywood people lived. It was impressive, but it wasn't quite my style, which was why I was never too interested in doing movies. Around that time, I had been offered a part as a bartender in a film with Sidney Poitier and Harry Belafonte, but I didn't want to spend that much time on the West Coast. Sammy was tired of all the "Superfly" movies going around at the time, and he had asked me out to his house to talk about a movie he wanted to make about a black jockey. It wasn't for me, though. Sammy was also interesting in buying the ball from my 715th home run for $25,000, but since Magnavox was paying me a million, I figured Sammy was a little short.

As much as Billye and I were traveling, I was happy to get back home for a few days now and then. But when we did, there were always reminders that it was still Georgia and I was still black. Billye and I stopped at a vegetable stand in the country one afternoon, and the farmer, with a big wad of tobacco in his mouth, said to me, "Hey, boy, I sure wish you'd have broke that record last year." He probably thought he was being friendly, but I was past the point of being called "boy," and I got so mad I had to go sit in the car until it passed. It helped to be with somebody as calm and gracious as Billye. Those days were hard on Billye, because when we were out together I was always on edge, and when I was out by myself, she was always worried.

Even now, I still worry about Henry if he doesn't check in with me periodically or let me know when he's going to be late. Since the assassinations of Martin Luther King and the Kennedys, I've been aware of how vulnerable anybody can be, particularly a public person and one who might have enemies, for whatever reason. There was an image I couldn't get out of my mind in those days: When my first husband was living, he was on a program at Atlanta University with Martin and a young African leader named Tom Mboya. There was a picture taken of the three of them up on the stage together. Later, Tom was killed, and then Martin was killed. Samuel wasn't killed, of course, but when he died after surgery, I kept thinking of that picture and how all three of them in the picture had passed from the scene. It gave me an eerie feeling of foreboding. That picture kept coming back to me like a nightmare when Henry was receiving hate mail and death threats.—Billye Aaron

After thinking about Billingham all winter, it looked for a while as though I might not even face him. In February, I had a meeting with Bill Bartholomay, the Braves' owner, and he told me that the Braves wanted to hold me out of the three games in Cincinnati so that I would have a chance to tie and break the record when the team returned to Atlanta. I might not have been willing to go along with it had it not been for that great ovation during the last game of 1973. That made me feel a little different about Atlanta, and if the Braves wanted me to hit the home runs there, I didn't have any objections. I sort of liked the idea of being able to show my grandchildren the spots where 714 and 715 landed.

The commissioner didn't see it that way, though, and neither did the New York sportswriters—although I'm not sure I have the right order there. As soon as Bartholomay announced his plan, the New York press ripped into the Braves like lunch meat. Dave Anderson of the *New York Times* wrote that keeping me out of the lineup was "a brazen defiance of baseball's integrity." Larry Merchant of the New York *Post* wrote that the whole thing was an "insidious fix." But the ringleader, as usual, was Dick Young of the *Daily News*, who wrote, "Baseball has gone crooked. There is no delicate way of putting it. There is no other interpretation to be placed on the Braves' announced intention of playing their first three games without Henry Aaron in the lineup. I would feel slightly better, and so would the fans, if the Commissioner of Baseball had come out with a blistering order to the Braves that Hank Aaron must play the first three games, under threat of forfeit." Sure enough, a few days later Bowie Kuhn told Bartholomay that I had to play two of the first three games in Cincinnati, which was at about the same rate I had played the year before. It was the first and last time I can ever think of that a player was actually thrown into a game.

There were plenty of precedents in which players going for milestones were held out of road games. After Ted Williams hit a home run in his last time at bat in Boston, he sat out three games on the road. Clemente's three thousandth hit was saved for Pittsburgh, and Stan Musial's would have been saved for St. Louis except that the Cardinals needed him as a pinch hitter in a key spot against the Cubs in Chicago. Bartholomay and Mathews were willing to do it that way—to hold me out unless the situation cried out for me to bat.

The debate carried on through spring training, which was a nightmare anyway. The press was so thick in the clubhouse that I had to dress in the coaches' room so that we wouldn't crowd out the other players. There were media from all over the world. A reporter from Tokyo wrote that I was the most popular man in Japan. A TV executive from Venezuela dropped a wad of $100 bills on Bob Hope's desk, thinking it would buy broadcast rights. The whole thing was a circus. To have a moment of peace and to keep the crowds away from the rest of the team, I had to live separately in a penthouse apartment. Even so, the autograph hounds always found me. I knew that it all came with the territory, of course, and I could tolerate it except for when I couldn't get where I was going or when people would act like they owned me: "Aaron, over here! Hey, Hank, sign this one! Hank, give me an autograph!" Fans kept jumping out of the stands to get their picture taken with me in the on-deck circle. It was a little disconcerting, because I was never quite sure what to expect when somebody came running at me. Every time it happened, Calvin Wardlaw had his hand on that binoculars case. The Braves had arranged for Calvin to stay with me through spring training, and although it seemed silly that a ballplayer would need a bodyguard, I wasn't going to argue.

One day, Calvin and I were at my apartment when the police came and told us there was a report that Billye and Ceci were missing. They were searching all over the area for them, and I was pretty frantic when suddenly Billye and Ceci walked through the door. They had been shopping on Worth Avenue in Palm Beach.

I was relieved when spring training finally ended. By that time, it had been decided that I would play on Opening Day in Cincinnati and we would take it from there, which was fine with me because I was eager to get the whole damn thing over with. I knew it wouldn't take me many swings of the bat, because I simply couldn't let it go on any longer. The writers were saying that it would be tough for me to break the record because of all the pressure, but they had it wrong. I felt the pressure, all right, but the only way to deal with it was to put an end to it. Pressure never bothered me at home plate because nothing ever bothered me at home plate. When I went up to hit against Billingham, I wouldn't be thinking about Babe Ruth or hate mail or TV cameras or autograph hounds or boarding the train in Mobile with my sack of sandwiches; I would be concentrating on the ball in Billingham's right hand.

> We stopped in Birmingham to play an exhibition game against the Orioles on our way to Cincinnati, and after the game Hank and I went back to the hotel to get ready to go out for dinner. We were in the room talking and jiving for a while, and when we opened the door to leave, there were two big policemen standing outside. They said they didn't want Hank going anywhere because there were rumors he would be killed or something. We went out anyway and had dinner and a couple of drinks, and when we got back to the hotel, Hank said, "Cassy, I'm sick and tired of this. When we get to Cincinnati, I'm going to tie the record in the first game. Then I'm going to take a little rest and when we get to Atlanta I'm going to break the record in the first game there."—Paul Casanova

When we arrived in Cincinnati, all bets were off. It was the day before the opening game and the day that Ohio, Kentucky, and Indiana were clobbered with some of the worst tornadoes in American history. We flew into Cincinnati in a terrible thunderstorm, and when I picked up Daddy at the airport late that afternoon, I saw funnel clouds in the distance. That made me forget all about Babe Ruth and Jack Billingham for a while. More than 300 people died from the tornadoes, a lot of them within an hour or so from Cincinnati. A town called Xenia, Ohio, right up the road, was practically destroyed. As I read the paper Thursday morning, the home run record didn't seem so important in the big picture. There was disaster in the Midwest and another kind of disaster in Washington, where Watergate was closing in around President Nixon. Suddenly, I didn't feel like the center of the world anymore.

I have to admit, though, it was hard to stay humble in those days. When I went downstairs to leave for the ballpark, I was met by a man who called himself Fabulous Howard, who escorted me to a huge black Cadillac limousine. Fabulous Howard said that he had driven all the way from Chicago just to carry me from the Netherland Hilton to Riverfront Stadium. He told me he had chauffered Babe Ruth, but I wasn't really impressed until he told me he had also chauffered Joe Pepitone. Pepitone had been with the Braves briefly, and I knew he had style. In fact, Pepi had left behind a nice pair of baseball shoes, and I had snatched them up. Those were the shoes I intended to wear when I broke the record. When Fabulous Howard told me he had driven Pepitone, I was sold. I started to get in the car, but Fabulous Howard wasn't ready for me yet. He reached into his trunk and took out a red carpet that I had to walk on. After I sat down in the backseat and he started the engine, bagpipe music came blaring out of the outside speaker. Then, as he drove away, Fabulous Howard picked up a microphone and started shouting: "Feast your eyes on royalty! The king is in this car! The king of baseball!" When we pulled up at the ballpark, I couldn't get out until Fabulous Howard stretched out that red carpet from the car to the clubhouse door.

I got to the ballpark early for a press conference to announce the Hank Aaron Scholarship Fund, which would be started by one dollar that Western Union would contribute for every telegram I received after tying or breaking the record. I also mentioned that I had requested a tribute to the memory of Martin Luther King. Ralph Garr had called it to my attention that Opening Day was on the anniversary of Dr. King's assassination, and I had asked the Reds' front office about providing a moment of silence. I should have known better. If nothing else, though, I got the message across that we should be more concerned with Dr. King's legacy and less with Babe Ruth's. I was doing my best to keep things in perspective.

My teammates helped in that respect. They kept me from taking things too seriously. When I got to the clubhouse, Ron Reed, a pitcher who also played professional basketball, had taped a can of Raid to my locker to ward off the press. When Dusty Baker saw me, he said, "Supe"—Baker and Garr and some of the others called me that, short for Superstar—"you playing today, brother?" Then Garr pulled me aside and said, "We'll sure be glad when you get this thing over with." I promised him I'd do it that day.

I lifted a lead ball in the clubhouse for a while, and when I went out to the field there were about 250 reporters waiting for me. There's something about being so conspicuous that makes a person feel cut off from everybody else. At one point, when the writers were about ten-deep around me, I called over to Davey Johnson by the batting cage and said, "Davey, come talk to me. I'm all alone here." I asked Davey if I looked nervous, and he said yes. Davey was no liar.

Billingham was obviously nervous, too, because he walked Garr leading off the first inning. Billingham was a control pitcher and Ralph was a very, very tough man to walk. It could have been that Billingham had a hard time loosening up, because it was a cold, damp day. Mike Lum got to him for a single with one out, which brought me up to bat with two men on base. It was a good situation to hit in, because Billingham couldn't walk me and I knew he would throw me sinking fastballs to try to make me hit the ball on the ground for a double play. Along with the other records I set, I also hit into more double plays than anybody else.

I went up there looking for the sinker, and I wasn't going to swing until I saw it. Fortunately, Billingham's pitches were just out of the strike zone, and the count went to three-and-one. I couldn't ask for a better setup: Billingham had no margin for error, and I knew what he had to throw me and where he had to throw it. It was all just as I had imagined it on the beach in Jamaica and in the penthouse at West Palm. The three-one pitch came in low and hard, and instinctively I turned into it for my first swing of the season. It was like about 600 of my other 713 home runs, just high and far enough to drop over the fence. Babe Ruth's were so long and high that people talked about them for the rest of their lives, but here we were, both with 714.

I managed to keep my composure as I trotted around the bases, except that my eyes were moist and I made it around a little faster than usual. This time, there was no thought of Bobby Thomson, like there had been when I hit the home run to win the pennant in 1957, or even Ruth. I just wanted to find home plate somewhere in the middle of the mob that was waiting there, because when I did, the long, excruciating chase would at last be over. I still had one more home run to go to set the record, but for the first time in several long years, I wasn't chasing anybody. It was like I had landed on the moon. I was there. All I had to do now was take the next step. From that point on, every home run I hit would set an all-time record.

Johnny Bench congratulated me as soon as I touched the plate, and all my teammates were out there shouting and grabbing at me. There's no greater feeling in sports than the one a player gets when his teammates are genuinely excited over one of his own personal accomplishments—excited just to be his teammate. In baseball, it happens on no-hitters and almost no other occasion except all-time records, and in other sports it happens even less frequently. Words don't matter much at moments like that—I couldn't hear anything anyway, and wouldn't remember it if I had. What I remember is that everybody was right there celebrating with me, as if my record was their record, too. A player can't ask for any more than that.

After I went to the stands and hugged Billye and my father—my mother was waiting to meet up with us in Atlanta, and my children were at their great-grandfather's funeral in Jacksonville—Gerald Ford, Nixon's vice president at the time, came onto the field and shook my hand. Bowie Kuhn did, too, although in retrospect I have to wonder whether he would have been there if it hadn't been Opening Day in Cincinnati, the first game of the season in either league. Since it was the first game, incidentally, it meant that at the moment I caught Ruth, I led the league in home runs and RBIs. It also meant that number 714 was the first cowhide home run in major-league history, since the leagues switched that year from horsehide to cowhide baseballs. The only thing wrong was the main thing—after leading 6-2 going into the bottom of the eighth, we lost the game in extra innings. Pete Rose tied it with a double in the ninth, then doubled again with two outs in the eleventh and scored from second on a wild pitch to beat us, 7-6.

At the press conference afterwards, the reporters asked me about the pitch from Billingham, about the pressure, about what I'd been thinking at the plate and going around the bases, about what I did that morning and what I was going to do that night, and they even asked about the moment of silence for Dr. King. I was glad that they gave attention to my request, but there didn't seem to be a lot of sympathy for it.

I was standing next to Henry when they were asking him these questions, and it almost seemed as though they were attacking him about the moment of silence. Before I knew it, I was talking. I blurted out something to the effect that he shouldn't have even had to ask for the moment of silence and that we should take the occasion to remember Dr. King. It was probably the biggest mistake I ever made in regards to Henry. As soon as I said it, I realized, "Hey, you should stand up here and be seen, not heard." But they were coming after him. It was an instinctive reaction.

Looking back, I think that incident planted the seed of suspicion that maybe I was putting ideas into Henry's head. From that time on, we kept hearing and reading that I had changed Henry, that I had made him speak up more about social issues. I don't particularly mind being held responsible for that, but the fact is, I didn't have a thing to do with his speaking out. I was proud and pleased that he did, but it was not at my urging.

Anyway, I learned my lesson from that incident. Since then, I've never offered any more unsolicited comments.—Billye Aaron

I couldn't seem to stay clear of controversy. The wet weather continued in Cincinnati, and Eddie Mathews said that he didn't intend to play me in either of the two remaining games there. He knew he was in defiance of the commissioner, and also of Bartholomay and Eddie Robinson, our general manager, both of whom had reached an understanding with Kuhn about me playing two of the Cincinnati games, but Mathews wasn't the kind of man who would be pushed around. He resented the fact that he was being told whom to put in his lineup. He knew that there were plenty of precedents for what he was doing, and it irked him not only that he was being dictated to by the commissioner, but that the commissioner was being dictated to by the New York sportswriters. He also recalled a rainy night in 1973 when the umpires asked him if I was in the lineup that night, and when they were told that I was not, they went ahead and called off the game. Eddie was battling everybody that weekend—the commissioner, our own management, and the press. Part of it was that he was truly upset about being told how to manage, and part of it was that he was taking the heat off me. It's not often that a manager is such a loyal friend of a player.

There was no game Friday and no objection Saturday when I was on the bench. But Kuhn still insisted that I be in the lineup on Sunday, and Saturday night he called Eddie to tell him there would be serious repercussions if I did not start Sunday. Eddie had no choice but to go along, but he didn't have to like it.

Naturally, I wanted Hank to break the record at home. All the New York writers were saying how terrible it was to be thinking of the gate, but to me, it wasn't a matter of money. It would do our ball club a lot of good to play in front of big crowds at home, because we didn't see them very often. I was thinking of Hank and the ball club. The whole thing wouldn't even have come up if the people who scheduled the damn season hadn't started us out with three games in Cincinnati. I knew Hank was only going to play ninety or a hundred games that year, so why should I put him out there in the cold weather in Cincinnati to break the record? Then the commissioner got involved and I had to play him, and I'll be damned if he doesn't tie the record the first time up at the plate on Opening Day. On the day off Friday, I said to him, "Damn, Hank, if you don't break the record in Cincinnati, we've got an eleven-game homestand coming up, and we can put a lot of people in the stands." So I said I wasn't going to play him anymore in Cincinnati, and that's when the commissioner got pissed. And I mean pissed. He was gonna suspend me, suspend the owners, the integrity of baseball was at stake, blah blah blah. So I had to play him Sunday. Knowing Hank, I figured he'd probably break it then, and even if he didn't, he was bound to do it in the first game back in Atlanta.—Eddie Mathews

A righthander named Clay Kirby pitched for the Reds on Sunday. Kirby was not one of the best pitchers in the National League, but he had one of the best sliders, which was a pitch that consistently gave me more trouble than any other because it was hard to identify as it came toward the plate. I struck out twice against Kirby and grounded out a third time. By then, we had a good lead and Mathews sent somebody in for me. I couldn't believe it after the game when the writers suggested, and later wrote, that I might have deliberately struck out against Kirby. The last thing I wanted to do was to look bad in that situation, or, worse yet, ruin my reputation by going into the tank. If I was going to do something crooked, I sure as hell wouldn't do it with 250 reporters watching every move I made. I had always taken a strong stand against anything that wasn't within the spirit and rules of the game—like spitballs. I believed in the integrity of the game as strongly as anybody, and it irked me to have my own integrity assaulted. The fact is, on both strikeouts I was called out by John McSherry, and one of them was a bad call that I argued. Even Kirby said that he thought the pitch was a ball.

I was in a foul mood when we got back to Atlanta, but Atlanta was in a good mood. The annual Dogwood Festival was going on, and the Braves had planned a big Hank Aaron Night for the home opener on Monday. There were almost 54,000 people at the ball-park that night—still the biggest crowd in team history. Bob Hope, the Braves' publicity man, had been working on the special night since the year before, not knowing that I would be tied with Ruth at the time. There were balloons and cannons and marching bands and a program that was like the old "This Is Your Life" television show. Important people from my past took their places on a map of the United States that covered the outfield—Ed Scott, my manager with the Mobile Black Bears; John Mullen, who signed me; Charlie Grimm, my first big-league manager; Donald Davidson, who had seen more of my home runs than anybody. Pearl Bailey sang the national anthem because she wanted to. Sammy Davis, Jr. was there and also Jimmy Carter, who at the time was still governor of Georgia. It seemed like the only people not there were the President of the United States and the commissioner of baseball. Nixon had a pretty good excuse—Congress was on his back to produce the Watergate tapes—but I couldn't say the same for Bowie Kuhn. He was in Cleveland speaking to the Wahoo Club. Kuhn sent Monte Irvin to stand in for him, and the Atlanta fans just about booed poor Monte out of the park. Kuhn knew that he would have been the one getting booed if he had come to Atlanta, because the whole town was mad at him for intervening in Cincinnati. He said later that his presence at the ballpark would have been a distraction and he stayed away so as not to blacken the occasion, but his absence was a much greater distraction. I was deeply offended that the commissioner of baseball would not see fit to watch me try to break a record that was supposed to be the most sacred in baseball. It was almost as if he didn't want to dignify the record or didn't want to be part of the surpassing of Babe Ruth. Whatever his reason for not being there, I think it was terribly inadequate. I took it personally, and, even though Kuhn and I have met and talked about it since then, I still do.

I thought the commissioner was way out of line on the whole sequence of events. First of all, to dictate our lineup in Cincinnati was a big overstep on his part. After that, he felt awkward

about coming to Atlanta. In fact, we never saw much of him in Atlanta. Since he had been baseball's lawyer in our move to Atlanta, I think he was concerned about his involvement with our club and went overboard to disassociate himself with that. I could understand his feelings in that regard, but he was way out of line on the Aaron thing. I think he missed the moment.
—Bill Bartholomay

My father threw out the first ball, and then we took the field against the Dodgers. Their pitcher was Al Downing, a veteran lefthander whom I respected. Downing always had an idea of what he was doing when he was on the mound, and he usually pitched me outside with sliders and screwballs. I crowded the plate against him to hit the outside pitch, but at the same time, I knew he would be trying to outthink me, which meant that I had to be patient and pick my spot. It didn't come in the second inning, when Downing walked me before I could take the bat off my shoulder. I scored when Dusty Baker doubled and Bill Buckner mishandled the ball in left field. Nobody seemed to care too much, but my run broke Willie Mays's National League record for runs scored—Willie had retired at the end of the 1973 season—and put me third all-time behind Ty Cobb and Ruth. I had always put great store in runs scored ever since Jackie Robinson pointed out that the purpose of coming up to the plate was to make it around the bases. The way I saw it, a run scored was just as important as one batted in. Apparently, though, Jackie and I were in the minority on that score.

I came up again in the fourth, with two outs and Darrell Evans on first base. The Dodgers were ahead 3-1, and I knew that Downing was not going to walk me and put the tying run on base. He was going to challenge me with everything he had—which was what it was going to take for me to hit my 715th home run. I knew all along that I wouldn't break the record against a rookie pitcher, because a rookie would be scared to come at me. It had to be a pitcher with some confidence and nerve—a solid veteran like Downing.

Downing's first pitch was a change of pace that went into the dirt. The umpire, Satch Davidson, threw it out, and the first-base umpire, Frank Pulli, tossed Downing another one of the specially marked infrared balls. Downing rubbed it up and then threw his slider low and down the middle, which was not where he wanted it but which was fine with me. I hit it squarely, although not well enough that I knew it was gone. The ball shot out on a line over the shortstop, Bill Russell, who bent his knees as if he were going to jump up and catch it. That was one of the differences between Ruth and me: he made outfielders look up at the sky, and I made shortstops bend their knees.

I used to say that I never saw one of my home runs land, but when I see photographs or films of myself hitting home runs, I'm always looking out toward left field. I never realized I was doing it, though, and I still don't think I was watching to see the ball go over the fence. I think it was just a matter of following the ball with my eyes. From the time the pitcher gripped it, I was focused on the ball, and I didn't look away until it was time to run the bases. Anyway, I saw this one go out. And before it did, I saw Buckner run to the fence like he was going to catch it. During the pregame warm-ups, Buckner had practiced leaping against the fence, as if he planned to take the home run away from me, and I believe he was thinking about doing that as he ran back to the wall and turned. But the ball kept going. It surprised him, and it surprised me. I'm still not sure I hit that ball hard enough for it to go out. I don't know—maybe I did but I was so keyed up that I couldn't feel it. Anyway, something carried the ball into the bullpen, and about the time I got to first base I realized that I was the all-time home run king of baseball. Steve Garvey, the Dodgers' first baseman, shook my hand as I passed first, and Davey Lopes, the second baseman, stuck out his hand at second. I'm not sure if I ever shook with Lopes, though, because about that time a couple of college kids appeared out of nowhere and started running alongside me and pounding me on the back. I guess I was aware of them, because the clips show that I sort of nudged them away with my elbow, but I honestly don't remember them being there. I was in my own little world at the time. It was like I was running in a bubble and I could see all these people jumping up and down and waving their arms in slow motion. I remember that every base seemed crowded, like there were all these people I had to get through to make it to home plate. I just couldn't wait to get there. I was told I had a big smile on my face as I came around third. I purposely never smiled as I ran the bases after a home run, but I suppose I couldn't help it that time.

> Since I was hitting third ahead of Hank, I knew there was a good chance that I'd be on base when he hit the home run to break the record. You get fantasies about things like that. My fantasy was that I would be on first base and the home run would be about twenty rows up in the stands so that I could stay near the base and be the first one to congratulate him. But with two outs and the ball hit on a line the way it was, I had to be running hard. I was already past second when it went out. I stopped right away and figured maybe I still had a chance, but by that time Garvey and Lopes and all the coaches and everybody had already gotten to him. After that, I just wanted to get to home plate and turn around and soak up the whole picture. I'm still in awe of that whole thing. To know how hard it is to hit a home run in the big leagues, and for him to do it in those circumstances . . .
>
> I was on deck before him when he tied the record in Cincinnati, and when he came out of the dugout he said to me, "I'm gonna do it right now." I was on deck when he came out before he broke the record in Atlanta, and he said the same thing that time. He said, "I'm gonna get it over right now." He didn't say it the first time he batted that night, when he walked. But he said it before he went up there and hit number 715.—Darrell Evans

As I ran in toward home, Ralph Garr grabbed my leg and tried to plant it on the plate, screaming, "Touch it, Supe! Just touch it!" As soon as I did, Ralph and Darrell and Eddie and everybody mobbed me. Somehow, my mother managed to make it through and put a bear hug on me. Good Lord, I didn't know Mama was that strong; I thought she was going to squeeze the life out of me. About that time, Tom House, a young relief pitcher, came sprinting in with the ball. He had caught it in the bullpen and he wasn't about to give it up to anybody but me. When he got to me, he stuck it in my hand and said, "Hammer, here it is!" Then they stopped the game for a little ceremony, and I stepped up to the microphone and said exactly what I felt: "Thank God it's over."

It started to rain while the ceremony was going on. Since it was only the fourth inning, the game would have been wiped out if it had kept raining. That would have meant that the whole moment never really happened and I still had 714 home runs. But the fates were with me that night. The rain stopped, and we went on to win the game, 7-4. By the look of the crowd, though, you'd have thought there had been a flash flood in the grandstand. By the next time I batted, there couldn't have been more than 20,000 people left in the park. It seemed more like a Braves game. I guess that's when it hit me that the whole thing was really over. As I walked out to the on-deck circle, Ralph Garr said, "Come on, Supe, break Hank Aaron's record." God, that sounded good. But I couldn't do it.

> *All the sportswriters were mad at me that night because they wanted to get to Hank after the game and I closed the clubhouse to everyone but the team and families. At that point, I didn't give a damn about the sportswriters, the way they had treated Hank and me and the Braves in Cincinnati. I cared about Hank. When everybody was in and the door closed, I stood up on a table and said what I thought about Hank, which was that he was the best ballplayer I ever saw in my life. Then we had champagne and everybody toasted him.*—Eddie Mathews

There were already hundreds of telegrams piled up by the time the game was over. And President Nixon had called. I suppose with all that he was going through, he welcomed the chance to talk to a ballplayer for a few minutes. He phoned when I was in the outfield, and Donald Davidson disconnected him while they were trying to patch the call into the clubhouse. Donald tried to call him back, but the operator at the White House wouldn't let him through. Finally, Nixon called again and said some nice things and invited me to the White House. If I'd known he was such a baseball fan, I might have voted differently.

After the party in the clubhouse, there was one more press conference. It was a happier one this time, except that the reporters had to ask about Bowie Kuhn's absence and I had to tell them what I thought about it. And I had to have one more say about the Clay Kirby game. I wanted no misunderstanding about what had happened Sunday in Cincinnati. I had to get that off my chest before I could take my record home.

We had a little party at the house that night, mostly family and close friends. Billye and I were alone for a little while before everybody arrived, and while she was in the bedroom getting ready, I went off downstairs to be by myself for a few minutes. When I was alone and the door was shut, I got down on my knees and closed my eyes and thanked God for pulling me through. At that moment, I knew what the past twenty-five years of my life had been all about. I had done something that nobody else in the world had ever done, and with it came a feeling that nobody else has ever had—not exactly, anyway. I didn't feel a wild sense of joy. I didn't feel like celebrating. But I probably felt closer to God at that moment than at any other in my life. I felt a deep sense of gratitude and a wonderful surge of liberation all at the same time. I also felt a stream of tears running down my face.

The record brought Hank Aaron into the blinding light that bears down upon America's most visible people, but it left the better parts of him still obscured. He had become famous as something he really wasn't: Hank Aaron, Home Run King. Or Home Run King Hank Aaron. It was a reversible title that stuck to him like a paper raincoat. More than a description, it was a definition—three words and a name that would say it all for posterity. He was the home run guy.

Except that he wasn't. The fact is, Babe Ruth was still the home run guy and Aaron was a hitter who along the way hit the most. But in a numbers game in a numbers world, that made Aaron the Home Run King, which shrouded the fact that he was a Gold Glove outfielder, an expert baserunner, an impeccable player who rarely blundered, and the all-time leader in total bases and runs batted in, both of which are more significant than home runs in the deeper baseball scheme but just don't market as well: Total Base King Hank Aaron.

By the time he finished playing in 1976, Aaron had an astonishing 722 more total bases than the next guy (Stan Musial), which translates to 722 singles or 361 doubles or 240 triples (plus a double or two singles) or the equivalent of 180½ more home runs than anybody else who ever played the game, which says just about everything there is to say or could possibly be said about him as a hitter, to wit, that he hit the ball to greater effect— far greater—than anybody else. There is nothing subjective about the total-base statistic, no arguments about Ruth or Cobb or Mays or Rose or Hornsby or Williams or Musial or Mantle or anybody, no quarrels about parks and pitchers, nothing black and white about it except the number on the page. It accounts for singles hitters, doubles hitters, day hitters, night hitters, black hitters, white hitters, switch-hitters, pinch hitters, punch hitters, judy hitters, designated hitters, and undesignated hitters. There have been hitters with higher batting averages than Hank Aaron, with higher slugging percentages, higher home run ratios; there have been players who struck out less often, who walked more, who hit the ball farther; a few may even have been feared more by pitchers and managers. But when every player has hit every ball he ever hit and run as far as those hits would take him— that is, when all the total bases have been paced off—and the dust has cleared, Hank Aaron is exactly 12.3068 miles in front of the next guy.

To get there required a man who hit home runs both prolifically and incidentally, one to whom the home run did not represent a career path but a fringe benefit. It did not require a Home Run King, but a Total Hitter. It also required a man who had persevered longer and more effectively than all the others, who had kept running after everybody else had showered and changed and put on weight, and who, most of all, kept swinging until there was nothing left to swing at.

Because it so surpasses the field and because full-service hitters are becoming endangered, Aaron's total-base record will almost surely stand longer than his home run record, if they don't both last forever. In the final accounting, it makes him the man who did the most with a baseball bat. His 6,856 total bases ought to be the signature record of Aaron's epic career, but of course reality won't have it that way. Legacy goes for the long ball. The home run record was Babe Ruth and Babe Ruth was it, and besides that, America reveres the home run; it is such a perfect and final thing, ending where it starts. Once a man has the home run record, he belongs to it. As regards Hank Aaron, the home run record did not make him the player that he was, it simply made him the Home Run King. That was all, really— although one might have thought it would make him something else: a hero perhaps, a national icon, a local institution. At the very least, the toast of the town.

◆ ◆ ◆

The first thing I did the next morning was call Carla at the Braves' offices. She asked me if I felt any different, and I said, uh-huh.

But I didn't realize—there was no way I could—how completely different everything would be from that moment on. They say life begins at forty; well, for me, it began all over again at forty years, two months, and three days. I would never again be just another ballplayer who went to the park, took his times at bat, showered, and went home. I was no longer Henry Aaron of Mobile, Alabama—husband, father, private person, outfielder, fastball hitter, fish eater, blues fan; I was the Home Run King. For better or for worse, I had to learn to live with that, because it would be that way for the rest of my life.

My new life started when I got to the office on April 9. The phone lines were backed up, and sacks of telegrams were stacked on top of each other in Carla's office. We raised a lot of money for the scholarship program that day. There were 20,000 telegrams.

Dear Hank,

Your race is proud and I am one in a million among them.
—Bronx, New York

Dear Hank,

Mazel Tov, which means in Jewish congratulations, from the white population that's been with you all the way. We love you and are thrilled for the entire black population.—Miami, Florida

Dear Hank,

715 is more important than the moon shot.—Crawfordsville, Indiana

Dear Mr. Aaron,

Congratulations, far out. Bowie Kuhn can take a flying leap.
—Redding, California

Dear Hank Aaron,

You have reached the public's pinnacle at a time when this country needs somebody desperately to lead us out of the current quagmire of despair. You are truly a paragon. On April 5th our principal announced that the east wing of the third floor would be named the Henry Aaron Wing of Morris High School. —Bronx, New York

Dear Hank,

I am particularly happy for you since I followed your career from Jacksonville on. You see my uncle was Ben Geraghty. I know that wherever Uncle Ben is today his spirit will always be rooting for you.—Beverly Hills, California

Dear Hank,

I am confident that a man of your caliber will instill in others the spirit and love that you have given to major league baseball. My heart and feelings are with you and your kind friendship will mean more to me than any other person in my life. Proud to be your friend.—Ernie Banks

It was hard for me to believe how much the record affected people. I received copies of newspaper stories from all over the world, and some of them made me shiver. A Mexican paper said, "We lived through this historic moment, the most fabulous in the world. Thanks to God we witnessed this moment of history." A Japanese reporter wrote, "In my Atlanta hotel room I now begin writing this copy. I know I have to be calm. But I find it impossible to prevent my writing hand from continuing to shake." In Jacksonville, a cab driver was sitting down to watch the game on television, and when his wife insisted that he get up and go to work, he shot himself.

Atlanta was not quite so worked up about it, though. The lead headline in the afternoon paper the next day was: President Nixon Again Faces Tapes Deadline. The story about the record was below. Two nights later, we had all of 6,500 people at the ballpark. It was obvious that being the Home Run King did not make me a star attraction in the capital of Georgia. When the mayor, a black man named Maynard Jackson, started a campaign to have the stadium renamed for me, the city fathers all but laughed him down. The official statement was that it would be contrary to Atlanta tradition to name something for a person who was still living.

I was honored to learn, though, that there were some proud new parents who were not bound by the same tradition. A woman in Iowa wrote to tell me that their baby son had been named Aaron Black, in my honor. I received several letters like that, and I was touched by all of them, but there was one letter that, more than all the others, helped me to see and appreciate the enormous power that ballplayers are entrusted with—the power to make a difference in people's lives.

Dear Mr. Aaron,

We were watching as a family from Room 306 at Morton Research Hospital in Dallas when you broke Babe Ruth's record. Our grandson died just a short time later. The little 8-year-old boy kept saying "Hank can do it tonight," and when you did, this child with needles in his right arm couldn't move the right hand, but his little left arm saluted straight up toward the TV and he yelled, "He did it, Daddy! I knew he could!" He had been very ill for quite a while with leukemia, cancer, appendicitis, and pneumonia. I'm telling you this so you will know how much joy you brought to this courageous little boy. We all love you for it. And we wish you could have seen that little fellow jump and yell "He did it, Daddy!" The entire third floor knew about it. He was so proud of you. Thanks very much for giving him the chance to see you do it.

When Hank was chasing the record, all sorts of people were calling the Braves and saying they had kids with cancer, or a Little League team, or anything that could get them in to meet Hank. There were twenty kids every day wanting to meet him. Some of the parents would tell me that their kids were on their death beds, and when I'd see them, they looked okay to me. Finally I told Hank that the whole thing was getting pretty sus-

picious and that he didn't have to spend time with these kids every day. But he said, no, some of them were really sick and he wanted to do it. So he would sit there every day signing baseballs for these kids and then have his picture taken with them. Well, several years later I was walking through the Los Angeles airport and a man walked up and said, "You're Bob Hope, aren't you?" I didn't know him, but he proceeded to tell me that he had taken his son to New Orleans for open-heart surgery, and on the way there they had stopped in Atlanta to meet Hank. It turned out that the boy died during the operation. But his father said that meeting Hank was the thrill of his life. He said, "I can't tell you what it meant to us to see him so happy during the last few days of his life."—Bob Hope

Being a ballplayer carries with it a responsibility that not many of us fully understand. I felt it stronger than most for a couple of reasons—because of the home run record, naturally, and because I was black. I had to set an example for black children—and still do—because they need examples. A white child might need a role model, but a black child needs more than that in this society. He needs hope. People like Jackie Robinson and Jesse Jackson helped me understand that and take it seriously. There's nothing I can do that's more important than what I can do for children—black and white, but especially black. If the home run record gives me more power to inspire children—and I know that it does—then the ordeal was worth every moment of sleep I lost and every hurt I felt from every hate letter. I believe that I am a very lucky man to be able to influence children, because I happen to love children and there is nothing that would make me happier.

Of course, there was also a dark side to being the Home Run King, that being the complete surrender of a normal and private life. Although the media pressure diminished after the record was broken, the public pressure intensified. I was officially *somebody* now, which meant that I couldn't walk into a department store or an airport or a hotel lobby without drawing a crowd. I never tried going incognito—I don't like to wear sunglasses—but a time or two I put my right arm in a sling so that it would look like I couldn't sign autographs. In hotels, I would call down for room service in order to eat in peace, but even then, the waiters would bring in boxes of baseballs for me to sign. I was always amazed at how they managed to come up with so many baseballs at eleven o'clock at night.

It got to the point where I was almost afraid of crowds. I dreaded leaving my room on the road and started developing all sorts of defense mechanisms—most of which have stayed with me. It's mainly a matter of keeping your eyes open. You can always tell the people who want to approach you, because they'll watch you from a distance waiting for the right time to make their move. What they don't realize is that I'm usually watching them, too. The secret, though, is not to make eye contact, because once you do, they've got you. The easiest people to spot—and the ones you most need to avoid—are the autograph collectors, who are mostly in it for the money. In cities like New York and Philadelphia, you'll see the same guys every time you're there, and they always try to get you to sign as many things as possible. It's worse than ever now because the market for autographs has gone through the roof, but the collectors have always been around, and when I broke the record, I became a marked man. On top of that, I still had to keep up my guard for some crackpot who might be gunning for me. Even now, when I'm in a crowded room or a restaurant, I can practically describe every person in the room. I'm suspicious of everybody. I never leave my table unattended if I have a drink on it. It's probably my nature to be suspicious, but nothing in my experience has persuaded me that I should trust people. I've met a lot of bad guys and parasites along the way.

By the same token, as the Home Run King I've met important people I never would have met as Henry Aaron. I've attended state dinners at the White House with Gerald Ford and Jimmy Carter—I wasn't able to accept invitations from Nixon and Ronald Reagan—and sat at the same table as Emperor Hirohito of Japan and Helmut Schmidt of West Germany. I addressed Congress on Flag Day in 1974, where a few doors down the Senate was planning Nixon's impeachment. I've made friends with stars from other sports and movies and television, and I must have met every talk-show host in America.

All of that naturally was at a peak in 1974, and while I was humbled by it, I also had an eye out for tangible signs of acknowledgment and respect—something more than flattery, handshakes, and pats on the back. At the time, the chief issue for blacks in baseball was that there had never been a black manager. I had been saying for more than ten years that it was time for blacks to break into managing—Jackie Robinson had been saying it long before me—and now it was time to turn up the heat. With a black man in possession of the most sacred record in the game—although, once I broke the record, suddenly Joe DiMaggio's consecutive-game hitting streak became the most sacred record—it seemed more ridiculous than ever to keep us shut off from managing and front-office jobs.

I didn't have a deep desire to manage, but I thought it was vital that there be a black manager. If the opportunity came my way, I felt that I should accept it for that reason. I had no intention of forcing the issue, though, because I wasn't sure I was ready to quit playing. Then the Braves fired Eddie Mathews just before the All-Star break, and the whole thing came to a head.

I certainly wasn't going to campaign for a job that Eddie Mathews had just been fired from, and which I didn't really want anyway. So at first, I said nothing. Naturally, the local writers asked me if I would be seeking the job, and I said no, which was true. The issue came up again at the All-Star Game in Pittsburgh, and I said again that I wasn't interested in managing at that time. Then I did a television interview with Tony Kubek during the game, and I mentioned on the air that I thought I deserved the courtesy of being offered the job. I wasn't saying that I wanted it —just that I felt I should be given the opportunity. After the game, the writers circled me and asked if I would accept the job if it were offered. I said that I would, but that the Braves probably knew that, which could have been why they hadn't offered it. I didn't think I was contradicting what I had said earlier; I was just telling the rest of the story. In effect, it was the same thing I had been thinking and saying all along—that I wasn't seeking to be a manager, but if that was what it took to break the barrier, I was ready and willing. Still, the local writers believed that I had misled them. I can understand how they thought that, but I felt they carried it a little too far. The baseball writer for the Atlanta *Journal*, Frank Hyland, wrote that I had either lied to the Atlanta press or lied on national television. It bothered me that he would write such a thing, but I had invited controversy and I had to face it.

Dear Mr. Aaron:

You've pulled millions out of baseball without investing a dime. Why not plow some back in before you open your ungrateful mouth again about the overly generous owners who saved you from your fate as a natural born cotton picker?

Dear Nigger,

There are three things you can't give a nigger—a black eye, a puffed lip, and a job.

Before long, the whole situation turned rotten. When Eddie Robinson, our general manager, was asked if I were a candidate for the job, he said no. I actually thought that my brother, Tommie, was as a good a man for the job or better, because he was getting experience managing the Braves' farm team in Savannah and was doing well. When the writers asked Robinson if Tommie were a candidate, he said that Tommie was trying to win a pennant in Savannah and the Braves didn't want to take him away from the job he was doing. That was pure malarkey. In all my years in baseball—many of them overseeing the Braves' minor-league system—I don't think I've ever witnessed a situation where the organization considered the welfare of the minor-league club ahead of the major-league club. After he dismissed me and Tommie as candidates, Robinson was asked if he thought Atlanta was ready for a black manager. He said he preferred not to comment on that one—which was all the comment I needed to hear. As far as I could tell, nothing in baseball had changed but the name at the top of the home run list.

I was getting pretty angry with all of it, and then one morning I opened the paper to the sports section and hit the ceiling. The first thing I saw was a picture of Billye with a cutline underneath that said: "Wife Billye: Trouble?" There had been several stories in the newspapers about Billye putting ideas into my head and manipulating me, and I resented the implication that I couldn't think for myself—especially in light of the fact that I had been saying the same things for more than a decade. But the thing that set me off was seeing my wife scrutinized and criticized in public —seeing her picture splashed across the front of the section in such a reckless manner. Throughout the whole ordeal of the home run record, I had taken the heat and never lashed back at any of the media, but I drew the line when my family was under fire. I don't know if I've ever been so angry in my life. I went to the ballpark that day ready to take on anybody who got in my way.

That turned out to be Frank Hyland of the *Journal.* I wasn't happy with Frank because of the way he had written about the manager's situation, but I wasn't really mad at him. I knew he had nothing to do with the picture in the morning paper. But I was mad at everybody who had anything to do with Atlanta newspapers, and Frank happened to be nearby.

The Braves were playing San Diego in Atlanta, and there was a rain delay. I decided to go talk to Aaron, but on my way to the clubhouse, Bill Lucas of the front office caught me and said, "Frank, I wouldn't go down to the locker room if I were you." I guess that made me curious. Then Bill Acree, the clubhouse man, said, "Frank, I wouldn't go in there. Supe is hot." When I got into the clubhouse, Aaron called me over to his locker right away. I should have known it wasn't a good idea when Ron Reed and Paul Casanova sauntered over and stood there like bouncers, ready to jump in if there was any trouble. Then he got me.—Frank Hyland

It was Farmers' Night, and the players always received little baskets of strawberries on Farmers' Night. Most of the guys threw theirs away, but I figured mine might come in handy. When Frank came over to my locker, I just picked up my basket of strawberries and shoved them into his face. Then Cassy and Reed stepped in, and that was it. But it didn't end there.

Hyland didn't hold a grudge—which is to his credit, because there's no good excuse for what I did. But we had always gotten along pretty well, and he understood that I had no quarrels with him. At one point, he had written that I was the easiest superstar to cover. I don't know if he still thought that, but after I cooled off, we patched things up. Frank knew that I was just mad at the world, and he wasn't going to make a big deal out of the thing. But everybody else did. A syndicated columnist named Melvin Durslag wrote that what I had done was "a rotten and degrading act" and said that I was "the most revered and fawned over performer of this half of the century." I couldn't defend shoving strawberries in somebody's face, but I could only shake my head at the other part. He also wrote that I had embarrassed the club that had been so good to me. I had a hard time figuring how the Braves had been so much better to me than I had been to them; I didn't think I was such a bad investment.

Of course, Dick Young also got into the act. It doesn't make me feel good to talk about a man who has passed on, God rest his soul, but I can't ignore the part that Dick Young played in so many of my little dramas. I suppose the thing that bothered me so much about Young was that the New York press always seemed to fall in line behind him. He was a very powerful man —and not only with the press, but, as I found out in Cincinnati, with the commissioner. This time, Young wrote in the New York *Daily News* that Billye was behind my actions—dragging her into it even deeper. He also tried to get the National League to take disciplinary action against me, and about that time I received a telegram from Chub Feeney, the league president, warning me against further displays of temper.

After the strawberry incident, I got a call from Dick Young, who told me that he was going to file a complaint on my behalf with the Baseball Writers Association. I told him I didn't want to file any complaint, that the whole thing was forgotten. That's the way we left it. But Young got hold of Jack Herman, the president of the Baseball Writers, and they went ahead and filed a complaint. But it sure didn't come from me.—Frank Hyland

It didn't do much for my disposition to think that I had played in the big leagues for more than twenty years without causing a lick of trouble—in spite of some damn good reasons to—and after one mistake for which I was sorry, when my wife has been assailed in the press and I lose my temper at the expense of a writer who is willing to forgive me, they're almost ready to toss me out of the game. On top of that, the rednecks wanted to ride me out of town.

Dear Aaron,

I read about what you did in Atlanta to a REAL man . . .

Dear Nigger Aaron,

Some blacks we admire and respect—but we can't tolerate cocky niggers like you.

Dear Hank Aaron,

You are very fortunate that your ancestors were brought over to this country, even though they were slaves. Now don't you know that these slaves had a much better life over here than they would have if they had not been brought to America. Now these natives living in Africa need your help, they want you to send them money to dig wells, for you see by the enclosed paper that they do not have enough water. Knowing that you have been raking in the money from a good many sources and also knowing that you can well afford to help these people—your people. Also if you do want to manage then go over to Africa and manage to dig these wells that are so badly needed. They really need you in Africa and you should go by all means.

The Braves finally resolved the manager situation by naming a career baseball man named Clyde King. Meanwhile, I was playing left field about half the time and hitting decently, but not as well as I was accustomed to. All of my career, I'd had goals to shoot for—batting titles, home run titles, 200 hits, 500 homers, 3,000 hits, 700 homers, the Ruth record—and suddenly, there was nothing left. There was little chance to get back into the World Series, because although we had a competitive team, we were no match for the Reds or Dodgers. I could still break Ruth's RBI record, but that wasn't something that drove me on. In fact, nothing drove me on, except the fact that I was a ballplayer, and, in a backward sort of way, the fact that I wasn't hitting as well as I wanted to. I didn't want to be one of those guys who hung on past his time. Nobody does. The problem is, when you've pounded baseballs for twenty years, it takes a lot of convincing to make you believe you can't do it anymore. I didn't believe it yet. The way I saw it, I had three options—to hang on past my time, to do some hitting, or to retire. The option I preferred was number two. I had kicked around the notion of retiring—and a lot of other people had kicked it around for me—but it wasn't an easy thing to come to grips with. On one hand, I knew that it was time to quit when I lost my motivation, which I was obviously losing, but on the other hand, I had been so consumed with playing ball for so long that I just wasn't ready for something else. And let's face it, I had become a commodity. If I could make a lot more money playing ball than anything else, I had to consider it.

Since I hadn't completely made up my mind about retiring, I didn't bother to deny the reports that I would—I didn't want to get caught double-talking again—and around the league it was assumed that 1974 would be my last season. The Braves made the same assumption, and late in July they held a day in my honor, in which I received a Cadillac as well as a lifetime supply of pecans from Albany, carpeting from Dalton, a bowling ball from La Grange, rose bushes from Thomasville, twin beds from Macon, records from Nashville, a sewing machine from Anderson, South Carolina, and lifetime admission to the Alabama Space and Rocket Center of Huntsville. Other teams around the league had farewell presentations for me when we made our final visits of the season. There were over 50,000 in Los Angeles the night they honored me there, but the most memorable occasion was in New York, when I met the local dignitaries at City Hall— including Mrs. Babe Ruth and Mrs. Lou Gehrig—then rode in a motorcade through Harlem and spoke to a crowd of about 5,000 people at a city park. When I saw all those black faces staring up at me, I remembered being part of the Davis Avenue crowd staring up at Jackie Robinson when he came to Mobile. It was one of the high points of my career.

By this time, I had begun discussions with the Braves about 1975. I had pretty much decided that I didn't want to play for them anymore, and we were trying to work out an arrangement whereby I would move into a front-office job. In our preliminary talks, the Braves discussed a tempting position that would command a nice salary. Although I would be an executive with the Braves, a major part of the deal was that I would do promotional work for the sporting goods portion of the La Salle Corporation, which, in effect, owned the team. But that became complicated when I signed with Magnavox, because the Magnavox contract specified that I could not be a spokesman for any other company. I had already stopped doing commercials for Lifebuoy and Brut.

When they realized I couldn't be a front man for La Salle, the owners of the Braves seemed to lose interest in keeping me around. We continued to discuss a front-office job, but it wasn't much of a job. I would start at the bottom of the organization and learn my way around in various departments, with a vague understanding that I would eventually wind up as some kind of vice president or something. The salary was not in the executive range, and there were never any definite duties described for me. It all sounded as if their plans were to keep me around for the sake of public relations and make sure I didn't get in anybody's way. I had envisioned something more along the line of the arrangement Stan Musial worked out with the Cardinals, where he moved directly into a vice president's job that entailed some decision-making responsibility. It was important to me that I have an executive voice, and when I expressed this to Dan Donahue, the team president, he promised me I could look at everything that came across his desk. My response was that I didn't want to be a houseboy for the Braves.

> *Personally, I would not have understood the situation of Hank Aaron working up through the ranks. I'm not trying to duck responsibility—I knew what was going on. But Donahue was the one handling the negotiations, and he was a numbers guy. I think perhaps he was not as sensitive to Hank's situation as he might have been. There were some things about that situation that made it a little unclear. I was never quite clear about Hank's position on managing, for one—I didn't think he was interested in it, and then I would read in the paper that he was. There was also some confusion that had to do with the financial people who were representing him. But the fact remains, he should have been offered a chance to start higher in the organization. I wanted him with the Braves and happy. He was a class of one. If I had to do it over again, I would have been more hands-on. As it was, Hank probably felt I left him hanging, and I can't blame him for that—Bill Bartholomay*

We never really reached an agreement except that I would not play baseball for the Braves after 1974. In the meanwhile, there was some talk about the Braves trading me. Furman Bisher of the Atlanta *Journal* brought up the idea of Atlanta trading me back to Milwaukee to play for the expansion Brewers of the American League. I was intrigued by the notion of returning to Milwaukee. Also, Roland Hemond, the general manager of the White Sox, whom I knew from his days in the Braves' organization, was apparently interested in bringing me to Chicago, and there were also rumors that the Cubs would make an offer. It was beginning to look as though playing ball would be my best option for 1975, and I was confident that something would be worked out so that I could play somewhere other than Atlanta. There had been some unforgettable moments for me in Atlanta—I will always treasure the memory of the last day of 1973—but those moments were the exception more than the rule. There was no real warmth between the city and me, and it was time for us to go our separate ways.

The writers and television guys kept pressing me about my plans for 1975, so I called a press conference before the last game of the season. When I did that, everybody assumed I would announce my retirement. CBS-TV delayed the start of eight football games to get the announcement live on the air, but when I got to the microphone, I said that although I would be playing my last game as a Brave, I was not retiring. It was vague and confusing, but it was all I knew.

There were only 11,000 people at Atlanta Stadium for the final game. Although there was still some confusion about what I would do the next year, I had said more than once that I would not be playing in Atlanta, and it hurt me to know that so few cared enough to buy a ticket for my last of 3,076 games over twenty-one years with the Braves—which was more games than any other player played for any team (until Carl Yastrzemski broke the record in 1982 with the Red Sox). I couldn't help but think how different it must have been when Musial played his last game in St. Louis, or Williams in Boston, or Mantle or DiMaggio in New York. If nothing else, though, it convinced me that I was doing the right thing by leaving.

We played the Reds that day and routed them as Phil Niekro won his twentieth game. I also hit my twentieth homer of the season. It came in the seventh inning against Rawly Eastwick, and as soon as the bat hit the ball, I knew that was it for me as a Brave. I circled the bases one last time, stepped on home plate, ran to the dugout and kept right on going into the clubhouse. The fans yelled for me to come out and tip my cap, but I wasn't going back on that field. I wanted the home run to be my good-bye. Besides that, I was too choked up to face the crowd. I needed to be alone. The Braves had been my life for twenty-one years, and there was a lot to think about. I took off my uniform, got dressed, and drove off in the Cadillac I'd received on Hank Aaron Day.

I was sentimental for a few days; then I hit the road. My off-season itinerary that year included eighteen states and three countries, with the highlight being a trip to Japan, where I was scheduled to compete in a home-run-hitting contest with Japanese record holder Sadaharu Oh.

It was a seventeen-hour flight to Tokyo, and when Billye and I got there, we went right to our hotel room to get some rest. I was just about to lie down when the phone rang. I was due at a press conference. Press conferences had become almost a daily ritual for me, but not like this one. When I arrived, there must have been 2,500 reporters waiting for me and more cameras than I've ever seen in one place. Fortunately, I had picked up some gifts for Oh before I left the States, but unfortunately, I had done some miscalculating. Oh was not a large man—certainly not large enough to fit into the size-13 baseball shoes I had brought him. He was also left-handed, which I discovered when I presented him with a right-handed glove. It was pretty embarrassing, but he took it all in good humor. Then they started giving gifts to me. Everywhere I went, they gave me gifts. Among other things, I received numerous cameras and two or three television sets. Here I was on a million-dollar contract with Magnavox and carrying home Japanese televisions. My relatives were happy to have them, though.

I hadn't been able to prepare for the home run contest—I didn't have my own bat or spikes with me—but as soon as I arrived in Japan, I wished I had. I had thought of the contest as something on the order of the old Home Run Derby shows, but quickly realized that it would not be a casual exhibition—which I should have understood, because CBS was paying me $50,000 for the broadcast rights. Oh was much more of a national hero in Japan than I was in America. In fact, *I* was more of a hero in Japan than I was in America. The Japanese also took their baseball very, very seriously, and I saw that I had better approach the home run contest the same way. When I had agreed to it, Magnavox had told me it was fine with them as long as I won; they weren't paying seven figures for a loser. There was additional pressure because the Mets were over there playing games on a Japanese tour, and they were getting the stuffing beat out of them, something like six losses in a row. I had to win for the honor of American baseball and American televisions, and it was by no means a sure thing. Oh was a bona fide hitter. He had just won his second straight Triple Crown, and with more than 600 home runs, he was already a legend at the age of thirty-four. They called him "The Swinging Scarecrow." Although he was small, and I don't believe he would have been a big home run hitter in the States, Oh was a skillful and stylish batter who would have been a star anywhere. And he was on his own turf.

There were 50,000 people at Korakuen Stadium for the contest and the Mets game that would follow. The only things I had going for me were adrenaline and the size of the field. It wasn't far at all down the left-field line, and once I got loose, I felt like I could have stood up there all day poking fly balls over the fence. Joe Pignatano, a coach for the Mets, pitched to me—we each had twenty swings coming—and he knew where I needed the ball. Oh hit nine home runs on his turn. I hit my tenth on the eighteenth swing and stopped. After that, the Mets went out and won big. Our honor was preserved.

Back in Milwaukee, meanwhile, Bill Bartholomay and Bud Selig, my old Packers friend who had become owner of the Brewers, were meeting to talk over a deal. They had a lot of negotiating to do and stopped just long enough to watch the home run contest on television. They finished their discussions later in the day, and that night, at about 3:00 A.M. Japanese time, Selig woke me up in my hotel room with a phone call. I had been traded to Milwaukee for an outfielder named Dave May and a minor-league pitcher named Roger Alexander. I was going home.

The trade wasn't a complete surprise to me, because I knew that Bartholomay and Selig had been talking. But it was news, and great news. I still loved Milwaukee, and unlike Atlanta, Milwaukee loved me. I knew I would be going to a place where I was wanted, and that sounded awfully good.

The fact is, I had talked to Bartholomay about purchasing Hank as early as 1972. I knew how popular he was in Milwaukee. Beyond that, when we had brought the Brewers to Milwaukee in 1970, we had underestimated the bitterness of Milwaukee people over the loss of the Braves. They felt rejected by the Braves leaving, and to a lesser degree, they feel it even today. In some quarters, people were still calling us the Braves. It was a hard

*thing to overcome in a town like Milwaukee, and we had gotten
to the point that we needed to do something dramatic. I said at
the time of the trade that there was nothing I was more proud of
than bringing Hank Aaron back to Milwaukee, and that included giving the town a new franchise. Hank Aaron gave us
credibility and momentum. He legitimized us.—Bud Selig*

There were some negotiations to work out with the Brewers
before I signed, but there was little doubt about what I would do.
The money they offered was more than I had ever made,
$240,000 a year for two years. Even more than the money,
though, I was drawn to the attitude that Bud Selig and the front
office displayed toward me. They consulted me on things. It was
as if I were an equal party, a status I had never felt with the
Braves. And most important, they talked about setting me up
after my baseball career was over, possibly with an executive job
but more likely with a business deal. Selig indicated that he
could get me a Schlitz beer distributorship, which was exactly
the sort of thing I wanted to hear. With that, the deal was done.

I might have retired if I had been traded to any other team—
although, because of their fans and day baseball, I was intrigued
by the idea of playing for the Cubs—but I couldn't resist Milwaukee. To me, Milwaukee was the most comfortable place in baseball. Not only did I know and love the city, but both my bosses
were my friends—Selig off the field and the manager, Del Crandall, on the field. Crandall and I hadn't socialized together when
we played for the Braves, but he was a good, honest man, and we
had been teammates through some memorable years. On top of
that, we shared one thing that linked us in a way only ballplayers
can be linked—we used the same bat. I never had to worry about
ordering from Louisville as long as Del was around.

I also knew I would have a good time with the Brewers as
long as Bob Uecker and George Scott were around. Uecker had
come a long way since I loaned him fifty dollars to get back to
Atlanta after the Braves released him. He was already becoming
popular as a comedian, but his regular job was announcing for
the Brewers' radio broadcasts. He and I also teamed up on a daily

radio show in Milwaukee, which meant that he got to try all of his jokes out on me. As for George Scott—well, everybody in baseball knew the Boomer. He was one of the great characters of the game, always talking about the long taters he hit and wearing his rhinestones and his necklace of beads that he said were second basemen's teeth. The ballplayers from Mobile had become familiar with Boomer over the winters, because he used to come down from his home in Mississippi to work out. I hadn't been around him too much because I was ten years older than George, but I'd heard plenty about him from Tommie and the others. I suppose he'd heard about me, too.

> When people ask me about the greatest thing to happen to me in my baseball career, they always expect me to talk about some long tater I hit or about some fancy defensive play, but the greatest thing to happen to me in baseball was getting the opportunity to play alongside Hank Aaron. That was something I'll always carry with me. The day after they announced he was joining the Brewers, I went into the Brewers' office and sat there for a while talking with a couple of the front-office guys and just thinking about Hank Aaron. Finally I got up from my chair and said, "I can't believe it! The Boomer gets to play with The Hammer!"
>
> I had the best season of my career that year, and I believe it was because of Hank Aaron—not only the fact that he batted in front of me, but because of the way we used to sit and talk about baseball. He taught me what to expect from pitchers in certain situations—if a man is on base, or on second as opposed to first, or if it's late in the game, whatever the situation. When he joined the club, the first thing I did with him was to sit down with him and pick his brain. I asked him what he attributed all his good years to, year in and year out, and he said one word: concentration. I think that was the greatest thing he had going for him. Year in and year out, day in and day out, no matter what he was going through—his divorce, the hate mail, injuries, anything—that man never lost his concentration. You could still see it when he came to the Brewers. His skills had diminished, but you could see that tremendous concentration he had. I only wish I'd been able to play with him just a few years before. But I didn't need to play with him in his glory years to know how

great he was. A lot of times ballplayers will get into arguments about the best players, and I don't let anyone dog Hank Aaron. I stick up for Mays, too, because I love Mays. He could do more things than any player I ever saw. But I'm a firm believer that you have to lay the chips where they are. Nobody accomplished the things with the bat that Hank Aaron accomplished. Every time I talk about the man, I get very humble.

Whenever I see him, though, it's the same thing all over again. I saw him at an old-timers' game last year, and as soon as our eyes met he broke out in that big old grin I used to see all the time. He had the kind of grin that would light up the whole clubhouse. I used to love to see him laugh. And it was still the same way when I saw him at that old-timers' game. It gave me goose bumps. I get goose bumps every time I talk about that man.—George Scott

The Boomer was the best player on the ball club. People tended to overlook his talents because he was such a character, but the Boomer had a purpose for everything he said or did. He even had a good reason for calling home runs "long taters." The way the Boomer tells it, in Mississippi there are short potatoes that are nothing special and long potatoes that taste better and sell for a higher price. To George, the home runs that barely made it over the fence were short taters, and the big blasts, when the hitters really got their money's worth, were long taters.

We also had a young shortstop who turned a lot of people's heads that year, a nineteen-year-old kid named Robin Yount. Yount was just the kind of player I wanted to be around—a talented, impressionable kid who might be able to benefit from my experience. I was already hitting .300 in the big leagues by the time Yount was born. He was too shy to ask me for any advice when I first arrived—he called me Mr. Aaron—and I never gave advice when it wasn't asked for, but the Boomer made sure that all the young players took advantage of having me around. So did Crandall. One of the first days of spring training, Crandall gathered the team together and had me give them a hitting lesson. I wasn't accustomed to having a ball club turn to me for wisdom. It felt good.

It felt even better when 48,000 people—the most the Brewers

had ever drawn—showed up on a frigid day for our home opener and sang, "Hello, Henry . . . It's so nice to have you back where you belong." I'll never forget walking out on that County Stadium field, the same field my teammates had carried me off when we won the pennant in 1957, and hearing those fans screaming and singing for me. It made me realize how much I'd missed that place—everything from the musty old clubhouse to the smell of beer and bratwurst, and, most of all, the fans. One fan told me it was the first time he had been to the park since the Braves left.

I had a hit and drove in a run that day. A few days later, I hit my first American League home run, although it came against an old National League rival, Gaylord Perry. I explained to the press that Gaylord and I had come to an understanding over the years —if he made a good pitch, he got me out, and if he made a bad one, I hit a home run.

But I wasn't hitting well. Instead, I was finding that a ball-player ages fast when he loses his motivation. I was sluggish and inconsistent, and I was hitting so poorly at the end of April that I suggested to Crandall that he sit me down for a few games. It hurt me to have to say that. I never thought the day would come. But we were a young team trying to find itself, and it didn't do us much good to have a forty-one-year-old designated hitter batting .200.

At least I was driving in a run now and then, and on April 27 I hit a two-run double to tie Ruth's all-time record for RBIs. I broke the record on the first day of May when I went four-for-four and drove in Sixto Lezcano with a single against Detroit's Vern Ruhle. The wire services mentioned the record, but no fuss was made. The out-of-town writers didn't see fit to witness the record being broken, and needless to say the commissioner didn't. It seemed a little cockeyed to me that the RBI record would change hands so quietly after all the hullabaloo over my 715th home run, but I had quit trying to figure out the baseball establishment.

If the reporters weren't coming to our games, at least the fans were. Despite a poor showing in the pennant race, we brought in more fans than the team ever had before. We drew especially well on the road, where I was playing for the first time in American League cities like Boston and Baltimore and Cleveland and Detroit—the first time since my days in the Negro League, anyway. In fact, the fans turned out in big numbers in every town we were scheduled to play in, except for one—Atlanta. We had an exhibition game with the Braves scheduled there in June, supposedly to commemorate my 715th home run, but by the time the game was just a few days away, the Braves had only sold about three or four hundred tickets, and they had to call it off. I suppose I hadn't helped matters by saying that I was having a great time in Milwaukee and it was nice to be back in the major leagues. That touched off a little feud between me and Atlanta— although, as far as I was concerned, it really went back long before that.

I'd never really expressed my feelings about Atlanta, but when the exhibition game fell through, I said that I would never play there again. I was tired of being abused in Atlanta, and I wasn't going to hold back any longer. After that, the local writers opened both barrels. They wrote that I had worn out my welcome in Atlanta and that I should have broken the record in 1973 and retired "in a blaze of glory." The Braves even got into the action. One of their officials said that I would have been another Joe DiMaggio if I had known when to quit, which was the first time in my career that I had been compared to DiMaggio.

I couldn't help but think back to the year before, when the Braves had played an exhibition game in Milwaukee and we drew 21,000 on a night when the temperature was near freezing. I hit a home run that night, and I was told that people had tears in their eyes as I ran the bases. It was a different circumstance, of course—at the time, I hadn't played in Milwaukee in almost ten years—but the bottom line was that I was a favorite in Milwaukee and something very different in Atlanta. The whole thing seemed peculiar and backwards to me, because when the Braves moved to Atlanta, I had been the headline player, which I hadn't always been in Milwaukee. On top of that, I was a Southerner, and I brought a lot of attention to Atlanta when I broke the home run record. It was hard to figure. When I tried to analyze what had

gone wrong—why it was that Atlanta never really cared for me—
I kept coming back to the same things. I could only see two
reasons why I would be treated differently in Atlanta than Milwaukee. One was that Atlanta was in the South, and the other
was that I spoke my mind when I was there. That's all I could
come up with—a black man speaking his mind in the South. I
suppose it's enough.

The mutual affection between Milwaukee and me, on the
other hand, called attention to the fact that famous players have
had a history of returning to their original towns—Ruth to Boston, Hornsby to St. Louis, Mays to New York, and, later, Pete
Rose to Cincinnati. In every case but Rose's, we went back to play
for different teams in the cities where we started—Ruth for the
Boston Braves, Hornsby for the St. Louis Browns, and Mays for
the Mets. There's something magical about going back to where
it all began—as if it will make everything begin all over again. I
think the fans feel it, too. Everybody wants to turn back the clock.

But I discovered the same thing that Ruth, Hornsby, and
Mays did—you can't do it. The Milwaukee fans were kind to me
the second time around, but I couldn't show them the player they
remembered. It was only due to the fans' charity that I was voted
onto the All-Star team for the twenty-first year in a row. I didn't
deserve it. I batted only .234 with twelve home runs in 1975,
which again brought up the question of quitting.

I was still in no hurry to retire, though. My contract called for
another year at $240,000, and in my heart I felt I could earn it. I
convinced myself that I was not a .234 hitter, and I didn't want
to go out that way. I thought that I could turn things around if I
rededicated myself. I had become a player without a purpose.
For all of my adult life, I had been programmed to play baseball
and to strive for the next goal. Every year—every day—I had
been reaching for something. When I broke Ruth's record, it was
like I came unprogrammed. Nothing computed anymore. I didn't
know where I was going or what I had to do.

The problem was compounded when I crossed over to the
American League. As a designated hitter, it was more difficult to
keep my mind in the game. It shouldn't have been, because a

player can always make himself concentrate—that was something on which I prided myself—but I just didn't have the focus
I'd always had before. In addition, I didn't know the pitchers in
the American League. After twenty-one seasons in the National,
I had gotten to the point where I knew what every pitcher liked
to throw me, where, when, and how fast. I also knew the strike
zones of the umpires—which ones were likely to give me the
benefit of the doubt and which ones weren't. In the American
League, I knew nothing. All I had to go on was the scouting
report, but a scouting report doesn't compare to a career of face-
to-face confrontations. That's the only way to really get to know
a pitcher.

For Del Crandall's sake, not to mention my own, I wish I
could have hit better in 1975. If I'd been able to carry the Brewers
over some of the rough spots, maybe I could have saved Crandall's job. But I wasn't up to it. The Boomer did his best, leading
the league in home runs and RBIs, but the team had a very disappointing season and Del was fired on the last weekend of the
season.

When that happened, the speculation was that I would get
the job. In fact, the Brewers did talk to me about it, and I could
have accepted the position. But by that time, I didn't feel the
urgency to manage. Frank Robinson had been named the manager of the Cleveland Indians at the beginning of the year, so the
color line had been broken. I didn't want to rule out the possibility of managing in the future—obviously, one black manager
wasn't the end of the rainbow—but I didn't think the situation
was right just then. I would have had to quit playing and take a
pay cut, and I would have had to move into Del's office before he
could get the pictures off his desk. I figured there would be better
opportunities down the road.

Alex Grammas was our manager in 1976, and I was still the
designated hitter—although Grammas designated me less often
than Crandall had. I played about half the games and really didn't
do any better than I had the year before. There was no mistaking
it this time—I couldn't go on another year. I knew it was over
when I couldn't hit consistently in batting practice. My eyes had

deteriorated to the point where I needed glasses to read, my back still gave me trouble, and my knee was weak after I jammed it getting back to the base on a pickoff attempt. I was like an old pitcher who can just throw his good fastball a few times every game. The best I could manage was a little surge every now and then. In one stretch in June, I hit five home runs in a week, but every time I hit one, I wondered if it would be my last. About midway through the season, I started collecting the souvenir balls from my home runs. I knew there wouldn't be many of them, and I intended to give them to my mother and father. I thought that was a better place for them than Cooperstown.

Actually, the Hall of Fame had sent me a nice letter apologizing for the way they had mishandled my mementos, but I owed my parents more than I owed the Hall of Fame. I also had a commitment to Magnavox, which was sending my souvenirs around to the dealerships as a promotion. Anyway, the Hall would get the ball from number 714 when Magnavox was finished with it. I would keep 715 for myself. In the meantime, they were touring the country on the Freedom Train, which was a Bicentennial project designed to honor 200 years of American achievement. My souvenirs were just insignificant trinkets compared to some of the other things they had on board—George Washington's copy of the Constitution, airplane drawings from the Wright brothers, Jesse Owens's Olympic medals, the journal of Lewis and Clark, a piece of the flag that inspired "The Star-Spangled Banner," and on and on.

I didn't have many big moments in 1976, but the biggest came in July, when I hit a home run in the tenth inning to beat the Texas Rangers. It gave us a sweep of the five-game series, and the fans were so charged up that they called me out of the clubhouse for a standing ovation. That's the way I like to remember Milwaukee. As far as I was concerned, it was the second biggest home run I ever hit there, after the one in 1957. I'd had others that won ball games, but at the age of forty-two, every home run took on a little extra meaning to me. And it meant even more to hear the fans chanting my name one last time. I knew I might never hear that again. As it turned out, the souvenir I got from that home run would be the last one in my collection.

There was only one more home run in me. It came in Milwaukee on July 20 against Dick Drago of the California Angels, my tenth of 1976 and 755th over twenty-three seasons. A kid on the ground crew named Dick Arndt picked up the ball, and he wouldn't give it to me. The Brewers fired him over it, but he still wouldn't give me the ball. Every few years I call him and try to buy it from him—I've offered him as much as $10,000—but he won't part with it. To me, that ball is just as important as the one from number 715, because it's the one that established the record. The record is 755, not 715.

I didn't play much late in the season because of my knee. One night in September, it collapsed under me as I was walking up the dugout steps to the field. Appropriately, it was the day before the Brewers had a Hank Aaron Day at County Stadium, my official retirement party.

We raised a lot of money for the Hank Aaron Scholarship Fund that day. We also had a good time. Some of my old Milwaukee Braves buddies showed up—Mathews, Bill Bruton, Johnny Logan, Charlie Grimm, and Felix Mantilla—as well as Willie Mays, Ernie Banks, and Mickey Mantle. Believe it or not, Bowie Kuhn even came. The fans booed him. My teammates, showing their deep respect for my accomplishments in baseball, gave me a battered car from Crazy Jim's Demolition Derby, and written on the side it said: 755 Home Runs—Who Cares? How Many Strikeouts? They also gave me a shotgun. The Brewers retired my number and established a showcase of my memorabilia in the corridor of County Stadium. It's still there, and it includes one of my prized possessions—the shower shoes I wore for more than twenty years.

By September, I had already announced that I would be returning to Atlanta the next year as player development director for the Braves. The whole situation with the Braves had changed in the spring of that year when Ted Turner bought the club. I had known Turner when he was an upstart in the local television business, and I had an idea that he would be nothing like the conservative old guard I was accustomed to dealing with in baseball. Shortly after he bought the club, he had made a point of contacting me about coming back to Atlanta. It was the first time

I had talked about a front-office job with somebody who was willing to make me a solid offer. Despite my strained relationship with Atlanta—and as much as I loved Milwaukee—deep down I was a Southerner, and I was prepared to go back. So was Billye. She had her own television show in Milwaukee—I was her first guest—and she enjoyed the city as much as I did, but her life was in Atlanta. There is no other black community in the world like Atlanta's, and Billye thrived in it. Knowing the city as she did, Billye made me realize that I could accomplish more there than anywhere else. Moving back to Atlanta also meant that I would get to see my children more. It was the right place for us, and Turner's offer was the right offer.

Even so, there would have been no occasion to talk to Turner if things had worked out as I thought they would in Milwaukee. Bud Selig had said something about a front-office job being available to me, but we didn't get into it too deeply because my heart was set on the Schlitz distributorship. When it came time to work out the details of the arrangement, however, it didn't resemble the kind of deal I had been counting on. The territory offered to me was Baltimore, and I had to put up a million dollars to get it. I hadn't recalled hearing anything about a million dollars when Bud first brought up the possibility of a distributorship, and I certainly didn't know anything about Baltimore. I had understood that the territory was to be Atlanta. Eventually, they offered to sell me part of another distributor's territory in Atlanta, but the dividing line sort of juked around to give me all the vacant lots and cemeteries.

At any rate, I'd finally arranged to do something other than play ball, and after Hank Aaron Day, it was just a matter of finishing out the season. It was a long September. Not even the Boomer could get us out of last place. There was absolutely nothing to play for except memories and one more milestone—I had a chance to pass Ruth in runs scored and fall in second behind Ty Cobb. I was fewer than a hundred behind Cobb, but that was one record I'd have to do without. I was more than content with the National League record and interested in catching Ruth only because it was Ruth. He and I went back a long way.

But I wasn't getting on base much in those days. I finished the season batting only .229. In my last game in Milwaukee, which we lost to the Yankees in extra innings, I was hitless in five times up, which disappointed me deeply because more than 40,000 people had turned out for the game. But if nothing else, it was more proof that the time had come to walk away, because in the past, I had always been able to respond to moments like that. And despite my failures at the plate, it was a day that I would cherish: It gave me one final memory of Milwaukee—all those great fans coming to the park just to say good-bye. Again, I couldn't help but hearken back to Atlanta, when nobody had seemed to care that I was playing my last game there. I suppose at that moment I had some second thoughts about returning to Georgia. Was I crazy to leave Milwaukee?

We ended the season in Detroit, and my eyes were wet before the last game even started. It was the 3,298th of my career, which was more games than anybody had ever played. When I came to bat in the sixth inning with runners on second and third, it was the 12,364th time at bat of my career, which was more times than anybody had ever batted. I hit a ground ball to the right of the shortstop, Jerry Manuel, who knocked it down but couldn't make a play. It was my 3,771st hit and my 2,297th RBI, which is where that record would remain for the foreseeable future. Also, if I could come around to score, it would be my 2,175th run and would break my tie with Ruth, but when it came down to it, I didn't care very much about breaking another tie with Ruth. I sort of liked the idea of sharing something with the Babe, and I wasn't upset at all when Grammas sent out Jim Gantner to run for me. I'm told I had a smile on my face as I trotted off the field.

12

The man played in the major leagues from Williams to Yount, from Kiner to Schmidt, from Eisenhower and Khrushchev to Carter and Khomeini; from Hemingway and Steinbeck to Woodward and Bernstein; from James Dean to Jack Nicholson, Elvis to Elton John, Nat Cole to Natalie, and Sugar Ray to Sugar Ray; from Jackie Robinson to Jackie Onassis; from the fifteen-cent hamburger to the fifteen-cent stamp; from the four-minute mile to the four-minute dinner.

The baby boomers grew up and the modern social movements—peace, women's, and civil rights—dashed and bobbed along the national landscape all the while Hank Aaron was grazing the tops of fences with his low-slung home runs. The country changed much more than he did in those twenty-three years. To the deep chagrin of the Home Run King, it changed more than baseball did, as well.

By the time Aaron retired as a player, there was a black manager in Cleveland and two black executives in Atlanta, counting him. There were black infielders and outfielders all through the American League, including a few who were not required to hit .305. Millions of dollars were being paid to black sluggers and base stealers. In visibility and impact, the black presence in baseball was sufficient to enable the game to applaud itself as a model for reform in civil rights, and yet, appearances and public relations notwithstanding, its record in that arena reflected a pattern that had little do to with progressive leadership and much to do with reluctant pragmatism. Baseball accepted Jackie Robinson only because a visionary from Brooklyn and a commissioner from Kentucky wouldn't take no for an answer, and proceeded haltingly from here. By and large, major-league teams integrated only as fast as competitive and/or social pressures mandated it.

Owing to roots, customs, and baronial ownership, the process was ponderously slow—much slower than its occurrence in sports such as basketball, track, and boxing. Boxing and track, by their individualistic natures, have invited the most autonomy and consequently the least discrimination, not depending on franchises to hire and designate. Basketball has been the least encumbered by tradition, and its racial amalgamation happened so swiftly and thoroughly—embracing coaches, chief scouts, and general managers—as to leave baseball embarrassed in comparison.

But it is to baseball, the most institutional of American sports, that the country looks for symbols of social progress. Who was the first black player in the National Basketball Association? The first black coach? The first black player in the National Football League? There are answers to these questions (Chuck Cooper, Bill Russell, and, arguably, Bill Willis), but they certainly don't leap to mind as fast as you can say Jackie Robinson. Baseball is the game that tells America about itself, its social commentator. There are no television news specials to discuss the effects of Chuck Cooper on the anniversary of his signing and no national crusades if a football executive makes a misguided racial remark on the air. Significance of this sort is reserved for the national pastime. It is from baseball that America expects the best of itself.

In the more winsome particulars, the game has met the challenge famously. It has succeeded as no other pastime in its service to a season, its devotion to drama, its enhancement of hot dogs and regional beer and AM radio and rocking chairs and pot-luck suppers on the lawn. But while all of this would represent a spectacular final score for most sports, baseball's unique responsibility goes beyond the aesthetics. It goes into the streets and issues.

As the great populist sport, baseball has obligations. Its mandate calls for more than reluctant pragmatism; it calls for conscience, vision, and rolled-up sleeves. It calls for the national pastime to be an example, to give back something that really matters, and, most urgently, to deliver on the trust that is bestowed upon an august, metaphoric, and inherently public institution.

◆　　◆　　◆

Ted Turner was the best thing that could have happened to me. As much as I had wanted the Schlitz deal to work out, I doubt that I could have been happy out of baseball. Now, maybe; but not then. I was too attached to the game. A sudden split might have left me exposed and tender.

Frankly, I wasn't prepared for the world outside baseball. I had left Mobile as a teenager who still answered to his daddy and mama, and my whole adult life I had never been anything but a ballplayer. A ballplayer doesn't have to be self-sufficient, because most of the day-to-day details are taken care of by business managers and clubhouse managers and traveling secretaries. Besides that, in my early years as a player my color kept me out of the mainstream of society, and in my later years my notoriety did the same thing. I lived on an island, and the only thing there was baseball.

The job Turner offered me was ideal. It carried real responsibility, although nobody seemed to believe it. My bailiwick was the Braves' farm system, and I was accountable for coordinating the reports, organizing the teams, and signing the players. Invariably, though, when an agent or an official from another team would contact us about a player, he would assume that I was just a figurehead and take his business to Bill Lucas—who had held the job before I took it—or somebody else in the front office.

But I took my job seriously, and to get off to a good start, the first thing I did was recommend that my brother Tommie be promoted to manager of our top farm club at Richmond. I could do that without being accused of favoritism, because everybody agreed that Tommie was one of the bright lights in the organization. I trusted Tommie's judgment, and he helped me in an area where I needed it—making player evaluations. That was the most difficult aspect of the job for me, because I couldn't go to Durham or Savannah or Greenville or Richmond and quietly watch a ball game without being distracted by fans or reporters. As a result, I sometimes stayed away from the minor-league ballparks or looked at a few innings and left early.

I took some criticism for that—especially from Jim Bouton, who ripped into me in an article he wrote for *Sports Illustrated*—but it was a fact of life. I didn't pay much attention to what Bouton had to say, anyway, because there was nothing we agreed on—especially his value as a thirty-nine-year-old knuckleball pitcher trying to make a comeback fifteen years past his prime. I have to admit that it didn't upset me to release Bouton. I respected the fact that he had once been an outstanding pitcher for the Yankees and had kept himself in good shape—especially for a writer—but he didn't seem to understand that my job was to develop promising prospects just out of high school and college. I suspected that Bouton was working on a scheme to land a job with WTBS, and I didn't appreciate him taking up roster space at the expense of a young kid trying to make his way up the ladder.

Another criticism I sometimes heard was that I was jealous of Bill Lucas, who became our director of player personnel when I joined the front office—in effect, the general manager. The fact was, I believed there was no one in baseball more deserving of his job than Bill and no one I would rather see as a general manager. I was thrilled every time a black man was appointed to a position like that. When Frank Robinson was named manager of the Indians in 1975, I was so excited that I found myself shaking. My only difficulty with Bill was that he was the brother of my ex-wife. When Barbara and I were going through rough times in our early years in Atlanta, it naturally caused some tension between me and Bill. He was very loyal to his family—just as he was very loyal to his employer. Professionally, I never had a minute's trouble with Bill, and neither did anybody else with our ball club.

Bill was a college student when I spent half the summer of 1953 on his family's front porch. Before he went off to Florida A&M, he used to hang around the Jacksonville ballpark, which was just across the street from his house, and do any odd jobs that needed to be done. He swept the aisles, wiped the seats, sold peanuts, and counted tickets shoulder-to-shoulder with Spec Richardson, who was general manager. When he got out of school, he signed with the Braves and was a pretty good minor-league player until he hurt his leg and had to quit at Triple-A. Everybody in the organization respected Bill for his intelligence and work habits, and when the Braves decided to move to Atlanta, John McHale got in touch with him to help lay the groundwork for the move. At first, Bill's job was essentially to be a liaison between the team and the black community. He was hired because he was black, but he was promoted because he was good. He worked his way up through the departments of the front office, and after Turner took over, Bill became his top baseball man. I think Ted trusted Bill more than anybody he ever had in the front office, and by 1979 the organization was really on the rise.

One night in May that year, when the team was in Pittsburgh, Bill watched on television at his home while Phil Niekro chalked up his two hundredth victory. He sent a bottle of champagne and a dozen roses to Phil's wife and telephoned Niekro in Pittsburgh to tell him to celebrate at the Braves' expense. A short while later, he had a brain aneurysm. I got a call around midnight, and I threw on some jeans and spent the night and the next day at the hospital. Bill was unconscious for five days before he died at the age of forty-three. The players were so upset that we didn't win a game the whole time he was in the hospital. Bill had been everything to the Braves—a brother to some of us, a father to others, and a friend to everybody.

I asked not to be considered to fill Bill's job, and the Braves brought John Mullen back to the organization to take it. Meanwhile, Ted Turner made sure he took care of Bill's family. He sent a check every month to Bill's wife, Rubye—he still does—and she used the money to send her three kids to college. Eventually, he put Rubye on the board of Turner Broadcasting.

I was already on the TBS board when Rubye joined it. Turner has never been reluctant to give opportunities to blacks, but our appointments actually came as the result of some racial pressure. About the time he was thinking about putting WTBS on the satellite, a TV station he owned in Charlotte was running into some trouble with the black community there. The controversy got a lot of local publicity, and a group of black preachers took up the cause. They were talking about a big lawsuit and causing such a fuss that one of Ted's big backers, Westinghouse, was thinking about pulling out of the deal. So Ted called me in to talk to them and appease them. I went down there and had some discussions and called Ted to report that we were making progress. That wasn't good enough for Ted, though, and he said he was coming down. I told him that wasn't a good idea, but the next day Ted showed up carrying a big box of plaques and commendations from the NAACP. He started going on about how he loved the NAACP. I told him those people didn't want to hear that, but Ted kept going on about the NAACP. They were just watching him, not saying anything. Finaly, I got him to leave and we worked out a settlement. The deal was that two blacks would go on the board of Turner Broadcasting, with me going on immediately. Ted named Rubye as the other, and we've both been on the board ever since.

Ted is one of the most enlightened and fair-minded business tycoons I've ever seen, but that hasn't kept him out of his share of racial situations. He had a dinner appointment once with Jesse Jackson at the Atlanta ballpark, and when Jesse showed up about an hour and a half late, Ted became very agitated. He and Jesse got into one of the damndest arguments in front of me and a whole room full of people. Jesse was trying to persuade Ted to do business with black-owned companies, but every time he would try to make his point, Ted would cut him off and yell at him for being late. Finally, Ted got up in the middle of the salad and said it was too late to carry on a conversation because he had to get down to his seat to watch the ball game. After the incident, Jesse wrote Ted a very strong letter—and sent a copy to me—saying, among other things, "Your irate and bizarre behavior was a source of embarrassment to everyone present. As your consumption of alcohol increased, your personal obsession drowned out your rational processes, and you cancelled our dinner abruptly . . ." Later, Ted visited Jesse's office in Chicago to straighten things out, and they've been friends since then. At one point, Jesse even presented Ted with an award for his efforts on behalf of equal opportunity.

In 1977, my first year in the front office, Turner was suspended by Bowie Kuhn for tampering with a player on another team. That was the year he won the America's Cup with *Courageous*. Since then, Ted has been blamed for much of the ridiculous escalation of player salaries, but I don't think he is nearly as responsible for that as George Steinbrenner. Of course, I can't deny that Ted has made his share of colossal mistakes. As far as I'm concerned, the worst thing he ever did was to fire Donald Davidson as traveling secretary because Donald made a practice of reserving a suite for himself, which he also used as team headquarters in the hotel. I think that was just a case of Ted being unfamiliar with baseball and insensitive to the legend of Donald. But whatever mistakes he has made, I still believe that Ted is in a class by himself as an owner—that he has done more for the game than any other. I'm certainly biased about this, but I've seen firsthand what Ted Turner has done for Atlanta and for the television industry and, in turn, for baseball. I think that if the Bartholomay group had not brought the Braves to Atlanta, another team would have come, but if Turner had not bought the Braves and promoted them on his superstation, they might be gone by now, leaving the South without a team.

Ted is a brilliant man, committed to his goals and always poised to make a fast decision. I don't know where he finds time for hobbies, but he has plenty of them—sailing and fishing and hunting and ranching and who knows what else—and he takes his leisure time very seriously. He has large ranches—plantations, he calls them—all over the country. I spent a weekend with him on one of his plantations in South Carolina, and while we were there we went deer hunting together. After a while I spotted a deer and got him in my sights, but before I could shoot, Ted pushed my gun down and said, "No, that's Janie's favorite deer." Janie was his wife. We went on a little ways, and I spotted another deer and lined him up to shoot, and when I did, Ted pushed my gun down again and said, "No, no, that's Janie's favorite." After two or three times, I got the message and started wondering why we had brought guns.

Something interesting usually happens when you're with Ted, and I've learned a lot about business just by being around him. More than that, he has always treated me like a man, which is the best thing I can say about anybody. I don't know what role, if any, baseball might have had in store for me if he hadn't come along with the Braves' job, and I only hope that the Braves have benefited from having me in the organization. A lot of people seem to have their doubts about that. Our farm system has been taken to task over the years for not producing enough big-league stars, and I certainly have to answer to that, but I'd like to think that people can look a little deeper before they judge my years as director of player development. While it's true that we were not as consistently successful as I would have liked, there are a lot of things that go into the equation—scouting, trades; it all works together. We developed several good players that we traded away —guys like Brett Butler, Brook Jacoby, and Steve Bedrosian. When I finally gave up the job in 1990 to move over into a vice president's position under Stan Kasten, our farm system was considered to have the best pitching talent of any in baseball. We also produced the National League Rookie of the Year in 1990, Dave Justice. And again, just like our failures have to be shared, much of the credit for that has to go to the scouting department.

I do know and appreciate the fact that Turner trusts my baseball judgment. Since I've been in the front office, he has twice offered me the manager's job. Near the end of my first year, 1977, he called me into his office and said, "Why don't you go down and manage the damn team?" I was just getting acclimated to my new job and hadn't been thinking in terms of managing, so I didn't take him very seriously. Ted actually went down to the dugout and managed one game himself that year. He offered me the job again a few years later, but I wasn't really interested. By that time, I was thinking in terms of becoming a general manager. In retrospect, though, it's probably best that it hasn't happened, because I would have some conflicts with a job that's so demanding on my time. I make a lot of speeches and charity appearances and do a lot of business traveling, and I wouldn't want to give up any of that. The way I look at the situation now is the same way I looked at the prospect of being a manager in 1974: I'm not seeking to be a general manager anymore, but if I felt at the time that it was important to get a black man into the position, I'd have to consider it.

Because I've been in the front office for such a long time, and because I haven't been timid about expressing my views in recent years, it has worked out to my satisfaction that whenever a racial issue comes up in baseball, the press turns to me as an unofficial spokesman. To his credit, Ted Turner has never tried to censor me. I appreciate that, because I feel very strongly about the need for baseball to employ more blacks in the front offices and also the need to speak up about it. There is no acceptable excuse for the fact that there have only been a handful of black managers and no general managers since Bill Lucas. As I write this, the integration of baseball's coaching staffs and front offices is probably further behind than was the state of player rosters when I broke into the game almost forty years ago. Progress seems to be a dirty word in baseball circles. It makes no sense whatsoever that black players are still systematically excluded from key executive positions four decades after they began dominating on the playing field. How long is this going to take?

I've heard all kinds of lame reasons why retired black players have a harder time finding work in baseball than retired white players. The reason you hear most often is that black players are often stars who are unwilling to take pay cuts to start out at the lower levels of an organization. First of all, that only emphasizes the point that black players are generally required to be better than white players to stay in the big leagues, the effect being that fewer of the fringe players are black. I don't believe that one discrimination is an excuse for another. Second, it's simply not true that black players are unwilling to start low and work cheap. I have too many friends with different stories.

I've sent letters and resumes to everybody I know in baseball. Some answer, some don't. One of my friends sent back a little two-line letter saying there was nothing available right now but he would keep my name on file. Two or three weeks later, he goes out and hires somebody.

The Dodgers gave me a shot at managing a low minor-league

club in Arizona. They gave me the shittiest club they had, but I believe you can make chicken salad out of chicken shit if you play baseball the right way. We kicked ass and took names, won the league with that team. I proved to myself that it could be done, but it didn't seem to mean a tinker's damn to the powers that be. I was also a minor-league hitting coach for a while until my director, Bill Schweppe, invited me to lunch to fire me. When he said they were not going to renew my contract, I just laid my credit cards on the table and said no thanks to lunch. Afterwards, Peter O'Malley, the club president, called me in and asked me why I reacted that way. They might have had another spot for me in the organization at some point, but I said that I wasn't going to sit around for ten or twelve years and keep watching less qualified people jump right over me. I said, "Peter, they're not going to kill me the way they did Jim Gilliam." Gilliam was one of the headiest baseball men there ever was, and they put him on first base and left him there for ten years while they brought in guys like Danny Ozark and Preston Gomez to coach third base and then Tommy Lasorda to be manager. Gilliam was still a first-base coach when he died. I told Peter I was getting to the point where I was about to kick somebody's ass, and if I did that, I would be out of baseball for good. So Peter said, "John, if you feel that way, maybe it's best that you do leave." But I still can't get it out of my system. My wife tells me to give it up, but I can't. My fantasy is to manage a major-league ball club before I die.—former Dodger John Roseboro

I played professional baseball for twenty years, and when I was done, I wrote to every club in the major leagues for ten straight years seeking some kind of employment. I was willing to do anything, because baseball is my life. I'd have gone to work for $15,000, maybe less, just to be in baseball. Even today, I'd take a job in baseball for a lot less money than I'm making out of baseball, working for Amtrak. I understand that not everybody is going to be a manager, but do you mean to tell me that I played twenty years and I can't stand next to third base waving my arm around for somebody to score? You mean to tell me there aren't more than two black guys who can swing their arms around and tell runners when to run? It's just like quarterbacks *in football. Black quarterbacks can throw the damn ball, they can think, they can read defenses. It wasn't that anybody thought they couldn't do it, but it was a case of, well, we'll give you running back, and we'll give you wide receiver, and we'll give you defensive back, and we'll let you play the line, but we're not gonna give you quarterback. It's the same thing in baseball. They figure, give the blacks too much rope, and pretty soon they'll be buying teams.*

How do you think it makes you feel to keep applying for jobs and then see them hire somebody who never even played professional baseball? You give your life for something you love, and it gets you nowhere. If I had to get out of bed in the middle of the night to help kids learn to play baseball, I would. I love it that much.—former Brave Lee Maye

I keep waiting for the opportunity to get back in baseball in some capacity. Hitting instructor, coach, scout, whatever. I just want to get back in baseball. I've talked to every general manager, every farm director, every scouting director, and I haven't gotten a call back yet. I'm going to hang in there, though, because sooner or later the time will come. I'm a baseball man. You cut me open right now and I bleed baseball. If somebody got on the phone right now and said, "George Scott, we need a scout in Mississippi," I would not ask the man how much the job pays. I would say, send me a contract, and I would sign it.

God knows, I hope baseball is not keeping me out because I'm black. Many people tell me the reason I don't get a job is the color of my skin, but I swear I don't want to believe that. Some times you're better off not knowing the truth, but I don't even want to think about the possibility of that being true. I just don't want to believe it.—George Scott

When it comes to being managers and general managers, you're always hearing that this black guy wasn't hired or that black buy wasn't hired because he didn't have the experience. But I can't figure out why it is that only black men need experience. You see Lou Piniella step right into a manager's job with the Yankees and Ted Simmons walk off the field into a big front-office job with the Cardinals, and guys like Dal Maxvill and Tom Grieve and Lee Thomas land general manager's jobs with little or no experience. That really hurts. When the Blue Jays fired Jimy Williams as manager in 1989, they did all they could to keep from giving the job to Cito Gaston. When Cito kept winning as interim manager, they had no choice. There were two black managers in baseball that year—Gaston and Frank Robinson of the Orioles—and they went down to the last weekend of the season battling for the division title.

I sometimes think how easy it would be to staff a team with black coaches and executives. If I owned a team, I wouldn't go out of my way to hire only blacks in those positions, but I would see to it that everybody got an equal opportunity. If you did select from blacks only, though, there would be an incredible supply of talent to choose from. It would almost be like Branch Rickey having his pick of black players before the rest of the teams integrated. All of this great talent is just sitting there waiting to be utilized.

Hardly a week goes by that I don't talk to some old baseball friend who is either looking for a job in the game or depressed because he has just been fired or passed over. Billy Williams was barely considered for the Cubs' managing job the last time it opened up, despite the fact that he was their hitting coach and knew the players as well as anybody in the organization. Billy was so discouraged that I had to talk him out of quitting. I happen to think it's important not to get mad and leave baseball over these injustices, because we'll never get anywhere unless we stay with it. I've even had to give pep talks to Ernie Banks, if you can believe that. Ernie is the most optimistic, enthusiastic man who ever played baseball, but after he retired he couldn't seem to find the right niche with the Cubs. We'd talk at my apartment in Atlanta, and I'd say, "Ernie, you've got to tell them what you want to do. You're Mr. Cub! Don't let them shove you around!" Eventually, he did some speaking for the Cubs, but after the new owners took over, they let him go. After all that Ernie has done for that organization, it's hard to imagine that the Cubs can't find a place for Mr. Cub.

I feel a responsibility to help my friends and I do what I can by speaking publicly about the situation and working behind the scenes, but I'm not in a position to find jobs for them and don't believe I should, anyway; there would be too many personal and professional complications. Occasionally, a different kind of opportunity will come along for me to include an old buddy or two, but even then I have to be very cautious—which I learned after I took Ernie and Billy on a trip to play a series of exhibition games in Korea in the late seventies. The team I took was made up primarily of players from the Braves' farm system, but the Koreans wanted a couple of big names for the tour. Ernie was pushing fifty at the time and Billy was over forty, but the promoters were thrilled when they agreed to come along.

I knew we were in for a long trip when we got to the airport in Korea and the local authorities broke open the big trunk that we carried our equipment in. I said, "Wait, I'll get a key," but they just busted it open. I guess they thought we were smuggling drugs into the country. They turned that thing inside-out looking for drugs and cut open every one of our baseballs. I should have put the team back on the plane and gone back home right then, but things started looking a little better after we got settled in at our hotel. The Koreans have a way of making their guests feel awfully comfortable. It wasn't my style, but I got a kick out of watching Ernie sitting back like a king as the Korean girls dropped grapes in his mouth.

After a few days, though, our hosts stopped being so hospitable. Our players weren't very good, and neither were the crowds. When they saw that, the promoters started putting pressure on us. One night in my hotel, the phone rang and a man told me in a very urgent voice to come downstairs. When I got down there I found a man in a blue suit pacing the floor waiting for me. He told me in no uncertain terms that I had to play Billy Williams and Ernie Banks every day—especially Ernie. I told him that Ernie couldn't play every day because he was almost fifty years old. He said, "No, no, Ernie Banks, every day, every day." A couple days later, I got another call in the hotel, and the man in the blue suit told me he had a big bet on the game the next day and we had to lose. I told him if I did something like that I'd get thrown out of baseball. He kept saying, "big bet, big bet," and I kept telling him no way. The next day we went out there and, wouldn't you know it, we started pounding the ball for the first time on the whole trip. Before you could turn around we were ahead 12-0. Ernie even had a grand slam. After that, the guy in the blue suit said he wanted to stay with me because he was afraid for his life. I said, "Hey, if you're afraid for your life, what do you want to stay with me for?" When it was finally time to leave the country, the promoters wouldn't give me the money they owed me. I'd put up my own money to pay for the trip, and I couldn't leave without being paid back. They kept giving me excuses, but when I finally said I was going to contact the U.S. Embassy, my money was waiting for me the next day.

About the only good thing that came out of that trip was that it gave me a chance to spend some time with my son Lary, who was one of the players on my team. Lary had just signed with the Braves out of Florida A&M, even though he'd had a late start as a ballplayer. In high school, he had been a better football player. So had Hankie, who was all-city in Atlanta and played college football at Tennessee-Martin. But Lary wanted to concentrate on baseball in college, and he and Bill Lucas, Jr., had done well as teammates at Florida A&M. The Braves drafted them both in the low rounds after they graduated, and they were eager prospects. But after two years, they were still in Class A ball, and it was obvious they weren't going any further. I had to release them. They were both hurt by it, and naturally it hurt me, too, but it really wasn't that difficult a decision. If there had been any earthly chance that they could have made it to the big leagues, I would have kept them. But it was time for them to get on with their lives. A year or two later, both of them thanked me.

Except for moments like that, I enjoyed being a farm director. I realized I was the exception to the rule of black players being unable to find places in the front office, and I didn't take my position for granted. After Bill Lucas died, I was the highest-ranking black in baseball until Bill White was named president of the National League. It was a quiet job, which was a pleasant change after so many years of facing the press and public. Actually, the job was so quiet that I felt forgotten sometimes. When the Atlanta newspapers held a contest a couple of years ago to determine the most popular Atlanta Brave of all time, the winner was Dale Murphy. I'd be lying to say that didn't bother me a little, but I guess I made a career decision a long time ago that popularity wasn't the thing I was after—especially not in Atlanta. Anyway, my job provided other rewards, the best of which was watching kids develop into big leaguers. Sometimes, you could almost see them change from spring to spring.

Spring training is the most important time for a farm director, and I developed my own routine in West Palm Beach. I stayed at the Days Inn with the minor leaguers, the only difference being that I reserved an extra room for my work table and my microwave oven. Most of the players were just a few rooms away, and I was like their house father. I had to keep the guys in after curfew and out of trouble, which was almost a full-time job in itself. In fact, keeping Steve Bedrosian out of trouble was almost a full-time job. Bedrosian had a big painted-up van that he would park out in the lot, and every time I'd walk by that van there would be a party going on inside. But he was the best pitcher we had in the system and nothing seemed to slow him down. The problem was that his buddies tried to keep up with him and they just couldn't do it. Over the years, I had to cut three or four guys who did themselves in trying to stay up with Bedrosian.

My own pace at West Palm Beach wasn't quite so fast. There were a few restaurants where I liked to go for a quiet dinner—I ate at the Okeechobee Steak House eighteen nights in a row at one point—and after dinner I'd just return to the Days Inn to keep watch over my boys. At the spring-training complex, where we spent our days, I stayed in my office most of the time because the autograph hounds made it impossible for me to walk freely around the fields. My office was just an empty little room in the back of a low cinder-block building a couple hundred feet from Hank Aaron Drive. After a while, people figured out where I was, and they would walk right up to my window and stare in at me.

I was sitting in that office one day in 1982 when my brother

Tommie walked in and told me that he had some kind of blood disorder. They didn't know yet that it was leukemia, and I didn't think anything of it until I was in New York several months later and received a message to hurry back to Atlanta because Tommie was in the hospital. At that point, he had about another two years to live. He stayed in the hospital the last few weeks, and I used to cook fish to bring down to him. We'd just sit there eating fish and watching the Braves on TV. I'd tell him that Dale Murphy was up, and he would try to answer, but you couldn't understand him. The whole time, Tommie never demonstrated any pain until the very last night before he passed away. I was there with his wife, Carolyn, when he died. It was the hardest night of my life.

Ralph Garr was one of Tommie's pallbearers, and the rest were from Mobile—Cleon Jones, Tommie Agee, and an old Toulminville friend named Robert Driscoll. At the funeral, John Mullen said, "We will miss him more than anybody we could have lost. If there ever was an organizational person, Tommie was it." They named the indoor batting cage facility at West Palm Beach for Tommie. He was a very popular and respected man in the organization, and I'm certain Tommie would have managed in the big leagues if he had lived. I'm just as certain that he would have been an outstanding manager.

I was glad, at least, that Tommie got to see me inducted into the Hall of Fame. I was elected in 1982, nine votes short of unanimous. Ty Cobb was the only player to ever get a higher percentage of the votes than I did, which made me feel for the first time that I had really been accepted by the baseball community. My old nemesis Dick Young even tore into the nine writers who didn't vote for me: "I am going to plead temporary insanity for the nine numbskulls. It can't be a racial matter. Nobody can be that blindly bigoted. The grand-dragon of the Ku Klux Klan would have voted for Hank Aaron." It puzzled me why anybody wouldn't vote for me—or for Frank Robinson, who was elected at the same time—but it didn't upset me, because eleven writers hadn't voted for Babe Ruth, and forty-three for Mickey Mantle.

The Hall of Fame weekend was one of the most satisfying

occasions of my baseball life. It especially pleased me to be inducted along with Frank Robinson, who was in our little fraternity of black All-Stars back in the fifties and sixties and had been the first black manager. It also warmed me to see Happy Chandler inducted at the same ceremony, elected by the veterans committee. Chandler was the commissioner who went against fifteen of the sixteen major-league owners to put Jackie Robinson on the Dodgers, and I was very interested in what he had to say about it at his induction. He said, "I felt I was doing what justice and mercy required. I knew one day I would have to face my maker and He would ask me why I wouldn't let this black man play baseball. If I said it was because he was black, I didn't think He would feel that was a satisfactory answer." My speech was the shortest, as you might expect, but I said what I came to say. I said it was true, as I once read, that the way to fame is through tribulation. I said that it wasn't fame I had pursued, but to be the best player I could be with the generous talent that God gave me. I said that I was standing up there only because players like Jackie Robinson had paved the way, and that my presence there, and Frank's, proved that a man's ability is limited only by his opportunity. Then I introduced my family and friends, thanked everybody, and sat down before I started crying in front of all those people.

When I sat down, by the way, I sat down next to Bowie Kuhn. I had played tennis with him the day before—beat him badly, I might note—and we were learning to respect each other a little more. Even so, I still couldn't swallow any reason he could give for missing my 715th home run. My feelings about that were so strong that they had led to a nasty incident a couple of years before. It started when *Baseball* magazine voted the home run as the most memorable moment of the 1970s and invited me to receive an award that would be presented by the commissioner. I sent back a telegram saying that I would not be there to accept an award from Bowie Kuhn. The New York press seemed to think that I was avoiding the ceremony because I was offended that Pete Rose had been named Player of the Decade instead of me. That wasn't it at all. I was clearly and simply returning a favor that the commissioner had extended to me six years before. If he hadn't thought that the home run was worth a trip to Atlanta in 1974, why should I go to New York in 1980 so that he could give me a plaque for it? I didn't see the logic. I would have felt like a hypocrite receiving an award from Bowie Kuhn for the best moment of the decade.

The writers, as usual, had no sympathy for my position. A columnist in Florida wrote that "Henry Aaron has chosen to wallow in the clutches of tastelessness . . . Those close to Aaron suggest this is no longer Hank Aaron speaking, but rather his wife Billye, formerly married to a militant civil rights leader." Will Grimsley of the Associated Press jumped in and wrote, "It was a thoughtless, ugly act. It was ill-advised and unwarranted and only sullied Aaron, not the commissioner. The commissioner deserved better." Back home, Lewis Grizzard of the Atlanta *Constitution* really let me have it: "Did I miss something? Did Henry Aaron get hit in the head with a foul ball? . . . Too many days in the hot sun of West Palm Beach? Too many lunches with Captain Dingeroo, Braves owner Ted Turner? Maybe it's his wife . . . Oh, Henry, how you have changed . . . Suddenly, you're Henry Aaron, activist. Who put you up to that? Jesse Jackson? . . . Frankly, Henry, why don't you cool it? . . . You have a terrific job because you really don't have anything to do. Show up at an occasional minor-league game, pop a beer, watch an inning or two, and take the rest of the day off. You could give us another great moment, Henry—a moment of silence." The way it came down was that the commissioner was excused for snubbing the record, but I was thoughtless, tasteless, and out of line for snubbing his banquet.

While all of this was still brewing, I was in New York for another purpose and ran into Monte Irvin at a crowded restaurant. Monte had accepted the brunt of Atlanta's hostility toward Kuhn when he showed up in the commissioner's place on the night I broke the record, and I was sorry about that. I had no beef with Monte. But when I declined to go to the banquet, he thought it made him look bad, since he had been the liaison between me and the commissioner. My conversation with Monte that night reminded me of the one I had with Mrs. Gibson after we moved out of her house in Bradenton to be with the white players. I told him that sometimes you just have to make a statement. Monte didn't think it was the right statement to make, though, and we had a pretty strong difference of opinion. I shouldn't have taken my anger out on Monte, but I did. In turn, he cursed me, and we got into a ferocious argument, which left neither of us feeling any better. It was a regrettable night, because Monte Irvin is a good man who has done a lot for baseball and for blacks in baseball.

The early 1980s were a turbulent time for me. I was trying to carve out a role as some sort of leader, trying to do and say things that would make a difference, but everything seemed to backfire. At one point, I spoke to a writer for a newspaper in Minneapolis and poured out some of my feelings about the bigotry in baseball. Among other things, I said that I would not recommend to young black boys that they pursue baseball as a career. I had made that statement in a speech to college students, and I believed it. I thought they would be better off studying to be doctors or law-yers or teachers and that if they entered baseball, they would be setting themselves up to be shafted one way or another. When the article came out, it was as if I had burned down the commis-sioner's office. A young, ignorant columnist in Chicago wrote that I had suddenly discovered that baseball was racist and that I hadn't noticed this in twenty-three years of playing. He posed the question of where I was when Dr. King marched on Washing-ton and Schwerner, Chaney, and Goodman were murdered in Mississippi? Then he criticized me for doing so little to change the country when I could have done so much. In the same col-umn, he managed to damn me for speaking out and damn me for not speaking out.

I was getting it from all sides. In Atlanta, somebody called the FBI and told them that I was the one responsible for the string of child murders that devastated the city. That was around the time that a group of private citizens formed a committee to erect a statue of me in front of Atlanta Stadium, commemorating my 715th home run. It was an undertaking that flattered and hum-bled me and also embarrassed me a little before it was finished.

The statue project was initiated by Bob Hope, who was the former public relations director of the Braves, and my old teammate Pat Jarvis. They got the idea that it would be appropriate to put up a memorial similar to the one of Stan Musial at Busch Stadium in St. Louis. Already, there was a statue of Ty Cobb in front of Atlanta Stadium. Cobb never played for the Braves, but one of the Atlanta civic leaders had decided it would be nice to have a series of statues at the stadium honoring Georgia-born athletes. Most of them would have been of football players like Fran Tarkenton and Charlie Trippi. Putting one of me out there would have changed the concept, which made it more difficult to raise money. But the NAACP jumped in and held a fund-raising dinner that got the project rolling. With that to start on, the committee hired a sculptor from Denver named Ed Dwight, who had also been the first black astronaut. But they still needed more than $100,000, and Bob Hope got on the telephone and started drumming up individual donations. I was a little uncomfortable with the idea of private citizens being solicited to pay for a statue of me, but I was touched and honored that so many people contributed. The committee received checks from hundreds of people—from everyday baseball fans to former teammates like Felipe Alou, Tony Cloninger, Eddie Mathews, Warren Spahn, Lew Burdette, Johnny Logan, Joe and Frank Torre, Bob Uecker, Tom House, Dusty Baker, Ralph Garr, and Davey Johnson. The Dodgers even sent a check, and, in a great show of sportsmanship, so did Al Downing. My nemesis in the front office, Paul Richards, made a contribution. So did my secretary, Susan Bailey. And my father and my brother Tommie. Money came in from celebrities like Bill Cosby and Flip Wilson and Burt Reynolds and politicians like Andrew Young. Bert Lance was even on the list. For some reason, so was Vidal Sassoon. So was Bowie Kuhn. But even with all those contributions, it took a painfully long time to raise all the funds that were needed, and all the while there were articles in the newspapers about whether the project would ever be completed. It dragged on for so long that at one point I thought about paying the rest myself just to get the thing done and over with. Ultimately, Ted

Turner said he would put up the last $10,000 if necessary. But the checks kept trickling in, and the statue was erected on the stadium plaza just before I was inducted at Cooperstown.

Everybody agreed that the statue itself was perfect, and in the end, I was profoundly grateful that it was done. Occasionally, when I'm feeling down about something, I'll drive around the stadium to look at the statue from the car, and it picks up my spirits. It reminds me that I've accomplished something and that people appreciate it. I'm indebted to all my friends who were so generous, and especially Bob Hope, Pat Jarvis, and the NAACP.

The statue is only one of many reasons why I'm so loyal to the NAACP. There are plenty of social organizations that do a lot of good in the area of civil rights—including Jesse Jackson's Rainbow Coalition—but I've always felt closest to the NAACP because it was there at the beginning. I had been involved off and on with the NAACP ever since Mal Goode took me to a meeting in Pittsburgh back in the late fifties, and for the past several years I've been on the national board. Billye also serves on the national board of the NAACP's Legal Defense and Education Fund. My connections with the NAACP keep me in regular touch with the chairman, Dr. Benjamin Hooks, who tries to stay abreast of the baseball situation.

I'm fortunate to work for an organization that has a very good record in racial matters, but there are still occasions when I get caught in the crossfire between my job and my extracurricular commitments. That happened in 1987, when the Atlanta chapter of the NAACP, for which I served on the board of directors, began pushing the Braves, the Atlanta Hawks of the NBA—which Turner also owns—and Turner Broadcasting to sign a fair-share agreement. At that point, no sports franchise in the country had entered into a fair-share agreement, which is a contract stipulating that the organization will grant minorities a fair share of everything from executive positions to professional services. As accommodating as Ted Turner is, a man in his position naturally doesn't like an outside organization dictating to him, and the whole thing turned into a real knockdown-dragout fight. It came to a head during basketball season, late in 1987, and the NAACP called a press conference to announce that it was going to boycott one of the Hawks' biggest games of the year. In NAACP affairs, the local chapter generally works independently in its own community—Jondelle Johnson was the executive director in Atlanta and she spearheaded the drive—but the Atlanta situation was so explosive that Dr. Hooks flew in from Baltimore to be there. Finally, they hammered out an eleventh-hour solution. When it was completed, I was proud to work for the only baseball team with a fair-share agreement.

Through the years, I've found that it's almost futile to try to accomplish anything constructive for minorities without the clout of a group like the NAACP. Not long after I retired as a player, I got involved in the formation of an organization called the 755 Foundation, which was created primarily to help place more blacks in baseball front-office jobs, but without the brand of the NAACP, it just wasn't taken seriously. That's why I haven't been involved in the Baseball Network, which was also formed with the purpose of securing more front-office jobs for blacks. A lot of good friends and good men signed up with the Network, however—Frank Robinson, Willie Stargell, Dusty Baker, Don Baylor, Curt Flood, Vada Pinson, and many more—and because of the quality of their membership, they have a chance to make a difference. I applaud their efforts. I also sympathize with them because of the resistance they have met. They have found, as I have, that baseball is a lot like the ivy-covered wall of Wrigley Field—it gives off a great appearance, but when you run into it, you discover the bricks underneath. At times, it seems that we're dealing with a group of men who aren't much different than others we've all run into over the years, except they wear neckties instead of robes and hoods. A black woman who works for the Oakland A's named Sharon Richardson Jones was talking on the phone with an owner of another ball club once about the racial situation, and the owner, not knowing Sharon's color, said, "I'd rather hire a trained monkey than a black in my operation."

I really believed that baseball was going to address its discrimination problem when Peter Ueberroth came in as commissioner. I met with him just a few days after he took over and offered him tangible ideas about how he could implement some necessary changes, including the creation of a position in his office to oversee a program of hiring minorities. We kept up the communication, had another meeting or two, and he listened politely to all of my points and grievances. I told him he was sitting on a time bomb—which is exactly what Al Campanis turned out to be.

> *I was just relaxing at home watching "Nightline" with my wife one night. Al Campanis was on talking with Ted Koppel about the fortieth anniversary of Jackie Robinson. I knew Campanis well from my days with the Dodgers. He was as good a man as any. Well, I was just watching quietly and all of a sudden Campanis made his statement about blacks not having the necessities for certain baseball jobs. When I heard that, I sat straight up in my chair and said, "Goddamn, the door just swung open, babe."*—John Roseboro

I could have gone on "Nightline" every night for a year screaming about the bigotry in baseball, and it wouldn't have done as much good as those two minutes from Al Campanis. The script couldn't have been written any better. Campanis was a high-ranking official of the team that integrated baseball—the most progressive and respected organization in the game. He wasn't a backward bigot. Just the opposite, he had known Jackie Robinson since the minor leagues and been one of his biggest allies. Once, when an opposing player tried to get rough with Jackie in the minors, Campanis said the guy would have to go through him to get to Jackie. The Dodgers had numerous blacks in their front office—Roy Campanella, Don Newcombe, a former basketball player named Tom Hawkins, and others—and a solid record in the treatment of minorities. Campanis was on "Nightline" because he represented the organization that had led the way when it came to opportunities for blacks. That was the amazing irony of the whole thing. And that's what made it so powerful. Campanis was only saying what so many other baseball officials believed and practiced. It was a shame that he was the one who had to take the fall, but I've always said that God works in mysterious ways.

The Campanis incident put the spotlight on baseball's racial problem. It was all over the news for quite a while, and it rallied the activist groups. Jesse Jackson and I met with Ueberroth in New York, and then I attended a meeting with Jesse in Chicago, where he assembled athletes from every major sport in an effort to form an alliance and exert some pressure on the owners. Jesse also met with the commissioners of pro basketball and football, David Stern and Pete Rozelle. After he met with them, he told me he could give each one of them a grade: Stern would be an A, Ueberroth a B, and Rozelle an F. But the heat was on Ueberroth, and everybody was waiting for him to do something. He responded with a grand stroke, hiring Dr. Harry Edwards and Clifford Alexander as consultants with the alleged purpose of addressing baseball's hiring practices toward minorities—essentially, the kind of position I had discussed with him a couple of years before. I was skeptical about the timing and motives behind the move, but hopeful that it might be a step in the right direction. Harry Edwards, in particular, had a history of making noise and getting things done.

As it turned out, though, I honestly believe that Edwards and Alexander were hired as buffers to keep the activist groups off Ueberroth's back. They couldn't hire anybody. They had no real power whatsoever. At one point, Dr. Hooks and some other NAACP officials and I made an appointment in Washington with Alexander and Janet Hill, whom he worked with. Alexander couldn't tell us a single thing that he had done on behalf of blacks. When we pressed him, he said he didn't have to answer to us because he was employed by the owners. All he would give us was name, rank, and serial number. It was as if we were the enemy.

When all was said and done, I don't believe Alexander and Edwards made one damn bit of difference. After a couple of years, Ueberroth gave a report about the increased percentage of minorities in the front office, but his figure only reflected the women who had been hired as secretaries and a few blacks in low-level positions. The only significant hiring of a former black player in that whole period was when Houston signed Bob Watson as assistant general manager. Ueberroth was a terrific public relations man, but as far as I could tell, all he really did on the minority issue was a lot of shucking and jiving.

The worst part of it was that the owners didn't care. They were looking for a marketing man as commissioner, and Ueberroth was perfect for the job. They certainly weren't looking for a baseball man or a champion of minorities—which I had found out firsthand when I met with Bud Selig and two other search committee members to interview for the position before Ueberroth was hired. For a long time, I was the only one who stepped forward publicly as a candidate to replace Kuhn. But I was never a serious candidate in the committee's eyes, or in the media's. A lot of people seemed to be amused by the thought of me as commissioner. I didn't happen to think it was so outrageous. Certainly, I would have needed help in a lot of areas, but so did Ueberroth, and so did Bart Giamatti. I would have needed help in the business areas; they needed it in the baseball areas. It struck me as ironic that baseball was always saying blacks didn't have the experience for front-office jobs, and yet they hired consecutive commissioners who had no background in baseball.

I never heard back from the search committee after my interview. We talked for two hours at O'Hare Field in Chicago, and I told them then, as I'm sure they knew, that naturally I would be strong on the minority issue. I would advocate not only a program of equitable minority employment, but also contracting. Baseball is a very broad industry, and it could perform a valuable and crucial service by providing opportunities for black doctors and announcers and concessionaires and advertising agencies— not only at the major-league level, but throughout the system. Naively, I believed the members of the search committee might think that was important for baseball. But that wasn't my only priority. I proposed a plan to place a cap on salaries to stop men like George Steinbrenner from putting other owners out of business or driving them out of the game. I also lobbied for mandatory drug testing and for inter-league play. One of the things that had impressed me during my two years in the American League was that fans were hungry to watch a famous player they had never seen before in person. It's a shame that National League fans never got to see Ted Williams or Joe DiMaggio or Mickey Mantle or Bob Feller and American League fans never saw Stan Musial or Willie Mays or Warren Spahn or Sandy Koufax. When a team like the Braves is twenty games out of first place in September, you might get some people to the ballpark if you give them a chance to see Wade Boggs or Jose Canseco. Inter-league play would also create regional rivalries like the Reds and Indians, the Cardinals and Royals, the Giants and A's, the Dodgers and Angels, and the Rangers and Astros, not to mention the Cubs and White Sox and Yankees-Mets. I'm not talking about integrating the leagues entirely—just crossing over for a few games, maybe on an alternating home-and-home basis, like college football. It's staggering to think of the money that could be saved on travel expenses. The only downside is tradition, which baseball too often gets stuck in.

Although I had serious reservations about Ueberroth, I thought Bart Giamatti was on his way to becoming an excellent commissioner before his tragic death. When I met with him in New York and he told me he intended to improve baseball's hiring practices, I had faith he would. And, of course, I was thrilled when Bill White was named president of the National League. As far as I was concerned, White's appointment ranked right up there with Jackie Robinson breaking the color line. This was a man who had fought with bush-league fans in the South and had pushed for the desegregation of Florida hotels. He had seen it all. He was also the man who I thought might easily have become the first black manager. But this was even better. I made sure that I put aside a dozen of the first batch of National League baseballs with Bill White's signature. He made a collector out of me.

When Bill was named, I couldn't help but reflect back a couple of years to when I had seen him at an old-timers' game in Washington, D.C. It was shortly after the Campanis incident, and Bill had walked up to me that day, shook his head, and said, "Do you think these people are ever going to change?" I said, "Yes, sir, I do. Maybe not today, and maybe not tomorrow, but they will." Even in my best moments of optimism, though, I couldn't have imagined I was speaking to the next president of the National League.

With White in office, I began to reconsider my own future in the game. It seemed that there were fewer and fewer reasons for me to remain. After more than a dozen years in the same job, I was getting a little bored with it and more than a little discouraged that I had not moved up the ladder. At the same time, I was becoming increasingly occupied with activities outside baseball. In recent years, I've served on committees for leukemia and cancer research and executive boards of PUSH, the NAACP, and Big Brothers/Big Sisters. Through Big Brothers/Big Sisters and Arby's, I've been involved with a Hank Aaron Scholarship Program that has raised more than $5 million to send kids to college. I've also joined up with Sadaharu Oh in a program to develop baseball in Third World countries.

After we met in Japan, I maintained communication with Oh and taped a message to be played in Tokyo when he hit his 756th home run to set the international record. We have a lot of respect for each other and both believe that, through baseball, we can make a big difference for a lot of underprivileged kids—not to mention the enormous benefit that a worldwide program can have for the sport. Oh has inspired me. He is a very influential man in Japan and an entrepreneur, besides. Along the way, he and I have also begun to team up in business matters. We made a commercial together for a new coffee product in Japan, and the product soon became number one in its market.

Gradually, I'm becoming less dependent on baseball for income—mostly due to my involvement with Arby's. When Arby's was a sponsor of major-league baseball, I was their baseball spokesman. One thing led to another, and we worked out a franchise contract whereby Hank Aaron Enterprises would establish at least a dozen Arby's restaurants in Milwaukee and Wisconsin over a period of five years.

Although my baseball accomplishments haven't produced

the bonanza that they might have for other players—white play-ers, to be more precise—I've certainly been able to cash in on my name to a certain extent. Like most well-known athletes, I've had the benefit of making money simply by lending my name to a product or company. For instance, an automobile dealer in At-lanta issued a special edition Hank Aaron Cadillac—even though I usually buy less expensive cars. I also had an arrangement with Coca-Cola for several years in which I made two or three appear-ances a year and received an annual check for $30,000. Jesse Jackson had been on Coke's back about hiring minorities, so they put me under contract just to have me under contract.

Then, of course, there is the money that has become so avail-able to ballplayers through autograph shows. I don't care for au-tograph shows in principle, because they bring out a greedy side of the souvenir industry that doesn't help its image—but I haven't always been above doing a few for the payday. A player who is in demand can make as much as $50,000 in a weekend. One of the last shows I did was Pete Rose's in Atlantic City, which brought together all of the living players with 500 home runs. At one moment during that weekend, I looked around the room at Willie Mays, Ernie Banks, Harmon Killebrew, Frank Rob-inson, Ted Williams, Mickey Mantle, Eddie Mathews, Reggie Jackson, Mike Schmidt, and Willie McCovey, and I thought, "Damn, I hit more home runs than all of these guys. I must have been pretty good."

While I was in Atlantic City, I also managed to win a few thousand dollars at the slot machines. I love playing the slot machines—I also enjoy buying tickets for the state lotteries—and, in fact, I love Atlantic City, because everybody is watching their money so closely that I can walk around without being disturbed. But I don't enjoy card shows, and I decided after that one that I wouldn't do more than one or two a year. Instead, I entered into an arrangement with a company in Philadelphia named Scoreboard that sells memorabilia on TV. I sign so many balls and bats for a fee—it can go as high as six figures—and they take care of the rest. I have to appear on television occasionally, but the agreement is that I don't have to do any hard selling.

I've also decided to retire from the old-timers' tour. Those games depress me. I understand that the whole purpose behind them is to get everybody together and have some fun, but I can't have any fun playing baseball the way it's played in old-timers' games. When you get to the clubhouse, there are so many baseballs to sign that it seems like you never get out of your locker. When you finally make it to the field, everybody wants you to pose for pictures with their arms around your shoulders. All of that is fine, except that there's no chance to warm up and get ready to play. Then you go out there stiff and cold and make a fool of yourself. Maybe I have a different idea of fun than most guys, but I take baseball too seriously to enjoy playing it that way.

I also take football seriously—especially the Cleveland Browns. I've been a Browns fan ever since I used to watch Jimmy Brown play. I admired him as much as any athlete I ever saw. I also related to him, because Jim Brown played with absolutely no wasted motion. He ran as fast and hard as he had to, and when he had to come up with a little extra, it was always there. After the play, he would pull himself up and straggle back to the huddle like he would never carry the ball again, and on the next play he'd knock over three more tacklers. Like Sandy Koufax, he was still at the top of his game when he retired. By that time, I was hooked on the Browns. Several years ago, I found out that I could hop on a plane in Atlanta on Sunday morning and make it to Municipal Stadium in Cleveland in time to catch the game. I would dress up in ratty old clothes and a stocking cap, put some dog bones in a paper sack, and sit in the Dawg Pound with all of the crazies. Nobody ever recognized me—except possibly one time, when an older fellow looked over at me, did a double take, and looked again. I was afraid he had figured me out, but then I started barking and I'm sure he thought, "Nah, it can't be." I stopped going to the games when I got my satellite dish and found I could watch them every week from my easy chair at home. But now I try to visit summer training camp for a few days every year, and during the season I talk once a week to Ernie Accorsi, the Browns' director of football operations. When the baseball season is over, I live and die with the Browns.

For the most part, though, my life is no longer divided between the baseball season and the offseason, like it was for twenty-five years. These days, I get to see my family in the summertime. Ceci stays with us when she is not off at college, and all of my kids except Lary live in Atlanta. Hankie works for Delta Air Lines, Dorinda works for Southern Bell, and Gaile recently moved back from Los Angeles—with a little persuading from me—and took a job as an insurance analyst. Lary got married not long ago in Milwaukee, where he teaches school and does a little coaching. My only grandchild is Dorinda's boy, Raynal, who is in grade school in Atlanta. I frequently pick him up at school and take him to dinner or baseball practice or just hang around with him. He calls me Papa Henry, just like I called my granddaddy in Camden, Alabama.

My sister, Alfredia, also lives nearby, married to a state senator named David Scott. With so much family around, I'm very comfortable in Atlanta now. Not long after I took the job with the Braves, Billye and I moved into a Colonial-style home in southwest Atlanta, a very nice black neighborhood where a lot of ministers and civic leaders like Andrew Young and Maynard Jackson also live. Our house is low-key, and Billye has decorated it in an interesting way that is still comfortable. She collects cultural artifacts—mostly black art that she picks up in her travels. She has figurines and pictures from Africa, Haiti, Nassau, St. Thomas, Japan, Spain, and anywhere else she has been. Her collection also includes three paintings by Romare Bearden, a black artist whom she admires very much and happens to be a big baseball fan.

There's a five-acre lake behind the house where I can catch a fish now and then—actually, Mama does most of the fishing out there every time she visits Atlanta—but the best feature, as far as I'm concerned, is the tennis court that was built for us by Bud Selig and the Brewers as a gift from Hank Aaron Day in Milwaukee. Tennis is my sport now. Except for an occasional catch with Raynal, I don't play baseball at all anymore. After I retired, I tried playing on a softball team, but I couldn't hit that big, slow thing. I also found that you're expected to sit around and drink beer after every game, which means that you lose three pounds and then gain about nine in the same night. That wasn't doing me any good. But tennis is a game that makes you feel like you're really playing something, and I love every minute of it. I'm involved in an informal league in my neighborhood, which is the most competitive thing I do these days. Playing the game has also made me a fan, and I have come to respect professional tennis players as much as any athletes for their conditioning and mental toughness. For some reason, I seem to most appreciate the bad boys—guys like Lendl and McEnroe. I was talking to McEnroe's father once at a party at Madison Square Garden during the U.S. Open and mentioned that I would like to meet John some day. He said to wait a minute, then went over and picked up the phone. I could hear him telling John to come over because there was somebody who wanted to meet him. Then I heard him say, "You get your ass over here right now!" McEnroe was there within the hour.

If I hadn't discovered tennis, there would have probably been something else. I just don't feel right unless I have a sport to play or at least a way to work up a sweat. I love to tie on the tennis shoes, if only to jog. On days when I'm working in my office—it seems like I'm on the road about half the time—I run for forty-five minutes around the top deck of the stadium. I'm not in bad shape for a guy fifty-seven years old, although I probably eat too much ice cream and fried fish. In the summertime, I love to fry up a mess of fish and take it out on the patio, in front of the lake. That's my idea of a pleasant evening.

At times like that, I sometimes sit back and reflect on the nice life I have now, which, of course, I owe to baseball. I reflect on baseball, too, and my relationship with it. I finally feel that my place in the game is secure. The home run record will last at least long enough to suit me; recently, there was a national contest in which number 715 was voted the most memorable event in baseball history. My name is also on an award that is to be presented to the RBI champion of each league for the rest of baseball history. With all that in the bank, I wonder if I really need baseball anymore . . . and if it really needs me. But whenever I wonder about it, I usually come to the conclusion that I do, and it does—at least for the time being. Baseball needs me because it needs somebody to stir the pot, and I need it because it's my life. It's the means I have to make a little difference in the world. I made a decision at the age of eighteen to devote myself to baseball, and at the age of fifty-seven I have to live with that decision. I step outside of the game now and then to try to make a political statement—endorsing candidates or working through the NAACP—but I know that the only reason anybody listens to me is that I had 3,771 hits and 755 home runs. I also know that while it's great to help a politician and to maybe have a small part in a little civil rights strategy, my field is baseball. And that's okay, because people pay attention to baseball. Baseball counts. It counts a lot.

Some day, I might get out of the game. Maybe even soon. But I know that even if I do leave baseball in an official capacity, I'll still be in it up to my neck. I'll still love it as I always have and want to strangle it sometimes. And whatever I'm doing, I'll still be trying to carry on the job that Jackie Robinson started.

I once read a quote from Jackie that speaks for me, too. He said, "Life owes me nothing. Baseball owes me nothing. But I cannot as an individual rejoice in the good things I have been permitted to work for and learn while the humblest of my brothers is down in the deep hole hollering for help and not being heard." All I can add to that is, Amen.

Maybe the day will come when I can sit back and be content with the changes that have taken place in America, or, at least, in my part of it, which is baseball. Maybe in a few years, baseball won't need somebody like me anymore. But until that day comes, I intend to stay in the batter's box—I don't let the big guys push me out of there anymore—and keep hammering away.